For a list of other books in the Cambridge Latin American Studies series, see p. 331

CAMBRIDGE LAT

GENE
SIMO

ADVISO
MARVIN BERNS
CLARK W. REYNOL

THE POLITI
RULE II

THE POLITICS OF COALITION RULE IN COLOMBIA

JONATHAN HARTLYN

Department of Political Science, Vanderbilt University

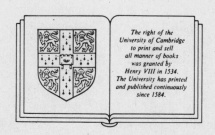

The right of the
University of Cambridge
to print and sell
all manner of books
was granted by
Henry VIII in 1534.
The University has printed
and published continuously
since 1584.

CAMBRIDGE UNIVERSITY PRESS

Cambridge

New York   New Rochelle   Melbourne   Sydney

Published by the Press Syndicate of the University of Cambridge
The Pitt Building, Trumpington Street, Cambridge CB2 1RP
32 East 57th Street, New York, NY 10022, USA
10 Stamford Road, Oakleigh, Melbourne 3166, Australia

First published 1988

Printed in Great Britain at the University Press, Cambridge

British Library cataloguing in publication data
Hartlyn, Jonathan
The politics of coalition rule in Colombia.
– (Cambridge Latin American studies; 66).
1. Colombia – Politics and government
I. Title
320.9861   JL2811

Library of Congress cataloguing in publication data
Hartlyn, Jonathan.
The politics of coalition rule in Colombia.
(Cambridge Latin American studies; 66)
Bibliography
Includes index.
1. Colombia – Politics and government – 1946–
2. Coalition governments – Colombia. 3. Political
parties – Colombia. 4. Colombia – Economic policy.
I. Title. II. Series.
JL2811.H37   1988   986.1'0632   87-25673

ISBN 0 521 34055 1

JL 2811

H37

1988

BO

To Amy

Contents

Tables

Acknowledgements

I have accumulated many debts as I have researched and written this book, more than I ever would have imagined. The chapters that follow are based upon research carried out in Colombia during 1977 and 1978, with subsequent visits in the summers of 1982, 1984 and 1986.

During each visit, my research "home" in Colombia has been the Universidad de los Andes. I owe particular thanks to Fernando Cepeda and to Dora Rothlisberger, department chair during my initial stay. Gabriel Murillo, subsequent department chair, Francisco Leal, Mario Latorre and other department members also have provided assistance and criticism. Bruce Bagley has been a supportive academic colleague, first at the Universidad de los Andes and subsequently in the United States, as we have continued to debate interpretations of Colombian politics. Similarly, Colombian colleagues at other universities and research institutes have also been generous with their time, as were the staffs at over a dozen libraries that I used during my different trips to the country. I owe a particular debt to the numerous people who generously agreed to be interviewed formally, as well as to the many others who shared impressions of their country with me in more informal ways.

In the United States, I need to single out Juan Linz and Alfred Stepan, my thesis advisers at Yale, for sharing with me their excitement about intense field research experience and their insistence on broad comparative perspectives. Others who provided valuable comments on earlier drafts of chapters or on the manuscript include Gary Hoskin, Daniel Levy, Samuel Morley, John Sheahan, Arturo Valenzuela, Alexander Wilde and Simon Collier, general editor of the Latin American series. Responsibility for the current version, of course, is mine alone.

The field research and writing of this book were made possible by generous financial support from a variety of sources. These include the Danforth Foundation, the Social Science Research Council, the Doherty Foundation and the Vanderbilt University Research Council. Vanderbilt's Department of Political Science provided a collegial and supportive atmosphere for research and writing. Emotional and financial support from Leila and Joel Hart and from Sue and Leonard Rosenthal is also gratefully acknowledged.

Some paragraphs in chapter 2 first appeared in "The impact of patterns of industrialization and of popular sector incorporation on political regime type: a case study of Colombia," *Studies in Comparative International Development*, 19 (Spring, 1984), pp. 29–60. A slightly different version of chapter 3 was previously published as "Military governments and the transition to civilian rule: the Colombian experience of 1957–58," *Journal of Interamerican Studies and World Affairs*, 26 (May, 1984), pp. 245–81. And sections of chapters 4 and 5 formed part of my article "Producer associations, the political regime and policy processes in contemporary Colombia," *Latin American Research Review*, 20 No.3 (1985), pp. 111–38.

In the final stages of completion of the manuscript, Elizabeth Wetton at Cambridge was especially helpful. And I owe thanks to Betty McKee and Mildred Tyler, who in their work on my bibliography were forced to perfect their ability to translate an indecipherable scrawl into neat typed copy, correct with accent marks.

This book is dedicated to my wife, Amy. Appropriately, her first gift to me was a pound of Colombian coffee, for she has been living with this project since we met. Amy has been a center of encouragement and a source of perspective while actively pursuing her own studies and her own career. To Liza and Zachary, who have also been forced to share their lives with this project, I can now promise to move the filing boxes from under my desk and computer terminal, to make more room in one of their favorite hiding places, even if only momentarily.

Abbreviations

ACOPI	Asociación Colombiana Popular de Industriales (Popular Colombian Association of Industrialists)
AD	Acción Democrática (Democratic Action)
ADO	Auto Defensa Obrera (Workers' Self-Defense)
AID	Agency for International Development (United States)
ALCO	Compañía Colombiana de Alcalis (Colombian Company of Alcalis)
ANAC	Asamblea Nacional Constituyente (National Constituent Assembly)
ANAPO	Alianza Nacional Popular (National Popular Alliance)
ANDI	Asociación Nacional de Industriales (National Association of Industrialists)
ANIF	Asociación Nacional de Instituciones Financieras (National Association of Financial Institutions)
ANUC	Asociación Nacional de Usuarios Campesinos (National Association of Peasant Users)
APRA	Alianza Popular Revolucionaria Americana (American Popular Revolutionary Alliance)
ASOBANCARIA	Asociación Bancaria de Colombia (Colombian Bankers Association)
ASOCAÑA	Asociación de Cultivadores de Caña de Azúcar (Association of Sugar Cane Growers)

ATLAS	Agrupación de Trabajadores Latino-americanos Sindicalizados (Group of Syndicated Latin American Workers)
BdelaR	Banco de la República (Bank of the Republic) (Central Bank)
CAJANAL	Caja Nacional de Previsión Social (National Public Social Security Agency)
CAMACOL	Cámara Colombiana de la Construcción (Colombian Chamber of Construction)
CFT	Corporación Financiera del Transporte (Financial Transportation Corporation)
CGT	Confederación General del Trabajo (General Labor Confederation)
CNG	Coordinadora Nacional Guerrillera (National Guerrilla Coordinator)
CNRA	Comité Nacional de la Reforma Agraria (National Agrarian Reform Committee)
CNT	Confederación Nacional de Trabajadores (National Workers Federation)
COLCULTURA	Instituto Colombiano de Cultura (Colombian Institute of Culture)
COLDEPORTES	Instituto Colombiano de la Juventud y el Deporte (Colombia Institute of Youth and Sports)
COLPUERTOS	Empresa Puertos de Colombia (Enterprise of the Ports of Colombia)
CONFECAMARAS	Confederación Colombiana de Cámaras de Comercio (Colombian Confederation of Chambers of Commerce)
CONPES	Consejo Nacional de Políticas Económicas y Sociales (National Council for Economic and Social Policies)
CORELCA	Corporación Eléctrica de la Costa Atlántica (Electrical Corporation of the Atlantic Coast)
CSTC	Confederación Sindical de Trabajadores de Colombia (Syndical Confederation of Colombia Workers)
CTC	Confederación de Trabajadores de

	Colombia (Confederation of Colombian Workers)
CUT	Central Unitaria de Trabajadores (Unified Workers Central)
CVC	Corporación Autónoma Regional del Cauca (Regional Autonomous Corporation of Cauca)
DANE	Departamento Administrativo Nacional de Estadísticas (National Administrative Department for Statistics)
DASC	Departamento Administrativo del Servicio Civil (Administrative Department for Civil Service)
DNP	Departamento Nacional de Planeación (National Planning Department)
ECLA	Economic Commission for Latin America (United Nations)
ECOMINAS	Empresa Colombiana de Minas (Colombian Mining Enterprise)
ECOPETROL	Empresa Colombiana de Petróleos (Colombian Petroleum Enterprise)
ELN	Ejército de Liberación Nacional (National Liberation Army)
EPL	Ejército Popular de Liberación (Popular Liberation Army)
FANAL	Federación Agraria Nacional (National Agrarian Federation)
FARC	Fuerzas Armadas Revolucionarias de Colombia (Revolutionary Armed Forces of Colombia)
FASECOLDA	Unión de Aseguradores Colombianos (Union of Colombian Insurance Companies)
FECODE	Federación Colombiana de Educadores (Colombian Federation of Educators)
FEDEARROZ	Federación Nacional de Arroceros (National Federation of Rice Producers)
FEDEGAN	Federación Colombiana de Ganaderos (Colombian Livestock Federation)
FEDEMETAL	Federación Colombiana de Industrias

	Metalúrgicas (Colombian Federation of Metal Industries)
FEDERACAFE	Federación Nacional de Cafeteros de Colombia (National Federation of Colombian Coffee Growers)
FEDERALGODON	Federación Nacional de Algodoneros (National Federation of Cotton Growers)
FENALCO	Federación Nacional de Comerciantes (National Merchants' Federation)
FNA	Fondo Nacional de Ahorro (National Savings Fund)
FNC	Ferrocarriles Nacionales de Colombia (National Railroad of Colombia)
FSD	Frente Sindical Democrático (Democratic Syndical Front)
FVN	Fondo Vial Nacional (National Highway Fund)
GDP	(Gross Domestic Product)
IBRD	(International Bank for Reconstruction and Development or the World Bank)
ICBF	Instituto Colombiano de Bienestar Familiar (Colombian Institute for Family Welfare)
ICCE	Instituto Colombiano de Construcciones Escolares (Colombian Institute for School Construction)
ICEL	Instituto Colombiano de Energía Eléctrica (Colombian Institute for Electrical Energy)
ICETEX	Instituto Colombiano de Crédito Educativo y Estudios Técnicos en el Exterior (Colombian Institute for Educational Credit and Technical Studies Abroad)
ICSS	Instituto Colombiano de Seguridad Social (Colombian Institute for Social Security)
ICT	Instituto de Crédito Territorial (Institute for Territorial Credit)
IDB	(Inter-American Development Bank)

IDEMA	Instituto de Mercadeo Agropecuario (Institute for Agricultural Marketing)
IFI	Instituto de Fomento Industrial (Institute for Industrial Promotion)
IMF	(International Monetary Fund)
INCOMEX	Instituto Colombiano de Comercio Exterior (Colombian Foreign Trade Institute)
INCORA	Instituto Colombiano de la Reforma Agraria (Colombian Agrarian Reform Institute)
INDERENA	Instituto Nacional de los Recursos Naturales Renovables y del Ambiente (National Institute for the Defense of Renewable Resources and the Environment)
INSFOPAL	Instituto Nacional de Fomento Municipal (National Institute for Municipal Development)
INTRA	Instituto Nacional del Transporte (National Transportation Institute)
M-19	Movimiento del 19 de abril (de 1970) (Movement of April 19 (1970))
MAN	Movimiento de Acción Nacional (Movement of National Action)
MAS	Muerte a Secuestradores (Death to Kidnappers)
MOEC	Movimiento Obrero Estudiantil de Colombia (Workers' Student Movement of Colombia)
MOIR	Movimiento Obrero Independiente y Revolucionario (Workers Independent and Revolutionary Movement)
MRL	Movimiento Revolucionario Liberal (Revolutionary Liberal Movement)
OECD	(Organization for Economic Co-operation and Development)
ORIT	Organización Regional Inter-Americana de Trabajadores (Regional Inter-American Labor Organization)
PCC–ML	Partido Comunista de Colombia –

	Marxista Leninista (Colombian Communist Party – Marxist Leninist)
PIN	Plan de Integración Nacional (National Integration Plan)
PROEXPO	Fondo de Promoción de Exportaciones (Export Promotion Fund)
SAC	Sociedad de Agricultores de Colombia (Agricultural Society of Colombia)
SENA	Servicio Nacional de Aprendizaje (National Apprenticeship Service)
SENDAS	Secretariado Nacional de Asistencia Social (National Secretariat of Social Assistance)
TELECOM	Empresa Nacional de Telecomunicaciones (National Telecommunications Enterprise)
UNIR	Unión Nacional Izquierdista Revolucionaria (Revolutionary Leftist National Union)
UP	Unión Patriótica (Patriotic Union)
UPAC	Unidad de Poder Adquisitivo Constante (Unit of Constant Acquisitive Capacity)
USO	Unión Sindical Obrera (Workers' Syndical Union)
UTC	Unión de Trabajadores de Colombia (Union of Colombian Workers)

Map of Colombia

1

Introduction

Colombia basks in relative obscurity, in spite of being the third most populated country in Latin America and its fifth largest economy. A small illustration is the fact that neither of two excellent texts on Latin American politics, Thomas Skidmore and Peter H. Smith's *Modern Latin America* (1984) and Gary Wynia's *The Politics of Latin American Development* (1984), have any discussion of the country. Colombia's continental neighbors have attracted more media and scholarly attention over recent decades because of their powerful populist or radical parties, successful or potentially successful revolutionary movements, brutal military regimes and widespread state-directed terrorism, galloping hyper-inflation, crushing debt burdens or draconian economic stabilization programs.

This book is about the contemporary Colombian political regime and its limited successes and current challenges. It analyzes its politics of coalition rule – consociationalism – in a comparative perspective. In a Latin American context, the Colombian case is an intriguing "puzzle." Although recent Colombian history has been marked by populism, guerrillas, repression, inflation, debt and economic stabilization, these have been present in a more attenuated fashion than in other Latin American countries. Since the establishment of civilian rule in 1958, Colombia has achieved modest progress in reducing social inequity while maintaining a comparatively enviable record of stable growth. At the same time, the regime has generally maintained limited democratic rights and, until the 1980s, moderate patterns of socio-political strife. Its occasional use of repressive policies, though condemnable, have not compared to the brutal excesses of the bureaucratic–authoritarian regimes of Argentina, Brazil, Chile or Uruguay. Yet, with increased violence from guerrilla movements, drug traffickers and right-wing reaction, and growing challenges to the coherence of state institutions in recent years, the regime remains some distance from consolidation. As many of the countries that had bureaucratic–authoritarian regimes and others on the continent return to civilian rule and seek a stop to the pendular swing of their economic and political cycles, the Colombian case demands increased attention.

Scholars have been challenged in attempting to characterize the Colombian political regime:

Marxists are frustrated by the lack of social class conflict. Liberal democrats don't understand why a country that has so many of the trappings of liberal democracy often does not act like one. Students of Latin American politics, expecting a praetorian state like those of the Southern Cone, do not find the military in power. Others, with the idea of the cultural fragment of corporatism brought by the Spanish to the New World, find that fragment weak or nonexistent. (Kline, 1983: xiii)

Most analysts have viewed Colombia since 1958 as a qualified democracy, using adjectives such as "controlled" (Williams, 1976; Bagley, 1979); "oligarchical" (Wilde, 1978) or "traditional bipartisan elitist" (Cardoso & Faletto, 1979: 179). The Colombian regime has been characterized as "elitist rule" (Berry, 1971) or as a "near polyarchy" (Dahl, 1971).[1] Still others have characterized the country from the other side of the democracy–authoritarianism continuum, as "inclusionary authoritarian" (Bagley, 1984) or simply because of its National Front electoral restrictions, as "authoritarian" (Huntington & Moore, 1970: 509–10). The only justification for insisting on another term that overlaps with but is not equivalent to these qualified descriptions of Colombia's political regime is because of its analytical appropriateness and usefulness.

The major thesis of this book is that Colombia's comparatively favorable economic and political patterns over the past few decades and the serious problems it currently faces in consolidating stable, legitimate rule have been shaped by the predicaments and "rules of the game" of the country's limited democratic political regime of two-party coalition governments – its *consociational* regime. In developing this thesis, the book has three principal goals. It seeks to contribute to the consociational literature by analyzing a paramount Third World example. It aims to provide a deeper understanding of the economic and political evolution of the relatively ignored Colombian case in a comparative context. And, it also intends to establish the value of "middle-level" political variables as central explanatory factors in a regime-centered analysis. In doing so, it does not aspire to develop yet another global conceptualization to characterize the whole of the region; as Arturo Valenzuela has argued in a useful review of the study of Latin American politics, we have had those to excess (Valenzuela, 1985: 25–6). Theoretical frameworks have drawn too much on broad cultural or economic determinants, focusing on explanatory factors from "above" (the state), "outside" (the international political economy) or "below" (the urban poor and peasants). While not ignoring these factors, this book places the role of the political regime and of parties, state institutions, interest associations, policy processes and electoral dynamics at the center of analysis.

The consociational literature analyzes countries in which violent conflicts across major segments of society have been resolved within the context of open political regimes by means of over-arching elite cooperation. In Colombia, the consociational National Front regime established in 1958 was an elite response to a perceived crisis stemming from the fear of exclusion from power by the military government, potentially revolutionary violence in the countryside and economic stagnation. This response is analogous to the way in which corporatism has been employed in other Latin American countries (Stepan, 1978). In Colombia, consociationalism was caused and made possible by a factor that sets Colombia apart from most of its continental neighbors: the complete dominance of political life by the two traditional parties established in the nineteenth century, the Conservative and Liberal. The two-party system both divided the country's population and provided for national integration while leading the Liberal and Conservative parties to become functional alternatives (though not exact equivalents) of the ethnic, linguistic, religious, ideological, regional or other segmental divisions analyzed in the consociational literature. The history of these two parties has included periods of hegemonic one-party rule, violent civil wars and coalition government. The political regime established in 1958 came after an intense decade of primarily rural bloodshed, *la violencia*, that left 200,000 dead, included unsuccessful efforts at compromise between the parties and two different failed experiments in corporatist rule. Given the immediate past history of intense violence between party faithful, a return to civilian rule in 1958 was inconceivable without the extensive mutual guarantees between the parties embodied in the National Front agreement.

As it finally emerged, the parties' National Front agreement sharply limited the operation of mechanisms of majoritarian representative democracy in the country. It stipulated that from 1958 to 1974 the presidency would alternate between members of the two parties, and that all cabinet offices, legislative and judicial posts and other government jobs not covered by civil service were to be divided equally between the two parties. In addition, most measures would require a two-thirds vote in Congress for approval. A 1968 Constitutional Reform was only able to program a partial dismantling of the agreement. The Reform reinstituted simple majority vote rather than by two thirds in Congress. It also opened elections to all parties and eliminated parity in the legislative branch at the municipal and departmental level in 1970 and at the national level in 1974. Competitive presidential elections were first held in 1974, although parity in the cabinet and public employment was extended until 1978. From 1978 on, the majority party has been required *to offer* "adequate and equitable" representation in the executive branch to the party receiving the second highest number of votes in elections. Thus, a potential feature of consociationalism has been retained by constitutional fiat. From 1958 to 1986, when Conservatives refused participation in the newly inaugurated Liberal government, Colombia had a political regime based on coalition rule.

The political regime and the state

This book focuses both on the independent impact of the political regime's policies and features on the country's economy and society as well as on the role of economic and societal factors in establishing and subsequently affecting the regime. In doing so, it is partially inspired by some of the growing literature on the "state" in comparative politics, especially that of Krasner (1984), Skocpol (1985; see also Evans, Rueschemeyer & Skocpol, 1985) and Stepan (1978). This literature views the state as an "intervening variable"; it is interested not only in how domestic and international factors shape the contours of the state but especially in how the state affects these factors even as they continue to have an impact on it. Thus, a key tenet of this approach is that the state can also be treated analytically as an actor in its own right, as an "independent variable" which itself shapes major economic and political outcomes, unlike previous approaches which gave it a far more passive role. The autonomous contribution of the state to domestic policy-making is being discovered even within "weak states" (Skocpol, 1985; Finegold & Skocpol, 1982). Thus, the concrete manifestation of the state – what I refer to as the political regime – can play a major role in shaping key economic and political patterns in the country. This is true in two different ways: first, because of the intended and unintended consequences of the independent efforts of state institutions and elites to enact and implement policies and processes of change; and second, because of how their structures and activities channel and encourage some kinds of political activities and not others and stimulate discussion of some kinds of political issues and not others (see Skocpol, 1985: especially 21). In sum, even if state institutions are not powerful enough to determine or impose specific policies or actions, their efforts to do so and the ways in which the political regime acts upon and reacts to social forces and its environment are crucial to understanding a country's economic and political evolution. At the same time, this approach suggests that institutional readjustment will not occur smoothly, for political institutions do not adjust easily to societal change, just as societies tend to resist efforts from above at forced change. As Krasner notes:

Institutional change is episodic and dramatic rather than continuous and incremental. . . During periods of crisis politics become a struggle over the basic rules of the game rather than allocation within a given set of rules. . . (Krasner, 1984: 234)

The analytical focus in this book, though, is on the "political regime" rather than the "state." The literature on the state has tended to ignore the question of the political regime, either taking it as a "given" because it analyzes states in which regimes have high levels of legitimacy and effectiveness, or as "epiphenomenal" because of the level of analysis, theoretical bias or focus on structural economic issues. As I am employing the concept *political regime*, it refers to the structures of governmental rules and processes, including such issues as the basis for legitimacy of rule, patterns of leadership recruitment, mechanisms of representation and forms and scope of domination and control (cf. Collier,

1979: 402–3). If one accepts the distinction made by Cardoso between the regime and the *state*, the latter is a more general and abstract concept encompassing a basic alliance or "pact of domination" of certain social classes or parts of social classes (Cardoso, 1979: 38–40). At this high level of abstraction, there appear to be some basic similarities in regard to the state across Latin American countries, particularly at similar levels of development, in terms of the major social groups that form part of the dominant coalition supporting the state and in terms of general patterns of international and domestic actors that influence state policy. State rule for these Latin American countries involves issues of altering or transforming capitalism domestically while still essentially maintaining it (cf. Collier, 1979: 370–1). Even under this conception of the state, similar kinds of states may have a wide variety of political regimes with significant consequences for patterns of influence, linkage, policy, legitimacy, growth, domination and control (cf. Cardoso, 1979). But in my view there is no inherent theoretical justification for inevitably linking state power to control by economically dominant classes. Rather, I share the view of Skocpol that "state power has a separate basis from dominant class control over the means of production: States are compulsory associations that claim control over territories and the people within them" (Skocpol, 1982: 16). This makes the ways in which economically dominant classes employ the state an empirical issue, rather than one partially resolved "theoretically" in an a priori fashion – even if in thoughtful and sophisticated fashion as in some of the neo-Marxist literature on the state (see the analysis by Carnoy, 1984).[2]

At this level of abstraction, though, many important questions can be missed and useful comparisons and distinctions across country cases can be blurred. Changes in political regimes lead to modifications in political structures and to changes in the ways that policies are determined; these can have significant consequences in terms of political liberties and implications ultimately for regime legitimacy. They may or may not lead to changes in the substance of social and economic policies as similar kinds of political regimes or the same regime through time may pursue very different economic and social policies. To understand the extent to which regime changes will have an impact on political patterns and economic and social policies, it is crucial to understand the major causes and forces that lead to the establishment of a new regime as well as how regime actors seek to impose their views and how the new regime structures patterns of conflict and decision making in the country.

This is the approach employed in this book. The political regime structure in Colombia is not the center of the analysis because it represents a powerful state autonomous from economically dominant groups (as in the analyses of Stepan, 1978 or Trimberger, 1978), though it was reformed following a serious crisis. Consociationalism was a mechanism that elites could employ because of past historical developments in the country. Once in place, the consociational regime placed certain constraints and limits on the scope and nature of political activity and fomented certain kinds of political channelling over others, even as regime actors sought to carry out their policies. Historically, the Colombian state has been a weak state, although during the past few decades state autonomy and capacity have increased unevenly, and the intended and unintended consequences of different administrations' efforts in this direction are an important part of this study.[3] Through time the regime found itself increasingly vulnerable as societal changes were not met by appropriate regime modifications.

The theoretical emphasis in the following chapters is thus at the "middle-level" of the regime and political factors are viewed both as central explanatory factors and as factors that are themselves to be explained by other political, cultural, social or economic determinants. The analysis seeks to avoid the two extremes of economic determinism and of political voluntarism, though the emphasis is on regime and political factors that have tended to be underplayed in many interpretations of Latin American politics. The explicit and implicit comparisons are made principally to the most likely alternatives the Colombian state, regime or particular administration confronted at critical junctures and to the actual development pattern of other Latin American and consociational country cases, rather than to some idealized pattern of development. The economically deterministic views of many versions of world-systems or dependency analyses that would consider the economic and political phenomena analyzed here as largely unimportant or epiphenomenal are rejected. This does not mean that the existence of domestic and international constraints to state or regime action or to the possibilities of full development are not viewed as significant. It is to say, though, that in my view the role of these constraints in shaping economic policy responses and political patterns – particularly in inhibiting the possibilities for establishing and consolidating liberal democratic politics – has often been overplayed in this literature, when the question has not simply been dismissed.[4] In the burgeoning work on democracy and redemocratization in Latin America in the 1980s, scholars have appropriately placed great emphasis on studying governmental institutions, parties, elections, leadership, statecraft and other issues cast at the analytical level of the political regime.[5]

Having explained the logic of the book's regime-centered approach, I turn now to the more specific argument that the contemporary Colombian political regime has been a consociational regime. This must rest on a more careful understanding of what is meant by "consociationalism." Although some scholars have studied the consociational establishment of the Colombian regime, none have systematically pursued the analytical implications for the country's major economic and political patterns and for regime consolidation in an integrated fashion.[6]

Consociationalism and democracy

The term "consociational democracy" was adopted by Arend Lijphart in his seminal work to describe the nature of the political process and the type of political regime found in the Netherlands, as well as other countries such as Austria, Switzerland and Belgium (Lijphart, 1969; 1975; 1977), which he characterized as plural societies. In these countries actual or potential violent conflict across the major segments of their societies was avoided within the context of democratic political regimes by means of over-arching elite cooperation. Thus, the two essential features of consociationalism according to Lijphart are a plural society and elite cooperation. This elite cooperation is usually characterized by the formation of governments of a grand coalition of leaders representing the major segments; other common elements are a mutual veto, proportionality in bureaucratic appointments and public expenditures and segmental autonomy regarding internal affairs (Lijphart, 1977: 25). These institutional arrangements tend to go considerably beyond the forms of cooperation and compromise found in all democratic regimes. This complex of traits has been presented both as an empirical model of how democracy has worked in particular nation-states in certain periods as well as a normative–prescriptive model for societies antagonistically divided along ethnic, religious, linguistic or class lines in which employment of more competitive democratic norms would exacerbate the existing social and political divisions (see especially Lijphart, 1977). Lijphart has also analyzed the experiences with consociational democracy of three less-developed countries, Cyprus, Lebanon and Malaysia, as well as the more dubious case of Nigeria (Lijphart, 1977: 142–61).

A vast literature, often critical of particular arguments, has developed around consociationalism. In the next few paragraphs I will present my perspective on three critical debates and argue that a crucial issue has been largely ignored in the literature. Scholars have disagreed on whether the consociational literature should be restricted only to what Lijphart terms "plural societies," on the relationship between consociationalism and democracy and on what factors are conducive to the establishment of consociationalism. At the same time, analysts have largely ignored the vital issue of consociational transformation and its relationship to regime consolidation. Since the initial literature largely considered Western European cases, the tacit assumption was that these regimes would become consolidated democratic regimes. Yet, evidently consociational regimes can also transform themselves into more authoritarian systems or can break down, generating renewed violence. A rigid consociational agreement may be necessary for establishing a regime but increasingly inappropriate in light of subsequent societal change. More attention must be focused on the reasons regimes take alternative paths.

The application of consociational analysis only to "plural societies" is unduly restrictive and complicated by the difficulty in separating plural from non-plural societies. Nordlinger, whose work on conflict regulation in the context of open societies overlaps with that of Lijphart and other consociational theorists, develops an approach that allows for broader, yet still meaningful analysis. He advances the view that a segment exists when a large number of people who share a class or communal characteristic become subjectively aware and value positively their similarity to other such individuals, attributing some importance to it in defining their relations with individuals who do not share that social characteristic (1972).[7] As discussed in chapter 2, the Colombian political parties satisfy this criterion. Furthermore, I would join

Steiner (1981) in arguing there is no reason to limit consociational theory to "plural societies" as Lijphart does, though not for the same reason. Steiner bases this view on the argument that it is difficult to distinguish plural from non-plural societies in an analytically satisfactory fashion. Indeed, it is difficult and "impressionistic judgements based largely on qualitative data" are required.[8] In my view, it is best to discuss the nature of a country's relevant societal segments in the overall context of the appropriateness, viability and consequences of consociational rule or of aspects of consociationalism in a given country, rather than seek to limit the cases. This is important not only in discussing the need for and possibilities of establishing consociational rule but also in terms of its subsequent transformation. In some cases, as in Colombia, consociationalism may reduce the strength and viability of the societal segments in conflict, whereas in others, such as Lebanon, it may not.

Another critical question revolves around the relationship of "consociational" and "democracy." Though the two concepts have traditionally been joined, they are conceptually distinct. The central defining element of consociational rule – over-arching elite accommodation in the context of a society divided into antagonistic, politically salient segments – in itself represents a compromise with democratic norms (Lijphart, 1975: 179; Stiefbold, 1974: 146).[9] A key feature that distinguishes the extent to which consociationalism is democratic revolves around the nature of relations between elites seeking accommodation and their mass following. For cooperation to succeed, segmental elites must have substantial independent authority without being challenged for ignoring, dominating or coercing their followers. The more this structured elite predominance is non-coercive and the procedural safeguards of democratic rule are respected the more democratic the political regime. Thus, although consociationalism inevitably compromises democracy to some extent, there are variants that are more or less democratic, just as the consociational elements may vary.[10] Nevertheless, especially in the Third World, to the extent consociational regimes replace military regimes or governments in which ethnic, religious or other social groups are repressed, they often represent a shift to more open – if not always clearly democratic – regimes.[11]

There is little consensus within the literature regarding what factors are conducive to the establishment of consociational rule.[12] Lijphart perhaps represents an extreme version of political voluntarism in suggesting that all that may be necessary for consociational democracy is a deliberate change in elite behavior (Lijphart, 1977: 16), though he does analyze various other societal factors that tend to change very slowly through time as conducive to such rule.[13] An opposing view, leaning toward societal determinism, is that in some cases consociational mechanisms may not have been necessary at all to manage conflict but were instead largely a consequence rather than a cause of peaceful elite accommodation (Daalder, 1973; 1974). This latter argument points to a particularly difficult analytical question because of its counter-factual nature and that is how to establish convincingly in specific cases that consociational mechanisms were necessary in order to prevent open conflict. In addition to being a consequence of elite cooperation, it may also be possible that elites acquiesced or encouraged consociational practices unnecessarily (cf. Barry, 1975b). Is it possible that in those societies where they are truly needed they are not feasible (e.g. Northern Ireland) and that in cases where they have been implemented they haven't really been needed? In my view, the argument that in fact consociational mechanisms are necessary to prevent or stop violence, and thus that consociationalism is more than just a description of a particular set of political arrangements is strengthened in cases such as Austria or Colombia where actual violence broke out between the segments just years prior to the agreed upon pact (on Austria, see Stiefbold, 1974; for an opposing view, see Barry, 1975b). Although the importance of political leadership and statecraft are central to my analysis, I consider it is essential to discuss what social, economic and political factors facilitate conciliatory practices where before they may not have existed. An understanding of these factors may also be important in understanding the eventual transformation or breakdown of consociational regimes. It is also true that even if these mechanisms of accommodation may have been necessary initially in order to establish an open political regime they may become less important through time as the saliency of the original segmental source of conflict declines in importance. The continuance of shared rule may or may not strengthen the particular segmental divisions upon which it is built, depending upon the specific political arrangements, the nature of the segmental cleavage, and the impact of societal change upon both.

This focuses attention on the relatively ignored issue of the transformation of consociationalism. As the literature originated with the examination of Western European cases in which democratic regimes had persisted for long periods and which were still consociational when the analyses were first carried out, the relationship of consociationalism to regime stability and consolidation has been glossed over more than analyzed.[14] There are at least four different ways in which consociationalism may fail. The country may revert to violent conflict of the same type between substantially the same groups over largely the same issues. This may be a result of a failure to maintain elite cooperation or due to an inability of group leaders to retain the loyalty of their mass following or both. The country may also erupt into violent conflict as a result of the interjection of new groups and new issues. In Lebanon, both of these appear to have played an important role in explaining the breakdown initiated in 1975 (see Dekmejian, 1978). A third possibility is the imposition of rule by one or more of the groups over the other(s).[15] A fourth possibility is that consociational mechanisms are maintained increasingly as an exclusionary means against other forces that are emerging and gaining widespread appeal, or in an attempt to prevent them from doing so. Counter-elites within the groups in conflict may be brutally repressed, until finally all pretenses of democratic rights are dropped. Or, as may be the case in Colombia, this response may be generated by the decline in the original segmentation that led to the agreement and the unwillingness of regime leaders to respond to the demand for new political arrangements, as well as demands on social and economic issues.[16] If embattled elites turn increasingly to repressive means to maintain their control of government, then consociational democracy becomes a form of authoritarianism with a consociational component, as appears to have occurred in Malaysia (see von Vorys, 1975; Huntington, 1984).

In contrast to these four scenarios, in the Western European cases as the danger of intersegmental conflict declined shared rule continued because it was in the interest of elected politicians, because the danger of a return to competitive rule was overestimated or due to institutional inertia. Eventually, though, a return to a more competitive model of democratic politics occurred, more smoothly in some cases (as in Austria) than in others (as in the Netherlands).[17] In sum, a concern with consociational democracy cannot stop simply with its establishment, but must look at how and why it evolves through time. The Colombian case starkly illustrates this issue.

A look ahead

The book proceeds by analyzing the historical antecedents, the establishment and the subsequent evolution of the Colombian consociational regime. Chapter 2 discusses certain critical "constants" that emerge from the country's historical development and have played a major role in the process of establishment or the subsequent evolution of the regime. These include the emergence and consolidation of the two political parties, a weak state and military, strong regionalism and a pattern of attenuated populism and controlled incorporation of popular sector groups primarily through party rather than state ties. In reviewing the country's history, the chapter indicates the importance of bipartisan coalitions in major transition points that led to state and regime restructuring. Chapter 3 analyzes the period of transition from military to civilian rule in 1957–8 and the establishment of the National Front. It argues that in the Colombian case the mutual guarantees of the consociational National Front agreement were necessary for a return to civilian rule, and discusses the crucial role of political leadership and statecraft. At the same time, the excessive political voluntarism of some consociational theorists is qualified as additional structural and environmental factors are identified as crucial to facilitating the transition process.

The following three chapters analyze how the consociational regime structure, the efforts of regime leaders to circumvent its predicaments and the interaction of these leaders with major domestic and international groups affected the country's major economic and political patterns in the period from 1958 to 1978. Chapter 4 presents three predicaments common to many open political regimes but inherent to the political formula of consociationalism: threatened immobilism, lack of popular responsiveness and policy incoherence. The chapter describes the major actors and their relationship to the regime and discusses the way in which the regime sought to manage the political problems resulting from these predicaments by certain "rules of the game." It concludes by examining how these "rules" operated in the central political process of presidential selection and in one of the most critical efforts to affect the "rules" themselves, the 1968 Constitutional Reform.

Chapter 5 discusses the country's economic evolution and major policy patterns during this period. It provides evidence that Colombia's recent economic record has been comparatively "moderate," avoiding extreme populist policies or radical freemarket ones similar to those of the more "pendular" Latin American countries such as Argentina, Chile and Peru. Its growth record has been smoother and stronger and its inflation levels and budget deficits have been lower and have fluctuated less. The central argument advanced in this chapter is that the domestic regime structure, with its uneven shifts in state capacity and its interplay with major groups, played a central role in the country's particular economic evolution. Coalition rule inhibited populist politics and facilitated the emergence but not the dominance of a technocratic state sector. Thus, it is argued that factors often considered as sufficient explanations by themselves – features of the country's prior historical evolution, structural economic factors such as the country's natural resources and world markets, and the effects of earlier policy choices – are important, but provide an incomplete explanation for Colombia's comparatively surprising economic performance during this period.

The ways in which the regime sought to maintain continued legitimacy and popular support are examined in chapter 6. The central theme of this chapter is the declining effectiveness of the regime in maintaining legitimacy and support. A primary "lesson" the political parties learned from *la violencia* was to fear popular mobilization out of concern they could no longer effectively channel it. Coalition rule encouraged demobilization and facilitated a decline in party segmentation but provided powerful incentives for political leaders to continue extending shared rule. Clientelism and brokerage, effective in reaching a small but salient percentage of the population though economically inefficient, were challenged by an expanding "technocratic" state sector, itself encouraged by certain political leaders, international agencies and by structural economic pressures. Facing opposition from powerful social groups and fearing uncontrolled mobilization, regime-sponsored (corporatist) efforts at organization of the lower classes were ambivalent, as the regime also pursued "divide and conquer" strategies toward popular sector organizations. The most significant regime impact was on party segmentation. The National Front requirements of alternation and parity, combined with socio-economic changes, led to a decline in party identification, the emergence of an independent electorate and increased abstention, particularly in urban areas. The political parties, though, became dominated by regional leaders responding to the logic of coalition rule and high abstention elections. Thus, as the danger of intersegmental conflict declined with time, there were still powerful political–electoral incentives for coalition rule to continue. Under the more difficult economic conditions of the 1970s and with the weakening of state authority due to drug trafficking, this led to the emergence or the strengthening of significant non-electoral opposition: labor organizations independent from the traditional parties and the regime, particularly in the state sector, civic protest movements and guerrilla groups seeking to overthrow the state.

The political realities that led to the establishment of consociationalism had been superseded and regime arrangements required transformation. Chapter 7 analyzes the alternative repressive, exclusionary "strategy" of the Turbay administration (1978–82) and the limited successes of the more reformist, inclusionary one of the Betancur administration (1982–6) implemented in a context of economic decline, growing military autonomy and increased violence. Consociational transformation – postponed for so long – was hesitantly and tentatively underway in Colombia in 1986, following the passage of potentially significant decentralizing political and fiscal reforms, with a fragile truce in place with the country's largest guerrilla organization and with the landmark decision by the Conservatives not to enter the Liberal government inaugurated in August of that year.

The politics of coalition rule had finally ended, at least in a formal sense. The chapter concludes by considering the likely future evolution of Colombia's political regime in light of the different scenarios of consociational transformation. In the conclusion (chapter 8), the value of the consociational literature and the Colombian case to issues related to the establishment of democratic regimes and to the question of consociational transformation are considered in comparative perspective.

2

Political parties and consociational practices in Colombia: a selective history

The formal, constitutionally mandated and electorally agreed upon pact for equally shared rule between two political parties established by the National Front had no exact precedent in Colombia or in other countries. In that sense, it was unique. But Colombia's history of sustained violence, party development and party-linked conflict and coalition behavior is strikingly similar to experiences of conflict regulation or consociationalism in other societies wracked by violence or threatened by it. The country's two major political parties, the Liberal and the Conservative, came to represent functional equivalents of the segmental divisions along religious, linguistic or ethnic lines identified in other consociational cases. Political party identification became an ascriptive trait in Colombia and the parties have been central actors in all significant social processes in the country. The unfolding of the complex processes generated by capitalist development and social change in Colombia cannot be understood separate from the history of the interaction across these two parties. Processes of industrialization and of working-class integration into the political life of the country inevitably occurred in the context of and were conditioned by (even as they, in turn, also affected) the two parties and their interrelations.

This chapter analyzes the development of certain "constants" or crucial features of Colombia's political landscape which played a central role in the establishment of the National Front or in how it subsequently evolved. The essential feature of the National Front and post-National Front political regime has been the political dominance of the country's two traditional parties formed in the nineteenth century. The country's contemporary political turmoil reflects the difficulty of moving beyond traditional bi-partyism. Other features that emerged in the nineteenth cen-

16

tury and have had a sustained impact on the country's historical evolution, in addition to entrenched party identification, have included strong regionalism, occasionally pandemic violence and a weak state and military. As a result of the nature and landholding patterns of Colombia's primary export crop, coffee, and the country's process of initial industrialization, there was little sectoral conflict between the agro-export sector and early industrialists as occurred in a number of other Latin American countries (see O'Donnell, 1973). Combined with the process of early labor organization in conjunction with the established party structure and very limited foreign investment, this meant that the country's experience with populism was attenuated. Both political parties became multi-class parties, though the process of urbanization that accelerated in the 1930s led to a substantial Liberal majority still evident to this day. In addition, these various factors played a part in limiting the role and autonomy of the state in the country, though there was a strongly centralized presidential system, state ownership of utilities and considerable growth in its importance from the turn of the century to the present.

In discussing these "constants," the pages below inevitably provide a selective history, focusing especially on the country's political evolution and emphasizing events since the 1930s. They illustrate the traumatic process of state development and regime modification in Colombia. Unlike chapters 5 and 6, which emphasize the impact of the National Front political regime on Colombian society, this discussion places greater emphasis on how regime readjustments resulted from international or societal challenges. This provides the historical material necessary for the argument developed in chapter 3 that a return to civilian rule in 1958 was practically impossible to conceive without the extensive inter-party mutual guarantees of the consociational National Front agreement.

In approximate quarter century cycles beginning in the 1880s, political parties and the state in "episodic and dramatic" (Krasner, 1984) fashion established new institutional arrangements in the face of economic change and societal challenges (cf. the preface to Santamaría & Silva (1984) by Alvaro Tirado Mejía). These arrangements were preceded or surrounded by sometimes intense violence channelled via the two parties. At the same time, the country's two-party system helped limit the development of more class-based organizations within the peasantry, the working-class or the middle sectors even as it occasionally divided leaders with essentially similar material interests against each other and led to outbreaks of severe violence. Inter-party coalitions based on shared economic interests or ideological beliefs sometimes emerged, although the intense identification with either of the two parties inhibited the consolidation of these coalitions as third parties. Following the Liberal reforms of the 1860s, bipartisan coalitions were significant in facilitating major transition points that led to significant institutional readjustments, as will be explored below in brief discussions of the centralizing reaction of 1886 and the reforms of 1910 which helped establish the country's oligarchical democracy. More space will be devoted to the reforms of the 1930s which sought greater incorporation of the popular sector into the political life of the country. Significant social and political changes were associated with these reforms and with the country's continuing industrialization and urbanization, including an expanding role of the state in the economy and a growing number of politically salient groups in society. This raised the stakes between the parties regarding control of the country's governing apparatus even as the history of their interaction fueled further distrust. The stage was set for the failure of accommodation between party leaders in the 1940s, their brutal confrontation in *la violencia* and its complex evolution, including regime breakdown leading to a military coup.[1]

Political parties, regionalism, a weak military and civil wars

One is Liberal or Conservative as one is Catholic, as one is Colombian–by birth. One does not even consider *not being* Liberal or Conservative, just as one would never think of not being Catholic or Colombian through a simple act of will. (Leal Buitrago, 1974: 1)

Although the origins of the country's two political parties still remain a controversial historical issue, by the 1850s both parties were established and capable of generating extensive electoral turnouts as well as mobilizing for violence (see Bushnell, 1970 & 1975; Colmenares, 1968; and Tirado, 1978). The parties were loose confederations of large landowners and merchants who possessed considerable autonomy in their region rather than tightly knit organizations. The country's rugged topography impeded effective national integration and aided the development of a number of regional centers significant to this day.[2]

Ideological differences between the two parties were more significant in the nineteenth century than in the twentieth. In general, the Conservatives were wedded to a view that approximated the previous colonial order, emphasizing close cooperation between the Church and the state, a strong, central administration and protectionism. The Liberals, more influenced by the industrial, liberal–democratic powers of the nineteenth century, generally argued for federalism, separation of church and state and free-trade economic policies (see Tirado, 1978: 102–30; Dix, 1967: 231–55). These ideological differences blended with and at times were superseded by more purely personalistic and regional disputes. Although the parties in the nineteenth century were essentially factional divisions within the small ruling oligarchy, the lower classes were drawn into the intermittent violent conflicts between them, especially in rural areas because of their dependence on local landowners. Both parties were heterogeneous in terms of their regional bases and the socioeconomic origins of their adherents. A regional survey of party alignments in the nineteenth century suggests lowland areas such as the Cauca valley and the Atlantic Coast states, with concentrations of blacks and mulattos, tended to be more Liberal, whereas highland areas with higher proportions of Indian population, such as those around the cities of Bogotá, Pasto and Tunja (Boyacá), tended to be Conservative. Santander was the bastion of Colombian Liberalism, and the movements of Mosquera from Cauca and Núñez from the Coast can be understood at least in part as Liberal regional reactions to its predominant role. Antioquia was the most staunchly Conservative region, though Conservatives from eastern Colombia and Cauca played a more influential role in the national political arena (see Delpar, 1981: 14–42; 189–91).

Aiding the establishment of the political parties as primary actors was the fact that the military establishment was relatively weak and insignificant. The Colombian elite distrusted Simón Bolívar's predominantly Venezuelan liberation army and after the break-up of the Gran Colombia federation in 1830 the army was further reduced in size and influence (Ruhl, 1980: 182). In subsequent decades, the civilian bands the parties were able to mobilize were often larger than the national army itself. The inability of the army led by General José María Melo to sustain its overthrow of a civilian government during the 1850s in the face of an armed *coalition of Liberals and Conservatives* led to further reductions in the size of the army. This was the only major conflict of the nineteenth century in which popular sector groups, in this case urban artisans, struggled in their own name.[3] Thus, as the political parties began to consolidate themselves in the 1850s, the military institution was practically non-existent. The army remained small throughout the 1800s and no professional corps of specialized military personnel ever developed until the beginning of the twentieth century (Ruhl, 1980: especially 182; Maingot, 1969: especially 145; see also Helguera, 1961; Payne, 1968: 111–33; and Leal, 1984).

The civil wars of the nineteenth century in Colombia played a central role in generating population-wide identification with either of the two parties. As presented in Table 2.1, following the major post-independence conflicts of 1827–32 and 1839–42 in the early decades of the nineteenth century, *seven* major civil confrontations were fought in the country in the second half of the century: 1851, 1854, 1861–3, 1876–7, 1885, 1895 and 1899–1902.[4] Numerous other smaller-scale regional conflicts were also fought during this period. Some 24,600 lives were lost in the civil conflicts between 1830 and 1876 and 100,000 lives in the turn of the century War of the Thousand Days (Payne, 1968: 4). The regional, economic and ideological bases of these conflicts are briefly sketched in Table 2.1. In spite of the complex and sometimes structurally based causes for the eruption of these conflicts, they were channelled via the parties, not easily restrained by a weak central state or its military establishment.[5] As noted above only in the 1850s did civil conflict have clear overtones of inter-class conflict. Subsequent civil wars revolved principally around inter-elite and regional rivalries (see Table 2.1).

The Liberals emerged victorious at mid-century, dominating the national political scene from 1863 to 1885. A lengthy, regionally differentiated civil war ultimately led to the defeat of Conservatives who had been in central government. Two major consequences were the enactment of anti-Church reforms and of a Constitution in 1863 which was extremely federalist, secularist and politically liberal.[6] At least nominal observance of constitutional procedures became more important. Although fraud on the part of incumbents and abstention on the part of opposition groups was common, of the eleven men who occupied the two-year term federal presidency between 1863 and 1886, only one attained his post by irregular means (Delpar, 1981: 15, 97).

Table 2.1 *Emergence and consolidation of the traditional political parties through civil wars, 1827–1910*

I *Caudillismo* and emergence of the Conservative and Liberal political parties (1810–62)

Years	President or ruler and party/faction affiliation	Supporters	Opponents	Nature and outcome
1827–32	Francisco de Paula Santander (President) and José Ignacio de Márquez (Vice-President) (a moderate Boliviano) (1832–7)	Santanderistas or Constitutionalists; moderate (civilian) Bolivianos	Bolivianos or Bolivarianos	*Major conflict.* Break-up of Gran Colombia: defeat of primarily Venezuelan Boliviano military.
1839–42	Conflict and eventual election of General Pedro Alcántara Herrán (1842–5)	Ministeriales (evolved from Republicanos and formed core of Conservative Party)	Uncoordinated regional movements, of which the most important was in Nariño, eventually supported by "Progressives"	*Civil war.* "War of the Supremes." Defeat of pro-federalist regional movements, continued rule by conservative forces.
1851	José Hilario López (1849–53)	Gólgota Liberals (artisans)	Conservatives (Slave-owners and clergy)	*Civil war.* Begun by pro-slavery and anti-separation of Church and state opponents shortly after slavery abolished. They were defeated.

1854	General José María Obando (1853–4) (Draconiano Liberal)	Draconiano Liberals (evolved from Progressives); artisans	Gólgota Liberals and Conservatives – blocked government by controlling Congress. Pro-federalism, free trade and anti-army	*Civil war.* Sparked by *coup d'état* led by General José María Melo and supported by Draconiano Liberals and artisans.
	General José María Melo (1854)	Draconiano Liberals; artisans	All others	Opposed by "Constitutionalist" Conservatives, Gólgota Liberals and anti-coup Draconiano Liberals. Artisans crushed. Significant defeat for the military.

II Liberal dominance and federalism (1863–85)

1861–3	Victory of Tomás C. de Mosquera (1861–4)	Radical (evolved from Gólgota and became anti-Mosquera) Liberals and Draconiano Liberals	Conservatives	*Civil war.* Defeat of Conservatives who had been in control of government. Church property nationalized, enactment of other anti-Church reforms and federalist Constitution.

Date	Election	Winning party/government	Opposing candidate	Notes
1876–7	Election of Aquileo Parra (1876–8) (Radical Liberal)	Radical Liberals	Rafael Núñez – "Independent" (evolved in part from Mosquerista) and some Radical Liberals, backed by some Conservatives and Army leaders. Other Conservative candidate	*Civil war* after election. Conservatives hoped to take advantage of Liberal division, instead led to temporary Liberal unification and Conservative (clergy) defeat As a result, Conservatives more open to alliance with Liberal faction, supporting Núñez (Independent Liberal) for presidency, 1880–2.

III Conservative dominance: *La regeneración* and civil war (1886–1910)

Date	Election	Winning party/government	Opposing candidate	Notes
1884–5	Election of Rafael Núñez (1884–5) (Liberal)	"Unión Nacional" Cabinet (3 Independent Liberals, 2 Radical Liberals and 2 Conservatives). Electoral support from Independent Liberals and Conservatives	Solón Wilches – Radical Liberals	Liberal division and economic crisis placed country near civil war in 1884.

1885	Rafael Núñez and *La Regeneración*	Independent Liberals (in process of disintegration) and Conservatives fuse into *National Party* – evolved into a major faction of Conservative party	Radical Liberals	*Civil war*. Núñez joined by Conservatives defeats Radical Liberals. Leads to increased centralization (1886 Constitution) and closer Church–state relations (1887 Concordat).
1892–5	Election of Rafael Núñez (President but did not assume office and died 1894) and Miguel Antonio Caro (Vice-President – Conservative) (1892–8)	National Conservatives	Vélez – Historic Conservatives. Liberals politically excluded (only one in Congress) and divided into Civilista and Revolutionary Liberals	*Civil war* in 1895. Brief and regionally concentrated. Revolutionary Liberals, unsupported by other Liberals, led to temporary Conservative unification and Liberal defeat
1899–1902	José M. Marroquín (Historic Conservative) (1900–4)	Historic and Nationalist Conservatives	Civilista and Revolutionary Liberals	*Civil war*, "War of the Thousand Days". Both sides divided, 100,000 casualties, economic collapse, no decisive military victories and Conservatives retain control. Party identities consolidated

Sources: Delpar, 1981; Oquist, 1980; J. León Helguera, personal communication.

The constitution's recognition of regional autonomy to some extent made a virtue of necessity given the central government's inability to extend its control over the entire country. Yet it also exaggerated the tendency. In 1870, the national government actually took in less revenue than state and local governments (McGreevey, 1971: 88). Federalism and free trade nearly brought the country to the brink of economic ruin, destroyed its incipient industrial base and further impeded national integration (see McGreevey, 1971: 146–81).[7]

This long-term crisis eventually resulted in a new institutional re-accommodation, a centralizing reaction with considerable *bipartisan support*, known as *La regeneración* (see the sketch of the 1885 civil war in Table 2.1). This movement, spearheaded by Rafael Núñez, sought to establish the authority of the central state and of the Church. The 1886 Constitution, the basic text still in effect to this date, strengthened considerably the powers of the central state and of the presidency. The presidential term was lengthened and the central executive was given the right to appoint departmental governors.[8] The role of the Church in all areas of national life was entrenched by the signing of a Concordat with the Vatican in 1887. In addition, by the 1890s, the parties had established more formal structures, with party directorates and party conventions (Delpar, 1981: xi). However, in spite of the initial bipartisan guarantees of the new constitution, the Liberals were almost completely excluded from political power. Between 1880 and 1904, only two Liberals were elected to Congress, in different periods. Conflicts regarding Núñez' political and economic reforms and political exclusion led to a brief civil war in 1895 and then from 1899 to 1902 to one of the longest and by far the bloodiest of the country's civil confrontations, known as the War of the Thousand Days. In the turn of the century bloodletting, both Liberals and Conservatives were internally divided and profiteering and speculation encouraged the conflict to continue. The war essentially ended in a draw, though the Conservatives retained power. A major consequence was that it consolidated the grip of the two traditional parties over the population – following this war it became practically unthinkable to switch party loyalties.

Throughout this period, divisions within the governing party at times led to partial inter-party alliances, either to promote common material interests or to weaken a particular party or party faction. Conflicts were amalgamations of disputes over material interests (though with the exception of the conflict in 1854, the lower classes did not fight to defend their interests), ideological issues, and regional and personal interests. In some cases, the party out of government or elements of it sought to regain power by going to war taking advantage of divisions within the governing party. Conservatives failed in this attempt in 1876–7, as did the Liberals in 1895 and again in 1899–1902 (Table 2.1). Instead, their actions largely served to unite temporarily the party in government.

The early 1900s were marked by the country's emergence from the end of the century civil war and the loss of Panama. This was followed by the dictatorial government of the conservative Rafael Reyes, who sought unsuccessfully to emulate Porfirio Diaz in Mexico (Tirado, 1978: 132). Frustrated by Conservative opposition in Congress, Reyes closed Congress and called for a National Assembly. He reached out to Liberals by including a small number in his cabinet, permitting them representation in the National Assembly and promoting passage of a measure that would guarantee them representation in Congress. Following the civil war, many Liberal leaders rejected violence as a means of promoting their aims or seeking political office. They sought political reforms such as the adoption of electoral reforms to guarantee proportional representation of the parties and related economic reforms such as increased sectional autonomy (Delpar, 1981: 188–9). Violent conflict was followed by consociational practices in an attempt to prevent renewed violence.

The stage was set for a new institutional re-accommodation. A bipartisan opposition movement which flirted with the idea of creating a new party, the Partido Republicano, emerged and led a political struggle to depose Reyes and his Concordia Nacional movement. It promoted certain reforms to encourage conciliation. A Constituent Assembly, established by the Republicanos in 1910, confirmed minority representation. It also decreed direct presidential elections for a four-year term with no immediate presidential re-election and extended to the Supreme Court the power of judicial review regarding the constitutionality of legislation (see Gibson, 1948). Supported particularly by merchants and industrialists, the movement never developed a popular power base (Abel, 1974: 21). Nevertheless, in coming after a period of extensive violence, and seeking bipartisan consensus and political demobilization, it foreshadowed the National Front.

The centrality of the political parties

The country's history of violence channelled through partisan bands played a central role in establishing party affiliation as an ascriptive trait inherited by families of all social classes. In some regions of the country, adjoining municipalities became locked into blood feuds, giving overwhelming majorities to the opposing party at election time. In that way, it was not only different factions of the oligarchy, but all social groups including the peasantry that became socialized into identification with one or another political party. In his landmark study of rural Saucío, the sociologist Orlando Fals Borda noted:

vendettas and other expressions of group action cause the Saucite to be born into a party. . . Party allegiance runs in the "blood," and one who changes party in his adulthood is looked upon as a despicable traitor.[9]

In this way, in Colombia the *political parties came to represent functional alternatives of the segments* formed due to conflicts over religion and language in Western European cases of consociationalism, or which in other societies have been generated by ethnic differences. As one Colombian analyst has noted, the parties are better characterized as "deeply rooted *subcultures* than [as] distinct programs for the conduct of the state or of economic development" (Sánchez, 1985: 796). As another Colombian wrote: "Among the most remote childhood memories of a Colombian are . . . those of political parties similar to two races which live side by side but hate each other eternally" (Hernández, 1962: 168, cited in Dix, 1967: 211).

The Conservative "Republic" and export-led growth

In contrast to the years surrounding the end of the century, the period following 1910 was an era of remarkable political stability. Between 1910 and 1949, Colombia had an oligarchical democracy, a political system, as Wilde has argued, "of notable stability, openness, and competitiveness" (Wilde, 1978: 29). These decades also brought Colombia into far more extensive contact with the outside world. A sustained coffee boom in the late 1800s and early 1900s set the stage for industrialization. Significantly, it incor-

porated groups from *both* the Liberal and the Conservative Party
into the export trade, even as its characteristics helped block the
development of a more radical nationalist politics. Coffee maintained itself as the predominant export item, as foreign trade
almost quintupled in value between 1914 and 1929. Representing
49.4% of total exports in 1914, coffee increased to 79.8% of all
exports in 1924 (Urrutia & Arrubla, 1970: 209). Throughout this
period, coffee production in the latifundia of primarily Liberal
landowners eventually came to be challenged by production in
small family-owned farms established in the Western highlands by
colonizers from the predominantly Conservative department of
Antioquia. By the 1920s, most coffee in Colombia was grown on
small and medium size farms.[10] Many of these landowning small
growers were less receptive to radical ideologies which had made
inroads in other countries where agrarian wage earners were more
prevalent, or in which the major landowners were foreigners.[11]
The fact the country's major export product was largely in local
hands further inhibited the development of nationalist radical
political movements built around opposition to foreign
penetration.[12]

Economic growth and social differentiation picked up in the
1920s. Total foreign trade grew from 57 million pesos in 1914 to
268 million pesos in 1929. United States private investment grew
from a paltry US$21.5 million in 1914 to the still modest sum of
US$214 million in 1929. Led by the coffee boom, the first install-
ment of the US indemnification to Colombia for the loss of
Panama in 1923 of US$25 million and a rapid increase in foreign
loans, the gross domestic product grew at an average annual rate
of 7.3% between 1925 and 1929, primarily as a result of investments in public works and transportation. Central government
revenues grew from 24 million pesos in 1922 to 75 million pesos in
1929 (McGreevey, 1964; Urrutia & Arrubla, 1970: 128; Dix, 1967:
79; Drake, 1979).

Similarly, Conservative rule came under increasingly greater
challenge in the 1920s. In 1918, the Liberals did not even present
their own presidential candidate; rather, they supported a dissident Conservative hoping to promote a division within the
governing party. In 1919, though, a newly formed Socialist Party
published a platform. In the Congressional elections of 1921, it
received a respectable percentage in urban areas, actually outpoll-
ing the Liberal Party in Medellín with 23% of the vote (Orlando,

1978: 88). The Liberal Party, influenced in part by young Liberal intellectuals with socialist leanings, responded to this new challenge to its urban electorate by incorporating socialist planks into its own platform. Its ability to attract this new constituency appears to have been facilitated by the fact that it was an opposition party that could promise substantial reforms (Tirado, 1978: 107). In the 1922 campaign, though, massive fraud, traditional partisan appeals, Church support and violence guaranteed a high rural vote and electoral victory for the Conservative candidate, though the Liberals did extremely well in urban areas. Following the election, the Liberals withdrew from government and refused to participate in the 1926 presidential elections.

The dramatic economic changes of the late 1920s caught the Conservative government, as most governments in Latin America, unprepared. They paved the way for an unprecedented constitutional transfer of power from one political party to another, facilitated by a bipartisan coalition. Peasant squatter movements and land invasions emerged in the late 1920s in various regions (LeGrand, 1984: 43–6). A strike against the United Fruit Company in 1928 was brutally repressed, seriously affecting the reputation of the Conservative government (see Urrutia, 1969: 99–108). And, with the onset of the depression, foreign credits dried up, budgetary deficits mushroomed, unemployment rose and food scarcities emerged. What assured the Liberal victory at the polls in 1930, though, was the split within the Conservative Party over candidates, mirrored within the Church which was also unable to commit to one candidate over another. The Liberals wisely chose the moderate Enrique Olaya Herrera as their candidate. Although a Liberal, Olaya had been active in the bipartisan Republican effort two decades earlier, and had served Conservative governments for eight years as representative in Washington. He spearheaded a bipartisan electoral campaign and upon his inauguration, formed a bipartisan Concentración Nacional government. However, as with earlier transitions, this one was not totally peaceful.[13]

Partisan violence, particularly in rural areas, marked the 1930 elections and intensified during the 1931 elections for departmental assemblies in February, for Congress in May and for municipal councils in October (see Horgan, 1983). Liberals attempted to consolidate their electoral victory and remove Conservative office-holders, and Conservatives attempted to protect their position. Yet, civil war did not result as partisan violence remained localized. As in the nineteenth century, the links between national leaders and regional and local ones were so tenuous that national leaders could not fully control the actions of lower-level leaders. However, by the 1930s the strength of the regions *vis-à-vis* the central government had eroded considerably as a result of expanding central government revenues, of stagnating departmental and municipal budgets and of regional elite migrations to the capital city. The possibility of a region rebelling against the central authority and seeking support from other regions, as had occurred in the previous century, was very small (Abel, 1974: 388). The emerging party violence came to an end as the country mobilized for a brief border conflict with Peru in 1932 (Horgan, 1983; Oquist, 1980: 106). The path had been opened for a new institutional re-accommodation.

The Liberal "Republic" and initial industrialization

By 1934, a Liberal "Republic" had emerged. Mindful of past Conservative fraud and exclusivism, Liberals employed highly fraudulent elections to place Alfonso López Pumarejo, in any event the only candidate, in the presidency.[14] Responding to two major factors, the massive societal changes induced by the growing economic ties to the outside world and the challenging economic circumstances of the Depression, López' years in the presidency became a period of tumultuous reform, known as the Revolution on the March (*Revolución en marcha*). Constitutional reforms and measures to modernize the state and expand its role were approved, legislation to deal with peasant unrest was enacted and labor organization was supported. López effectively co-opted or neutralized dissident political movements from the radical and progressive left (the Communist Party founded in 1930 and Jorge Eliécer Gaitán's short-lived UNIR (1933–5)),[15] and struggled against those of the fascist right (Gilberto Alzate and Silvio Villegas' Acción Nacionalista Popular).

As with institutional re-accommodation earlier in Colombian history López' reforms were a pragmatic response to "an incipient crisis of the old order" (Dix, 1967: 85). Yet they also served more narrow partisan purposes, consolidating the position of the Liberal Party by limiting the influence of the Church, expanding the electorate in urban areas where it was strong, and increasing the party's support base within labor (Dix, 1967: 85).[16]

At an ideological level, López' 1936 constitutional reforms symbolized a dramatic philosophical shift toward an increased role for the state. New constitutional clauses asserted that "[p]roperty is a social function that implies obligations," and that "the State may intervene in the exploitation of public and private businesses and industries for the purpose of rationalizing production, distribution and consumption of goods, or to give labor the just protection to which it has a right" (Gibson, 1948: 367–8, citing Articles 26 and 28 of the 1936 Codification of the 1886 Constitution). The reform also expanded the right of the state to expropriate private property and reduced the links between the state and the Church. A constitutional clause giving the Church a privileged position in Colombia was removed.[17] The changes were attacked as "bolshevik, socialist and atheist" from the right while they helped promote popular support for the "revolutionary Liberal government" (Tirado, 1978: 145–50).

Significant political and economic reforms were enacted. Universal male suffrage resulted from the elimination of electoral restrictions based on literacy and property requirements. Conservatives did not actively protest because they hoped the measure would potentially help them more than the Liberals mobilize voters in the still predominantly rural country with assistance from the local clergy (Abel, 1974: 285). López implemented a tax reform that placed government budgets on a firmer basis. Reform measures included direct taxation, progressive rates, differential treatment of industrial firms based on their size and nature and deductions for depreciation (Poveda, 1976: 60). State revenues were augmented, though on a per capita basis the state's share of the nation's income and gross product did not increase until the post-war economic boom, and then only slightly (UN/ECLA, 1957: 88). These measures intensified opposition by industrialists against the López government (Palacios, 1983: 508–9), as the progressive income tax became a more important source of revenue than customs duties (UN/ECLA, 1957: 92–106; Drake, 1979: 57).

López' land policies were also conflictive. They represented an effort to address the growing unrest of the 1920s and 1930s in the countryside. The sharp drop in public spending on labor-intensive public works in the late 1920s, the steady decline in coffee prices and peasant grievances regarding dispossession or control of land combined with legal precedents regarding land titles had led to various forms of protest and unrest in rural areas.

In some regions, tenants claiming to be long-term settlers of public lands illegally appropriated by private landowners stopped paying rent; in others, settlers occupied uncultivated land they knew was privately owned. Other conflicts had arisen due to the efforts of peasant-tenants to be allowed to plant coffee trees as well as traditional crops on their plots and the resistance of landowners fearful that the cash income would free the peasants from their control (Hirschman, 1973b: 95–106; LeGrand, 1984: 40–7). In many cases, landowners evicted tenants, settlers and squatters. López' refusal to oust peasant squatters occupying coffee estates in areas of Cundinamarca and Tolima gained him the enmity of many traditional landowners.

In 1936, López enacted legislation (Law 200) which was bitterly opposed by landowners, though in effect it struck a compromise between landlord and tenant rights. Measures were directed at clarifying who had proper title to the land in different situations (often validating the status quo in favor of large landowners), while calling for all privately held lands that remained uncultivated for ten consecutive years to revert to the state. However, the state never enforced the latter measure that most directly affected traditional large landowners. In addition, an unforeseen consequence of the law was the eviction of tenants by landlords fearful of losing their land titles. Similarly, some landlords became convinced that cattle-grazing was a safer pursuit than the growing of crops (Hirschman, 1973b: 107–11). At no point, in spite of their more or less simultaneous emergence in different regions of the country and the great fear they generated among landowners, did peasant movements or organizations move beyond relatively localized protest movements. In a pragmatic fashion that demobilized the emerging movements, the government responded by expanding colonization programs and in some of the cases of protest on large coffee haciendas by purchasing them from their landowners (usually at commercial prices) and subdividing them among tenants and squatters. [18]

Significant industrial growth and organization and incorporation of the working class came during this period. Yet, because of the nature of the country's party system, of its leading export product and because the prior level of industrialization was so low in Colombia, the depression years did not result in significant sectoral clashes between agriculture and industry nor an often concomitant "state project" of industrialization that could have spawned more dramatic increases in state autonomy and state capacity, led to a more powerful labor movement or to the emergence of new primarily middle-sector or labor-based political parties.

Instead, the initial industrializers were closely allied to the dynamic exporting sector, which retained its autonomy from the state, and bipartisan participation in the coffee trade was reflected as well in industry. Although many industrial interests identified with the Liberal Party, much of the country's incipient industrialization occurred in Antioquia, a traditionally Conservative region in politics (Poveda, 1967; Palacios, 1983: 506–7). The coffee exporters, organized in the Federation of Colombian Coffee Growers (FEDERACAFE – Federación de Cafeteros de Colombia), were the single most important actor in the private sector. By the mid-1930s, the Federation had consolidated itself as a powerful representative for large coffee producers and exporters. Throughout the 1930s the Federation and national private interests with government assistance continued to garner greater control over commercialization of coffee. The Federation sought to rationalize the market, creating an internal market structure that could operate with some autonomy from the external one.

Both internal and external factors helped determine that the Federation would remain relatively independent from the state and that conflict with industrial interests would be muted. The bipartisan export sector strove to prevent sectarian partisan interference, which meant in practice that it sought independence from the state (see Oquist, 1980: 158, 192n; Machado, 1977: 80–1). The fact that coffee was produced by so many growers also made politically (and electorally) more difficult any attempt by the state to control the trade and transfer surpluses to the industrial sector, while it strengthened the centrality and the clientelist nature of both parties. Colombian growers also benefited from the price-support efforts of Brazil, the world's largest producer. Because of the Brazilian efforts, Colombia was never forced to curb production in its own coffee sector. The precipitous drop in world coffee prices during the 1930s was more than offset for local producers and exporters by the series of devaluations of the peso during these years (Bergsman, 1970: 21–2; Furtado, 1963: 193–213; UN/ECLA, 1957: 42, 263; Poveda, 1976: 58).

Industrialization was largely initiated by large landowner-merchants and the state played only an indirect and relatively minor role. The annual growth rate of industry between 1933 and 1939 was 10.8%. Domestic production of import substitutes during these years became more profitable as the prices of imported manufactured goods became more expensive primarily because of devaluations.[19] During this period industrialization proceeded from a very low initial level and diversification was limited. In contrast to other Latin American countries, there was no rupture between industrialists and export-oriented landowners during the 1930s and none of the Liberal Presidents developed a conscious industrial policy (Palacios, 1983: 507).

One reflection of this low sectoral conflict was the industrialists' ambivalent relationship with labor which inhibited creation of a clear populist coalition and brought Liberal reformism to a halt. In the early years of unionization, in comparison to other Latin American countries, labor was largely not an important center for radical activity. This was due in part to low rates of immigration (a focus for anarcho-syndicalist movements in many other Latin American countries), to low levels of foreign investment in these years of initial industrialization, and to the nature of landholdings in the coffee sector.[20] The first major labor federation, the Confederation of Colombian Workers (CTC – Confederación de Trabajadores de Colombia), was founded in 1936 with important Liberal, Communist and socialist factions. Its creation was aided by the Communists' policies of collaboration and accommodation with the Liberals in the late 1930s and early 1940s (for a "self-criticism", see Comité Central del Partido Comunista de Colombia, 1960). The essential element, though, was political support from President López. Between 1935 and 1939 only 44 of 218 labor–management conflicts were resolved without government intervention which was usually on behalf of labor (Urrutia, 1969: 118–21, 160). Even during this initial period of state sponsorship of labor, the union movement never became fully dependent on the state (see Pecaut, 1973: 149–54) though labor organization was concentrated in public services.

President López' sponsorship of labor organizations, as well as his other reforms, met intense opposition from landowners, merchants, industrialists and leaders from both parties. Indeed, the organizational looseness of the parties that permitted factions of differing viewpoints to co-exist within the same party also helped preclude implementation of the various reforms. The government had little control over local and regional party officials many of whom were resistant to recently enacted measures. Opposition from Conservatives, expressed in strongly ideological language, intensified particularly because of the massive dismissals of Conservatives from government. Yet, even within his own party López experienced such intense opposition that he agreed the country now required a "pause" in reformism. The victory of his Liberal opponents in the 1937 Congressional elections assured the nomination and subsequent election of the moderate Eduardo Santos (founder of the major Liberal daily *El Tiempo*).

Although Santos inherited the Republican tradition of Restrepo and Olaya, he was unable to re-establish a bipartisan coalition. Regional Liberal leaders did not wish to share government patronage with Conservatives, particularly in a period of budget retrenchment, and Conservative leaders feared they could once again be supplanted as had occurred during the Olaya presidency (Abel, 1974: 53).

López regained the presidency in 1942, in an election which pitted him against a moderate Liberal supported by Conservatives. This term, though, was far different from his first. Polarization between the more ideologized elements of the two parties intensified, even as the Liberal Party split over ideological and economic issues. López confronted a Congress dominated by opposition Liberals and Conservatives, an economy buffeted by inflation and lacking needed inputs due to the war. The war-constrained economy and related increases in government regulation generated opportunities for corruption, and scandals erupted regarding import licenses, exchange controls and the confiscation of German properties (Fluharty, 1957: 66–77; Martz, 1962: 38–42). After surviving a military coup attempt by Conservative sympathizers in 1944 and in spite of continued labor support, López resigned in August, 1945.[21] The attacks by Conservatives, led by Laureano Gómez, and Liberals, particularly Gaitanistas (supporters of Jorge Eliécer Gaitán), were too much for him. He hoped his resignation would pave the way for interparty accord. Indeed, his successor, Alberto Lleras Camargo, formed a bipartisan "National Union" Cabinet.

Political polarization and regime breakdown

In explaining the political polarization, regime breakdown and descent into violence of the period from 1946 to 1949, a focus on regime politics and electoral dynamics appears necessary. In strict economic class terms, national-level Liberal leaders probably shared more in common with their Conservative counterparts than they did with the rapidly emerging populist figure of Gaitán. Yet, partisan identities, personal enmities and the regional dynamics of patronage and clientelist politics drew them apart.

The 1946 elections represented the second transfer of power between the two parties in this century and occurred in a mirror image fashion of events in 1930. The Liberal Party was irreparably split with the more traditional, regional leaders and moderate national elements of the party and most Liberal CTC labor leaders and Communist leaders pursuing a "Popular Front" strategy, supporting Gabriel Turbay. Many rank-and-file CTC members and Communist sympathizers supported the populist Gaitán. Gaitán continued to attack the government, the "oligarchy" and the "*país político*" (the traditional politicians), identifying himself with the "*pueblo*" and the "*país nacional*." His bases of support were in the urban poor, blue collar workers, frustrated employees, professionals and youth. His speeches and slogans– "I am not a man! I am a people!" "The people are superior to their leaders!" "For the moral and democratic restoration of the republic!" – identified and intensified the feelings of economic dislocation and political polarization of the times. Gómez' paper, *El Siglo*, in tactically shrewd but ideologically muddled fashion, initially supported Gaitán, as Conservatives prepared to abstain from the elections. Just six weeks before the elections, the Conservatives nominated Mariano Ospina Pérez, a far less acerbic and more compromising figure than Gómez, whose candidacy would almost certainly have unified the Liberals (see Lleras, 1975: 452; Martz, 1962: 44–6). Ospina won with a plurality of votes due to the Liberal split and entered office with a bipartisan National Union government as he pledged he would during the campaign, in spite of Gómez' opposition.[22]

Politicization, polarization and violence accelerated following the unexpected, pivotal Conservative victory in the 1946 elections. The implacable logic of patronage politics was felt in massive turnovers of government personnel throughout the country. In some cases, Liberals began the conflicts resisting Conservative efforts to gain control of government at the local level (see Oquist, 1980: 115; Sharpless, 1978: 161–7). In addition, Conservatives had resented Liberal efforts to strengthen the police as a partisan base to counterbalance the largely Conservative military. Once in power, Ospina began replacing Liberal police personnel by sectarian Conservative personnel, using these new recruits to repress Liberal regions and groups. Though resembling the violence that followed the 1930 elections, the stakes were now higher. Liberals feared the Conservatives, as a minority party, would attempt to consolidate a permanent grip on power by force. Conservatives, mindful of exclusivism by the Liberals in power, feared that if they were to lose the presidency, they would be able to regain it only with great difficulty if at all (cf. Payne, 1968: 159–82). With the socio-economic changes of the recent decades, there were now more economically integrated and politically mobilized groups. Although the state did not expand its relative share of the country's economy, it now touched more people. Control of the state retained its importance for politicians due to patronage and for party supporters due to the state's growing importance in terms of contracts, administrative decisions, judicial rulings, police action and jobs. Thus, individual-level economic interests across all social groups and political sectarianism began to reinforce each other, polarizing the country in the opposing figures of Gómez for the Conservatives and Gaitán for the Liberals.

The country's growing politicization was apparent from the sharp increase in electoral turnout. In 1946, 60.2% of the electorate voted, in contrast to 39.4% in the previous year's Congressional elections. The two subsequent Congressional elections, in 1947 and 1949, had even higher turnout rates, of 63.7% and 72.9%, respectively (Tables 6.1 and 6.2 on pp. 150–1 and 152–3 respectively; Colombia, DANE, 1970: 152–4). Table 2.2 provides another indicator of the country's intense and sustained party polarization. Contrasting electoral results at the municipal level for the 1930 and 1946 elections (chosen because the split in the party in power allowed the opposing candidate to win, suggesting opposition was meaningful and fraud minimized) show that in *over three-quarters* of the municipalities (77%), one party or the other won with *60% or more* of the vote. This polarization appeared to have been sustained relatively unchanged for the 16 year period, for there is a high correlation ($r^2 = 0.62$) between the votes for the two elections, although in 1946 there was a larger Liberal vote, especially in urban areas (Oquist, 1973).

Another significant consequence of the advent of Conservatives to power was the reshaping of government–labor relations.

Table 2.2 *Party polarization*

Party polarization by municipality for the 1930 and 1946 presidential
elections (average percentage vote)

Winning party received:	Number of municipalities	Percentage	Group percentage
80%–100% of total vote:			
Conservative	150	17%	
Liberal	167	19%	36%
60%–80% of total vote:			
Conservative	129	15%	
Liberal	227	26%	41%
40%–60% of total vote:	205	23%	23%
TOTAL	878	100%	100%

Source: Oquist, 1973: 68.

The process had begun during the brief presidency of Alberto
Lleras. Lleras had repressed a strike by the Federation of River
Workers, destroying what had been the stongest labor union in
the country and weakening the CTC (Pecaut, 1973: 149–54). Yet
the decimation of the CTC and the move away from a regime-
protected labor movement accelerated much more under Ospina.
The CTC attempted a nationwide strike against the government
in May, 1947 that failed dismally. Interpreted as part of a Liberal
plot to overthrow Ospina's government, it led to further repression and decline of the Liberal labor confederation and
government encouragement of a new confederation being
formed under Jesuit auspices, the Union of Colombian Workers
(UTC – Unión de Trabajadores de Colombia) (Urrutia, 1969;
Medhurst, 1984). The UTC was oriented toward more localized
company-level collective bargaining, had a much more centralized organization and firmly rejected state syndicalism. Given
these characteristics, the UTC prospered under Ospina, who saw
this as an alternative to the Liberal and Communist-linked CTC.
The UTC's initial successes in organization came in the manufacturing sector and in the creation of peasant leagues in the

countryside (Urrutia, 1969). The result was a labor movement which was relatively independent from the state and linked to the political parties, yet neither powerful nor autonomous.

Liberal divisions remained severe. As a result of the 1947 Congressional elections, Gaitán emerged as the leader of the party and almost certainly its sole candidate for the 1950 Presidential elections. He opposed Liberal participation in Ospina's government. Finally, in March 1948, the moderate Liberals left the government, claiming lack of guarantees for fellow party members around the country.

On April 9, the assassination of Gaitán on the streets of Bogotá led to the *bogotazo* – mobs burned commercial buildings, destroyed churches and attacked government buildings in Bogotá. Riots spread to other cities. The government blamed the violent demonstrations on a Communist conspiracy to disrupt the Ninth Inter-American Conference then taking place in Bogotá. Gómez accused the Liberals of conspiring with the Communists. Perceiving a civil war as inevitable, he called for formation of a military government and fled the country. The intensity of the outburst can be explained in part by the deteriorating economic situation. High inflation and a decline in real wages preceded the April riots (see Table 2.3).

The regime survived, barely. Moderate Liberals, confronted with Ospina's refusal to resign, agreed to re-enter the government which imposed a state of siege. Ospina agreed to institute a "cross-over" pattern (*cruce*) in the administration, whereby Cabinet-level officials, governors and mayors would name secretaries of the opposite parties.[23] Yet, it was imperfectly implemented as recriminations between members of the two parties increased even as violence continued in small towns and in the countryside. Neither party had coordinated, much less centralized, decision-making capabilities. Party moderates were finding it difficult to disassociate themselves from the statements and actions of the more extreme elements within their party without endangering their own position and capacity for influence. Liberals sought to link the Conservatives with international Falangism; Conservatives accused the Liberals of passivity or worse in the face of the Communist menace (cf. Abel, 1974: 111). Their flirtation with violent and exaggerated rhetoric fed upon and in turn nourished the increasing violence over regional and local-level stakes.

Table 2.3 *Selected economic series 1945–53*

Year	1 Annual change GDP	2 Annual change cost of living (Bogotá)	3 Wages, agricultural laborers (pesos/day 1958 prices)	4 Real wage index working class
1945	4.7%	11.3%	4.04	110
1946	9.6%	9.3%	4.20	115
1947	3.9%	18.2%	4.42	120
1948	2.8%	16.4%	4.74	112
1949	8.7%	6.7%	4.53	120
1950	1.1%	20.1%	4.46	119
1951	6.0%	9.3%	4.55	115
1952	6.9%	0.0%	4.85	120
1953	8.2%	7.4%	4.66	113

Sources: Column 1, United Nations, Economic Commission for Latin America (1970: Table 1); Columns 2 and 4, Urrutia & Arrubla (1970: 82, 76); and Column 3, Berry & Urrutia (1976: 100–1).

The conflict between Conservatives and Liberals became a struggle between the Executive and the Legislature. In May, the Liberals once again left the government. The following month's congressional elections confirmed their control of Congress. Gómez, back in Colombia, called for Ospina to close Congress, while moderates in both parties established a "Pro-Peace Committee" with industrial, commercial and financial representation. Relations between the parties were poisoned by events such as the fatal shooting of a Liberal representative on the House floor in September. The Liberals sought to assure their victory in the upcoming presidential elections by means of a series of "heroic projects." Foreshadowing aspects of the subsequent National Front agreement, Ospina proposed postponing presidential elections by four years and that the government be ruled in the interim by a bipartisan four-man government council, with major organs of the state under equal control and with a two-thirds majority requirement for legislation. Yet, even as this proposal was being transmitted to the Liberals (by Gómez, who personally opposed it), hardliners were replacing moderate Conservatives in government and official repression against Liberals continued. Following Gómez' nomination as the Conservatives' presidential candidate and the failure to reach an accord, the Liberals decided to withdraw entirely from the elections they had moved up to November and began impeachment proceedings against Ospina (Wilde, 1978: 51–8).

The result was regime breakdown. The President responded on November 9 by declaring a state of siege, closing Congress, banning public meetings and imposing censorship of the press and radio. Colombia's oligarchical democracy had come to an end until its restoration in 1958. Liberal leaders encouraged a national strike by the CTC and conspired ambiguously with sympathetic military and police, with disastrous results. The continued violence and conflict, though fueled by social and economic changes, was essentially the result of partisan polarization and not class conflict.

Unopposed, Gómez was elected President. His sectarian partisan rule was to lead to a military coup. Under Gómez, censorship tightened, repression against labor increased, and violence against Liberals and Protestants, sometimes with the cooperation of the local clergy, intensified. Additional efforts to establish inter-party accords failed. In September, 1952 mobs ransacked the offices of the major Liberal newspapers, destroyed the party's headquarters and burned the homes of two of its major leaders, Alfonso López Pumarejo and Carlos Lleras Restrepo. Gómez' government (headed by Roberto Urdaneta Arbeláez since Gómez' 1951 heart attack) convened a National Constituent Assembly (ANAC– Asamblea Nacional Constituyente) in order to impose a new falangist–corporatist constitution that would free the presidency of most Congressional constraints, further centralize power and convert the Senate into a corporatist body (Martz, 1962: 147–54; Fluharty, 1957: 127–35). Yet this constitutional counter-reform divided Gómez' own party, as some feared it was a means of perpetuating his grip on office and others thought it unnecessary or irrelevant in the face of more crucial national issues, including *la violencia*. Conservative leaders, particularly former President Ospina, began conspiring with the military against him. This eventually led to Gómez' overthrow by General Gustavo Rojas Pinilla in June, 1953 (see Martz, 1962: 155–69).

General Gustavo Rojas Pinilla and the Colombian military did

not have the capability or the inclination to govern the country
without civilian assistance. Rojas, as much of the officer corps,
strongly identified with the Conservative Party and sought
Church support and approval. Initially, Rojas' goal appeared to be
to broaden and improve the Conservative Party (Dix, 1967: 116).
Rojas' government was staffed heavily with Conservatives, particularly Ospinistas, and his major economic and political advisers
were civilian. Yet as it became clearer that he was not intending a
rapid return to civilian rule, but was instead seeking to consolidate and probably prolong his stay in office, opposition began
to intensify. The opposition crystallized in the bipartisan movement that led to the National Front. The backdrop to this were
the continuing violence and Rojas' failed populism.

The politics of regime breakdown and *la violencia*

The period from 1946 to 1958 is one of tragic violence and intense
drama in Colombian history. The causes of regime breakdown
and of *la violencia* remain complex and controversial subjects. I
share the perspective that emphasizes the importance of political
factors – the nature of the dynamic between the political parties –
over more purely class-based or economic factors in explaining
the breakdown and the initiation of the violence. At the same
time, regime-based and political factors alone are incapable of
explaining the evolution of *la violencia* once it was unleashed.

Regime breakdown in 1949, although fueled by social and
economic change, and particularly by mass mobilization following Gaitán's death, was fundamentally a result of elite fragmentation and the breakdown of elite negotiations. Extensive
negotiations were carried out by party leaders and consociational
practices were suggested and partially implemented throughout
1946–9 and even subsequently.[24] However, national intraparty
leadership was fragmented and conciliatory attitudes among
several crucial conflict group leaders were lacking. Although
Ospina was President and ostensibly leader of the Conservative
Party, Gómez controlled the party machinery. Gómez, an inflam-
matory orator, with an unyielding and acerbic character, consistently blocked Ospina's attempts at mediation with the Liberals
and was not strongly committed to the preservation of democratic rule (see Henderson, 1985a). Ospina could not control the
excesses of Conservatives at the local level, and Gómez was not

interested in doing so. Many Church leaders, especially following the attacks on Church property and symbols during the *bogotazo* and the attacks on priests that followed in rural areas, allied with the Conservative Party and attacked the Liberals as "communists ... the enemy of Christ and the Church."[25]

The Liberals were also divided between regional "war" leadership groups and the national "peace" faction. Yet, many national Liberal leaders attacked Ospina, further undermining his already weak position. They neither condemned their own party members' acts of violence nor felt they could stand by as the Conservative-dominated police and (less often) army counterattacked. Ultimately, especially after the Liberals left Ospina's government for the second time in early 1949, most national party leaders probably aided their rural associates (Wilde, 1978: 51–8). Liberal guerrilla groups began to form in the Eastern Plains (*llanos orientales*) in late 1949. Nevertheless, in contrast to all previous civil wars, *not one* national Liberal political figure took to the field during *la violencia* (Oquist, 1980: 203).

The violence that began in the countryside after the 1946 elections had no central coordination and was similar to the feuding that followed the 1930 elections. However, it gained greater intensity because the stakes were now higher and more actors were involved. National Conservative leaders and the Church opposed a Liberal Party which had governed exclusivistically and was viewed increasingly as a majority party dominated by populist Gaitanismo (including large elements of the working class and a partially mobilized peasantry) even as regional Conservative figures enjoyed their return to power and feared the consequences of a new Liberal victory. National Liberal leaders, torn between populism and their base of support among landowners, industrialists and merchants, responded in partisan terms, fearing permanent exclusion from control of the state by Conservative maneuvers. Moderate party elites were unable to disassociate themselves from the more extreme positions voiced by other leaders who shared the same party label (particularly the case of Ospina with Gómez), and there were numerous cases of uncontrolled violent activities by local party subordinates which subverted the attempted pacts. Yet ultimately what led regional conflicts to spiral into the breakdown of the regime, a "partial collapse of the state" (Oquist, 1980) and one of the "greatest armed mobilization of peasants ... in the recent history of the western hemisphere" (Hobsbawm, 1963: 16), was the inability of some and the unwillingness of other elements of the top leadership in both parties to negotiate in good faith with each other. With their direct or ambivalent support for the violent activities of their regional party subordinates, given the country's ideologized condition they had helped to create and all the other circumstances of social and economic dislocation, they soon found they had helped unleash a wave of violence they were unable to control.

Oquist's notion of a partial collapse of the state somewhat exaggerates the extension and coherence of the Colombian state in the 1940s. With economic growth and diversification and more extensive commercial linkages into rural areas had come greater state institutional complexity and state presence throughout the national territory. But, the role of the state in the economy was roughly the same in the late 1940s as it was in the early 1920s. Similarly, the proportion represented by the central government and by departmental and municipal governments – roughly 60%, 20% and 20% respectively – changed very little over this same 25 to 30 year period (UN/ECLA, 1957). The key characteristics of the police forces, politicization and decentralization, did not change dramatically until the Rojas years. Neither was there a disproportionate increase in the size of the Colombian armed forces or of its budget. Violence began less due to the collapse of an active presence of the central state or its repressive arms – rather tenuous at the time in many rural areas – and more due to the encouragement of regional party figures with the active or passive acceptance of national leaders. And there is little to indicate *la violencia* was an aborted social revolution. Most conflict revolved around partisan goals or partisan revenge or the seeking of narrow economic goals cast at the individual level revolving around acquiring land or expropriating crops.[26]

Violence was *unleashed* because of the breakdown of relations between party leaders and was initially and predominantly carried out in partisan terms. Yet it also had very different characteristics in different regions of the country, even as it left some largely untouched (much of the following discussion of the regionalization of *la violencia* comes from Oquist, 1980; excellent regional studies of *la violencia* include Arocha, 1979; Henderson, 1985b; and Ortiz, 1985). The worst casualties were suffered in the earlier years, when the partisan motivation was strongest: an estimated

145,000 deaths are attributable to *la violencia* between 1948 and 1953. Another 25,000 are believed to have been killed between 1954 and 1960 (Oquist, 1980: 17–18). The most affected departments include larger Caldas, Tolima, Antioquia, the Santanderes and Valle. Remarkably, the country experienced healthy economic growth during most of this period, as export crops reached the ports and urban industrial areas were little affected (see table 2.3). This may help to explain why reaction against the continued violence grew so slowly under the Gómez presidency.

Liberal guerrilla groups were most prominent in the Eastern Plains, and in parts of Tolima, Huila and Cundinamarca. Initially, the army remained apolitical and many Liberal villages perceived them as a neutral force in contrast to the police who had been politicized under Ospina.[27] As the guerrillas became more of a threat, however, the army became more heavily involved in the fighting. By 1950, there were major battles between Liberal irregulars and the army on the Eastern Plains. Further illustrating the partisan nature rather than the class basis of the early violence, these Liberal forces were initially supported by wealthy Liberal cattlemen in the region as well as ambiguously by the National Liberal Directorate. By the end of the year, however, they had lost the support of both these groups even as they suffered important defeats. There was a resurgence of open conflicts in the region in 1951 and 1952, and the guerrillas were gaining greater autonomy and organizational coherence as the Rojas government took power in 1953 and offered an amnesty which many of them accepted (Oquist, 1980: 201–10).

In minifundia areas of the country, particularly in the departments of Boyacá and the Santanderes, partisan conflict often took the form of rivalries between adjoining villages and struggles for control over local power structures, the major source of wealth in these impoverished areas. Many of these conflicts had strong historical ties to past periods of partisan violence and erupted into brutal incidents in the absence of effective governmental authority to prevent it. Confronted by more serious challenges to central state authority elsewhere, national authorities viewed the management of these conflicts as a low priority.

Some of the most intense violence occurred in the western coffee-growing areas of the country. Liberals organized into self-defense groups to defend themselves from state repression and Conservative paramilitary groups and assassination squads (*pájaros*), who were especially active in Valle and Caldas (see Ortiz, 1985: 184–95; 214–46). These departments and surrounding regions of Cauca, southern Tolima and northern Huila were also the scene of intense conflict over control of land. The descent into violence was taken advantage of by some and actively promoted by others to expropriate entire harvests and force sales of land at bargain prices.[28] Partisanship and personal enrichment became confused. Many small-holding peasants were driven from their plots, intensifying urban migration. In other areas with a tradition of organized peasant struggles for land, conflict took a different orientation with a focus on "self-defense" of local communities. Thus, communist guerrilla groups were active in the Viotá and Sumapaz regions of Cundinamarca and in southern Tolima. Yet these guerrillas probably represented no more than 10–15% of the country's groups mobilized in conflict (Henderson, 1985b: 146–7; Dix, 1967: 370). As in the *bogotazo*, some Conservative and Church leaders were quick to blame "communism" for the violence even as they accused Liberals of communist tendencies. In the most virulent periods of *la violencia*, army and police troops joined by irregular Conservative forces fought Liberal and Communist guerrillas and more apolitical bandits, all of whom also fought among themselves, as paid assassins killed targeted opponents. In 1952, the Communist Party helped sponsor a National Guerrilla Conference, but efforts to unify the guerrillas in ideological or strategic terms failed. Most bands were spontaneous in origin and had limited, defensive goals or were oriented toward revenge understood in partisan or narrow economic terms (Dix, 1967: 370).

Levels of violence dramatically declined shortly after Rojas assumed power. Rojas called for "[n]o more pillage, no more war, no more hatred," among Colombians and declared a general amnesty for those involved with violence (Oquist, 1980: 186). Efforts were made to depoliticize the national police, and army officers negotiated the handing over of arms with guerrilla leaders. Those areas, such as the Eastern Plains, in which Liberal irregulars viewed themselves primarily as defending themselves from official, Conservative aggression most successfully responded to the amnesty. Some 3,540 guerrillas on the Eastern plains accepted the amnesty in August and September of 1953, and the national total for this period was 6,500 (Alape, 1985: 130). Elsewhere, however, where violence was localized with adherents of the two parties living side by side and where the absence of state authority had permitted other conflicts to emerge which would be more complicated to control, such as struggles for land, the amnesty largely failed. In late 1954 and in 1955, government troops clashed with Liberal and Communist-organized peasant groups in Tolima. Violence further escalated in 1956. Some guerrilla groups as well as bands involved in local-level rivalries moved into banditry as others became radicalized and began espousing revolutionary objectives.

The violence tragically demonstrated significant regional differentiation as well as the crucial role of the political parties as channels of conflict. Those areas of Colombia which escaped violence, particularly the Caribbean Coast and Nariño, were ones in which local Liberal and Conservative political elites were able to reach local-level political agreements.[29] The centrality of partisan and national–regional conflicts as the central state sought to reimpose its authority in the National Front period is also apparent in the evolution of the "late violence" (notwithstanding their own interpretation, this is what comes through clearly in Sánchez & Meertens, 1983: especially 42–61). The numerous groups of bandits that operated from the late 1950s into the mid-1960s initially received support from local peasants as well as local party leaders. The local power structure often supported them, not only out of partisan reasons, but also for economic benefit and in an effort to resist state centralization. The National Front, however, was able to integrate most local leaders politically, helping to isolate the bandit leaders, some of whom were becoming more radicalized and others almost pathologically violent. Out of desperation, many bandits ended up repressing the local peasantry that initially had provided them with support, until they were captured or destroyed by the armed forces.

The evolution of *la violencia* provided both motivation and justification for leaders across both parties to seek accommodation anew. Both the inability of the Rojas government to bring violence to an end and the fact that some groups of insurgents were taking on a more radical revolutionary purpose helped generate opposition to Rojas among important civilian sectors and support for restoration of civilian government. During these years, as a result of the violence, there was also large-scale migration (perhaps 1 million people) and numerous land parcels changed hands. At the same time, commercial agriculture expanded in many of the lush plain areas of the Andean valleys, creating a broader alliance in favor of a political alternative that would end the violence.[30] The consociational alternative found strength in the context of the increasingly populist Rojas regime, to which we now turn.

The Rojas regime and failed populism

General Gustavo Rojas Pinilla was essentially thrust into power in the midst of *la violencia* by a segment of the Conservative Party and elements of the military and with the approval of the Liberals, many of whose national leaders were in exile. His only initial opposition came from Laureano Gómez, whom he had deposed, and from the small Communist Party, which he eventually outlawed. Rojas came to power with no organizational infrastructure and was to find himself incapable of finding the allies to develop one. The major groups Rojas courted included the military and the Church, as well as government employees, labor and urban marginal groups. He failed to gain substantial institutional or mass support in any of them, even as he alienated nearly all producer groups.

The weakness of Rojas' effort to build a new political movement reflected the most important "constant" in Colombia's political life: the continued centrality of the traditional parties. As he moved ambiguously and ultimately unsuccessfully toward attempting to build his own political base within labor as well as his own political organization, he alienated the political actors and the church leaders who had initially supported him. The Church began to reconsider its active role in partisan politics following Gómez' bitter attacks on the institution after his fall from power as well as in reaction to the horror of *la violencia* in a country it had considered *cristiano y culto*. The Church further distrusted Rojas' government due to its increasingly Peronist trappings.

Other factors also contributed to Rojas' weakening base of support. He alienated broad sectors of the population by government brutality, incompetence, corruption and continued press censorship; his Peronist leanings and economic policies gained him US and World Bank opposition; and Rojas lost the support of powerful domestic economic actors by his statist and populist economic policies even as economic transformations during his period in office strengthened their organization and coherence (for general descriptions of this period, see Martz, 1962; Dix, 1967; Williams, 1976; and Tirado, 1978).

Between 1953 and 1955, favored by expanding export revenues, the country experienced the most dramatic increase in production and industrial employment in its history. In 1955 alone, 18,000 new industrial jobs were created, a figure rarely equalled since (Poveda, 1976: 72). These dramatic changes helped strengthen producer associations such as the National Association of Industrialists (ANDI – Asociación Nacional de Industriales) and provided an industrial core more vulnerable to subsequent foreign exchange scarcities and thus more likely to oppose populist policies perceived as inimical to their interests. At the same time, Rojas unsuccessfully attempted to levy a stiff export tax on coffee in April 1954. Indeed, in spite of talk of land reform and threats to increase taxation on land and agriculture, tax burdens on landowners remained very low under Rojas, as many close to the government acquired landholdings of their own (Martz, 1962: 194–6; Hirschman, 1973b: 124–5).

By the second half of 1956, the country's economic situation had suffered a serious downturn. Private external debt was greater than the country's international reserves. Coffee prices that had peaked in May 1954 at 99 cents a pound dropped to 73 cents in September of that year and continued declining. Public investment grew sharply from 1954 to 1955 and only declined slightly the next year. Businessmen increasingly complained about unnecessary imports for government agencies such as SENDAS (Secretariado Nacional de Asistencia Social),[31] increased foreign loans for excessive public expenditures and corruption in the management of import licenses. They were also unhappy with what they perceived as state encroachment into areas of private economic activity. Particularly troublesome was perceived unfair competition in areas such as banking, where Rojas established two new public banks. International agencies also were displeased with growing government deficits, reliance on international suppliers' credits, and the overall deterioration in the country's balance of payments.[32]

Rojas' most significant failure was his inability to establish a political movement outside of the two political parties. He failed in his effort to create a corporatist labor organization and a "Third Force" (Tercera Fuerza) political movement. The organizational space already occupied by the political parties and existing labor organizations as well as domestic implications of the international environment weighed against his success. The weak CTC, still linked to the Liberal Party, had been nearly decimated by the Ospina and Gómez governments and was not anxious to be incorporated into a state structure dominated by the military and by Ospinista Conservatives. The Catholic-inspired UTC grew substantially during the Rojas years as the General courted Church support. Although some UTC leaders did support Rojas, due to the confederation's orientation toward collective bargaining, its independent revenue base and its international and Church ties, it was basically not open to state incorporation. Furthermore, Rojas never substantially increased wages and benefits for workers (see Urrutia & Arrubla, 1970: 76–9).

Rojas tried to establish a new National Workers Federation (CNT – Confederación Nacional de Trabajadores) in 1954 with support from several UTC leaders. The CNT was linked to the Peronist movement by its rhetoric and by its formal (and probably financial) ties with the Argentine-sponsored Group of Syndicated Latin American Workers (ATLAS – Agrupación de Trabajadores Latinoamericanos Sindicalizados). It was soon attacked by the Church hierarchy in Antioquia, seat of its greatest strength, as "Peronist and anti-Catholic" (Fluharty, 1957: 245–9). Although the Colombian Church had its own reasons to be cautious in its ties with Rojas due to its concerns over the fate of the UTC, Rojas' close connections with Perón further inclined Colombian Church officials to oppose him.[33] Both the UTC and the CTC remained linked internationally during this period with the United States-dominated ORIT (Organización Regional Inter-Americana de Trabajadores) which bitterly opposed the Peronist ATLAS. By August 1955 Rojas was forced to order the CNT dissolved (Moncayo & Rojas, 1978: 163–70).

Another failure was the attempt to build a "Third Force" in politics. In February 1955, insurgent Conservatives, a few Liberals and some socialists joined Rojistas and the CNT in forming the Movement of National Action (MAN – Movimiento de Acción Nacional). However, the CNT's identification with MAN combined with the condemnation of MAN by the Church, led the dissident party groups and others to abandon the newly formed movement. Shortly after Perón's fall in September, MAN was disbanded (see Fluharty, 1957: 246–7; Martz, 1962: 191–3). In

November, yet another effort to create a government-sponsored umbrella labor organization also met with failure. Rojas' official proclamation of a "Third Force" in Colombia on the third anniversary of his coup in June 1956 also led nowhere.

In the end, Rojas' ties to labor were so weak and the party alternative so strong that both the UTC and the CTC supported (though they did not help initiate) the national strike that led to Rojas' fall. In contrast to the experience of other Latin American countries such as Argentina and Brazil, the post-Depression and post-World War II periods in Colombia did not spawn an urban popular sector with organizational forms capable of pressing its demands, or with political allegiances and ideological tendencies hostile to the central political and economic actors.[34]

Concluding reflections

This chapter has addressed the emergence and the role played by certain "constants" in Colombia's historical evolution while focusing on the major changes in regimes and in the state. Because of a weak military establishment and the history of violent interaction between them, the two political parties established in the nineteenth century in Colombia became functional alternatives of segmental divisions along religious, linguistic or ethnic lines present in plural societies. Although the two parties initially represented distinguishable ideological differences, they did not come to divide the country by class or region, as party members could be found in all classes and concentrated in communities in all regions of the country.

In periods of crisis, limited consociationalism in the form of bipartisan governments dominated by one party often served as a transition to governments that instituted significant political and economic reforms (the Nacionales and the 1886 Constitution, the Republicanos and the 1910 Constitutional Reform, Olaya's Concentración Nacional and the 1936 Constitutional Reform). In two of these cases, the bipartisan movements ushered in new politically exclusivistic regimes (the Nacionales and Olaya's government). Thus, the efforts of centralization of the Nacionales and the political incorporation and socio-economic reforms of the Liberals in the 1930s fell short of their goals in part (though only in part) because they were viewed in politically sectarian form. The Republicanos, on the other hand, institutionalized the

earlier political compromise of guaranteed minority representation instituted by Reyes following the protracted War of the
Thousand Days and ushered in a period of relative political
stability.

Colombia's period of export-led growth and integration into
the world market began around 1910, somewhat later than in the
larger Latin American countries. Similarly, initial industrialization in the 1930s, although rapid, began from a much lower level
than in the other major Latin American countries. Lacking any
significant foreign presence around which to build nationalist
sentiment, large-scale immigration to spawn anarcho-syndicalist
ideologies within an emerging working-class, or agro-industrial
sectoral conflict, the possibilities for populism were limited. The
two-party system and the role the Liberal party played in opposition in the 1920s facilitated political incorporation of the
emerging social forces in the 1930s. The nature of the country's
coffee crop, particularly the fact it was grown by numerous small-
growers (as well as large landowners) and that its commercialization was essentially in private hands, in part out of desire to
reduce partisan manipulation, limited the role the state could
play in the process of industrialization. Structural factors,
though, did sustain the importance of the state in the economy, in
mediating social conflicts and as a source of patronage funds. This
pattern was superimposed upon the two-party system and a delicate national–regional arrangement.

In the 1930s, reflecting the concerns of powerful landowning,
industrial and commercial elites, there was Conservative opposition and insufficient agreement within the Liberal Party to pro-
ceed with López' reforms and corporatist strategy to incorporate
labor. His successor Santos, however, was incapable of bringing
Conservatives back into the government. Intra-party leadership
fragmented and ambivalence in the face of increased social
mobilization, economic dislocation and localized partisan violence
led subsequent efforts at consociational compromise to fail. The
result of what began as Conservative repression from government
and Liberal retaliation fearing exclusion from power was a new
round of intense civic strife, *la violencia*. Regionally differentiated,
shaped by multiple factors, *la violencia* weakened the state but
reinforced the central role of the parties. Much of the violence,
whatever its subsequent class basis or economic or vengeful

motives, was justified or perceived in partisan terms. Given the strength of the parties, the success of an effort by Rojas to supplant them appeared doomed. At the same time, the violence between them made a return to civilian rule difficult to imagine and without consociational guarantees, practically inconceivable.

3

The establishment of the National Front

In Colombia's past history, crises and challenges to elite rule were often met by the formation of bipartisan coalitions. By the mid-1950s, political party leaders were aware that their mutual intransigence had been the central cause of a totally unexpected and deadly spiral of violence and that the consequence had been their displacement from power – only partial for the Conservatives yet with the threat that it could become total. Inter-party violence was not new, but the threat of loss of power to a populist military officer and the challenge of revolutionary violence by some armed bands essentially were. The only way to displace General Rojas from power, block a potential if still weak revolutionary threat and end inter-party violence was by forging a consociational political alternative that provided for extensive inter-party guarantees and generated strong societal support. The response by party leaders built upon historical antecedents of compromise and the "political learning" that stemmed from the combination of their earlier failed negotiations and their mutual horror and fear in the face of *la violencia*. The necessary change of will by political leaders to enact such an agreement occurred and leadership and statecraft saved the process from calamity at crucial moments, though, at times, the consociational pact-making succeeded almost in spite of party leaders. This indicates how important various political, economic and social conditions were in providing a structural space and opportunity for the negotiations to be successful.

The underlying argument of this chapter is that a return to open, civilian rule could not have worked in Colombia without consociational guarantees: consociationalism thus is not merely a term describing particular political arrangements that emerged in Colombia in the 1950s, but a term with theoretical import, indicating these arrangements appeared necessary for the transition to occur and the regime to persist in its initial years. In other Latin American cases such as Venezuela or Uruguay, consociational mechanisms have been present and were evidently helpful for the transition though it is less obvious that their formal application was *necessary* as in Colombia.[1] At the same time, however, the kinds of factors cited as conducive to the establishment and maintenance of consociationalism by consociational theorists such as Lijphart, factors which change only slowly through time, do not appear to have played an important role in Colombia. Rather, the capacity and willingness of elites to compromise appear to have been shaped by a different set of social, economic and political factors identified below. The politically voluntaristic versions of the consociational theory – that such arrangements are possible if elites have the courage and wisdom to enact them – need also to consider the social, economic and political factors that encourage elites to be more conciliatory and reduce the likelihood of challenges to their authority.[2]

Unlike other cases analyzed in the consociational literature, in Colombia what was involved was a dual process of removal of a military regime and establishment of a new civilian one.[3] Thus, both these aspects are considered in this chapter. The two key elements in the ouster of any military regime are the transition coalition, the coalition of political, social and economic groups that comprise opposition movements dedicated to a return to civilian rule, and the military. Given the inevitable differences among the various groups, how can the transition coalition prevent serious divisions from opening up the way for a return of the old military regime or the establishment of a new one? Can sufficient guarantees be provided to the various central actors in the transition process to retain their loyalty and support? When are consociational guarantees necessary or helpful? Regarding the military, the major challenges are to convince them their best interests are served by a decision to withdraw from power and then to assure that groups within the military do not attempt a countercoup to stop the process of transition. The economy is a third element, as questions regarding its management can often threaten the coherence of the transition coalition or recreate opposition within the military to the transition process. Thus, after analyzing the process by which the consociational alternative was forged and the Rojas government fell, each of these major elements of a successful transition – political, military and economic – will be examined. The concluding section will briefly consider the consociational literature in light of the Colombian case.

Creation of the consociational alternative

By early 1956, a consociational alternative to General Rojas' regime was emerging. Indeed, it was a central cause of the erosion of Rojas' hold on power. Former President Alfonso López suggested that Liberals agree to support a previously agreed upon Conservative candidate for the 1958–62 presidential period and seek an agreement with the Conservative Party by means of which the parties would be represented in the executive branch in a manner proportional to their legislative representation. Alberto Lleras was chosen to direct the party in order to seek agreement with the Conservatives. [4]

Why would the Liberal Party that had received an electoral majority in the country since the 1930s take the negotiating initiative and agree to support a candidate of the opposing party for the presidency? There appear to have been two major reasons. The Conservatives were bitterly divided with one faction to a significant extent already in power. Thus, they were unlikely to sign an agreement that would require substantially relinquishing it. In addition, it was even less likely that Rojas, a "Conservative in uniform," would ever agree to hand power over to a Liberal. [5]

Yet, with whom should the Liberals seek an agreement? In the late 1940s and early 1950s, Mariano Ospina had been a conciliatory Conservative figure and Laureano Gómez an intransigent one. Thus, the Liberals approached Ospina first. However, they found he was reluctant to negotiate with them. He feared that if he reached an agreement with the Liberals, the wrath of Gómez would descend upon him further diminishing his standing within his own party already affected by his links to Rojas (Lleras, García and a prominent Conservative politician, interviews with Pinilla, 1979; interview with Villareal [Conservative politician and minister of government for the military junta], Summer 1982). Numerous Ospinistas also retained high positions in the government, although by 1956 Ospina personally had distanced himself from the Rojas Regime (Tirado, 1978: 183).

Rejected by Ospina, Lleras sought out Gómez in exile in Spain in July 1956. Because Gómez was unforgiving of the Conservatives and the military who had overthrown him, bitter toward the Church officials that had supported them, and increasingly convinced *la violencia* was a result of political sectarianism, he was open to the idea of negotiating with the Liberals (see Henderson, 1985 a: 63–7). Discussions between Lleras and Gómez led to the Declaration of Benidorm which called for a return to republican rule by means of one or more coalition governments (the text of this and subsequent documents are in Colombia, Cámara de Representantes, 1959). Simultaneously, a "Civic Front" of opposition began to grow within the country. By January, 1957, after the minister of war declared the armed forces had "irrevocably" decided that Rojas would remain as president for the next term (1958–62), Ospina provided his full support for the bipartisan alternative with a Conservative presidential candidate. Most Conservatives, including Ospinistas, now surmised they had less of a political future with their current military allies than with the Liberals. The two parties decided upon Guillermo León Valencia as their joint candidate and a symbol of their opposition to Rojas. His Conservative credentials, bravery and fiery rhetoric were requirements for a candidacy with an uncertain future (interviews with Liberal and Conservative politicians, Summer 1982).

The next stage was an agreement of all major political forces within the country. For that purpose an extensive "Joint Manifesto of the Liberal and Conservative Parties" (Pact of March) was prepared calling for free elections for the presidency, in which the two parties would present jointly a single candidate of the Conservative Party, and guarantees of inter-party *parity*. In addition, the pact reaffirmed the privileged position of the Catholic Church in Colombia.[6] As a harbinger of difficulties to come, Gómez from exile opposed parts of the Pact and therefore most members of the Laureanista Directorate ended up not signing the document (Vázquez, n.d.: 232; Betancur, interview with Pinilla, 1979). But the opposition movement pressed ahead. To place additional pressure on the Rojas government, Valencia's candidacy was officially launched by the two parties in April. As the crisis surrounding Rojas' efforts toward re-election brought increasing numbers of political leaders into the transition coalition, the country's growing economic crisis further convinced businessmen of their need to support the party alternative. Forced to choose between potential future presidential ambitions of his civilian and military advisers, Rojas opted for the military, thus losing the counsel of his major strategist and minister of government, Lucio Pabón Núñez, in April.

The fall of Rojas

The crisis surrounding succession and the country's economic problems came to its resolution in 1957 during the "days of May." On May 1, Rojas unsuccessfully tried to place the parties' candidate, Valencia, under arrest. Student demonstrations erupted in the country's major cities. On May 5, police tear-gassed the Bogotá church of an anti-government priest. Two days later, a nationwide civic strike led by the country's bankers, industrialists and merchants shut down the country's major cities. On May 8, Rojas desperately convened the Constituent Assembly which quickly approved his re-election for the subsequent presidential term. Rojas also nationalized a major bank and decreed that banks could not charge interest on outstanding loans while they were closed although deposits would continue to earn interest (see Ediciones Documentos Colombianos, 1957: 178–80; the decrees were annulled by the junta on May 11 (:226)). The next day, the Church hierarchy strongly attacked the regime. Businesses continued closed and massive demonstrations against the government continued. On May 10, a five-man military junta was placed in charge of government and Rojas flew into exile.

The large demonstrations reflected a different class base and orientation than earlier mobilizations such as the *bogotazo* of 1948. The popular sector largely did not mobilize in opposition to Rojas, though organized labor eventually joined the demonstrations. Plans to carry out a lockout and civic strike jelled in late March and early April in discussions between party leaders and the producer associations. To assure labor support, industrialists with the cooperation of the banks (which also were closed) paid the workers' wages for the period of the lockout.[7]

The only bulwark of support for the regime remained the armed forces which retained extreme loyalty to Rojas. Yet, the armed forces feared for their institutional cohesion and possessed serious doubts about their "mission" in the context of the Rojas government. Some military officers had been displeased by the corruption within the regime. Toward the end, most objected to the sudden turn to socialism indicated by the nationalization of the banks. Within the senior ranks, there was little desire to battle the unarmed middle-class civilian demonstrators in the streets and concern regarding the anti-military tone of public opinion mobilized by the "Civic Front." Elements of the air force appeared prepared to take violent action to force Rojas' downfall.[8]

Finally Rojas asked Antonio Alvarez Restrepo, manager of one of the public banks he had created, to convene a group of *Conservatives* to study formulas for his withdrawal from office. Yet, the Conservative–Liberal coalition could not be broken. Valencia and other opposition leaders demanded that the Liberals be included in any transition government. Since everyone in society was identified as either a Conservative or a Liberal, a Cabinet of "neutral" civilians was not possible. An all-military government was also unthinkable not only because of civilian distrust of the military but because of the military themselves. They had not felt confident even under Rojas of forming an all-military cabinet. At the same time, through their intermediary General Rafael Navas Pardo, they insisted on a military junta so they could dismantle the military government themselves. Finally, the civilians agreed to a junta as long as its Cabinet would have equal numbers of Liberals and Conservatives (see Ediciones Documentos Colombianos, 1957: 197–200; interviews with Antonio Alvarez, Rafael Navas, Carlos Lleras and others, Summer 1982).

The military junta consisted of high-ranking military officers, though seniority was not strictly respected. General Gabriel París, Rojas' former minister of war, became head of the junta. Probably the two most active and ambitious members of the junta were General Navas, former Commander of the Army, and General Luis Ordóñez, former head of the intelligence service. The fourth and fifth members were Vice-Admiral Rubén Piedrahita and General Deogracias Fonseca. Rojas apparently had the major role in determining the junta though senior military officers had some influence (interviews with senior military officers, 1982; see Martz, 1962: 249–50; Dix, 1967: 120–8; and Rojas' "explanation" of how he formed the junta, which should not be taken completely at face value, in Colombia, Senado de la República, Comisión Instructora, 1960: 758–74).

Many players harbored secret plans. Rojas expected the junta, which had several members who had been deeply loyal to him, would soon invite him to return. Some Conservatives hoped the transition would allow them to continue governing, largely excluding Liberals. A few military officers probably possessed presidential ambitions of their own. Yet, the strength of the alternative, the Civic Front, was immense. This was reflected in the junta's program announced the day of its creation: formation of a bipartisan Cabinet, temporary closing of the Constituent Assembly, re-establishment of freedom of the press, and the calling of elections to replace the junta at the end of Rojas' presidential term in August, 1958 (Junta Militar de Gobierno, 1957).

Consociational pact-making during the transition period

The junta and its bipartisan Cabinet confronted numerous problems. Violence continued in the countryside, spreading in some instances to the cities as several guerrilla leaders who accepted amnesty offers were assassinated, and explosions, probably set off by dissident military, rocked the homes and offices of anti-Rojista newspaper columnists and Liberals. And Rojas left behind an economy in shambles. Yet party leaders also had a continuing political problem. They needed to decide how they would provide mutual guarantees to each other and the process by which power would be transferred to them from the military junta. The major problem, apparent even before the fall of Rojas, was the split within the Conservative Party. The specific issues the parties faced were the particular mechanisms by which mutual guarantees would be provided and the presidential candidacy of Guillermo León Valencia.

The negotiations by means of which these two issues were settled were complex; different actors' intransigence and last minute crises fostered the hope of opposition movements. Yet, in spite of their differences, *all* the major political leaders were firmly opposed to any alternative political regime which did not comprise extensive mutual guarantees to the two parties – of that much *la violencia* and the Rojas government had convinced them. Thus, even as the difficulties mounted, none of the disgruntled actors were available as allies to forces opposed to the transition process. Furthermore, they did not have other significant differences relating to the socio-economic order or central political procedures and constitutionalism. Nevertheless, it is remarkable that agreements paving the way for crucial national elections – one on the plebiscite establishing the National Front and the other on a coalition presidential candidate – were reached just nine days and ten days before the date of each respective election.

The Liberals continued to identify with the presidential candidacy of Valencia. Yet Gómez communicated from Spain his total opposition to Valencia. Apparently, he wished to punish those Conservatives who had conspired to overthrow his government, he feared that a weak, divided Conservative Party in the presidency would provide a bad government from which the Liberals could derive advantage, and he had personal antipathy toward Valencia. At the same time, Valencia made several negative comments about the armed forces that fueled opposition to his candidacy within the military.[9] And, there continued to be no agreement on how coalition rule would work. Faced with these problems, Alberto Lleras travelled once again to visit Laureano Gómez in Spain.

The plebiscite and mutual guarantees

What form were the mutual guarantees between the parties to take? Fearful of the major alternatives of extended or unstable military rule or renewed partisan and intensified class-oriented violence, and confronted with a divided Conservative Party, Liberals and especially Conservatives were inclined toward a rigid agreement between the two parties. Thus, in the July 1957 Pact of Sitges, Lleras and Gómez agreed to parity in Congress and in the Cabinet for a period of twelve years. They also concurred that the most practical (that is, the most certain) method of instituting this agreement was by means of a national plebiscite, the first in the country's history. If congressional elections were held first and one party received a significant majority, that could complicate the successful passage of a constitutional reform imposing parity. An extra-constitutional agreement to present joint Liberal-Conservative congressional lists would not necessarily solve the problem, since existing electoral laws could not prevent those opposed to the National Front plan from presenting dissident lists (see the discussion by Alberto Lleras in *El Tiempo*, August 29, 1957). Lleras was wildly acclaimed upon his return from Sitges, and the military junta enthusiastically backed the new pact. The Pact of March disappeared from public discourse and the new agreement made no mention of presidential candidacies.

Because of the Conservative divisions, elaboration of the constitutional reform to be approved by the plebiscite required a complex three month process. A draft text was initially prepared by a Committee of Jurists (Comisión Paritaria de Juristas) based on the suggestions written down at Sitges. From there it passed to the Commission on Institutional Readjustment (Comisión Paritaria de Reajuste Institucional),[10] which revised the text in several places. New approval by the Commission of Jurists was sought by Lleras and then the draft text passed to the junta. The text was finally approved by the military junta and its bipartisan council of ministers in October and the plebiscite election was set for December 1, 1957.

The procedure further consolidated support behind the consociational formula engendered by the plebiscite text. From the first draft, the Liberals agreed to a special preamble affirming the centrality of the Catholic Church to the country. But, the core of the agreement were the consociational measures of parity in the Congress, a mandatory two-thirds majority vote until 1968, parity in the Cabinet, and a number of measures to depoliticize public administration. These measures included the creation of a civil service, restrictions on political activities of government employees, and prohibitions against political discrimination in hiring and promoting public officials. Other measures granted women the right to vote (a measure initially passed by Rojas), required that legislators be paid a daily stipend rather than a salary (to inhibit absenteeism), declared that all future constitutional amendments would have to be approved by Congress (underscoring the unusual nature of the plebiscite), and specified that presidential and congressional elections would be held on the same day.

The Commission on Institutional Readjustment instituted three changes, two of which were quite significant. The language was changed so it was clear that parity was meant to cover not only the Cabinet but the entire executive branch.[11] It was specified that members of the armed forces could serve in government independent of the requirements of parity. This increased military confidence in the process and in fact in all subsequent administrations, the minister of defense has always been a ranking military officer. Liberals were reassured and the confidence of the armed forces in the transition process increased. Finally, some flexibility was added to the absolute requirement of a two-thirds majority in Congress by permitting Congress to establish by that vote matters it could legislate on with a simple majority.

Other changes were incorporated by the junta. Parity in government was strengthened by extending it to the judicial branch and granting life tenure to judges in the highest tribunals. The use of simple majority in Congress was limited for specified issue areas to a period of two years without renewed congressional authorization. Finally, the only socially oriented measure of the plebiscite was placed there by the junta: a requirement that at least 10% of the national budget should be spent on education (interview with Villareal, Summer 1982; see also *El Tiempo*, September 20 and October 5, 1957).

Examination of the plebiscite reveals how clearly the immediate concern of the party leaders revolved around the provision of mutual party guarantees. Of the fourteen articles in the final version of the text, fully seven referred to consociational guarantees of some form between the two parties. That so much emphasis was placed on mutual guarantees is not remarkable considering that the agreement was made largely by the very same actors who had been involved in failed attempts at conciliation just years earlier, had seen the country submerged in partisan violence, had feared exclusion from power by Rojas, and now wished to limit mobilization and were concerned about the consequences of the continuing violence. Party leaders saw no other viable alternative to a formal constitutionally mandated pact for equally shared rule.

Presidential candidates

The issue that still threatened to torpedo the carefully constructed agreement remained Valencia's presidential candidacy. The Conservative Party remained divided as ever, reflected in their inability to hold a single party convention. Gómez returned to Colombia in October 1957 to excoriate Valencia who had just been acclaimed as candidate in an Ospinista Convention. Soon after, Valencia's candidacy was rejected at the Laureanista Convention. In November, Gómez wrote to the junta requesting that the plebiscite be postponed and threatening to pull out of the National Front agreement if congressional elections were not held first so that the Conservative faction with the majority could impose its presidential candidate (interview with Navas, Summer 1982). The junta called together the major political leaders at the Presidential Palace (Palacio de San Carlos). The Liberals put pressure on Valencia to concede to Gómez and an agreement was reached *just nine days* before the scheduled date for the plebiscite vote. The "Pact of San Carlos" established that congressional elections would be held prior to the presidential ones and that Valencia's candidacy would have to be ratified by the newly elected members of Congress of both parties (text of accord in Colombia, Cámara de Representantes, 1959: 89–91; interviews with Navas, Carlos Lleras and Jaramillo, Summer 1982).

Although these last-minute complications accentuated conspiratorial opposition (discussed below), the plebiscite was overwhelmingly approved by 4,169,294 voters; only 206,864 negative votes and 20,738 blank ballots were cast.[12] Given the confusion prior to the vote and the complexity of the agreement, it is likely that many voters were not certain for what they were voting. However, major organized groups in the country endorsed the plebiscite, many in large newspaper advertisements: the parties, the Church, industrial, commercial and financial firms and organizations and labor organizations. Only Gilberto Alzate and Jorge Leyva from the right wing of the Conservative Party opposed the constitutional reform.[13] The subsequent March congressional elections ruled out Valencia's candidacy, as Gómez had wished. Gómez' lists won 59% of the Conservative vote. Most of the remaining Conservative vote went to supporters of Valencia, although backers of Alzate, pro-Rojista and anti-National Front, did win a few seats (*El Tiempo*, March 13 and 18, 1958; *Semana*, September 6–13, 1958). The vote again demonstrated a Liberal majority in the country, as Conservative lists received 42% of the total vote.

The central question now became: who would be the National Front candidate for the May 4 presidential elections? The issue was resolved only *ten days* prior to the elections, when Alberto Lleras consented to be the nominee. In accepting, Lleras agreed to present a constitutional amendment to Congress providing for alternation of the presidency between the two parties for the subsequent three terms and extending the agreement on parity in Congress an additional four years. In that way, in the period 1958–74 each party would hold the presidency for two terms and the last National Front President would be a Conservative.

As with the previous negotiations, the steps preceding this determination were fraught with obstacles (Vázquez, n.d.: 312–20; Martz, 1962: 268–9). They fueled considerable Conservative dissatisfaction and a coup attempt two days before the presidential elections. Gómez offered the candidacy to Lleras in a letter on March 30 but then was forced to back off due to rejection by his fellow Conservatives. The Liberals then suggested several names– one Conservative businessman turned down the offer and the other Conservative names were not acceptable to Gómez. Leading Antioquian businessmen helped force the issue by urging Lleras' nomination and on April 2 Gómez received reluctant support from Conservative congressmen (64 of 115). Three days later, Lleras finally accepted the nomination. [14]

Lleras had been the public figure most identified with the bipartisan National Front effort and the opposition to Rojas. Yet, given the fact his candidacy was defined only days before the May 4 election, his margin of victory highlights both the dominance of the National Front actors and the weakness of their opposition. Lleras was opposed by Jorge Leyva, whose sectarian Conservative campaign supported by Alzate garnered only 20% of the total vote and won a majority only in the department of Norte de Santander. On August 7, 1958, Lleras was given the oath of office by the new President of the Senate, Laureano Gómez.

The armed forces during the transition period

The difficulties surrounding final negotiation of the plebiscite and determination of who would be the first National Front President offered opportunities to disgruntled Rojista military and sectarian Conservatives to try to overthrow the junta. Part of the mobilization against the Rojas regime resulted from opposition to the favoritism and corruption of the regime. Continued press about the "crimes" committed during the Rojas government could serve to mobilize support for the civilian alternative. Yet the country was now governed by military officers who had occupied central positions in the previous government and whose continued support was essential for the success of the transition process. In addition, vigorous investigation could also implicate civilians who were now defenders of the transition process. Thus, the central strategy pursued by the party leaders was the *de-linking* of the Rojas regime from the armed forces, suggesting that the attempts to create an independent political movement, his government's economic policies and most of the financial irregularities were committed by members of the "presidential family" and a few civilians closely tied to Rojas, not by the military.[15]

This strategy of de-linking was greatly facilitated by the fact that Rojas' dictatorship was relatively benign, even by 1950s standards (cf. Szulc, 1959). An official investigating committee was established to explore charges of alleged irregularities regarding coffee contraband, double-invoicing of imports, selling of import licenses, livestock transactions, land purchases, use of public agencies for private gain and bank loans for the Rojas family. However, the committee complained of official obstructionism, changed personnel several times and few arrests were made.[16]

The junta made a serious effort to prevent the success of counter-coup movements. Because of the strong pro-Rojas sentiment within the army's intelligence branch, a separate intelligence organization charged with keeping track of conspiracies to overthrow the government was established under General Navas (interviews with Gen. (ret.) José Joaquín Matallana and Col. (ret.) Hernando Forero, Summer 1982). Counter-coup movements found support within arch-Conservative and pro-Rojista groups. Some Conservatives were upset by the presence of Liberals in the cabinet and the fact that Liberals were slowly being appointed as mayors and governors. Some military officers felt a sense of betrayal against Rojas and the armed forces, as well as a loss of status.

The military remained concerned about the continuing violence. Communist guerrilla groups and Liberal bands which had passed over to their ranks in the Sumapaz and adjoining areas, and bandits with vague political coloration, particularly in the coffee-growing regions, remained active. The junta began to explore rehabilitation of areas most affected by the violence and appointed a special commission to study the causes of the violence (this led to the first major work on *la violencia* by Guzmán, Umaña, and Fals, 1963–4). Paid assassins continued operating with impunity, killing prominent amnestied figures such as Guadalupe Salcedo, the former head of the Liberal guerrillas on the Eastern Plains (see the eloquent testimony of Germán Zea Hernández in Alape, 1986: 208–10).

In the second half of 1957, coup conspiracies sought to bring Rojas back to the country. Four months after his fall from power, Rojas was stopped in the Dominican Republic. The junta threatened to suspend the license of any airline that brought

Rojas to Colombia. Another plan called for Rojas to enter Colombia from Venezuela (Cúcuta) and lead a march to Bogotá. Rojas apparently lost his nerve and did not appear.[17] The uprising by the regional police battalion was quickly controlled by loyal troops. In November, as the politicians argued over elections, the junta foiled another coup attempt, arresting and eventually purging many pro-Rojista officers (see *El Tiempo*, September 1 and 3, 1957, and November 18, 1957; interviews with Navas and Forero, Summer 1982).

The most serious challenge to the regime came only two days before the presidential elections. On May 2, 1958, four of the five members of the junta, and Alberto Lleras (the presidential candidate), were apprehended in the early morning by elements of the military police and the national police in Bogotá. The fifth, Piedrahita, avoided capture, and by a fluke, Lleras was released by troops not involved in the plot *en route* to where he was to be held. Lleras and Piedrahita rallied loyalist forces from the Presidential Palace and the support the coup leaders had expected did not emerge. The leaders of the coup, of whom the most important was Lieutenant Colonel Hernando Forero, Commander of the Bogotá Military Police Battalion, were allowed to seek diplomatic asylum in return for the safe release of the junta members.

Additional facts about the failed coup remain in dispute (the following details are from interviews with Forero, Summer, 1982). Two Conservative leaders knew at least the outlines of the coup plot. One, Gilberto Alzate, wrote a draft proclamation that he subsequently recovered when it appeared the coup attempt was failing. Many members of the Constituent Assembly which had re-elected Rojas in May, 1957 and had been dissolved by the junta were prepared to reconvene to provide some legitimacy for the coup. Furthermore, Forero noted the coup was discussed with two members of the junta who never openly rejected it, and that one had expressed interest in serving in a subsequent government if the coup were successful. In addition, the commanders of both the army and the air force were also involved in coup discussions. At the time, Forero accepted most of the blame for the coup, and no attempt was made to investigate his allegations then that higher officials were involved. The junta members denied any involvement, and Lleras absolved them of any responsibility (see also Dix, 1967: 127–8; Leal, 1970; and Revista de Historia, 1977). One plausible interpretation is that the coup was essentially the idea of ambitious middle-level officers in conjunction with a few arch-Conservatives, and that senior military officers may have listened to their plots, and in some cases even acquiesced to them, without seeking direct involvement. Indeed, officers in only four of the seven battalions in Bogotá were directly involved in planning the attempted coup.

Even if the entire junta and Lleras had been captured the outcome of the coup would have been in doubt. The post-coup plans of the plotters, their "mission", was vague. They had shelved the idea of calling for the immediate return of Rojas. There was, moreover, no significant economic or social plan (interview with Forero, 1982). If the coup plot had progressed, violence could have rapidly escalated within the country as civilian opposition expressed itself and the armed forces divided. Liberals had strengthened their organizations and only a minority of the Conservatives would have given their support; Laureanistas, in particular, would have rejected overtures from the military.

Senior military officers, impressed by the support for return to party rule by financial, industrial and commercial elites, fearful of the loss of prestige of the armed forces and the divisive currents within it, and confronted by civilians who appeared sensitive to their major fears, stood by their pledge to withdraw from power. As they perceived the country's situation, probably correctly, the other major alternative was a chaotic period of unstable governments with uncertain domestic or international support. The National Front did not threaten them personally or the armed forces as an institution. On the contrary, it would permit them to focus their attention on what they perceived as a growing guerrilla threat in the countryside and place responsibility for management of the polity and the economy on the civilians.

The economy during the transition period

The junta inherited a country whose economy was in disarray:

> The bad news included growing payment arrears, capital flight, tightening import restrictions, increasing use of bank credit to finance public deficits, as well as a generally expansive credit policy, growing inflationary pressures, a rising black-market peso rate, stagnant real output, and, last but not least, a falling dollar coffee price. (Diaz-Alejandro, 1976: 19)

In its fifteen months in office, the new government imposed a stabilization plan that cleared away many of the short-term economic problems they inherited, permitting the first civilian government to inherit a more positive economic picture. One of the country's central problems remained the external sector because of low coffee prices. The country's total exports dropped significantly in the period the junta was in office. As a result of the government's stabilization program, economic growth declined, industry went into recession, inflation climbed upward and public expenditures were cut back. Real wages, after a brief upsurge due to a decreed wage increase, soon fell due to inflation. Yet, when compared to other countries, the drops in growth rates resulting from the stabilization plan do not appear as sharp in Colombia during these years (Díaz-Alejandro, 1976: 20–1, 24).

Transition leaders – political and economic – viewed recovering Colombia's external credit as essential for economic recovery (see the analysis by the outgoing ANDI President in *El Tiempo*, May 22, 1957). Two weeks after the junta came to power, the International Monetary Fund was invited to visit the country. The most serious problem consisted of the backlog of unpaid short-term commercial loans taken out principally in 1955 and 1956. In June, the government devalued the peso significantly and reduced the differential between the import and export rates, cut public expenditures (including a reduction in the size of the armed forces by 10,000 men) and established a new agency to review import requests. The junta received significant external support for the country, including a $60 million dollar credit from the US Export–Import Bank as well as a $27 million dollar private bank loan. However, as coffee prices continued to drop, reserves also fell and the pressure on the peso intensified. This led, in March, 1958, to a second devaluation as well as to the establishment of a new coffee retention tax (Wiesner, 1978: 72–4).

As it became apparent that the country would need further external assistance, a commission led by Alfonso López Pumarejo and Mariano Ospina, ex-presidents from the two different parties with extensive financial experience, was sent to Washington, DC, just weeks prior to the presidential election. The composition of the commission was intended to reassure international creditors of bipartisan support for a continued stabilization effort, especially important given the uncertainties regarding which party would be in the presidency.[18]

Despite the effects of the stabilization program, opposition was muted. The Coffee Federation supported the devaluation as well as the reduction in the differential between the exchange rates for imports and exports, claiming the differential had discriminated against coffee producers, unfairly benefiting industry or commerce or being employed by the state to finance public works that did not necessarily benefit the country's coffee-growing regions (Zuleta, 1975). Although some industrialists grumbled about the mechanics of the import licensing scheme or argued government expenditures should be cut even further, there was an overwhelming sense that the country required a stabilization program. Much of their opposition to Rojas had been predicated on their belief that the country's *first* priority had to be the re-establishment of external credit, which concomitantly would provide the basis to attract foreign investment which they sought. Labor criticism was muted by modest wage increases, the establishment of new programs and the granting of additional legal suport for unions (*El Tiempo*, December 7, 1957; interview with Raimundo Emiliani [minister of labor during the junta period], Summer 1982).

The country's economic well-being was tied to the political formula of transition. Alberto Lleras told a group of military officers in February 1958 that those seeking to prevent the establishment of the National Front:

are prepared to ruin definitively Colombia's prestige in the world, her credit, her possibilities for foreign investment in our businesses, her possibilities for prosperity, including – without any exaggeration – the compromising of Colombia's fundamental industry; because, given the state of coffee prices in today's world markets, a *coup d'état* could be all that is needed so that, with the delicate control of international coffee policy lost, inventories which fourteen coffee-producing countries have been making to sustain the price will be brought onto the market, generating a crisis. (Junta Militar de Gobierno, 1958: 222–3)

The junta's economic stabilization program provided Alberto Lleras with the opportunity to initiate his government in August 1958 with a more expansive economic program. Future Colombian presidents were not to be so fortunate at their inauguration.

Consociational success

The transition to civilian rule in Colombia in 1958 was spearheaded by leaders of the country's two major political parties, the Liberal and the Conservative, who had committed themselves by a series of pacts eventually approved by a national plebiscite to govern the country jointly (and exclusively). Just a few years earlier, political conflict between the two parties paved the way for one of the bloodiest chapters in Colombia's already violence-stricken history, *la violencia*, whose effects were still being felt in the late 1950s. The national political leadership "learned" the value of conciliation and compromise.

There is little question that the result of the transition process was a consociational regime in a descriptive sense. The unique strength and nature of the two political parties in Colombia made them functional alternatives to segments in other conflict-ridden societies. And the mechanisms of parity, alternation and mutual veto of the National Front agreement as it finally emerged, of over-arching elite cooperation by means of a "grand coalition" form of government, were unmistakably consociational.

But the process also led to a consociational regime in the theoretical sense. A return to civilian, limited democratic rule in 1958 was essentially inconceivable without extensive mutual guarantees between the two political parties. Only by working together could they effectively oppose Rojas or prevent a succession of military governments, and only by promising to govern together could they prevent a rekindling of partisan violence with its increasing overtones of class conflict. The major alternatives to some version of shared two-party rule were extended and increasingly unstable military rule or an attempt to promote one-party (Conservative) rule with the likelihood of kindling renewed partisan violence. In both of these cases, there was also the possibility that class-oriented conflict by Communist guerrilla groups and radicalized Liberal ones combined with banditry and other forms of violence would have intensified, although their actual threat to the national state appeared to be relatively minor.

One can still ask if such a formal, rigid constitutional agreement was necessary. In most consociational cases, the mechanisms are not embedded in the Constitution but in party pacts and agreements. The rigidity of the agreement in Colombia reflected the fact that national politicians "learned" to distrust local level leaders and fear mass mobilization since it had gotten out of their control and led to *la violencia*, radicalization and banditry. Liberals, though the majority party, were bargaining from a disadvantageous position out of power and were thus more willing to pact on an equal basis with Conservatives. Rigidity was favored more by the minority Conservatives and was more easily imposed due to the division in the party with part of it in power and part outside. The peculiar mechanism of presidential alternation, in turn, was more directly a result of the Conservative division and the political calculations of Laureano Gómez.

Leadership, statecraft and political learning were crucial to consociational success. The key events of this period such as the fall of Rojas, the party pacts and their approval and the choice of president point to the fact that the most difficult problems revolved around reaching inter-elite agreement, not "selling" the solutions that were reached to the parties' mass following. The leaders of the two parties that had been in conflict with each other moved from intransigence and violence to compromise and conciliation. Yet, the analysis above has sought to demonstrate the importance of structural factors in providing the opportunities for the dual processes of removal of the military and transition to civilian rule to succeed. The perspective of consociational theorists such as Lijphart, who emphasizes that successful consociational outcomes are possible if the political elites have the will to work for them, though refreshing in its rejection of socio-economic determinism, appears incomplete and thus may be too politically voluntaristic.

In addition to political factors, then, what other factors help explain the establishment of consociationalism in Colombia? As other scholars have also noted, the factors Lijphart presents as conducive to the establishment and maintenance of consociationalism tend to change only slowly through time. Thus, they are not too helpful in explaining successful consociationalism in a case such as Colombia where agreement came only a decade after failed efforts and serious violence. The factors viewed as favorable by Lijphart are: over-arching trans-segmental loyalties; a smaller country; prior traditions of elite accommodation; geographical separation of the segments in conflict; a balance of power between the segments that preferably are more than two; and, least important, cross-cutting cleavages, especially of class (see Lijphart, 1977: 53–103). If we were to "score" these, ranging from −2 for "very unfavorable" to 2 for "very favorable", out of a possible high score of 12 (6 × 2), the Colombian case would score only a −1. Favorable conditions would include over-arching loyalties, as neither party considered secession or viewed itself as linked to another nation-state, and cross-cutting cleavages, as both parties have incorporated elements from all social groups. On the other hand, these factors were not sufficient to prevent *la violencia*. Given the past history of both violence and accommodation, prior traditions of elite compromise were ambiguous, thus meriting a neutral score. Similarly, the size of the country is neutral. As Liberals and Conservatives were found throughout the country, sometimes in the same communities and often in adjoining communities, there was little segmental isolation, thus this was unfavorable. Very unfavorable was the balance of power between the segments as these were only two and the Liberals were the majority (for a related critique, see Dix, 1980a: 310–12).

Certain factors contributed to the overthrow of the Rojas regime and to the establishment of the National Front and facilitated the necessary change in political will among national leaders. At the international level, the US opposition to the Rojas regime in part due to its Peronist trappings, including the withdrawal of credit by the US and by international financial institutions and the subsequent extension of credit and diplomatic support to the interim military junta and civilian backers were significant. However, the overall economic picture for Colombia during this period was clouded by the low world price for the country's major export product, coffee. The country's dependency on this product and the harmful effects of its low price on the country's exports did not change from the period of the Rojas government to that of the junta.

More significant factors of explanation for the fall of Rojas and for the successful establishment of the National Front must be sought at the national level. The key factor operating against Rojas was the fact that the two traditional political parties completely dominated the country's political landscape. International actors supported initiatives sponsored by domestic political and economic actors. A more organized and diversified industrial sector had increased capabilities and greater reasons beyond the ties of traditional party loyalties to oppose Rojas, for the civilian alternative promised greater stability and economic policies more consonant with their interests than Rojas' statist and populist policies. More immediately, the experience of *la violencia* was devastating to the Church and to party leaders, encouraging compromise which was made even more compelling by the efforts at *continuismo* of Rojas and the fear of incipient radical movements in

the countryside. As these factors led party leaders to seek an inter-
party agreement, they were aided by the fact that bipartisan coalition rule was rooted in historical antecedents.

Yet establishment of the National Front was not inevitable. At a
number of points the process appeared to be near a total impasse.
These critical junctures – the Pact of Sitges and the national
plebiscite, the Pact of San Carlos regarding congressional elections and the Valencia candidacy, the last-minute selection of
Alberto Lleras as presidential candidate – reflected neither
institutional or ideological problems nor problems with mobilization from below by party faithful, but the continued domination
of the political landscape by party leaders in control of collec-
tivities with entrenched loyalties. The solutions reached indicated
the creativity of the country's political leaders and their considerable capacity to reach agreements with opposing party leaders
and carry their party followers along. Gómez' imposition of the
Lleras candidacy, even if at eventual personal political cost, was an
excellent example of that capacity. The fact that counter-
movements were unable to take advantage of these moments of
near paralysis in the process – for example, the unraveling of the
conspiratorial movement prior to the plebiscite, the dismal
failure of the May 2, 1958 coup, the small percentage of votes for
the Conservative Leyva in spite of the sudden switch to a Liberal
presidential candidate – underscores how favorable the structural
and environmental conditions were and how weak the
challenges.

Once established, though, a regime must continue to strive for
legitimacy and support as it seeks to enact its policies. The predicaments of consociationalism took little time in emerging.

4

The National Front political regime: an introduction

Introduction: regime predicaments

The political regime established in 1958 contained numerous elements of historical continuity. The traditional parties, the country's regional structure, the limited state role in the economy and the controlled incorporation of the popular sector primarily through party rather than state ties were inherited from the past and would continue to have an impact on the country's political and economic evolution. Even many of the key individual players were the same. The regime "project" was essentially a defensive one. Two alternative means of political organization had been rejected: Gómez' efforts to form a corporatist–falangist state and Rojas' populist goal of creating a political movement outside of the parties. Though the National Front was born out of crisis, its purpose was neither to confront directly the socio-economic aspects of the breakdown and of the violence nor to seek to deepen political incorporation. Rather, the party leaders and their socio-economic allies saw the National Front at least in part as a restoration of their rule in a more secure, "civilizing" fashion, a rule that had been challenged due to their previous intransigence by *la violencia* and then by Rojas' rule. In that sense, the National Front represented a logical institutional alternative for economically dominant groups to support in terms of long-term concerns with capitalist development in a stable political environment. These concerns were to require rebuilding and modernizing the state apparatus and developing operating "rules of the game" to manage the new regime's predicaments.

The agreement was also enacted because it promised something for all major party groups and dominant economic actors in the short term. The Liberals regained a foothold in political power, the Ospinistas retained their position of power without the burden of their untrustworthy military allies, and the Laureanistas regained their position within the party and a chance at political power. The consociational arrangement of parity and alternation served the bureaucratic and pork-barrel interests of national and regional party leaders. The Church could view itself as a force of conciliation for all Colombians as both parties now recognized its privileged position and institutionally it preserved greater autonomy. The military were promised autonomy and respect, and producer groups could expect greater access to policy circles and thus economic policies more to their liking. Lacking was any autonomous organized presence of different popular groups. With the exception of the small pockets of armed struggle, most popular organizations had been destroyed in the *violencia*. Popular groups had played no direct role in the regime's creation, but for them the agreement heralded peace and held out the promise of social reform.

The regime sustained a precarious balance, a balance that became more precarious in the post-National Front period (1978 on) as the political parties sought to maintain the same political mechanisms in a societal structure changed by the National Front experience itself as well as massive population growth, continued rural to urban migration, industrialization and other socio-economic changes.[1] The conflicts generated by the contradictory reasons for supporting the regime by different key actors were reflected in two central points of tension found in all consociational regimes, similar to those that may be experienced in democratic regimes more generally. The first relates to inter-elite accommodation and the danger of immobilism, if elites cannot reach agreements because of inter-party or intra-party differences. The difficulties many democratic regimes find in establishing working majorities for policy purposes and managing executive–legislative relations can be considerably magnified in consociational cases such as Colombia when the need for inter-party support or a two-thirds congressional majority are built into a prior agreement.[2] Support could be held back due to intractable policy differences or for narrow partisan reasons, resulting in either case in immobilism. Another possibility is policy incoherence as the regime is continually forced to change policies as different groups successfully pressure for measures that further their interests or to prevent the implementation of policies they believe oppose them.

The second point of tension regards elite–mass relations or what Nordlinger terms "structured elite predominance" (Nordlinger, 1972) and the danger of a lack of popular responsiveness. Party leaders required considerable independent power and secure leadership positions to bargain with their counterparts; at the same time, they needed to retain popular support if regime stability was to rest more on democratic legitimacy than on coercion. Yet the regime also had to accommodate the interests of its key support groups. The tendency toward mutual vetoes inherent in consociationalism combined with the tendency in pluralist regimes for the more powerful to be better organized and have more potential influence, to thwart social reform and stimulate political protest. At the same time, policy incoherence also threatened from the tension between elected officials seeking to strengthen their positions by serving particularistic or regional demands and the desire for more general political orientations and effectiveness from central government. It was in response to these three predicaments inherent in the political formula of consociationalism –*threatened immobilism, lack of popular responsiveness and policy incoherence*– that certain "rules of the game," alternative institutional mechanisms and informal means were sought (cf. Lijphart, 1977: 122–3).

The major groups and actors domestically and internationally that most effectively placed demands upon and supported the regime – producer groups, the Church, the military and international agencies – and their relationship to the regime are sketched in the next section. The interaction of the political regime with these producer groups and international agencies is analyzed in chapter 5. The central political actors, the political parties, are examined in the next section. A major reason that the regime predicaments were felt so acutely was the fact that the serious division within the Conservative party was soon mirrored by an ideological split in the Liberal party even as ambitions responding to the logic of brokerage politics and coalition rule generated more extensive party factionalization. Thus, factionalization was a complex phenomenon that responded in part to the electoral incentives of the National Front structure and in part emerged as a form of expressing political dissent. The contradictory role of the regime structure and the political parties in seeking to strengthen regime legitimacy and support is addressed in chapter 6.

The principal "rules of the game" in Colombia, detailed in the subsequent section, have reflected the predicaments imposed by the structure of the regime, built upon historical antecedents and responded in part to the demands of some of the more powerful groups and actors domestically and internationally. The practices that emerged are not unknown in other political regimes, which reflects the fact that related regime types often confront similar kinds of predicaments and seek to resolve them in similar ways. However, the mechanisms and means devised in Colombia, taken as a whole, have reflected the particular nature of the country's political regime as it sought to prevent total immobilism and strike a balance between responsiveness and effectiveness. These various "rules" were informal, which meant that the use of mechanisms was never institutionalized and specific actors never clearly delineated. From its inception particularly due to the continual risk of immobilism, the regime had a sense of contingency existence and appeared continually to exist from crisis to crisis. The last two sections illustrate this by examining the operation of the "rules of the game" in two core regime processes, presidential selection and constitutional reform. Presidential alternation forced the parties to negotiate with each other regarding what became an increasingly more important office in the country, continuing to make the selection process of presidential nominees after 1958 as complex and conflict-prone as the nomination of Alberto Lleras had been in that year. Reform of the constitutional strictures that formed the National Front and impelled creation of the particular informal regime "rules" was also a difficult process. The stormy passage of the 1968 Constitutional Reform provides an example of the operation of the regime "rules," even as its final outcome exacerbated some of the political tensions that have plagued the regime into the present.

Supporting groups and actors

The political regime was established by the actions of political leaders with the active support of many economically dominant groups and Church leaders. The support of international actors such as the US government and international financial institutions such as the World Bank soon followed. And with the tense transition from military to civilian rule successfully achieved, the armed forces became a major supporter of the National Front regime. The support of these groups continued to be critical to the success of the National Front and subsequent coalition governments and depended upon such factors as their favorable access to the regime, the regime's overall policy orientation and its ability and willingness to maintain order.

Producer groups

The establishment of the National Front was made possible by the aggressive support of industrialists, bankers and merchants who through their interest associations helped organize a national strike that paralyzed the country and precipitated the final crisis that led to Rojas' overthrow.[3] The coffee sector and other agricultural interests, preferring a low political profile, offered more passive support. The ouster of Rojas and the return to civilian rule was perceived as assuring all these groups much greater access and influence over policy.

Reflecting the relatively late integration of Colombia into the world market and its somewhat delayed process of industrialization compared to other major Latin American countries, most producer associations in Colombia have been formed fairly recently, in the period from the 1940s to the present. Only the agricultural, coffee, banking and some professional associations were founded earlier (see Table 4.1). And reflecting the relatively weak state these groups faced, they have not developed a single peak association to represent private sector interests in Colombia.[4] The closest approximation to a peak association is the National Association of Industrialists (ANDI), which includes major industrial firms, as well as firms in agro-industry, finance, insurance and commercial distribution. Nevertheless, because it was founded and has retained its headquarters in Medellín, center of the country's textile industry (and originally largely national capital), ANDI has also sometimes been perceived as a regional pressure group for domestic industrial interests. The financial sector in Colombia was represented by the Colombian Bankers Association (ASOBANCARIA) and the Union of Colombian Insurance Companies (FASECOLDA) until the 1970s. Due to personality and policy clashes, a major financial conglomerate, the Banco de Colombia and associated firms, and other companies left ASOBANCARIA to form their own association, the National Association of Financial Institutions (ANIF).

In the agricultural sector, the Agricultural Society of Colombia

Table 4.1 *Principal producer associations in Colombia*

Interest group	Sector	Year Founded
Sociedad de Agricultores de Colombia (SAC)	Agriculture	1871
Asociación Bancaria de Colombia (ASOBANCARIA)	Banking	1936
Federación Nacional de Cafeteros de Colombia (FEDERACAFE)	Coffee	1927
Asociación Nacional de Industriales (ANDI)	Industry ("modern sector")	1944
Federación Nacional de Comerciantes (FENALCO)	Commerce	1945
Cámara Colombiana de la Construcción (CAMACOL)	Construction	1957
Federación Colombiana de Ganaderos (FEDEGAN)	Livestock	1959
Confederación Colombiana de Cámaras de Comercio (CONFECAMARAS)	Chambers of Commerce	1969
Asociación Nacional de Instituciones Financieras (ANIF)	Banking and Finance	1974
Unión de Aseguradores Colombianos (FASECOLDA)	Insurance	1976

(SAC) and the National Livestock Federation (FEDEGAN) have served as convenient mouthpieces for large landowner and livestock interests, but the two associations have been financially weak and technically deficient, with few if any professional staff. A gradual change within SAC occurred in the mid-1960s as traditional landowners were slowly displaced from positions of influence by commercial farmers, especially of rice and cotton (Gilhodès, 1979: 122). Not until the 1980s, though, were more technically proficient administrators being hired to direct these agricultural associations (a reflection of that is the SAC-supported history of its own association, Bejarano, 1985: see especially 328–39). In contrast, the powerful Coffee Federation of Colombia (FEDERACAFE) and to a lesser extent the associations for export crops such as sugar (ASOCAÑA) and cotton (FEDERALGODON), have been extremely well-organized and professional.

In the last thirty years, many more specialized interest associations have been formed, reflecting increased economic specialization and diversification. Although many of these groups had policy differences with various of the coalition governments, no significant coalition of groups withdrew support from the regime to seek another governing alternative. In fact, as we shall see in chapter 5, producer associations have provided a crisis-ridden regime important independent backing at critical moments. Furthermore, for these groups the country's experience of military government was overwhelmingly negative, a fact that served with diminishing intensity through time to hold back support for another military intervention. By and large, the individual associations have not been particularly powerful over their own sector and in that sense have not been effective representatives, though their capabilities evidently extend far beyond those of working-class or peasant associations. ANDI's abilities to negotiate authoritatively for its member firms has been limited and it has had no effective capacity to impose sanctions for non-compliance of agreements. Even the powerful Coffee Federation has had limited influence over private coffee exporters.[5].

Reflecting the heterogeneity of the two traditional political parties, *all* major producer associations have been bi-partisan in makeup. SAC briefly flirted with the idea of its own political party in 1909–10 and again in 1933–4, but then became the first major association to adopt consciously a bipartisan style with party parity on its board of directors.[6] Of the twenty-five managers who signed the initial charter forming ANDI in 1944, I was able to identify thirteen as Conservative and ten as Liberal (two could not be classified). And from its inception it was agreed ANDI would not express itself on partisan matters.[7] The Coffee Federation, which had always been careful to retain both bipartisan and regional balance, in 1958 increased the number of private directors on its board from five to six in order to insure partisan parity in keeping with the National Front spirit. SAC, ANDI, FEDERACAFE and the other major producer associations have sought to maintain a regional as well as a partisan balance on their boards of directors.[8]

In a complex *pas de deux*, more common in the agricultural sector than elsewhere, political figures have sometimes been appointed as managers of producer associations and previously non-political managers of these associations have occasionally been selected as cabinet ministers or for other high government posts. Weaker presidents have tended to rely more on party figures to fill their cabinets, whereas more autonomous presidents have recruited more broadly.[9]

Producer groups feared government immobilism, yet sometimes promoted it at the expense of what they viewed as excessive popular responsiveness or government efficiency which contradicted their interests. In other instances, they encouraged government effectiveness in areas that favored them. The regime structure particularly favored access to key policy-making circles by producer groups. Because of its bipartisan nature, coalition rule increased channels of access for them even as it fragmented power across party factions, particularly in periods of a weak presidency.

The Church, the military and international actors

Shifts in perspective of two other domestic groups were significant in the successful establishment of the National Front: the Church and the military. Changes within each of them and conciliatory gestures by the political parties guaranteed their support. After initially supporting Rojas out of growing concern over *la violencia*, the Church broke dramatically with his government and firmly supported his overthrow. Laureano Gómez' bitter denunciations of the Church from exile for its acceptance of the Rojas regime convinced many in the hierarchy of the dangers of continued close identification with a single party. Furthermore, many in the Church felt threatened by the experience of *la violencia* (Martz, 1962: 219–21). Changes in the Church hierarchy and conciliatory gestures by the Liberal Party contributed to the Church's readiness to withdraw from partisan politics and support the National Front.[10]

The Colombian Church has remained among the most conservative on the continent, opposing activist stands against societal inequalities. The country's experience with *la violencia* and the fact that National Front governments were never harshly repressive were important in consolidating the Colombian Church's rejection of conflict and violence (see Levine and Wilde, 1977: 220–49). One of the clearest examples of this was the condemnation of Camilo Torres as he advocated insurrection against the regime.[11] The Church provided the regime with legitimacy. Although Church officials often attacked the regime for immobilism, lack of reform or inefficiency, their clear condemnation of violence as a means of effecting social change and their appeals for participation within the regime structures reinforced regime legitimacy.[12] As a result of its withdrawal from partisan politics and due to urbanization, the centrality of the Church gradually declined in Colombian political life.[13]

The creation of the National Front was initially organized as an anti-military governing alternative, as its original name "Civil Front" (Frente Civil) intimated. Once the higher military officers ousted Rojas and pledged to hold elections permitting a return to civilian rule in the country, party leaders worked together with the military junta to rebuild the image of the military. The Civil Front became the National Front. Party leaders sought to de-link the military from the Rojas government and in the final negotiations of the National Front pact the military were given further assurances of autonomy in managing their affairs by changes in the plebiscite text that permitted a military figure to be appointed minister of defense (as indeed has been the case ever since 1958).

The military became a major prop of the National Front, although by continental standards their size and budget remained relatively modest.[14] Particularly in the early 1960s, they played a major role in combat against armed bands and remaining guerrilla groups, without totally eliminating them. The Army increasingly took responsibility for maintenance of public order, not only in selected rural areas but also in cities during major demonstrations and labor and civic strikes and on election day. The practice of naming military mayors in areas of guerrilla violence continued and, beginning with the state of siege of May 1965, certain crimes by civilians were channelled to verbal courts-martial under military justice rather than civilian courts, a practice which had also existed under Rojas. Under the National Front, the military became an increasingly more professional military, developing an institutional self-conception independent from the two traditional parties (Leal, 1984). This process of movement away from identification with either of the traditional parties fostered generalized support for the regime, permitting the regime to employ the military as an instrument to contain popular demands or confront guerrilla threats in the face of regime immobilism or lack of responsiveness. Yet, the slowly increasing autonomy of the military also meant that regime authorities needed to address its demands in a more systematized and less *ad hoc* fashion through time, particularly by the 1980s when other parts of the state were in disarray and the country confronted challenges from guerrilla movements and drug trafficking.

In addition to support from these key domestic groups, the National Front regime also found international backing. Regime survival in the 1960s was clearly facilitated by the "bonanza" of foreign aid it received. The return to civilian rule in 1958 was a welcome development in the eyes both of major international agencies and of the US government. With Colombia's return to democratic rule and willingness to meet Alliance for Progress "conditions" – paramount was preparation of a national development plan – Colombia became a "showcase" for the aid plan. In addition, during these years the country was the World Bank's fourth largest borrower. Consociationalism encouraged and the World Bank and other borrowers promoted state institution building in economic planning and implementation of programs that fostered a "syndrome of depoliticization" (see Cepeda, 1977). Colombia was also able to rely on international aid agencies for emergency funding to deal with its recurring balance of payments problems (particularly in the early and mid-1960s) which assured the country would not collapse economically. Thus, these agencies saw their central mission as promoting policy coherence and circumventing immobilism by depoliticization. Although the economic growth and employment their programs generated aided popular responsiveness, their approach weakened the perception that what little responsiveness existed was due to the regime's political agents even as the country's development model did not lead to substantial improvements in social equity.

The political parties and factionalism

If the role of producer associations and other supportive groups was important to the regime's continuing viability – even as the regime provided means for these groups to advance their interests – this was due in part to the fact that the political parties were not fully playing the ambitious role prescribed for them by the

National Front agreement. The agreement was written as if the two parties were coherent entities. Yet, historically the Colombian parties have been factionalized and have revolved around political clientele groups. And, as we saw in chapter 3, divisions within the Conservative Party nearly destroyed the agreement at key points during the negotiation process. During the National Front, party factionalism remained a central problem for the political regime. Factionalism contributed a small measure of regime legitimacy as it provided alternative electoral channels both for sectarian faithful who could not bring themselves to vote for the opposition party as well as for others opposed to the coalition governments on socio-economic grounds. Yet, most party factions were built around clientele groups or clusters of such groups and devoted their energies to patronage politics. Factionalism initially aided the regime objective of responsiveness, though ultimately in a counter-productive fashion as party leaders continued to collaborate in government and simultaneously attempted to serve as political opposition. As a consequence, factionalism also seriously threatened to induce immobilism and to prevent policy coherence.

Although the National Front rested upon the country's two traditional parties, it had features of both a one-party and a multi-party system. Presidential alternation required both parties to agree on an "official National Front candidate," which made the regime appear to be based upon a "single" party with hegemonic aspirations. There was no way to express inter-party dissent by "voting the rascals out" and each election became in effect a new plebiscite on the National Front. At the same time, party factionalism forced each president to create and recreate an effective governing coalition, making the National Front period resemble a multi-party system. Managing coalition politics was even more complex prior to 1968 because of the need for a two-thirds majority vote on most legislation. Table 4.2 summarizes information about the major party factions during the National Front based on electoral results and faction position at election time. Sub-factional dissidences created primarily for electoral purposes and which disappeared shortly thereafter are not included. Following elections, new factions were sometimes created and old ones disbanded as congressmen shifted allegiances and factions changed their position toward the National Front on the basis of electoral results. These changes are also not reflected in the table.

As is apparent from the table, anti-National Front forces increased steadily during the National Front to around 30% of the seats, declined in 1968 as the Revolutionary Liberal Movement (MRL – Movimiento Revolucionario Liberal) re-entered the mainstream Liberal Party, and jumped in 1970 back up to 33%. However, with the convincing Liberal victory in the 1974 competitive elections and the decline of the National Popular Alliance (ANAPO – Alianza Nacional Popular), opposition movements almost disappeared from Congress.

The logic of coalition rule combined with an electoral system that permitted each party to present multiple lists on election day sustained and encouraged additional factionalism. With both parties guaranteed a share of government, struggles over use of government resources and patronage participation shifted from inter-party conflict to *intra*-party factional disputes. Regional and local politicians sought to enact laws providing for particularistic benefits and fought among each other for patronage posts. They joined together to fight the aspirations of those political leaders, such as Carlos Lleras, who sought to restrict their access to resources and favored policies of a more rational "collective goods" allocation. The influence of national leaders over their parties declined, particularly in the Liberal party, and regional leaders more autonomously determined party lists. In 1962, for example, Ospinistas were able to present single lists for Congress in only fourteen departments, while the Liberals (without even considering the dissident MRL faction) were only able to achieve that in ten departments. Liberal Party statutes, written by Carlos Lleras in 1963, and which sought to rationalize party organization and broaden participation, were continually "suspended" as regional politicians successfully protested their implementation. Increasingly, national party organizations or leaders became simply "referees" in cases in which regional party leaders agreed to turn to them for assistance. Otherwise, relations were based more on mutual support and convenience. By 1982, the Liberal presidential candidate, López, sought to influence only the party list in the department of Cundinamarca (whose capital, Bogotá, was also the nation's capital) (Lara, 1983).

Party factions could be distinguished by their durability, by the extent to which they were dominated by a single leader and by the relative importance of ideology. The most durable party factions were found in the Conservative Party as a result of the historic

Table 4.2 *Seats held by party and faction in the House (%) 1958–74*

Party and faction	Year							
	1958	1960	1962	1964	1966	1968	1970	1974
Presidential period	A. Lleras 1958–62 (Liberal)		Valencia 1962–6 (Conservative)		C. Lleras 1966–70 (Liberal)		Pastrana 1970–4 (Conservative)	López 1974–8 (Liberal)
Pro-government								
Liberals								
(Oficialistas)	50%	38%	32%	32%	36%	38%	27%	57%
Conservatives								33%[1]
(Laureanistas)	33%							
(Ospinistas)		24%	27%	35%	18%	24%	14%	
SUB-TOTAL	83%	62%	59%	67%	54%	62%	41%	90%
Dissident								
Liberals								
(Dissidents)						8%		
(Belisaristas)							2%	
(Sourdistas & others)							7%	
Conservatives								
(Ospinistas)	13%							
(Alvaristas)		25%	25%	–	14%	10%		
(Belisaristas)							9%	
(Sourdistas)							6%	
SUB-TOTAL	13%	25%	20%	0%	14%	18%	25%	0%
Anti-National Front								
Liberals								
(MRL)		12%	18%	17%	11%	1%		
(ANAPO)				.5%	2%	3%	13%	
Conservatives								
(Alzatistas or Leyvistas)	4%	.6%		.5%	.5%			
(ANAPO)			3%	14%	17%	14%	20%	7%
Opposition								2%
SUB-TOTAL	4%	13%	21%	32%	30%	18%	33%	9%
TOTAL[2]	100%	100%	100%	100%	100%	100%	100%	100%
TOTAL (N)	148	152	184	184	190	204	210	199

[1]Joint lists.
[2]May not add to 100% due to rounding error.
Source: Registraduría Nacional del Estado Civil; *El Tiempo*, June 29, 1978.

division between Laureano Gómez and Mariano Ospina. Ospina was linked to coffee and construction interests and Gómez was associated with landowner groups and with falangist ideology.[15] The intense division between these two figures, though, stems more from their bitter political interaction in the 1940s and 1950s, discussed in chapters 2 and 3, than from profound programmatic differences. At regional and local levels, their political allies and clientele groups battled each other more around efforts to secure political resources and positions (patronage) than over policies. In some cases, party factions began loosely associated with national party figures, as regional leaders sought to build increasingly more independent power bases of their own, potentially to aspire to national leadership. Julio César Turbay was a national leader who worked his way up and built his power base primarily upon patronage politics. More ideological were party factions such as the Revolutionary Liberal Movement (MRL) founded by Alfonso López Michelsen (son of the Liberal president of the 1930s and 1940s) or the faction around Carlos Lleras Restrepo that sought to strengthen and rationalize the state and limit pork-barrel politics. And a heterogeneous populist movement gradually emerged around General Rojas. Finally, there were more ephemeral factions or sub-factions that were created around specific elections. A common cause for breaking away from one faction to join or create another was dissatisfaction with the placement of one's name on a party-faction's electoral list. Often justified on ideological or programmatic grounds, this kind of factionalism was almost always the result of tactical calculations by aspiring regional or local leaders.

In its early years more of an opposition movement than a Liberal party faction, López' MRL was initially formed to protest the requirement of presidential alternation though it also called for greater economic and social reforms. The MRL served as a means for more radical groups, including the Communist Party, to present candidates for elections: a prominent example was Juan de la Cruz Varela, leader of the Communist guerrillas of the Sumapaz, who was elected to Congress for the MRL.[16] The MRL was particularly strong in rural Liberal municipalities, especially those which had been affected by *la violencia* (Oquist, 1973). The MRL provided a peaceful way for former Liberal guerrillas and Liberal victims of *la violencia* to channel distrust of Conservatives and desires for social change through electoral means. The most serious threat to the National Front posed by the MRL came in the form of López' candidacy to the Presidency in 1962. With Liberals being asked to vote for a Conservative candidate and the Conservative Party divided, National Front leaders fearing a possible López victory had his candidacy declared unconstitutional. Following that election, President Valencia pragmatically gave the MRL a cabinet seat, though the MRL left government only a month later. Yet López gradually shifted from a position of total opposition to the National Front to one of partial opposition. [17] This helped cause a split in the MRL between his larger *linea blanda* and a smaller *linea dura*. Several of the founding leaders of the ELN guerrilla movement also came from the MRL youth movement (Behar, 1985: 54–5). López officially ended his opposition in 1967, negotiating his "re-entry" into the mainstream of the Liberal Party with then Liberal President Carlos Lleras (see Ramírez Aljure, 1986: 45–55). From 1958 to 1967, the rest of the party was nominally unified under the Oficialista banner, though strains among national leaders and regional and sub-factional dissidences were apparent.

Factionalism and opposition posed its most serious challenge to the regime in 1970 when two regional figures competed against the official National Front candidate. Without question, the most significant opposition movement during the National Front was the heterogeneous populist National Popular Alliance (ANAPO) which nearly won these elections. ANAPO first presented party lists under the Conservative banner in the 1962 elections. Eventually, it also presented Liberal lists, though these were never as successful. The movement's steady growth through the 1960s was a source of tremendous concern to the National Front party leaders and its near victory in the 1970 elections was a major regime crisis. From its high point that year, ANAPO rapidly declined. [18]

It is impossible to understand coalition formation or behavior within the two traditional parties solely or primarily on group (or class fraction) interest over patronage-oriented regional or clientelistic grounds; the latter played a substantial role. The Laureanista electoral losses in 1960 appear to have been due in part to Gómez' decision to support a Liberal for president in 1958, as well as to a clever opposition campaign by the Alza–Ospinistas. Gómez' decision to leave the National Front coalition at that point appeared to result more from personal pique and a hope that this would permit his faction greater electoral victories in the future than to ideological differences, which could have been expressed as easily within the coalition.[19] Subsequent decisions by his movement to enter and then to leave the Valencia government seemed equally motivated.

Similarly, in the Liberal Party, various political calculations shaped the major contours of factional politics. Although there were "programmatic" discussions between Alfonso López and Carlos Lleras before the MRL re-joined the pro-National Front Liberals, by that period patronage and electoral issues were also significant. As noted, López' stridency had diminished following the 1962 elections; the issue of presidential alternation was not relevant to the Liberals for the 1966 election. The division in the Liberal Party between Carlos Lleras and Julio César Turbay dated back at least to the early 1960s when their personal political ambitions clashed. They intensified during the Lleras presidency as Turbay sought to protect regional and clientelist forces from the centralizing and rationalizing Lleras reforms. Lleras and López shared a more reformist view, though López was more skeptical of land reform (expropriation and redistribution) and of import-substituting industrialization (a useful summary of López' ideas is Gómez Buendía, 1978) and more willing to compromise with traditional pork-barrel politicians, as had been his father in the 1930s. The coalition between the "reformist" Lopistas and the "conservative" Alvaristas during López' presidency, illogical if viewed in "ideological" terms, was facilitated by the affinity between the two leaders (and, some would note, of the unusual friendship between their fathers) who had both been "outcasts" for many of the National Front years, and by some of López' more market-oriented and export-oriented economic policies.[20] Similarly, opposition to López from Ospino-Pastranistas was not ideological but was generated primarily by López' attacks on the record of the previous Pastrana administration; Llerista opposition to López stemmed in part from López' success in gaining the party's nomination over Lleras for the 1974 race and in part from principled opposition to pork-barrel politics.

As this review illustrates, all National Front presidents faced considerable opposition as a result of party factionalism, albeit of varying nature. Some factions or movements opposed the regime, whereas others opposed specific governments for electoral, regional, personalistic or tactical reasons. And pro-National Front forces often expressed programmatic differences on specific bills or issues. Factions across parties often found themselves in closer agreement with each other during the National Front than with factions from their own party.[21] Party factionalism intensified problems of governance and thus the need for "rules of the game" to manage the regime predicaments of threatened immobilism, policy incoherence and lack of popular responsiveness.

Rules of the game

The National Front political regime managed conflictive policymaking issues and political crises by employing processes and mechanisms which were largely unforeseen in the pact itself and which were not written down, a "mixture of procedural rules and general orientations toward politics" (Lijphart, 1977: 122). The immobilism generated by the consociational agreement and the party factionalism that it further encouraged initially weakened the political parties, one of which entered the National Front already divided, and led to numerous executive-legislative deadlocks. To deal with these deadlocks, *presidential authority* was increased as Congress was marginalized from many key decisions. As we shall see below and in chapters 5 and 6, the 1968 Constitutional Reform expanded presidential powers, Congress occasionally ceded extraordinary powers to presidents to legislate on specific issues, and presidents also legislated after declaring a state of siege or after the 1968 Constitutional Reform by declaring a state of national economic emergency. Nominal but only rarely substantive bipartisan participation was assured by the fact that the signatures of the entire Cabinet were required on all such presidential decrees. The use of special powers by the president has been common to Latin American presidentialist systems. In Colombia, it took on added importance because of the consociational arrangement, an ironic situation since Colombia has been unique among consociational regimes in having a presidential system. The parties sought to limit presidential powers by requiring that the sensitive post of minister of government (which is legally empowered to appoint all governors) be of the opposite party. Similarly, during the National Front the attorney-general (*procurador*) and the comptroller (*contralor*), both elected by Congress, were also of the opposite party.[22] The latter two often served less as a check on presidential authority than as a brake on efficiency and as an important source of congressional patronage.

Presidents, however, were not all-powerful, and there were significant variations in their effectiveness from one administration to another. Presidents were constrained by the need for bipartisan participation and limited by the pressures exerted by the organized forces in society. No single institutional forum emerged in lieu of Congress to serve as the locus for bipartisan discussion. Because party factions were sometimes not represented in a cabinet or because ministers identified with a particular faction were sometimes more "technical" than "political," the Cabinet, which logically might have served such a function, did so only occasionally. Thus, on specific issues such as agrarian reform or during periods of acute economic or political crisis such as in 1965, *ad hoc decision forums* and *summit negotiations among top party leaders* were often employed in seeking to break apparent deadlocks.[23] Attempts to create institutionalized decision-making structures in Colombia essentially failed. They failed at the congressional level and at a corporatist state–society level. Efforts to establish congressional input into national development plans were unable to clear factional and regional obstacles within Congress, even as international agencies and government technocrats feared excessive politicization would result from greater congressional involvement. Major policy decisions were often worked out by presidents in negotiation with factional party leaders and sometimes ex-presidents, many of whom held no formal elected office. These various mechanisms operated in *secrecy*. Thus, many measures brought for congressional approval had essentially already gone through an extended accommodation process.

The press in Colombia has been an important participant in this process of secrecy. The country's major newspapers have a clear partisan and sometimes factional identification. The two dailies with the largest circulation, *El Tiempo* and *El Espectador*, have been owned and managed by members of two different prominent Liberal families, the Santos and Cano families, respectively. Each of the major Conservative party factions has published dailies in Bogotá as well whose importance has been far greater than their limited circulation: the Ospinistas, *La República*, and the Alvaristas, *El Siglo*. Regional newspapers and most weekly magazines have been similarly linked to political parties or factions (cf. Melo, 1978). Because of inter-factional disputes, the newspapers have sometimes provided a glimpse of the "invisible politics"; yet, by and large, they have remained supportive of the National Front system, indulged in very little serious investigative reporting and largely ignored the activities of opposition figures. The directors of the major dailies (particularly of *El Tiempo*) have also provided discreet behind-the-scenes communications links within their own parties or sometimes between the parties in efforts to settle political crises.

Politicians relied extensively on *patron–client* and increasingly *brokerage* ties to consolidate their electoral position and felt threatened by increased state capacity and centralization which increased the programs and investments channelled through various state agencies controlled from Bogotá, weakening their regional bases of strength. There were also ambivalent and only partially successful efforts at *regime-sponsored organizations of the lower classes*. In the end, the National Front did not create loyal popular sector organizations by corporatist mechanisms, in part because presidential alternation and partisan fears worked against it. The regime sought to pursue more of a policy of demobilization and of "divide and conquer" in relation to the popular sector than one of mobilization, centralization and control. Some popular sector groups were able to influence policy or attain limited goals by various means, including political ties (through government bureaucrats or through clientelist or brokerage connections with politicians), mass occupations, civic and labor strikes, demonstrations and appeals to the press. Nevertheless, the regime at times employed or condoned the use of non-democratic practices. Certain practices responded to multiple pressures. For example, the constitutional mechanism of a state of siege, usually invoked in response to labor and student protest, civic strikes or rural conflict, was retained for long periods of time to permit the executive to sidestep congressional immobilism.[24]

These rules of the game permitted somewhat contradictory processes to co-exist. For example, state capacity grew as the state's role in the economy became more significant, and as the executive branch, through its ministries, departments, boards and decentralized agencies also increased its role as regulator. The dramatic growth in state bureaucracy also facilitated continued clientelism and increasingly brokerage politics, though its nature changed due to the declining economic and administrative role of departments and municipalities. And, as regional party leaders came to depend upon coalition rule and small captive electorates for patronage guarantees, unionization, labor radicalism and militancy all increased dramatically within the public sector due to low pay and poor working conditions. At the same time, the operation of the rules of the game is apparent in core regime processes such as leadership succession and constitutional reform.

The presidential selection process

The tensions generated by the predicaments of threatened immobilism, policy incoherence and lack of popular responsiveness inevitably focused on the office of the presidency as the major site of conflict resolution within the regime structure. As a consequence, the presidential selection process during the National Front never became regularized but was governed by many of the "rules of the game" also employed for other policy decisions. In part, this reflected the fact that consociationalism is more difficult to implement in a centralized, presidential system than in a federal, parliamentary one. Presidents became the focal point of policy activity even more than they might have otherwise.

In the four selection processes that fell under the National Front requirement of alternation, determination of an "official" National Front candidate required intra-party approval and then bipartisan acceptance. Liberals were able to play a larger role in the selection of Conservative candidates because of the bitter split within the Conservative Party; as the majority party, they could also seek to exercise their right to have more "nonsectarian" Conservative candidates selected. The presidential selection process reflected the parties' historical oligarchical nature even as the consociational requirement of alternation reinforced it. The process illustrated the power of key party leaders as well as their creativity and skill in accommodation; at the same time, it demonstrated the fact that as in other policy areas, no regularized processes nor mechanisms were developed nor were appropriate participants ever explicitly determined. Deals were struck among national party leaders, some of whom were also potential candidates, in secrecy, in summit negotiations and by *ad hoc* processes with little or no input from party members. After 1958, party conventions were then usually held with the idea that they would ratify decisions largely made elsewhere. Convention participants usually included elected party officials and departmental and municipal delegations largely chosen by the major regional politicians (for details on each of the major conventions, see Lara, 1983).

The events in 1957–8 which led to Alberto Lleras' election as president have been discussed in chapter 3. It was a consociational process, negotiated across leaders of both parties, and his candidacy was joined to a pledge to seek a constitutional amendment implementing alternation in the three subsequent elections. Gómez' ability to block Valencia's candidacy and then to promote Lleras' election illustrates the considerable independent powers of party leaders. With the entry of the Ospinistas into Lleras' government in 1960 and the continued opposition of Laureanistas (and later Alvaristas) through the years of presidential alternation, "official" National Front candidates for 1962, 1966 and 1970 were negotiated between the Liberals (who themselves faced factional opposition particularly in the 1962 elections) and the Ospinistas.

In 1962, National Front leaders were particularly concerned that the dissident candidacy of Alfonso López could siphon off considerable numbers of Liberal votes in an election in which Liberals were being asked to elect a Conservative President. They feared he could even win an upset victory because of the split in the Conservative Party. For that reason, Alberto Lleras had López' candidacy declared illegal, and all ballots cast in his name were counted as blank ballots. To counteract López' anti-National Front and sectarian Liberal appeals it was crucial to select a Conservative candidate who would not appear threatening to Liberals. Because the Liberals played a larger role in designating Conservative candidates and sought out figures with a non-sectarian image, none of the major Conservative Party leaders (*jefes naturales*) were selected as candidates for the presidency during this period.

The Laureanistas refused to negotiate with the Liberals over candidacies for the 1962 elections and the two Conservative Party factions could not agree between each other on a process that would lead to a single nomination supported by both of them. The only option became for Ospinistas and Liberals to come to an agreement. In a complex process, a Conservative convention ratified a list of five names headed by that of Guillermo León Valencia to be sent to a Liberal convention, in which one of the names would then be selected, to be acclaimed at a subsequent joint convention. Unsurprisingly, Valencia was the candidate selected as the candidate of the "Great Coalition" (Gran Coalición); for the Liberals he appeared to project the least threatening image.[25]

Liberal presidential candidates did emerge from the *jefes naturales* of the party. After Alberto Lleras, Carlos Lleras appeared to be the logical candidate.[26] The Liberal convention of February, 1964 ratified the party's support for Lleras' candidacy in 1966, a candidacy which was also acceptable to Ospinista Conservatives. Given Lleras' statist, technocratic and reformist positions there was some opposition to his candidacy within the Liberal Party. Lleras had a stormy crisis-ridden campaign punctuated by a brief resignation in May 1965 due to Valencia's reluctance to endorse his nomination. However, Carlos Lleras' standing within the party and his recognition nationally and internationally as a hard-working and effective administrator precluded serious consideration of any alternative candidate. Alberto Lleras and Belisario Betancur formed a bipartisan committee to support Carlos Lleras' candidacy, which was widely endorsed by the Church, professional and producer associations and labor unions. This contrasted sharply with the events surrounding the 1970 nomination.

The 1970–4 period was a particularly sensitive one, since whoever sat in the office would oversee in 1974 the first competitive presidential elections since 1946. There were numerous aspirants. Alvaristas initially backed Belisario Betancur, who evolved into a regional Antioqueño candidate, with middle-class and labor support and with former President Valencia as a key backer. Ospina decided to promote the relatively young rising figure of Misael Pastrana, thus ending the hopes of other key aspirants such as Hernán Jaramillo Ocampo. Many traditional politicians, particularly from the Atlantic Coast, threw their support behind Evaristo Sourdís. Sourdís, a politician from the Coast, a region which felt politically under-represented in the Andean center of the country, had strong ties to landowning interests mobilized in opposition to Lleras and had incurred numerous political obligations as head of the key congressional patronage position of comptroller general. For the Liberals, Sourdís represented too sectarian an image compared to Pastrana who had played a major role in seeking approval of the 1968 Constitutional Reform as Carlos Lleras' minister of government.

Once again, the decision regarding candidacies was decided in the rarefied circles of top party leadership. Ospina accepted the Liberals' wish that the candidate be Pastrana, a personally difficult decision due to his close links with both individuals.[27] The critical moments came in the Conservative convention held jointly by both party factions in November 1969. Betancur, and Rojas who had to run as a Conservative, did not seek the Party's nomination. The delegates had to choose between Pastrana and Sourdís, toward whom the Alvaristas were now leaning. Ospina served as President of the convention and Alvaro Gómez as Vice-President. Ospina unilaterally rejected the first convention vote in which Sourdís received a 276–272 majority, declaring a second *public* vote was required. Incredibly, both candidates received exactly 278 votes. Both their names went to the Liberal Convention which ratified Pastrana as the official National Front candidate. Sourdís was relegated to the condition of a regional, dissident candidacy.[28] Sourdís' dissident candidacy, particularly due to its regional strength, and to a lesser extent Betancur's presence in the election, almost certainly saved the National Front from an overwhelming defeat by Rojas.[29]

Presidential selection was elitist and consociational in that elements of both parties needed to concur regarding the nominee (although elements of one or both also opposed him). The process was *ad hoc* and crisis-ridden, dependent upon the capabilities of a select number of key party leaders. The requirement for alternation robbed the regime of the promise of continuity in some critical areas and sometimes led to the choice of weak candidates. The fractious process of selection and lack of opposition were to generate problems among the parties' mass following, of which the 1970 election was a dramatic example. Yet, the "rules of the game" worked, breaking stalemates and generating results around which leading elements of both parties could coalesce.

Toward consociational transformation: the 1968 Reform

Presidential alternation and legislative parity had clear end points in 1974, but executive power-sharing did not. If no changes were made to the measures approved by the 1957 plebiscite, even after the return to competitive elections in 1974 the president would be *required* to grant executive power-sharing to all parties proportionally based upon their congressional representation. The

1968 Constitutional Reform was intended to address this issue, as well as some of the predicaments generated by several other National Front features that had become evident under Alberto Lleras and Valencia, such as an excessive reliance on the state of siege to legislate. The Reform was intended to pave the way for a return to a model of competitive politics and to strengthen presidential powers while providing Congress with a more limited but clearly defined role in the nation's economic issues. It was one of the most significant pieces of legislation enacted during the entire National Front period. As it finally emerged, the Reform consolidated some of the emerging "rules" confirming the growing importance of the presidency and of the executive branch in general and incorporating measures to improve administrative efficiency. It also set the stage for a partial dismantling of the National Front and sought to address questions of legislative efficiency, but in both these areas its effects and consequences fell considerably short of its desired results.

The approval process for the suggested reforms to the constitution was laborious and provides an example of how the "rules of the game" operated in Colombia's political context. In order to be enacted, the reforms required approval in both the House and the Senate in committee (*primer debate*) and by the chamber as a whole (*segundo debate*) by a *two-thirds* vote in *two* consecutive sessions. The measures were initially presented to Congress as three different packages in 1966 and 1967. The first referred to planning, budgeting and administrative capabilities of the presidency; the second to political questions and the dismantling of the National Front; and the third, to the strengthening of aspects of departmental and municipal administration (for a summary, see Vidal, 1970; for the complete texts, see Colombia, Presidencia, 1969).

Congressional opposition to the suggested reforms was found among many Conservatives and some Liberals. It was concentrated among the Alvarista Conservatives and the Anapistas. Their two central concerns were the strengthening of the executive and of the state in terms of its capacity for planning and intervention in the economy and on the formula for the dismantling of the National Front. In the House in the 1966–8 session, together they held sixty-three of the 190 seats; the 1968 elections, however, reduced their numbers to forty-eight of 204. In the Senate, they numbered thirty-two of 106. The first two packages were initially presented and debated in the Senate; the third one in the House.[30] Basic opposition to parts of the reform was also found among some independents and MRListas, but negotiations between Lleras and López brought the MRL back into the governing coalition in 1967, assuring Lleras of a narrow two-thirds majority. Opposition from other Conservatives centered around formulas to guarantee continued Conservative participation in government following the National Front and on the size and composition of Congress. Other Conservative and Liberal (Turbayista) groups were most concerned about congressional loss of control over regional financing as well as other aspects more directly relating to Congress: pork-barrel funds (*auxilios parlamentarios*), autonomy to determine its own budget and congressional salaries.

Of the numerous changes introduced to the first package in the Senate at this time, perhaps the most important was the addition of a "state of national economic and social emergency" upon the recommendation of then Senator Alfonso López Michelsen. Approved by the Senate in March 1967, some members of the House sought unsuccessfully to amend this first package to extend the term in office of representatives from two years to four years beginning with their own term in office, rather than in 1970. There was also an attempt to assure Congress of 5% of the national budget to spend autonomously but this measure was even more short-lived than the former. The full House finally approved this package in September 1967.

The second package of reforms contained conflictive political elements relating to the dismantling of the consociational arrangement. Approved by the full Senate after some changes in July 1967, it was extensively revised by the House and sent back to the Senate for a new vote. *The initial bill had called for the end of legislative and executive parity in 1974.* However, after *summit negotiations* between Lleras and Ospina in November 1967 this was substantially modified due to Conservative opposition. Ospina insisted that "the defeated party [be called] to share power in a certain way" (from an editorial in *La República*, November 8, 1978) with the party winning elections. It was agreed that legislative parity would end at the municipal and departmental level in 1970 and for Congress in 1974; that bureaucratic parity in the executive would be maintained until 1978 and that thereafter the party receiving the second highest number of votes would be provided "equitable participation" by the winning party (Vidal, 1970: 34). This package passed in the House in February 1968. In the meantime, the third package of measures had been approved in the House in December 1967.

The locus of conflict shifted to the Senate and June 1968 was to be the critical month. If the full Senate did not approve the modifications of the second package of reforms and the complete third package before its recess, then the reforms could not be considered for the mandatory second vote in the new congressional session beginning on July 20 and passage of the reforms would be delayed at least a full year. In early June, in an all-night session, the Senate voted down certain measures supported by the government, including the one about "equitable participation" in governments following the end of parity in 1978. With its defeat, *mandatory executive power-sharing was extended indefinitely.*

Unwilling to accept indefinite power-sharing, in a classic but still dangerous maneuver, Lleras offered a letter of resignation to the Senate on June 11, 1968 (text of letter in Vidal, 1970: 109–17; a justification by Lleras in *Nueva Frontera*, December 3, 1979). As he had hoped and expected, his resignation was rejected. After he promised that modifications to the entire package would be considered in the second round the package was finally approved one week later. Shortly after, the third package was also approved.

The three packages were incorporated into a single bill and a review committee was formed composed of congressmen from both parties (though only Ospinista Conservatives), and of the minister of government (Misael Pastrana) and the president's legal adviser for the government. That committee re-wrote various provisions, giving congressmen an expanded role in the approval of the government's economic plans and programs by means of a special commission that was to be formed (to be known as the Comisión del Plan). The requirement for the president to offer equitable participation to the opposing party was changed slightly so that if that party refused to accept it the president would be free to make other appointments and his government could still function.[31]

The carefully crafted agreement met opposition in committee in the Senate, where it was first presented. Turbayista Liberals refused to vote the bill out until congressmen were given greater guarantees regarding expenditures of pork-barrel funds[32] and limited control over tax laws (see Leal, 1970: 168). Even as this compromise was reached, Ospinistas balked at the reduction in congressional size built into the new formulas. Lleras, asserting this meant the end of the coalition, asked for and received the cabinet's resignation (it was later withdrawn). A new *summit negotiation* between Lleras and Ospina led to a compromise.[33] In addition, congressmen were given a fixed salary, rather than payment based upon attendance at sessions and Congress was permitted to increase its salary during the remaining years of the term. At the last minute, ANAPO supported the reform because of political concessions that were granted to it. It was agreed that until 1974 officers of Congress, departmental assemblies and municipal councils would be determined by a two-thirds vote rather than a simple majority, thus providing a minority group such as ANAPO greater possibilities of attaining one or more of these positions with its related patronage (see Leal, 1973: 168; Vidal, 1970: 51). The 1968 Reform finally passed and shortly afterwards on December 16, 1968, the state of siege was lifted.

The 1968 Constitutional Reform, whose passage was shaped by the regime's "rules of the game," itself modified these rules, particularly as related to presidential authority and increased state capacity. The Reform substantially strengthened presidential authority, especially in economic matters. Congress lost the power to initiate legislation dealing with social and economic development (except for its limited pork-barrel funds) or with the modification or creation of new administrative structures. Furthermore, the Reform strengthened presidential control over many decentralized agencies.

The Reform sought to organize relations between the executive and the legislative branches so as to obviate the need to declare or maintain a state of siege simply in order to allow the executive to legislate due to congressional immobilism. While a state of siege is in effect, a president may issue decrees with the force of law and may suspend laws incompatible with the state of siege, though laws may not be repealed. Because extraordinary decrees issued during a state of siege cease to be in force once it ends, National Front governments, faced with an inability to have the legislation they desired passed by Congress, often kept the state of siege in effect.[34] The president's powers under "state of siege" were modified, while the power to declare a "state of national economic and social emergency" was created.

The Reform also sought to bolster congressional agility and

increase its oversight capacity, although here the results fell far short of these intentions. The two-thirds vote rule was reduced to one of simple majority for most legislation and the growth in the size of Congress was slightly trimmed. Yet, efforts to bolster the technical staff and administrative services of the Congress failed as money earmarked for these purposes was misspent or channelled into more partisan purposes. Furthermore, the special permanent Commission to review and oversee the executive's plans and programs was never formed. Congressmen could not agree on the appropriate partisan and regional criteria for membership in what was viewed as a commission rich in patronage potential (interviews with a leading Liberal and a leading Conservative politician, November 1978 and July 1978). And, finally, as will be analyzed in chapter 7, the compromise wording agreed to by Lleras for moving away from coalition governments failed to achieve its purpose until nearly two decades later, in 1986.

This chapter has provided an introduction to the National Front political regime, with an overview of the major groups supporting the regime and of the traditional parties. It has argued that inherent in a consociational regime are three principal predicaments – immobilism, policy incoherence and lack of popular responsiveness – that the National Front regime sought to circumvent by a set of "rules of the game" that emerged from the nature of the regime, past historical patterns and pressures from major domestic and international actors. The importance of these "rules" was illustrated in discussions of two core regime processes, presidential selection and regime modification by constitutional reform.

In the next two chapters we will extend our analysis of these regime predicaments and their implications. We turn first to an examination of the ways in which regime leaders and the regime structure affected economic policy-making and growth patterns and then to their impact on patterns of political participation and support.

5

Economic policy-making: thwarted reformism and moderation

Colombia is a clear example of a Latin American country that, in comparative terms, has pursued "moderate," "eclectic" economic patterns during the National Front period (1958–78). In that sense, Colombia is similar to a number of other Latin American countries that in their process of industrialization in the past several decades, until the effects of the external debt crisis were felt, have appeared to pursue largely "moderate" and relatively continuous economic policies, such as Mexico and Venezuela, in contrast to others that have followed more "pendular" patterns, such as Argentina, Chile and Peru. This reflects, in part, differences in their historical experiences with populist movements and governments.[1]

Colombia's historical evolution – its political party structure, regionalism and weak state and particularly its process of initial industrialization and popular sector incorporation into the political process – is very important in understanding the relative absence of a "pendular" pattern in Colombian policy-making. As we saw in chapter 2, Colombia has had periods of tumultuous change in economic policy (as well as considerable violence), yet in comparative terms these have often been neither as sharp nor as intensely implemented as in other countries. López' reforms of the 1930s were met by a "pause" in the subsequent presidential period and Rojas in the 1950s was relatively timid in his more populist policies and overthrown after a relatively short period in contrast to Perón in Argentina or Vargas in Brazil. In Colombia, as a result of the two-party system and a process of industrialization that incorporated elements from both parties, the popular sector was integrated into the political process in a relatively non-mobilized fashion with attachments to the two parties and with low levels of organization. Initial import-substitution industrialization was not as protectionist as in many of the larger South American countries.

Although these historical factors are crucial in setting a context for "moderate" policies, they are not fully determinative. A pattern of "moderate" policies in Colombia was not simply foreordained because of these favorable initial conditions or because of the broad support for the establishment of the National Front in 1958. The consociational regime was a natural extension of many of these conditions and once established it structured, legitimized, blocked, permitted or encouraged processes or actions by various domestic and international groups, and was able to respond to adverse international circumstances. Thus, while not avoiding economic problems and shifts in policy, the regime has sought to maintain policy continuity in terms of attention to variables such as inflation, fiscal deficits and growth, a greater consistency of control of the money supply, and since the late 1960s has tended to reduce tariffs in partial and negotiated, if irregular, steps. In this sense, it has avoided extreme populist policies – with high inflation, extreme protectionism, dramatic wage increases and extensive fiscal deficits – or radical neoliberal ones – brusquely eliminating state subsidies and fiscal deficits, imposing massive devaluations, sharply curtailing wage increases, and indiscriminately slashing tariffs.

Colombia's economic record on growth, inflation and budget deficits is contrasted with larger or comparably-sized neighbors in Tables 5.1 and 5.2. The tables provide strong evidence for the existence of a "moderate" pattern in Colombia. The country's growth record has been less spectacular yet smoother (Table 5.1), in that way outperforming Argentina, Chile and Peru. Its inflation level has been lower and has fluctuated much less than in all the "pendular" cases (Table 5.1). And, for the years for which data are available, Colombia's budget deficits (as a percentage of GDP) have been lower and also have fluctuated less (Table 5.2).[2]

Certainly, the historical legacies examined in earlier chapters and noted above and crucial economic factors such as resources and world market conditions also have played a major role – sometimes the primary role – in determining the country's recent economic growth pattern. This chapter, though, seeks to highlight the role of the political regime structure, as some presidential administrations sought to increase state autonomy and capacity, in interaction with influential domestic and inter-

Table 5.1 *Selected Latin American countries: average growth rates and changes in the consumer price index*

	Average annual change in real GDP (%)[1] 1957–81	Standard deviation from the mean (%)[2]	Average annual change in the consumer price index (%)[3] 1958–80	Standard deviation from the mean (%)[2]
Argentina	3.03	4.7	60.98	98.7
Chile	4.04	4.8	77.22[4]	155.5
Peru	4.17	2.8	17.99	18.8
Brazil	6.94	3.8	37.74	21.5
Colombia	5.15	1.7	14.99	9.2
Mexico	6.37	2.2	8.97	8.9
Venezuela	5.31	1.9	4.60	5.1

[1] A geometric mean calculated from annual percentage change in real GDP (OECD series) in Wilkie & Perkal, 1984: 393–409. The assistance of Greg Michaels is gratefully acknowledged.

[2] Calculated from the arithmetic mean.

[3] A geometric mean calculated from annual percentage change in the consumer price index in IMF, 1981: 64–5.

[4] For 1964–80 only.

national groups, in resolving policy differences internal to it and in generating economic policies. The central argument is that consociationalism – coalition rule and muted inter-party conflict – facilitated an essential policy focus on key macro-economic variables and a relative absence of populist politics at the national level, though at a risk of increasing regime delegitimation across some middle-sector and popular sector groups. This also meant that the ongoing consequences of prior policy choices in areas such as export promotion, import controls and taxation, themselves an important component of a country's economic evolution, would likely strengthen "moderate" over "pendular" policies.

Regime policies were substantially influenced by producer groups that possessed multiple points of access and means to pressure the regime. In contrast, the direct influence of organized labor, peasant movements or other popular sector organizations

Table 5.2 *Selected Latin American countries: public sector deficits (% of GDP) 1970–81*

	Argentina	Chile	Peru	Brazil	Colombia	Mexico	Venezuela
1970	−1.1	−5.2	−0.8	−2.4	−4.0	−1.9	−2.6
1971	−3.8	−12.4	−1.4	−2.1		−2.3	−2.6
1972	−4.6	−16.7	−2.9	−1.4	−3.8	−4.1	−7.1
1973	−6.6	−15.8	−4.5	0.4		−5.3	−5.1
1974	−6.9	−6.8	−6.8	−0.1	−2.9	−5.8	2.2
1975	−14.0	−1.7	−9.6	−2.3	−2.5	−9.1	−7.6
1976	−9.8	3.7	−10.0	−2.6	−2.5	−7.5	−13.2
1977	−3.2	1.3	−9.8	−1.8	−1.1	−5.2	−11.4
1978	−3.8	1.7	−6.2	−3.4	−1.1	−5.5	−12.1
1979	−3.5	5.2	−1.1	−1.7	−0.3	−7.5	−16.5
1980	−4.3	5.9	−6.5	−9.1	−1.4	−7.9	−13.5
1981	−7.1	3.2	−8.2	−7.1	−1.5	−14.5	1.3
Average 1970–81 (%)	−5.7	−3.1	−5.7	−2.8	−2.4	−6.4	−7.4
Standard deviation (%)	3.5	8.2	3.5	2.7	1.3	3.4	6.2

Source: IDB, 1984: 28, 154, 163–4, 168, 172–3, 177, 184, 190.

was considerably less. And, international agencies and foreign aid missions played a central role. Their support was facilitated by the "democratic" legitimacy of the political regime, and their willingness to provide resources was partially a function of appropriate governmental policy measures and the possibility for the relative insulation of certain economic processes – such as the purposes, disbursement and oversight of international loans, the determination of public utility tariffs and the staffing of key government agencies – from partisan–political considerations.

This focus on the evolution of relatively continuous "moderate" and "eclectic" economic policies fomented by a consociational regime contrasts with many analyses of Colombia which have emphasized crises and their management by means of short-term policies and dramatic maneuvers (see, for example, the articles in Berry, Hellman & Solaún, 1980). As the descriptions of various policy processes and policy results below illustrate, the political regime – with its predicaments of threatened immobilism, policy incoherence and lack of popular responsiveness– did make a style of crisis decision-making almost inevitable. However, the regime structure also largely constrained policy options, preventing sharply pendular policies. At the same time, though, this also had serious implications for the possibility of implementing more than modest social reforms.

In the section that follows, the regime's ability to manage its predicaments while the country evolved economically without the sharp disruptions of many of its neighbors is sketched in an overview of development policies from 1958 to 1978. One of the costs of a regime structure excessively open to mutual vetoes by the better-organized producer groups is a threatened lack of popular responsiveness. Case studies of major efforts of social reform in the next section were selected to illustrate the regime structure's complex role in permitting occasional formulation but not serious implementation of reform measures.

Economic crises in Latin America– balance of payments and fiscal problems associated with high inflation requiring economic stabilization programs – have often exacerbated political weaknesses and at times facilitated or precipitated regime crisis and change.[3] For this reason, the subsequent section examines how some of the regime's critical early devaluation–stabilization episodes were resolved, crises which resulted in 1967 in an important policy shift toward partial export promotion.

The varying efforts of the Carlos Lleras (1966–70), Pastrana (1970–4) and López (1974–8) administrations to manage the regime predicaments by their differing development emphases are analyzed in the final sections of this chapter. Structural pressures from the economy, the influence of international agencies and the drive to satisfy minimum levels of efficiency led to *increasing state capacity* in terms of planning, regulating and investing, particularly during the Carlos Lleras administration. At the same time, in order to avoid potential immobilism or politicization and to seek greater efficiency, or due to concerted efforts by particular producer groups, the regime continued with the past historical pattern of a kind of societal corporatism with a predominant role for private sector interests in certain economic areas and functions (particularly evident in the coffee sector).

I have termed this *selective privatization* to emphasize the predominant private sector role in what is an interactive process between
the state and certain major producer groups. Less evident in the
more statist Lleras years, this trend partially reasserted itself in
the subsequent Pastrana administration.

An overview of development policies: the case studies in context

Over the National Front period, Colombia underwent dramatic
economic, social and demographic changes (see Table 5.3). It
became a substantially younger, urban country with significant
shifts in its labor force from agriculture toward services and, to a
lesser extent, industry. Improvements in social conditions (for
example, life expectancy and education) were not paralleled by
significant changes in income distribution. One of the most
dramatic changes was a rapid decline in population growth
rates.[4]

In the 1950s and 1960s, Colombia's focus on import-substitution
industrialization was similar to that of its continental neighbors.
In contrast to countries such as Argentina, Brazil, Chile, Mexico
or Uruguay, however, industrialization began somewhat later,
not really expanding until the 1930s. And in the 1930s, the degree
and generality of industrial protection in Colombia was less
extreme than in countries such as Argentina and Brazil. Industrialization was further promoted in Colombia by tariff barriers
(new tariffs with higher and less uniform rates were imposed in
1950, 1959 and 1962), as well as other restrictions on imports
such as licenses, quotas and prior deposits (also employed to
manage situations of tight foreign exchange).[5] As in many other
Latin American countries during this period, the country's
exchange rate in the 1950s and 1960s was overvalued, initially
helping industrialists importing capital goods and inputs and
affecting possibilities for export diversification.

The sharpening economic problems that result from efforts to
move beyond initial import-substituting industrialization (the
"easy stages") in a period of poor export performance, generating
stop-go economic policies due to foreign exchange problems,
popular sector pressure and other factors were captured by
O'Donnell in his bureaucratic–authoritarian model (1973) which
built particularly upon the experience of one of the most extreme

Table 5.3 *Colombia: demographic and social indicators*

	Colombia		Average for middle income countries[2]	
	1960	1978	1960	1978
Total population (millions)[1]	14.5	25.7	—	—
Gross Domestic Product (per capita)[3]	479	922	—	—
Urban population (%)	48	70[4]	37	51
Labor force (%) in				
agriculture	52	30	58	45
industry	19	23	17	23
services	29	47	25	32
Life expectancy	53	62	54	61
Number enrolled in primary schools as % of age group	77	103	81	97
Adult literacy rate	63	81	54	71
Average annual growth of population (%)				
1960–70	3.0		2.5	
1970–8	2.3		2.4	

[1]Figures from Wilkie & Haber, 1981.
[2]As defined by the World Bank, comprising 52 countries with a per capita income of over $360 (including 18 Latin American countries).
[3]From IDB, 1982; 351, for 1960 and 1980 in 1980 US dollars.
[4]Figure for 1980.
Sources: World Bank, 1980: 110–57; Wilkie & Haber, 1981; and IDB, 1982: 351.

cases, Argentina. In the 1957–68 period, as world coffee prices remained low (see Table 5.4), Colombia partially resembled that picture.[6] The country did not totally escape the recurring balance of payments crises that affected many of its neighbors. As will be reviewed below, stabilization programs and devaluations with differing effectiveness were imposed in 1957–8, 1962 and 1965. The importance of the regime structure, the central role of the producer associations, the relatively lower level of popular demand-making, the nature of the agro-export (coffee) sector and the availability of international assistance (in part because of the nature of the regime) were all important factors in helping to mitigate the after-shocks of these programs, though with considerably more success in some cases than in others.

Following the resolution of the 1965 crisis and after the inauguration of President Carlos Lleras, the country once again confronted balance of payments problems. As the case study below of the resolution of this crisis illustrates, the result was the establishment of a new framework for trade and foreign exchange (Decree-Law 444 of 1967) that, although not entirely apparent at the time, provided the means for a partial reorientation of the economy from an import-substitution model to one of export promotion. This law provided for a shift to more orthodox policies encouraging realistic exchange rates and export promotion in a more gradual, though also more incomplete, fashion than occurred in the bureaucratic–authoritarian cases. This change thus occurred at a much earlier relative stage of the country's industrial development than for many other Latin American countries, and in this way Colombia avoided some (though not all) disastrous experiences in import-substitution. The timing of these policy changes was fortuitous for they permitted new exports to benefit from a booming world economy. After 1967, there were no more significant exchange crises and the early 1970s evidenced a boom in non-traditional or "minor" exports as is evident in the growth of recorded minor exports in Table 5.4 (cf. Hartlyn, 1984b: 42–7).

President Carlos Lleras had a comprehensive, reformist vision of development for Colombia which sought to create a coalition of industrialists, workers and peasant beneficiaries against traditional landowners, while establishing the basis for an active, interventionist state. A more vigorous state apparatus and a rationalized process of decision-making within it were to be employed to provide economic growth, redistribution of wealth and greater national autonomy. While eager to work with multilateral agencies (which helped strengthen the state) and to encourage direct foreign investment, Lleras also was an active participant in the creation of the Andean Common Market, sought greater state control over foreign investment and reestablished Colombia's diplomatic relations with the Soviet Union.[7] Lleras' efforts to create a new reformist coalition of forces left as a legacy a stronger state apparatus and a framework for a more efficient economy. However, his measures and style generated opposition from politicians concerned about the trim-

Table 5.4 *Coffee and minor exports 1957–78*

Year	New York price (US cents per lb)	Exports (thousands 60 kg bags)	Recorded coffee exports (US$ m.)	Coffee exports % total exports	Recorded minor exports (US$ m.)
1957	63.9	4,824	390.1	76.3	48.7
1958	52.3	5,441	354.7	77.0	40.9
1959	45.2	6,413	363.4	76.8	36.3
1960	44.9	5,938	333.5	71.8	51.1
1961	43.6	5,561	307.9	70.8	58.7
1962	40.8	6,561	331.8	71.6	70.8
1963	39.5	6,134	303.0	67.8	66.5
1964	48.8	6,412	394.2	71.9	78.9
1965	48.5	5,651	343.9	63.8	107.0
1966	47.4	5,566	328.3	64.7	108.7
1967	41.9	6,094	321.5	63.0	127.2
1968	42.6	6,588	351.4	62.9	170.6
1969	44.9	6,478	343.9	56.6	206.8
1970	56.4	6,509	466.9	63.5	210.1
1971	49.3	6,569	399.7	58.3	231.1
1972	56.7	6,528	428.1	52.2	392.1
1973	72.7	6,766	593.5	50.6	580.7
1974	77.9	6,906	623.1	44.0	792.5
1975	81.7	8,175	680.5	47.2	726.0
1976	157.7	6,289	996.0	56.1	777.7
1977	240.2	5,323	1,512.6	65.4	799.9
1978	185.2	9,034	2,026.8	68.9	914.9

Sources: col. 1, Avramovic, 1972: 265 (1948–69), *Revista del Banco de la República* (1979) (1974–8); col. 2, Palacios, 1979 (1948–72), *Revista del Banco de la República* (1979) (1973–8); col. 3, 4 & 5, Díaz-Alejandro, 1976: 35 (1948–72), *Revista del Banco de la República* (1976), p. 1505 (1972–5), *Revista del Banco de la República* (1979), p. 1895 (1976–8).

ming of pork-barrel funds and the rationalization of decision-making within the state, from numerous producer groups fearful of a more interventionist state, as regulator and as producer, and especially from landowners threatened by the encouragement of land reform and peasant associations. This produced a "political," "privatization" and "landowner" backlash that was felt both at election time and in the orientation of the subsequent Pastrana administration.

President Pastrana, after two years of general economic policy continuity combined with retrenchment on agrarian reform and co-optive policies especially in urban areas to prevent further successes for ANAPO, enacted a new development program oriented toward urban construction, known as the UPAC system, and toward encouraging further expansion of commercial agriculture and agro-exports. These policies were perceived to have helped foster higher inflation and were partially abandoned by the incoming López administration which returned to a more conventional strategy focusing on agricultural and manufactured exports as well as rural development and nutrition projects targeted more directly toward certain popular sectors. During the López years, the country experienced an unexpected bonanza of foreign exchange due to a boom in coffee prices and the rapid expansion of illegal drug exports. To ease inflationary pressures generated by the sudden influx of foreign exchange reserves, the administration slowed the rate of devaluation of the exchange rate (hurting prospects for minor exports), cut back on public investment and implanted a tight monetary policy. Prudently, it borrowed little on international capital markets. These years also saw the beginning of an industrial down-turn that was to continue into the early 1980s.[8]

As ensuing governments practiced different economic growth strategies and dealt with short-term pressures, there were also reform efforts directed at improving the distribution of wealth and income in the country. Of these, perhaps the most important was agrarian reform, first enacted in 1961. President Carlos Lleras sought to revive the reform in his term in office with limited results and it was effectively stopped during the Pastrana presidency. Subsequently, during the López presidency a major tax reform decreed in 1974 was largely dismantled over a five year period.

Thwarted reformism: agrarian reform and fiscal reform

The regime structure accentuated the power of established, organized interests that found expression in both parties and thus inhibited radical policy initiatives. Yet, reformist efforts apparently inimical to the core interests of major producer groups were promoted at times, although they were met eventually with counter-reform. Reformist efforts occurred during periods of more activist presidents who consciously sought to promote increases in state autonomy. Most reform efforts also enjoyed considerable international support and had been discussed extensively in policy-making circles. Their passage often relied upon various "rules of the game" as noted in the discussion.[9] In the end, however, the regime dominated by two hierarchical multi-class factionalized parties, while providing space for the formulation and occasionally the implementation of reform, also provided multiple opportunities for these reforms to be blocked, initially in the process of implementation and subsequently by new legislation.

The National Front began with a certain commitment to social reform and to agrarian reform in particular. Some party leaders were convinced that the continued social unrest, especially in rural areas, had to be countered by distributionist measures that would also ease the extremely rapid rate of rural to urban migration. This was viewed as essential due to the inability of industry to generate sufficient jobs to absorb the migratory flow with potentially serious political and social implications. The first National Front president, Alberto Lleras, was elected by an overwhelming margin and enjoyed considerable personal prestige due to his role in creating the National Front. He encouraged agrarian reform, although the chief force behind the measures in Congress was another prominent Liberal politician, Carlos Lleras. Furthermore, the United States, through its Alliance for Progress, promised financial support for the country's overall reform effort, and industrial and commercial groups generally accepted the need for reform.

Yet, as in other Latin American countries, landed interests were especially well-represented in Congress. Despite the political credibility and skill of the reformers and the promise of international resources, passage of agrarian reform legislation initially presented in January 1959 was not even achieved until late 1961. Resistance within *both* parties (though particularly from Laureanista Conservatives) and the steadfast opposition of both landowners (SAC) and cattle ranchers (FEDEGAN) slowed its passage. An *ad hoc* decision forum, the National Agrarian Reform Committee (CNRA – Comité Nacional de la Reforma Agraria), with members drawn from all major party factions (Laureanista Conservatives and MRL Liberals refused to participate), interest groups (landowners, labor and peasantry), the armed forces and the Church, was established in August, 1960 to try to break the Congressional deadlock. Subsequently, a secret summit negotiating meeting between Carlos Lleras and Mariano Ospina (each with one companion) was crucial in reaching compromise language to move the bill closer to final passage. [10]

The compromise worked out substantially weakened the final legislation, permitting expropriations of land only in limited situations and at high cost. In particular, a hierarchy of expropriability was established making it practically impossible to expropriate land that was deemed "adequately cultivated." The judicial process to make that finding and the process to assess the value of the land were complex and ambiguous. Furthermore, the agricultural associations continued to express their opposition to the reform during the implementation phase through their representatives on the government agency established to carry out the law, the Colombian Agrarian Reform Institute (INCORA – Instituto Colombiano de la Reforma Agraria). And, due to presidential alternation, the subsequent president was to be a Conservative. The weak government of Valencia was not committed to the law's implementation. In fact, his administration redrafted the law's regulations, substantially increasing the price of expropriated land. And numerous legal and illegal means were available to landowners to block or delay for years the expropriation of their land. Nevertheless, the fear of possible expropriation was sufficient, particularly when Carlos Lleras assumed office, to help induce a dramatic increase in the commercialization of agriculture in Colombia. [11] Carlos Lleras tried to accelerate the reform program during his presidency by pushing through additional legislation intended to facilitate the expropriation of land "adequately cultivated" but by tenants and sharecroppers. He also created a peasant organization, the National Association of Peasant Users (ANUC – Asociación Nacional de Usuarios Campesinos), to serve in part as a pressure group for agrarian reform (ANUC is analyzed more extensively in chapter 6). The legislation was opposed particularly by congressmen from cattle-ranching departments on the Atlantic Coast and from the Eastern Plains. It finally achieved passage in part because it also provided additional credit facilities and export incentives to commercial agriculture. [12] And, the new legislation and the emergence of the increasingly more radical ANUC stiffened the attitude of large landowners.

The next major piece of agrarian legislation would effectively prevent expropriation except in cases where the landowner acceded to it. President Pastrana, as Lleras before him, appointed a special committee to study the agrarian question and suggest new legislation to further clarify the remaining legal questions around expropriation and seek to foment increased agricultural productivity. The promise of greater accessibility in the Conservative administration of Pastrana, the increased importance of commercial agriculture (in crops such as sugar, rice and cotton) and an increase in peasant land invasions in 1970 and 1971, many organized by a radicalized ANUC, galvanized the agricultural interest groups to seek more iron-clad guarantees that "adequately" exploited land would not be expropriated as well as greater credit facilities. At the same time, there were concerns about government desires to impose a presumptive tax on the estimated income of agricultural land to encourage its productivity and address tax evasion. A deadlock in legislation was broken by means of an *ad hoc* meeting of government officials and leading congressmen (Lleristas and Anapistas were excluded) in Chicoral, Tolima, in January 1972. This agreement finally resulted in new legislation in 1973 (Laws 4 and 5) which contained major concessions by the government to landowning groups. Leaders of agricultural interest groups complained they were excluded from Chicoral, that the new credit mechanisms created for agriculture were insufficient and mired in red tape, and that they did not receive sufficient guarantees regarding the non-expropriability of "adequately" cultivated land (interviews with figures from the agricultural and livestock sectors, 1977 and 1978; for an analysis of the passage of Laws 4 and 5 of 1973, see Bagley, 1979: 227–57). Nevertheless, numerous congressmen, including many of those at Chicoral, had extensive ties with these associations and landed interests more readily employed congressmen to apply political pressure on the executive branch than did other producer groups. In fact, the new legislation was drafted in a manner that for all practical purposes made it impossible to expropriate any land without the landowner's consent (President Alfonso López made this point in an interview printed in *Revista Causa Común* 1 (March–April, 1977): 20).

Unconvinced of the wisdom of land redistribution even in the early 1960s, President López placed greater emphasis on the beneficial impact of a presumptive income tax on land (and independent professions) and on the use of augmented state revenues to fund social programs. He was elected in 1974 by an overwhelming margin in the first competitive inter-party election since 1946 and possessed a comfortable majority in Congress, a reputation as one of the party's key intellectuals, and a willingness to use patronage and work with regional politicians. Thus, López probably entered office with an even higher degree of potential autonomy and freedom to act than did Alberto Lleras in 1958, when the National Front began. Furthermore, international study missions (such as the Musgrave Commission Report, see Gillis, 1971) and the World Bank had urged Colombia to increase fiscal efforts in order to be able to increase public investments. Under Pastrana, public sector deficits were high (by Colombian standards) and during 1972 and 1973 were financed primarily by external loans. At the same time, inflation had jumped from 6.3% in 1970 to 25.0% in 1973.

The tax reform of 1974 and other financial reforms were enacted by presidential authority, making use for the first time of the executive power to declare a "state of national economic and social emergency."[13] By having the reform enacted by executive decree, the bipartisan nature of the reform was still maintained for the entire Cabinet was required to sign the measures. Conservatives might have mounted an opposition in Congress; but so soon after inauguration, following such a massive electoral defeat and with summit meetings between López and Ospina, they largely acquiesced to the measures. Congress probably also preferred that the executive take the blame for the added tax burden, in addition to which sidestepping Congress avoided the possibility of measures being changed due to pressure from producer associations and other groups (interviews with three principal economic policy-makers under López and a leading congressman, 1977).

A major increase in state resources was to come from a sales tax, but the most progressive innovations were the imposition of a capital gains tax and of a presumptive income tax on all sectors of the economy.[14] The subsequent outcry made it apparent that the producer associations had had no input or access in the drafting of the reform, although some informal consultations were held and a few changes were incorporated while the state of emergency was still in effect.[15] Unfortunately, a number of the decrees intended to reduce evasion were declared unconstitutional and only partially replaced by subsequent congressional legislation (Perry, 1977: 93–4; 130). Mounting protests over technical issues were accompanied by bitter political attacks on the López government, caused in part by unexpectedly high inflation in a context of presumed prosperity due to high world prices for coffee and the booming drug trade. These developments led López reluctantly to propose certain changes in tax legislation through the Congress in 1975. Although López supported these changes largely as an effort to minimize a potential counter-reform, the end result was that producer associations gained a more prominent role.

Continuing high inflation was not foreseen by either the original 1974 tax reform or the 1975 measures. The inflation led to sharp business protest over the increased capital gains tax generated by inflation, even as it sparked increased middle-class and labor opposition to the López government. To compound the problem, one of the government's major means of combatting inflation and the sharp expansion of the money supply (itself caused by the foreign exchange bonanza) that was fueling it was to cut back on public investment programs. This then left the government open to the charge that it was wasting increased tax revenues on "bureaucracy" instead of in worthwhile programs.

Although the tax reform was initially successful in augmenting state revenues, escalating rates of evasion became a serious problem. This difficulty caused the government to recognize that changes in the legislation were necessary, which opened the door to more substantial revisions. Thus, the continued evasion led to legislative retrenchment on key aspects of the reform, first in 1977 legislation sponsored by a new minister of finance, and even more substantially in 1979, by which time a new president had been inaugurated.[16] During his campaign, Turbay had promised the livestock interests that he would lighten their tax burden, and his government duly proposed new legislation after coming to office in 1978. Other associations also took advantage of this new opportunity to change tax measures through Congress. Indeed, an initial version of the 1979 tax law that passed in the Senate (although not in the House) was actually prepared in ANDI's Bogotá office (Urrutia, 1981: 294).

The 1979 tax law seriously emasculated the two major progressive elements of the 1974 tax reform. The presumptive income tax was saddled with limitations that reduced, if not eliminated, the tax burden on the livestock sector, and the capital gains tax on the sale of stock was virtually eliminated. The final bill that became law in 1979 was less extreme, though, due to the personal intervention of former President López.[17] But, when the impact of these modifications was combined with continued evasion (exacerbated by lax administration under Turbay), the growth rate of income tax revenues once again fell significantly below the inflation rate. The attempt to impose important changes in the Colombian tax system that would increase its progressivity and establish a firm fiscal base for the government to fund redistributionist programs was defeated in five years.

The regime structure restricted – without eliminating – the possibility for state autonomy sufficient for the enactment of redistributionist reforms, while providing numerous channels for affected groups to thwart their implementation. These two examples of agrarian reform and of tax reform (once presented to the legislature), illustrate that the political compromises necessary for successful passage led to legislation with significant flaws. In the case of agrarian reform, state capacity to implement the reforms was limited early on by the absence of regime coherence as the presidency passed from Alberto Lleras to Valencia and by limited administrative and financial capabilities. Both agrarian and tax reform were also subverted by a wide variety of individual legal and illegal responses which helped to undermine their effectiveness. At the same time, facilitated by the fact that they could find support within factions of both parties, producer associations exerted pressure to have the measures modified, convincing state elites of the need for legislative change. And in both cases input from labor and peasant organizations was nominal, or indirect and with undesired consequences. Peasant and labor groups had almost no role in drafting the 1961 agrarian reform legislation. The influence of peasant groups in the 1973 legislation was indirect, and the emergence of ANUC and land invasions mobilized landowners. The peasantry and labor were marginalized from any discussion about tax legislation.

The politics of economic stabilization: "success" (1957–8), "failure" (1962–3) and "crisis" (1965)

Balance of payments deficits and rapid inflation have been crucial economic problems that have plagued Latin American countries, often swamping ambitious reform programs and demanding economic stabilization programs, threatening regime crisis. These stabilization programs, which normally incorporate devaluation to help improve a country's balance of payments, a reduction in the growth rate of a country's money supply to slow down inflation, a correction and often attempted elimination of government budget deficits and attempts to let markets determine prices ("freeing" interest rates which usually increase and pushing wages down), have been difficult to implement successfully in most Latin American countries. As most economists have noted, efforts to improve a country's balance of payments (principally by means of devaluation raising the cost of imported inputs and encouraging exports) often partially counteract efforts to reduce inflation. As a consequence of depressed coffee prices, an emphasis on import-substitution industrialization and little effort at export diversification, Colombia also confronted balance of payments problems in the late 1950s and in the 1960s and the periodic need to stabilize its economy.

Colombia's "successful" stabilization effort of 1957–8, carried out during the period of the interim military junta was examined in chapter 3. It took place under exceptional circumstances which did not recur subsequently. Opposition to the economic program was muted as most social and political actors continued to strive for the completion of the political transition then in process. Under General Rojas, the World Bank had terminated its disbursements of funds to Colombia and balance of payments problems were paralyzing industries unable to import crucial inputs; thus, there was a consensus that recovering Colombia's external credit was essential for economic recovery. The promise of a return to democratic rule and of bipartisan support for needed economic measures was crucial for eliciting necessary support from the US in the form of credits from the Export–Import Bank and a private bank loan. Indeed, foreign aid to Colombia in 1958 was almost *triple* what it was in 1957.

President Alberto Lleras began his term in office under a relatively auspicious economic situation, both because of the stabilization efforts of the military junta and because of the external support the country could now expect with the return to civilian government. In fact, the economy did grow at a healthier pace (GDP grew at an average annual rate of 5.5% in 1959–62, as compared to 2.3% in 1957–8 (Díaz-Alejandro, 1976: 16)). Yet balance of payments pressures were felt, as the government's expansionary policies generated an increase in imports even as exports continued to decline. Coffee prices for this same period were over one-third lower than what they had been in 1955–6 (Díaz-Alejandro, 1976: 24).[18] By early 1962, however, renewed pressure on the country's balance of payments generated by an increase in imports generated by the government's more expansionary policies combined with a decline in exports placed renewed pressure on the country's balance of payments.

The government confronted a difficult economic situation, complicated by the challenge of the forthcoming congressional and presidential elections. Seeking to avoid the need for another devaluation right before the elections, the Lleras government sought to restrict imports. As pressures built up, the government was aided by timely foreign assistance. In April 1962, between the congressional and presidential elections, a \$30 million dollar loan from Alliance for Progress funds was signed and immediately released, primarily to aid with balance of payments problems (\$8 million dollars of outstanding Colombian debt to the Export–Import Bank were also rolled over) (US Senate, 1969: 10).

The winner of the presidential elections, Conservative Guillermo León Valencia, faced a difficult problem of governance due to the increased congressional representation of forces opposed to the National Front or to his government (particularly the Liberal MRL and the Conservative Laureanistas). The Valencia administration politically was the weakest of this entire period. Valencia did not possess a two-thirds majority in Congress and he sought to govern by allowing representation of most party factional interests in his cabinet, with little central coordination, and was uninformed and uninterested personally regarding economic matters. Balance of payments problems continued throughout 1962 as pressures for a devaluation built. The 1962 devaluation was widely discussed and debated prior to its occurrence. As one economist has noted, it was also "a textbook example of how *not* to manage a devaluation" (Díaz-Alejandro, 1976: 195). The devaluation became associated with a veritable explosion of inflation which jumped from 6% in 1962 to 35% in 1963.[19] In the same quarter in which the devaluation took place monetary expansion grew dramatically (by 17.4%, in contrast to 5.3% in the first nine months of the year) in large part because of the overextended position of commercial banks.[20] In late 1962, Valencia was forced to accept a decreed wage increase by his minister of labor Belisario Betancur which had not had his prior approval (Diaz-Alejandro, 1976: 194–5; Dix, 1967: 159–60). In early 1963, the government raised public transportation fares over 50%, gasoline prices by 20% and price ceilings for cement, cigarettes, milk and sugar between 15 and 20%. The sharp domestic inflation wiped out practically all of the intended incentive on exports. Furthermore, in spite of the decreed wage increases, inflation generated a perception (and for some the reality) of losing ground economically over 1963. As a consequence, numerous strikes occurred in early 1963. Devaluation became identified with inflation and political turmoil.

As a result of the disastrous economic policies, growing fiscal problems and continued foreign exchange difficulties, pressures grew for a second devaluation, which President Valencia simply refused to consider.[21] In 1963, the Congress ceded the executive extraordinary powers to deal with the government's critical fiscal situation, itself a result of the impact of inflation and increased government expenditures. The government decided to raise revenues quickly by imposing a 20% surcharge on income taxes to be paid in 1963 and 1964. Subsequently, revenue was to be generated by a general sales tax enacted at that time but not due to be implemented until January 1, 1965. Throughout 1964, as the date for imposition of the sales tax neared, opposition based upon its feared impact on inflation (and to a lesser extent, its regressive impact) increased. In addition a decision to devalue was actually agreed to in December 1964 by Valencia who then drew back. At this point, unhappy about the policy decision but fearing the political consequences of holding back, the US released US$40 million to help the country's balance of payments. The country's failure to devalue led to the resignation of the finance minister in February 1965 (Dunkerley, 1968: 135).

By early 1965, the country had reached a crisis point. Balance of payments problems, inflationary pressures, declines in real wages, and an upsurge in student protests, kidnappings and guerrilla activities all formed a backdrop to a threatened national strike by the two tradiitonal labor confederations (the UTC and the CTC), primarily protesting inflation and the imposition of the sales tax. Furthermore, as the UTC and the CTC proceeded with their plans to call a national strike for the end of January, talk of a possible coup by the controversial minister of war, General Alberto Ruiz Novoa, increased. Ruiz Novoa, who had earlier emphasized the importance of civic–military efforts to improve rural living standards as part of the anti-guerrilla struggle, widened his criticisms of the Valencia presidency.[22]

The country's major producer associations were instrumental

in resolving this crisis. Several days before the date fixed for the general strike, a number of them formed a Comité de Mediación Nacional to serve as intermediaries between the government and the workers. The bitterly factionalized political parties had lost influence within the confederations, and they were relying on the associations to find a way out of the impasse or in at least one case were passively watching events, having accepted the inevitability of a coup. Under an ANDI initiative, a Comité Privado de Cooperación was formed of representatives from FENALCO, ANDI, ASOBANCARIA, SAC, and the Popular Colombian Association of Industrialists (ACOPI – Asociación Colombiana Popular de Industriales), which met with the UTC and the CTC.[23] Four days before the specified strike date, the CTC withdrew from participation in the strike, claiming the government had satisfied its major complaints. Then, only hours before the strike was to begin, the UTC also refrained as the government succumbed to many of its demands.

A Gran Comisión was formed by members of the major factions of the two political parties, the producer associations, the unions, and government official to consider a variety of economic, labor and administrative reforms. Subsequently renamed the Comisión Especial de Estudios Económicos y Sociales, this was perhaps the most prominent example of an *ad hoc* decision forum created during the National Front to mediate a political crisis. A few days later, the president ousted minister of war Ruiz Novoa, and rumors of a coup subsided.[24]

In meetings held in secrecy, the Comisión addressed a broad range of labor grievances and economic issues related to fiscal weaknesses and balance of payments issues. Proposals emanating from the Comisión were transformed into labor legislation and presented to Congress in early 1965 as promised. However, Valencia could not muster the necessary two-thirds vote in Congress. Presidential authority was employed, as Valencia enacted the legislation by executive decree using state of siege powers.[25]

There was less success, however, in terms of dealing with the government's fiscal situation and the country's continuing balance of payments problems. The government entered into protracted negotiations with the World Bank, the IMF and the US government, who all insisted upon the need for devaluation. For Valencia that was still unthinkable, because it was linked to high inflation, violent political protest and a growth in the electoral strength of opposition movements such as ANAPO. The result was an informal suspension of loans and disbursements by the foreign agencies in 1965.[26] An effort by the new minister of finance to put a financial package together in May, 1965 failed as details leaked to the press and the president backed away from it (Dunkerley, 1968: 137). By mid-June, President Valencia was looking for his third finance minister in 1965.

As the international agencies pressured the government to devalue, carry out administrative reforms and generate additional public revenues, the same issues were being debated within the Comisión Especial and within the principal private sector organization, ANDI. A "*laissez-faire*" wing of industrialists was opposed to higher taxes or more government intervention in the economy, preoccupied by the emergence of opposition groups such as Camilo Torres' "United Front" and sought a more aggressive military response to kidnappings of prominent businessmen (see Bailey, 1965). However, less predictably, a vigorous "statist–reformist" wing also existed which sought to modernize the state, rationalize the running of the economy and humanize development. It argued that the state needed a sounder fiscal base upon which to build a stronger public investment program, including social reforms. The reformists' point of view was reflected in the commission's reports, drafted essentially by ANDI's technical staff and which reiterated in part recommendations made by international agencies also dedicated to state institution building and economic modernization. These recommendations included a revision of the sales tax; a tax on gasoline; a valorization tax; and a revision of the income tax, including improved administration to crack down on evasion.[27]

The uncertainty and the expectation of a major devaluation accelerated capital flight throughout these months. Finally, a new minister of finance was able to put together a package of strict import licensing and restrictions with a "hidden devaluation" involving modifications to the exchange rate. Most imports were now to be purchased at a rate of $13.50, rather than the "official" rate of $9.00. The devaluation was presented to the country as a "revaluation" because the higher "free rate" was brought down.[28] Before agreeing to resume aid flows, the World Bank prepared a memorandum of understanding signed by the government specifying quarterly targets for economic variables such as the government current account surplus, net foreign exchange reserves, import liberalization and public utility tariffs (see Cepeda, 1977; also IBRD, 1972).

The crisis-ridden period of 1965 illustrates well the regime predicaments of threatened immobilism and lack of policy coherence and the use of "rules of the game" such as presidential authority, secrecy and *ad hoc* decision forums. The stop-go policies of the latter Alberto Lleras and particularly of the Valencia periods reflected uncertain leadership and sharp political divisions within the regime in a difficult economic context. The efforts of producer associations committed to maintaining the civilian regime in a context of declining party influence due to immobilism and factionalism, the political allegiances and organizational weakness of the labor movement and the provision of aid funds at critical moments by international agencies were all significant factors in aiding the regime in its crisis periods.

President Carlos Lleras: stabilization, export promotion and increased state capacity

As Carlos Lleras assumed the presidency in August, 1966, his government faced a renewed crisis in the country's balance of payments due to a further drop in coffee prices combined with an inherited program of import liberalization which had led to a dramatic increase in imports even as minor exports had stagnated. Shortly after Lleras' inauguration, the IMF began pressuring for a new devaluation. Lleras was haunted by the disastrous consequences that had faced Valencia after he had devalued soon after his inauguration in November 1962. Furthermore, Rojas and the ANAPO movement had made devaluation a political issue during the campaign, accusing Lleras and the National Front regime of being instruments of the US and the international agencies. In the Congressional elections of March 1966, ANAPO had increased its percentage of the vote to 17.8%, while abstention in presidential year elections continued to increase (see Maullin, 1967: 16–17; election results from Table 6.1).

Lleras initially hoped he could separate the World Bank and AID from IMF demands. However, by late November 1966, both AID and the World Bank had made it clear to the Lleras government that their continuing aid depended upon an agreement of the Colombian government with the IMF, including a devaluation timetable (Díaz-Alejandro, 1976: 204–5; interviews, July 1982; IBRD, 1972). Lleras responded to the IMF in a dramatic gesture, appearing on national television and announcing the breakdown of negotiations and the refusal of the government to devalue. However, he did reinstate controls on all imports; in effect, a partial, *de facto* devaluation. In a masterful stroke, Lleras had "a public difference with the IMF, while in effect agreeing to terms it would accept" (Currie, 1981: 97; see also Maullin, 1967: 202–9 and Díaz-Alejandro, 1976: 204–5). Then after several months of feverish activity and employing extraordinary powers granted the executive by a somewhat reluctant Congress, the Lleras government enacted by decree a new framework for trade and foreign exchange (Decree-Law 444 of 1967) in March 1967.

This new law was ostensibly imposed as an alternative to the demands from international lending agencies for a large devaluation. The reality is more complex. World Bank officials, as "'honest brokers'" (Díaz-Alejandro, 1976: 205) and the IMF were involved with the Colombian technical staff preparing the new framework; at the same time, the IMF allowed itself to appear as a "Goliath" brought to its knees by a Colombian "David" (cf. Currie, 1981: 97). The law's enactment was followed almost immediately by the signing of a US$60 million standby agreement with the IMF. Although the standby credit was publicly announced, the numerous commitments the Colombian government made in order to receive it, related to quarterly targets for exchange, internal credit and money supply, were not (Currie, 1981: 97–8).[29]

It was not entirely obvious at the time that the law had established the means for a partial reorientation of the economy from an import-substitution model to one of export-promotion. One of the major elements of the law was the establishment of a "crawling peg" devaluation mechanism controlled by the Junta Monetaria and the central bank by which devaluations would occur constantly and gradually, rather than brusquely (and tardily) as in the past. Although the real increase in the exchange rate due to devaluation from 1967 to 1975 was only 2.7%, this still marked significant progress. In the past, significant declines in the exchange rate had been common (Wiesner, 1978: 93–4).

The same 1967 law established an export promotion fund (PROEXPO – Fondo de Promoción de Exportaciones) financed by a tax on imports. Its many activities have included generous lines of credit, insurance plans, information about foreign markets, and other promotional measures. In the opinion of one prominent economic policy maker, its most important function was probably that of a "pressure group" for export interests within the government bureaucrcy in the face of opposing fiscal, monetary or even social considerations (interview, November 1977).

The results, following these policy changes, were impressive. In sharp contrast to the previous period, after 1967 there were no significant exchange crises, even as the rate of inflation grew in the 1970s. A major reason for this in the first part of the 1970s was the dramatic increase in the value of non-traditional or "minor" exports, which nearly doubled in value from 1967 to 1971 (see Table 5.4). This rapid expansion in exports was due in part to a booming world economy, but was unquestionably aided by the domestic inducements established by previous policy efforts and particularly those offered along with the devaluation measure.

A shift, moderate rather than pendular, to more orthodox policies encouraging realistic exchange rates and export promotion occurred without a change in political regime as in the bureaucratic–authoritarian cases of the southern cone. Ironically, the political adroitness of a president committed to building a stronger state combined with the state's limited autonomy (its openness to influence by international agencies) to result in a felicitous outcome.[30]

Increased state capacity

Under President Carlos Lleras the state undertook its most significant transformations during the National Front period. The consociational National Front pact, by eliminating the struggle for control of the state, permitted both parties to benefit as the state increased in size and importance. The extent to which this increase in state bureaucracy would be "colonized" for clientelist purposes by different party factions or be relatively immunized from partisan influence and staffed by more technocratic elements was a source of tension within the political regime. Consociationalism fostered conditions for both trends, with party factions and leaders in the two parties occasionally preferring one more than the other. Thus, the crucial factor in explaining increased state capacity is the interaction of state elites with international aid agencies in the context of economic growth with its associated diversification and complexity. Only when increased state capacity was a priority of key state elites, particularly the president, were significant advances made in this area. The president most identified with this goal has been Carlos Lleras Restrepo. He was convinced that the state needed to develop a more vigorous planning capacity and a more agile administrative apparatus.

Although Lleras was in a weaker political position than he wished to be because of the nature and outcome of the 1966 elections, as a vigorous politician with a vision of what he sought to accomplish and as a leader in the country's majority party, he was able to carry out an impressive array of measures and reforms in his period of office. Nevertheless, as was evident in the discussions of the 1968 Constitutional Reform in chapter 4 and of agrarian reform above, he was also to be constrained by the regime structure, which permitted effective expression of political and private sector opposition to many of his measures.

There are numerous indicators of the growth in state capacity under Lleras. Total public expenditures expanded dramatically from 16% of GDP in 1960 to 32% of GDP in 1970 (Amézquita & Fernández, 1977: 265). And public investment was increasingly channelled through the national-level decentralized sector as investment at the departmental and municipal levels stagnated.[31] This decentralized sector grew substantially in size and in terms of number of agencies.[32] Expenditures of the decentralized sector as a percentage of total public expenditures grew over 300% from 8.5% in 1959–61 to 34.4% in 1969–71; expenditures at the departmental, municipal and central government levels declined as a share of total public expenditures during this same period by 39%, 30% and 26%, respectively (calculated from Amézquita & Fernández, 1977: 263). Finally, Lleras also increased the role of the National Planning Department and of technocrats in determining public investment patterns.

Lleras' measures led to a significant transfer of functions from the central ministries to the newly-created agencies. A number of these agencies were given economic independence and thus greater autonomy by having their budgets come from earmarked taxes or funds (interview with a former head of the National Planning Department, July 1978). Such was the case with the Colombian Foreign Trade Institute (INCOMEX – Instituto Colombiano de Comercio Exterior), PROEXPO and the decentralized agencies in the electrical sector. In this way, Lleras and his advisers sought to reduce the impact that partisan interests could have in the running of these agencies and to increase the rationalization of the distribution of public funds by the creation of technical entities that would be independent of political pressures.[33] International aid agencies were attracted to and sought to reinforce a discreet, technocratic, depoliticized state structure through which to channel their loans. The concerns of international agencies for proper identification and specification of projects, pre-investment studies, tight institutional control, professional staffing, clear operating regulations, proper auditing, prior review of selected loan disbursements and independence from partisan-political influence (Congress, civil service, local political or budgetary control) in loan disbursements were significant in the creation of planning and many decentralized agencies.[34] International aid agencies sought to manage their affairs with the various National Front governments in secrecy, without debate. Thus, major economic policy issues, including development plans, public utility tariffs and public investments were not debated in Congress, much less departmental assemblies, municipal councils or even other public forums.

Increased state capacity was also sought by enlarging the role of the state in monitoring and processing information and in regulating the economy. Planning was still in its infancy in Colombia when the National Front began. It advanced modestly under President Alberto Lleras, who instituted wide-ranging administrative reforms and created a planning agency that underwent various reforms and name changes until it became the National Planning Department (DNP – Departamento Nacional de Planeación) as a result of the 1968 Constitutional Reform. Alberto Lleras also created a special council, which also underwent modifications in 1963 and 1968, to emerge finally as the National Council of Economic and Social Policy (CONPES – Consejo Nacional de Políticas Económicas y Sociales). CONPES has been responsible for approving major programs of economic and social development in the country.[35]

With the establishment of the National Front, international agencies such as AID had political reasons to provide aid flows to Colombia. As a result of Carlos Lleras' numerous administrative reforms and the increased professionalism of the country's state agencies, the country became especially attractive to the international lending agencies (see Table 5.5). From its inception, the planning effort in Colombia was viewed primarily as an effort to acquire international financing for projects. Furthermore, similar to major reform efforts in fiscal and other areas, it was heavily influenced by international experts.[36]

Producer groups tended to be more ambivalent toward the Lleras government, in part because they now confronted a more imposing actor. Landowners and commercial farmers were bitterly opposed to Lleras' land reform measures. ANDI, as the representative of private sector – particularly industrial – interests in the country, has always expressed support for government planning. By that it has meant greater predictability and policy continuity regarding matters such as credit, tax incentives, price controls, tariffs and import controls. Yet, ANDI, like other private sector groups, has also feared increased government intervention.[37] This concern balanced ANDI's enthusiasm for Lleras' attempts to rationalize decision-making, for Lleras also sought to strengthen the state. For example, by the early 1970s, the association opposed agrarian reform, which it had initially supported. It feared that the reform would disrupt production and that state intervention in the rural sector might spill over into industry (Bagley, 1979: 238–9). In another instance, ANDI cooperated with organized labor to defeat an attempt by Lleras to create a centrally organized national savings fund with monies collected by both the public and private sectors for workers' pension funds. Opposition to this move derived from fear of the government possessing such a potent financial arm, concern of possible inefficiency and mismanagement and from the fact that most industrialists did not set aside funds for workers' pensions but paid them out of their operating budget. In the end, Lleras created a fund (the Fondo Nacional del Ahorro) to collect the pension funds of national government employees, employing extraordinary powers granted him by Congress to reorganize the executive branch.[38] A central part of ANDI's opposition to the Andean Pact's Decision 24 regulating foreign investment was a clause granting the state first option in the purchase of foreign companies (Urrutia, 1980).

Attempts to place consultation between the regime and producer groups on a more regularized basis though extensive during

Table 5.5 *Colombia: Official development assistance 1959–76 (in millions of current US dollars)*

Year	US/AID	US food aid	IBRD[1]	IDB[2]	Total aid[3]
1959	1.9	10.0	7.0	0	18.9
1960	1.9	11.1	12.2	0	25.2
1961	2.7	10.2	17.5	35.2	65.6
1962	35.7	13.5	26.8	12.8	88.8
1963	41.8	8.6	32.8	24.9	108.1
1964	49.0	11.5	46.8	28.0	135.3
1965	51.4	9.7	45.4	27.1	133.6
1966	36.7	5.5	32.9	22.7	97.8
1967	76.6	9.5	28.3	15.7	130.1
1968	82.2	9.3	36.9	112.1	240.5
1969	63.8	17.1	38.5	55.5	174.9
1970	92.7	15.9	40.2	23.1	171.9
1971	83.5	21.0	66.9	80.3	251.7
1972	55.1	20.9	61.5	49.9	187.4
1973	71.6	0	88.8	105.9	266.3
1974	53.4	0	75.1	0	128.5
1975	40.0	0	112.4	75.8	228.2
1976	18.9	0	80.1	109.0	208.0

[1]International Bank for Reconstruction and Development or the World Bank.
[2]Inter-American Development Bank.
[3]Other multilateral and bilateral sources of aid (e.g. from the UN or other OECD countries) are not included in this total.
Source: Wilkie, 1974 and Wilkie & Haber, 1981.

the Lleras presidency had only limited results. With the exception of relations between the state and the Coffee Federation, structured relations across the state, producer associations and labor organizations during the National Front were limited in scope and effectiveness. Business and to a much lesser extent labor groups have been represented on the boards of directors of public banks, and of commissions responsible for official purchases, determination of monetary and exchange policy, foreign trade policy, prices and wages; on numerous sector-specific advisory councils and decentralized agencies; and industrial sectoral committees.[39] This kind of public–private interaction expanded dramatically under Lleras, as a result of the creation of numerous decentralized agencies, sectoral committees (especially in industry) and other administrative reforms in the executive branch. Intended to help regularize public decision-making, the effects were mixed, reflecting both the relative weakness of the state and of the producer associations and the much greater weakness of organized labor and other elements of the popular sector. In the case of industrial sectoral committees there was little continuity into the next government. A number of committees came to meet sporadically, with businessmen holding back information from the government.[40] Furthermore, central state influence or coordination over the numerous agencies was often limited. Many state representatives were businessmen or other private sector individuals from the sector concerned appointed by the president, rather than state officials. In the case of many decentralized agencies ministers were required to serve on so many boards and had such high turnover that the agencies often had little effective oversight or were in fact controlled by sector-specific producer associations (interviews with high government officials in 1977 and 1978; see also Bailey, 1977).

During the National Front, there was not a unilinear process of increased formal consultation with the private sector, but a sporadic and incomplete process. Although industry felt favored by Lleras, it never gained a firm institutionalized voice within the state apparatus, as coffee had by virtue of its historical development and economic centrality for the country, nor did it gain the kind of support that private urban construction received, in a surprising turn of events, in the subsequent Pastrana government. In the Pastrana years, efforts to strengthen state capacity levelled off as the regime tilted away from a statist orientation.

President Misael Pastrana: urban construction and privatization

President Misael Pastrana assumed power in August 1970 under inauspicious circumstances due to his narrow victory over Rojas and the large contingent of Anapistas in the Congress, departmental assemblies and municipal councils around the country.

The Pastrana government immediately initiated a number of short-term measures in urban areas to attempt to reduce ANAPO's continued attractiveness (for a particularly interesting example, see Trapido, 1979). Pastrana inherited from the Lleras government a development plan for 1970–3, a report on fiscal reform based on a mission headed by Richard Musgrave (Gillis, 1974) and a report on employment based on a study mission of the International Labor Organization (Avramovic, 1972). However, a crisis in the National Planning Department in December 1970 led to a massive turnover of personnel and to the appointment of a political confidante of the president as the new head of the Department (for details of this dispute see Rivera Ortiz, 1975; see also Currie, 1981: 42–3). The new director asked Lauchlin Currie to return to Colombia and to advise the government on development plans, which Currie did in June 1971.[41]

A new development plan, the "Plan of the Four Strategies," was announced by the government in December 1971. The "four strategies" were urban development with particular emphasis on housing construction, export promotion, increased agricultural productivity and redistribution based on progressive taxation. The plan was a revised version of ideas that Currie had developed in 1961 in an alternative plan to the one prepared by the Alberto Lleras government. Urban construction was to receive the most concerted government attention. Export promotion was to be aided by the policy changes of the previous government, and commercial agriculture was to be favored by the legislation finally passed in 1973 ostensibly to foment agrarian reform discussed earlier in this chapter. The plan was heavily criticized for its inflationary tendencies, its overemphasis on construction (and within that of housing for the relatively wealthy) over other industrial sectors, its neglect of bottlenecks in construction inputs, its indiscriminate promotion of rural–urban migration to already overcrowded cities and its lack of quantitative analysis.[42]

In the meantime, Currie and other advisers were developing a means of implementing the plan to stimulate urban construction. The idea was to create new financial institutions to encourage increased deposits and thus provide increased loan flows for construction by providing for indexation (monetary adjustment) of the principal of deposits, as well as of construction loans and mortgages (Currie, 1981: 46) – the UPAC (Unidad de Poder Adquisitivo Constante) system. It was increasingly clear that a plan that so clearly singled out a "leading sector" would have difficulty finding approval in Congress, where the other affected interests would seek to block it. Furthermore, in this case the president would be seen as promoting a sector in which the head of his party faction (Ospina) had direct economic interests.

Pastrana enacted the UPAC system by decree using obscure presidential powers to regulate savings placed in the 1968 Constitutional Reform without any significant debate whatsoever.[43] The UPAC system soon channelled massive sums into the new savings institutions also established by presidential fiat. The enactment of the UPAC system represented a tremendous flow of funds toward the construction industry, though not due to public investment. In contrast to the statist strategy of Carlos Lleras, this plan called for a much more active role for the private sector (cf. Revéiz and Pérez, 1986: 277 and Findley et al., 1983: 87–120). The UPAC system was supervised by a Savings and Housing Board (Junta de Ahorro y Vivienda), in which the predominant influence was exercised by two "civilian" members and their alternates.[44] The rate of return provided by the UPAC system was so substantial in relation to other existing savings mechanisms in the country that by the end of 1973 36% of all savings deposits in the country's banking system were in the UPAC system (Findley et al., 1983: 89). However, this did not lead so much to an increase in total savings in the country as to a shifting of funds toward UPACs, permitting the construction sector to grow by 12.6% in 1973 (in contrast to 1.8% in 1972).

When President López assumed power in August 1974, he immediately took steps to prevent the continued growth and, in the view of his economic advisers, distorting effects of the system. Increased inflation and migration, and their negative impact on wages and employment levels in the cities, were blamed on the UPAC system, even as industrialists and others protested that they were suffering from lack of sufficient credit. Among other measures, López reduced the indexation to levels below the inflation rate and subjected savings to a capital gains tax (Findley et al., 1983: 104). With a greater "state" consciousness and desire to trim the UPAC system, the new president simply refused to name the "civilian" advisers to the board overseeing the UPAC system, and eventually the Monetary Board (again by presidential dictum) became the official adviser of the president in this area (cf. Currie, 1981: 50, 249n.). Given the substantial interests created by the

UPAC system – of major banks that partially owned the new Corporaciones de Ahorra y Vivienda, their depositors, the construction industry and its suppliers, workers dependent upon these industries and others – a total dismantling of the UPAC system would have been very difficult, although in theory López could have done so employing the same presidential powers Pastrana used to create it.

Selective privatization

An uneven but increasing trend toward greater state capacity is evident during the National Front and post-National Front period. Nevertheless, the trend began from a fairly low level and continued to meet considerable opposition. Colombia's export-led growth was based on a product, coffee, that remained out of state control and initial industrialization occurred with little direct state participation. The development of the country's agro-export and industrial sectors both reflected the lack of a "state ideology" in Colombia.

As noted earlier, the coffee sector represented by the Coffee Federation has one of the most formalized relationships with the state. The Federation is difficult to characterize. Although legally a private organization, it has carried out many public functions. The Federation has been responsible for overseeing coffee purchasing and export since the 1930s, though most coffee export has been carried out by private exporters. In 1940, the National Coffee Fund (Fondo Nacional del Café) was created by means of a tax on coffee exports and *the Federation* was charged with its administration. Since that time, the coffee fund has expanded its interests into the areas of finance, insurance, construction, shipping, and other kinds of agriculture as it continues to receive income from a variety of coffee taxes, coffee exports, and sales of coffee for domestic consumption. Only in 1972 was the Fund placed under the oversight of the Congressional Comptroller's Office. The Federation has represented Colombia in international negotiations among producing and consuming countries, and it maintains tight control on information about the country's most significant export (see Palacios, 1983 and Bird et al., 1981: especially 95, 292). In coffee regions, it has been responsible for development projects.

The Coffee Federation's ambiguous "public–private" status is reflected in the makeup of its board of directors. When its private directors were increased in 1958 from five to six in order to assure partisan balance, private directors constituted a majority on the board. Furthermore, whereas government board members have changed frequently due to cabinet crises, the private members have maintained an impressive continuity.[45] Few of the controversies between the government and the Federation have become public, and the Federation has rarely commented publicly on issues of general economic policy or on political issues and candidates. All major elements of coffee policy – domestic price support, marketing strategies, taxes, credits to coffee growers, and similar issues – have been determined either within the Federation or within the executive branch by organizations in which the manager of the Coffee Federation has been represented. Congress has played no significant role whatsoever, an arrangement that has insulated effectively this vital economic function from partisan and clientelist pressures and simultaneously afforded the coffee sector an unparalleled institutionalized voice within the state.

The relationship between the state and the coffee sector approximates that of "societal corporatism" (cf. Schmitter, 1974) or what can be termed *selective* privatization since the Federation operates as a private group when it is convenient – serving as a pressure group for the interests of its members and as a financial conglomerate managing massive investments – but also carries out numerous state functions related to coffee policy and also to regional development in coffee areas (a valuable discussion of the Federation is Palacios, 1983).

Consociationalism fostered the continuance of this pattern in the coffee sector and in other areas. Even as state capacity increased, the logic of the interaction between the two parties, the reliance of political clientele groups on the state for resources and the greater militancy of labor in the state sector all meant that strong arguments could be made on efficiency grounds that expansion of the national economy should continue to depend on "private initiative" as it had in the past.[46] Even Carlos Lleras, in campaigning for the 1978 elections, noted:

I am not in favor of a policy that would nationalize more companies. Experience is showing us that the fact that certain companies are owned by the state, by the community, does not reduce the intensity of social conflicts. On the contrary, it is believed that more can be asked of the

State than of private individuals, making nationalization anti-economic (in Delgado, 1978: 21).

To be sure, agriculture, industry and other interests have sought aid in the form of state assistance, such as tax breaks, credit, and refinancing in moments of difficulty, thus highlighting the *selective* nature of the privatization. Examples of relationships similar to those in the coffee sector but less institutionalized exist in other economic sectors. The case of urban construction under Pastrana and the political impossibility of López' dismantling the UPAC system has already been discussed. Regional and urban bus transportation have been privately-owned (except for a small number of buses in Bogotá), though prices have been carefully controlled and urban transport has been subsidized by the state. Urban transportation "strikes" have usually been carried out by the owners seeking to pressure the state to increase fares or the subsidy it provides them. The national airline, AVIANCA, is private, though it receives substantial government support (through a tax exemption and a monopoly on air mail) and has government representation on its board of directors (see Bird et al., 1981: 297). Although the country's major steel mill, Acerias del Paz del Río, was initiated by the state (through IFI), it was eventually sold to the private sector. Nevertheless, it continued to require – and obtained – significant financial support from the state (cf. Currie, 1981: 153–8). Some state enterprises that have almost continually operated at a loss justify their activities, not on the basis of employment or partisan considerations, but by the claim that they are subsidizing other (private) industries in the country.[47]

In agriculture, cotton cultivation provides one more example of selective privatization.[48] In 1960, the Federation of Cotton Growers (FEDERALGODON), in what it itself perceived as a major coup, received the right to market its own products, including the export of cotton, without state intervention. This assured the Federation a firm economic base, since members would now have to pay their quotas. Diverging economic interests (as cotton cultivators on the Atlantic Coast focused on export markets) exacerbated other regional and personality conflicts leading to the creation of various other cotton federations. Throughout the 1960s and 1970s, cotton growers did extremely well as they fully supplied the national textile industry and became one of the leading "minor" exports of the country. As cotton became increasingly the crop of the Atlantic Coast, cotton growers became a powerful regional pressure group. In the 1972–4 period this enabled them, after several years of high international prices for cotton, to press- ure the government and the textile firms successfully for increased prices (in effect, for the right to sell all cotton, including that for domestic consumption, at international prices). In their struggle over prices, the most important ally of the cotton- growers within the state was the minister of agriculture. However, they were aided at this time by the fact that the minister of development, the traditional defender of industrialists within the state, was from the Coast. Even as the cotton growers pressed for privatization (price deregulation) they continued to rely on the state for crop loans, for easy credit to purchase machinery and for export tax incentives.

Overcultivation and abuse of pesticides in 1977 and 1978 com- bined with low international prices was followed by a serious recession in the textile industry, submerging the sector in a severe production crisis from which it only began to emerge tentatively in the mid-1980s.[49] The cotton growers were able to exact relief from the government and the textile industry (which in turn also successfully sought government assistance) in terms of credit extensions, price supports, guaranteed quotas for export at government-supported prices and other measures. Reflecting the increase in state coherence over the National Front period, the final measures resulted from extensive negotiations *within the state* between the ministry of agriculture and other government agencies and were not entirely satisfactory to the associations (see Hartlyn, 1985).

Before the National Front, during the decades of hegemonic party governments, the protection of vital economic activities such as the coffee trade from the risks of sectarian partisan politics was a logical pattern. The National Front eliminated that need but buttressed practical and ideological arguments about government inefficiency compared to private management by providing both parties clientelist access to the state and then by the emergence of conflictive state–labor relations (both discussed in chapter 6). In spite of substantial growth in state capacity, the consociational regime also fostered continued selective privatization.

President Alfonso López: bonanza, stabilization and thwarted reform

López intended his presidency to be a period of vigorous development – with continued growth, increased national and state autonomy and social reform as goals. His aggressive enactment of the tax reform shortly after his inauguration reflected a shift in orientation toward a more important role for the state in the country's economic process, particularly to promote programs for the poor. However, López' economic policy also had neo-liberal components. His administration had initially hoped also to make Colombia a South American "Japan," promoting export diversification. It intended to encourage domestic industry to be more competitive internationally by liberalizing imports and reducing protection, reducing tax incentives for exports (prone to corruption and abuse) but maintaining an effective exchange rate by continued mini-devaluations. López' government also sought to strengthen the financial system by establishing more realistic, market-oriented interest rates, rather than continuing with the existing complex structure of subsidized rates. López sought greater national autonomy by "Colombianizing" the financial sector, requiring all banks to have the majority of their shares owned by Colombians. He also announced unilaterally that Colombia was foregoing any further AID assistance.[50]

A combination of factors soon ended the hopes of continuing diversification and growth in legal minor exports (for their decline, see Table 5.4). The 1975 world recession affected demand for these minor exports while their prospects were also hurt by a slow-down in devaluation in spite of the country's continuing inflation. This, in turn, was largely a result of the country's unexpected flood of foreign exchange generated by the unparalleled growth in coffee exports (Table 5.4) and in "services" (through which dollars generated by the drug trade were repatriated). The world price of coffee shot up beginning in 1976 as a result of massive frosts in Brazil. At the same time, the large-scale herbicide program against marihuana launched in Mexico in 1975 led traffickers to turn increasingly to Colombia as demand continued to increase in the US. In addition, by the Spring 1976, Colombia was cited in a UN study as the major world center for cocaine traffic (see Craig, 1983: 331).[51]

President López stated that the coffee bonanza was for the

cafeteros, although limited state efforts to control its inflationary effects fueled considerable coffee contraband in the 1975–8 period. At the same time, the drug boom was viewed benignly, and Colombia was seen as "a victim of its privileged geographic position" (López in a 1975 speech, cited in Craig, 1983: 329). Thus, unlike the oil-based "bonanzas" of the Mexican and Venezuelan cases, Colombia's foreign exchange bonanza of the 1970s was not channelled through the state. The government was unwilling to manage the bonanza by implementing new "excess profits" taxes on the coffee sector, even as it allowed rapid shifts in the internal price to reflect increases in international prices.[52] At the same time, the government sought to capture some of the incoming foreign exchange generated by illegal drug exports by creating a special window (*ventanilla siniestra*) at the Bank of the Republic (Lupsha, 1981). However, the dramatic expansionary impact on the money supply of the rapid influx of new foreign exchange required dramatic action in an attempt to curtail growing inflation. The government cut back on public investment especially beginning in 1976 and effectively revalued the peso in 1977 (though it maintained the exchange framework established in 1967). These moves, combined with high interest rates fostered by tight monetary policy further hurt the manufacturing sector. Many industrialists turned to the "underground economy" fed by drug and contraband money for credit at high rates, probably further fueling inflation (Junguito & Caballero, 1978: 103–39). If unable or unwilling to tax the coffee sector, the administration could have responded by dramatically liberalizing imports. This, however, was successfully opposed by an industrial sector fearful it could not compete against cheap imports. At the same time, textiles and other sectors were seriously affected by increased smuggling and contraband facilitated by the fact the black market dollar rate was below the official rate and by the lifting of import restrictions (interviews with businessmen associated with ANDI in Medellín, 1978 and 1982; see also Paus, 1982; and Gómez, 1987).

The López government began with an effort to employ its electoral mandate to increase state capacity and promote redistributionist programs. Confronted by unexpected economic events, its response reflected the regime structure's tendency to respond favorably to the powerful coffee sector and to a lesser extent other organized groups, while resisting "populist" pressures by implementing a tight monetary policy and cutting back on public investment. One particularly beneficial result of this outcome was that the government resisted the temptation to borrow extensively from commercial banks at a time when numerous other Latin American countries were doing so. This was a key factor in explaining why the continent's financial crisis hit Colombia much later and more moderately than the rest of the continent in the early 1980s. The government response to the coffee boom and particularly to the illegal drug boom both reflected and reinforced the fact that in spite of its impressive modernization over the previous twenty-five years, the state still possessed limited capacity to manage economic events within its borders.

Conclusion

The Colombian National Front political regime pursued eclectic economic policies. It shifted from import-substituting industrialization to moderate export promotion at a relatively earlier stage of its industrialization than other larger or comparable Latin American countries. Then, it concentrated briefly on urban construction as a leading sector, without giving up on industrialization or commercial agriculture. It ended with an export boom in its traditional export product, as well as in a new and illegal one.

It is difficult to ascertain what economic policies and patterns would have occurred if Colombia had not had a consociational regime. Colombia's historical evolution augured well for "moderate" patterns of economic growth. Yet, that is insufficient by itself, as is attested by the disastrous economic record of two previously "moderate" countries, Mexico and Venezuela, in the 1980s. Political regimes in general and in economically more dependent countries to an even greater extent have only partial influence over their country's economic evolution. Yet, much of the material discussed in this chapter supports the conclusion that the "moderate" pattern of Colombia's economic evolution was facilitated by political factors and in particular by the elements of coalition rule and muted inter-party conflict of consociationalism. These elements removed a major cause of violence and instability in the country and renewed the confidence of the Church, international actors and agencies and foreign and local investors in the country. The coalition nature and the institutional structure of the regime and its relative openness to domestic and international influence promoted both the relatively "eclectic" policy model as well as its "moderate" nature, inhibiting the application of any one economic theory ("ECLA" protectionism or "Chicago School" liberalism) to an extreme.

The patterns analyzed in the pages above illustrate an absence of radical policy shifts (lack of popular responsiveness) in a context of crisis decision-making (immobilism) and of continual short-term policy changes and shifts regarding development objectives (lack of policy coherence). Similarly, the creative use of the "rules of the game" discussed in chapter 4 to mitigate or partially circumvent these problems and consociational predicaments is also evident in the policy cases analyzed above.

"Moderation" was encouraged by the regime structure in various ways. The political regime, controlled by a coalition of two factionalized multi-class elitist political parties, inhibited radical policy shifts. Radical reform would have required a reorientation of policy combined with a dramatic increase in state capacity and state autonomy, neither of which took place. Presidential candidates were chosen from the mainstream of their parties and were either leading figures within them or closely allied to one. None, with the partial exception of Carlos Lleras, were particularly imbued with a "state" ideology and, further reflecting low "stateness," their cabinet ministers were largely politicians or figures from the private sector. Producer groups – coffee and other agricultural interests, merchants, industrialists, bankers and others – had representation within both parties and coalition rule facilitated the penetrability of the regime by these organized economic groups over and above weaker associations of workers, peasants or consumers (whose presence was often felt only "indirectly").

For the international agencies, Colombia had legitimacy as a "democracy," yet the National Front structure permitted them to maintain a discreet and relatively secret, though extensive, role in the state. International agencies provided crucial foreign exchange, and though willing at times to dispense funds to prevent feared political crises (USAID under Alberto Lleras and Valencia), they were also not reluctant to hold back funds to seek policy changes they desired (under Valencia and Carlos Lleras). AID was concerned about land reform, but until the 1970s the World Bank was largely unconcerned about the redistributive impact of its programs. The agencies played an important role in encouraging "moderate" policies by paying close attention to the country's exchange, trade and fiscal policies. Foreign advisers were often employed in domestic policy struggles to reinforce pressures for more "statist," "reformist" or "technocratic" – but not "populist" expansionary – positions.

Some elements of the National Front coalition were interested in reformist–redistributive goals. At the leadership level they were found primarily in the Liberal Party. Presidential alternation and coalition rule, as well as the opposition of affected producer groups, inhibited their capacity to enact reform, though not completely. Weak presidents were more the captives of party factions and open to producer group influence. Even stronger presidents operated under sharp constraints, but they could seek to put together an ideologically coherent government (even if a coalition one) due to the diversity of opinions within both parties. Then, as López did in 1974, they could employ mechanisms intended to circumvent immobilism in periods of crisis as a means of furthering a reformist agenda. Carlos Lleras' more careful, rational approach to decision-making almost certainly affected the chances of success for his policies, as it permitted the opposition to counter-mobilize effectively (cf. Hirschman, 1981: 163; and the analysis in Ascher, 1984). Furthermore, the expansion of state capacity under Lleras (facilitated by funds from international agencies pleased by his administration's professionalism), combined with the effective mobilization of landowner opposition and the expansion of commercial agriculture led the industrialists to back away from Lleras' objectives. Following the increase in state growth under Lleras, the size of the public sector has remained around the same, as the pressures for "privatization" partially reasserted themselves.

If the political regime inhibited radical policy shifts, it also kept opponents to reform within its boundaries. Unlike other Latin American countries, these did not seek out the military or promote regime change. In contrast to the "pendular" cases of Argentina, Chile and Peru, from the perspective of reform opponents in Colombia the likely political alternative to the reformists was *not* an even more unsatisfactory populist or radical movement (represented by the Peronists, the Popular Unity or

APRA, respectively in these countries), but a more centrist or conservative government from within the two parties (cf. Ascher, 1984: 221). In Colombia, both reformism and its opposition were channelled through the two-party system that dominated the regime. And the resulting economic policies promoted relatively stable economic growth and low inflation without discriminating excessively against any particular economic sector. Under somewhat different economic or political circumstances, Lleras and López could both have been more successful in implementing their land and tax reform efforts with important implications for the welfare of large sectors of the population. And speculating more broadly, a less rigid consociational agreement, one that permitted competitive presidential elections or called for coalition rule for a shorter period of time in a more flexible and open manner, might have permitted more reformist measures to be implemented and more continuity in some policy areas. Yet, given the nature of each of the two dominant parties, it is unlikely this would have provided for the kinds of policy shifts evident in the more "pendular" countries, or for the kinds of changes sought by Allende in Chile (1970–3) or by the Peruvian military (1968–75).

At the same time the regime precluded these dramatic policy shifts, successive governments came under sustained criticism from nearly all groups in society because of variations in economic strategies and because of short-term change in specific policy areas. To some extent, each president sought to put his personal stamp on his administration; in part, this is what led to new development plans with different emphases (Pastrana's replacement of plans inherited from Lleras with the "Four Strategies," to be replaced by López with "To Close the Gap", and so on). These shifts were facilitated by the country's diversified natural resource base, yet presidential authority and the regional concentration of costs and benefits generated by these changes provided the impulse for change and through time, channelled by the further inhibitory presence of coalition rule, generated the constraint. The constant short-term policy changes and apparent policy incoherence reflected the extent to which regime action could be blocked by mutual vetoes and changed as different groups found a way to promote their particular views in the policy process.

Overall, both coalition rule and the relative openness of the regime – its democratic structure of elections, division of powers, freedom of the press – have favored producer groups over popular sector groups. At the same time, the form of the regime has provided it with a limited legitimacy throughout all social groups. The National Front years did see considerable expansion in state capacity and economic development. Compared to the "spectacular failures" of the economic processes in countries such as Argentina, Chile and Peru, the management of the economy by the Colombian political regime stands out as moderate and prudent. Nevertheless, this "moderation" in economic policy and the capacity to keep conservative groups within the political process came at the cost of further democratizing the process in terms of other social groups. Under the impact of the political and social changes the regime helped to foster, and its extreme rigidity regarding the political inclusion of groups outside of the two political parties, this had serious implications for its continuing political viability.

6

Political support: elections, brokerage and popular sector organizations

Party leaders had considerable autonomy of action *vis-à-vis* their followers in the establishment of the National Front in 1958. The role of the popular sector in the overthrow of General Rojas was very limited. At the same time, fear of the consequences of mass mobilization, which had escaped the control of leaders and state institutions, was high among regime leaders. Party leaders sought to retain popular support for the National Front while ending potential revolutionary violence and depoliticizing to preclude new outbreaks of partisan violence. Their traditional means of mobilizing mass support by sectarian appeals were necessarily scaled back due to the National Front agreement and their horror over *la violencia*. At the same time, in spite of the inclination by some regime leaders to enact social reforms, these efforts – largely not the result of organized popular pressure – were essentially thwarted in their implementation, as we saw in the previous chapter.[1]

One of the regime predicaments was a threatened lack of popular responsiveness. The major means of seeking to maintain both legitimacy and control over popular sector groups were clientelism evolving increasingly into brokerage, and government-sponsored popular organizations and policies of "state pluralism," which sought to divide and co-opt emerging popular organizations. On occasion, these measures passed into non-democratic practices. In comparison to the country's experience during *la violencia* or to the state-sponsored brutality of the bureaucratic-authoritarian and many other regimes in Latin America, and as was true of the country's economic record, this regime can also be said to have had "moderate" patterns of socio-political strife. This was an enviable record of limited democracy, then, not by some absolute standard, but by comparison.

Control of the state for partisan-electoral purposes and to favor one's adherents was the major source of conflict between the parties in the 1940s. Parity insured that both parties would now have access to the state for that purpose. But the role of congressmen and of local authorities in the political regime suffered substantial modification as power became centralized in the presidency and in national-level decentralized agencies and as urbanization and the spread of commercial agriculture changed the country's social structure. At the same time, partially due to the regime structure but also due to structural pressures and encouragement from international agencies, more and more state resources were channelled through the central government and its agencies and presidential authority increased to circumvent immobilism. Congress lost its role in determining patterns of public expenditures and serious discussions on economic policy largely occurred elsewhere. As a result, the role of congressmen and of local political officials as policy-makers and as patrons declined as they became relegated increasingly to the role of brokers, intermediaries between their regions and the central government.[2]

Coalition rule, demobilization and brokerage politics reinforced each other in a way that grew counterproductive for the regime. As the role of legislators became increasingly relegated to focusing on public employment "quotas" and patronage funds, their interest in maintaining coalition governments beyond any need for them due to a fear of renewed party violence remained high so that access to these resources could be assured. Because of the administrative and financial centralization of the state the only guarantee of such access was by means of coalition rule. The logic of elections with low levels of participation, in which candidates needed to mobilize only a small part of the electorate sufficient for victory, further decreased incentives to develop strong party institutions or to seek to mobilize opposition movements and enhanced the role of regional party leaders and machine-style politics. In that context, it also became increasingly more difficult to develop national political figures. Thus, the parties did not employ the National Front years to develop more coherent organizations or to respond to the challenges of a more urban and better educated electorate as traditional sectarian party identification declined. Opposition came to express itself more in non-electoral channels.

At the same time, efforts to sponsor popular organizations

from government did not lead to effective corporatist patterns of control among popular sector groups, in part because of disagreements within the coalition reflected in different policies as presidential administrations changed. Rather, in a context of a weak state and of popular organizations with a potential for autonomy and radicalization, the pattern was akin to "state pluralism" in which control was sought more by the fragmentation and decentralization of popular sector organizations dependent upon state resources than by their full incorporation and organization.[3]

The underlying theme of this chapter is the declining effectiveness of the regime in maintaining legitimacy and support due particularly to its structure of coalition rule. The political institutions of the National Front regime resisted adjusting in the face of the country's massive societal change. The next section explores electoral participation and electoral results during the National Front period. Continuities from the pre-National Front period in overall participation rates and party shares are found alongside important changes in the electorate, changes induced partially by the regime structure. These led to one of the regime's most serious challenges, the near-victory of ANAPO in 1970. Throughout the 1970s, *party segmentation continued to decline* as mass identification with the parties dropped, a phenomenon particularly evident among urban and younger elements of the population. A floating electorate largely abstentionist but potentially mobilizable by different parties and movements gradually emerged for the first time in this century. Potentially a healthy process for the consolidation of a pattern of more open competitive politics, the traditional parties did little to reach out to this group. Instead, the parties became increasingly dominated by regional leaders more interested in maintaining small captive electorates by patronage and brokerage facilitated by coalition rule and by the logic of high abstention elections. Subsequent sections explore the mix of procedures and mechanisms of regime "rules" such as clientelism, brokerage and government-sponsored organizations for electoral purposes. The final sections focus on the contradictions that emerged leading to more significant non-electoral opposition through the 1970s, including new labor organizations, the emergence of civil movements and of new guerrilla groups.[4]

Elections and the organizational decline of the traditional political parties

Central to the success of the National Front has been the electoral performance of the traditional political parties. Elections in democratic regimes have generally been viewed as mechanisms that permit some degree of popular participation in decision-making and more concretely in selecting key governing leaders. Yet, even these "classical elections" where voters are free to choose among competing candidates and are assured that results will be correctly computed (Hermet, 1978) serve the purpose of specifying voter preferences very poorly. This is especially true in consociational cases where coalitions or party pacts may disregard electoral choices (for examples from the Netherlands, see Lijphart, 1975: 177–80). From the perspective of regime elites and party leaders, elections serve to build support and legitimacy as well as to provide a means for personnel turnover and readjustments in patronage shares (see Hermet, 1978 and the discussion in Collier, 1982: 12–28). Of course, the intended benefits may not result: low participation can undermine claims of legitimacy and electoral results may challenge established elites. In the short run, regimes may prefer low participation if the perception is that antiregime parties and movements suffer more; yet, this usually cannot serve as a long-term solution.

These problems were evident in Colombia. As a result of the 1958 National Front agreement, party leaders sought to pursue three principal goals in the electoral arena: to generate popular support for the National Front agreement, defuse continued inter-party conflict and prevent alternative populist and revolutionary movements from gaining support. These three goals were partially contradictory. Parity and alternation effectively eliminated inter-party competition and thus a major reason to vote, yet mobilizing the population to vote continued to be important for National Front party leaders for two reasons. First, the presence of factions opposed to the National Front turned each election in effect into a new plebiscite on the National Front, and a sufficiently large favorable electorate needed to be mobilized. In addition, declines in voter turnout could be viewed as a result of the declining legitimacy of the National Front.

There has been considerable debate about electoral behavior

during the National Front. In fact, in some key respects it was not much different from pre-National Front behavior. There were continuities in overall participation rates, and in party shares, especially in rural areas. Tables 6.1 and 6.2 give results for the legislative and presidential elections from 1930 to 1986. Regarding electoral participation rates, a first observation is that they have tended to be comparatively low and fluctuated dramatically both before and during the National Front period.[5] The common perception that abstention "grew" and was a "new" problem for Colombia, particular to the National Front, emerged from facile comparisons to the high turnout elections of the 1940s or to those of the plebiscite and early years of the National Front. Yet, these are not fully valid comparisons. The elections of the late 1940s occurred in a context of intense polarization and conflict. Taking the four competitive congressional elections prior to the 1946 elections, voter turnout was 42.5%; including the 1947 and 1949 elections, this jumps to 51.1%. Similarly, voter turnout for the early National Front elections was generated by the euphoria following the overthrow of Rojas and the fact that legal requirements for voting were lax. Participation rates for the congressional elections during the 1958–78 period averaged 40.3%.

Comparing electoral participation rates for presidential elections must also be done cautiously. Prior to the National Front, presidential elections were not held in the same year as congressional elections.[6] Prior to the National Front they were held in a variety of circumstances: in 1934 and 1938, Conservatives did not compete; in 1942, Conservatives did not compete but supported a dissident Liberal; and in 1946 the Conservatives defeated a divided Liberal Party in a polarized election. Discounting the unusual 1958 presidential election for the reasons noted above, average turnout for the subsequent three elections was 40.3%. Post-National Front competitive presidential elections (1974, 1978, 1982 and 1986) have a somewhat higher participation rate of 47.9%. The most valid pre-National Front comparison is probably with the 1942 and 1946 elections, which averaged the still higher 57.4%.

These comparisons suggest that abstention, already high prior to the National Front, did increase somewhat in this recent period. However, the incorporation of women (who voted for the first time in the 1957 plebiscite) and of the 18–21 year old group in 1976, added to the abstention rate. On average, women voted

Table 6.1 *Electoral results for the House of Representatives 1935–86*

Year[1]	Liberal %	Conservative %	ANAPO %	Leftist parties[2] %	Total votes	Participation rates[3] A	B
1935	100	—	—	—	430,728	33.4%	23.5%
1937	100.0	—	—	—	550,726	32.5	28.9
1939	64.4	35.1	—	—	919,569	—	46.4
1941	63.8	35.7	—	—	885,525	—	43.0
1943	64.4	33.8	—	—	882,647	—	41.2
1945	63.0	33.6	—	3.2	875,856	38.4	39.4
1947	54.7	44.4	—	0.8	1,472,689	56.3	63.7
1949	53.5	46.1	—	0.4	1,751,804	63.1	72.9
1951	0.6	98.6	—	0.5	934,580	—	37.4
1953	—	99.7	—	—	1,028,323	—	39.0
1958	57.7	42.1	—	—	3,693,939	68.9	60.7
1960	44	41.7	—	12	2,542,651	57.8	39.6
1962	35.0	41.7	3.7	19.5	3,090,203	57.9	45.6
1964	46.2	35.5	13.7	4.3	2,261,190	36.9	31.3
1966	52.1	29.8	17.8	—	2,939,222	44.5	38.7
1968	49.9	33.7	16.1	—	2,496,455	37.3	31.0
1970	37.0	27.2	35.5	—	3,980,201	51.9	46.5
1972	46.3	30.8	19.0	—	2,947,125	36.3	32.5
1974	55.6	32.0	9.5	3.1	5,100,099	57.1	51.0
1976	52.0	39.1	3.6	4.6	3,265,974	34.5	31.2
1978	55.1	39.4	—	4.3	4,180,121	33.4	33.2

1980	54.5	38.2	4.1	—	4,215,371	33.8	32.2
1982	56.3	40.3	2.5	—	5,584,037	40.7	40.8
1984	54.4	39.6	2.4	—	5,654,436	38.0	39.8
1986	54.2	37.2	4.4	—	6,909,851	42.9	47.1

[1] In 1935 and 1937, the Conservative Party officially abstained; in 1951 and 1953, the Liberal Party did. Small percentages for non-left minor candidates, and blank and void votes not included. In 1972, 1976 and 1980, the figures are for departmental assemblies (and in 1984 for municipal council) since no national elections were held in those years.

[2] Leftist parties: In 1945, 1949, and 1951, the Communist Party; in 1947, the Socialist Party. In 1960 and 1962, the MRL; in 1964, the MRL *línea dura*. In 1974, the Unión Nacional de Oposición (UNO); in 1976, UNO and the Movimiento Independiente y Revolucionario (MOIR); in 1978, UNO, the Frente Unido del Pueblo (FUP) and Unidad Obrera y Socialista (UNIOS); in 1980, UNO, FUP, Frente Democrático (FD), Movimiento Firmes and Coalición; in 1982, FUP, FD, Unidad Democrática, Liberal–FD and Movimiento Izquierda Democrática; in 1984, FUP; in 1986, Unión Patriótica (UP) and joint Liberal–UP lists, as Galán's Nuevo Liberalismo vote (6.6%) was included with the Liberal vote.

[3] Column A is based upon estimates by the Registraduría Nacional del Estado Civil of the total number of eligible voters; Column B is based on estimates of the population eligible to vote (male and over 21, 1935–53; over 21, 1958–74; over 18, 1976–86).

Sources: Colombia, DANE, 1972: 152–4 (for electoral results and participation rates 1935–53); Colombia, Registraduría Nacional del Estado Civil, for electoral results and participation rates, column A, 1958–82; Losada, 1976: 7, Losada, 1979: 9n and Losada, personal correspondence for participation results, column B, 1958–86. Dix, 1967: 140, for Liberal and MRL vote, 1960, 1962 and 1964.

Table 6.2 Electoral results for the Presidency 1930–86

A. 1930–49

Year	Liberal A	Liberal B	Conservative A	Conservative B	Total votes	Participation rates A	Participation rates B
1930	44.9% Olaya	—	29.1% Valencia	25.9% Vásquez	824,530	n.a.	n.a.
1934	97.6% López	—	—	—	942,309	n.a.	n.a.
1938	100.0% Santos	—	—	—	513,520	30.2%	26.4%
1942	48.5% López	41.3% Arango	—	—	1,147,806	55.8%	54.7%
1946	32.3% Turbay	26.3% Gaitán	41.4% Ospina	—	1,366,005	55.7%	60.2%
1949	—	—	100.0% Gómez	—	1,140,646	39.9%	47.4%

B. 1958–70

Year	Official National Front	ANAPO	Other A	Other B	Total votes	Participation rates A	Participation rates B
1958	79.9% Lleras C.	—	19.8% Leyva	—	3,108,567	57.7%	51.1%
1962	62.1% Valencia	—	11.7% Leyva	25.9% López M.	2,634,840	48.7%	38.9%

Year	Liberal	Conservative	ANAPO	Left	Other	Total votes	Participation rates A	B
1966	71.4% Lleras R.		28.0% Jaramillo	—	—	2,649,258	40.1%	34.9%
1970	40.3% Pastrana		38.7% Rojas	11.7% Betancur	8.3% Sourdis	4,036,458	52.5%	47.2%

C. 1974–86

Year	Liberal	Conservative	ANAPO	Left	Other	Total votes	Participation rates A	B
1974	56.2% López	31.4% Gómez	9.4% María Rojas	2.6% Echeverri	0.1% Duarte	5,212,133	58.1%	51.0%
1978	49.5% Turbay	46.6% Betancur	—	2.4% 3 candidates	1.3% Valencia	5,075,719	40.9%	41.2%
1982	41.0% López	46.8% Betancur	—	1.2% Molina	10.9% Galán	6,815,660	49.8%	50.7%
1986	58.3% Barco	35.8% Gómez	—	4.5% Pardo	0.6% Liska	7,229,937	n.a.	n.a.

Note: Participation rate A based on estimates by the Registraduría of the total number of eligible voters; participation rate B based on population estimates of the number of eligible voters.
Sources: Colombia, Registraduría Nacional del Estado Civil; Colombia, DANE, 1972: 152; and Losada, 1976: 7, Losada, 1979: 9n and Losada, personal correspondence (for participation rate B).

19% less than men between 1957 and 1970 (Harkess & Lewin, 1975: 442). In presidential elections between 1958 and 1974, they participated 18.6% less than men (Losada, 1976: 17n). In the 1978 elections, the 18–21 year old group was considerably more abstentionist than older age cohorts.[7] In sum, average participation rates both before and after the National Front were very low. In both periods there was considerable fluctuation based upon the nature of competition. And, regardless of the independent *political* effect that the perception of low reported participation rates during the National Front had on the country, *average* participation rates were *not substantially lower* than those of typical competitive elections held in the 1930s and 1940s.

A second element of continuity between these two periods has been in terms of continued Liberal dominance. Colombia has appeared as an unlikely case for consociational rule due to the predominant support in the country for one party over the other. As we saw, however, the Liberals totally excluded from government in the 1950s were willing to concede a full "half" and then presidential alternation to the minority Conservatives in order to regain a share of power. Subsequently, as in discussions surrounding the 1968 Constitutional Reform, Conservatives in particular were unwilling to give up the possibility of continued coalition rule as politicians had come to rely upon access to executive power so much. Prior to 1974, Liberals lacked the congressional seats to change the Constitution even if they so desired. And even after 1974 such a unilateral move would have had extremely high political costs with few offsetting benefits and would have been very difficult to muster through a faction-ridden Congress.

The Liberals were clearly the majority party before the National Front period. In the six competitive congressional elections between 1939 and 1949, the Liberals averaged 60.6% of the vote and the Conservative 38.1%. Votes for other parties were insignificant (see Table 6.1). During the National Front period (1958–78), the average share of the vote of both parties fell in contrast to the earlier period. Opposition was colored by the nature of the agreement itself. Until 1974, congressional lists and presidential candidates were required to be either Liberal or Conservative. Rather than serving solely as a straitjacket for the opposition, this requirement may paradoxically have increased its strength, as a comparison of opposition electoral strength before and after

1974 indicates. During the National Front there were two major electoral opposition movements: the MRL which always retained a Liberal identity, and the ANAPO, which began as a Conservative faction, then presented Liberal lists and ultimately declared itself a separate political party. Both the MRL and ANAPO benefited from the fact they could run as opposition movements, yet retain identification with the traditional parties.[8] In comparison to the 1939–49 period, the Liberal share of the congressional vote during the 1958–78 period fell 12.3% to 48.3%. For the Conservatives, the average vote declined only by 2.4% from the earlier 1939–49 period to 35.7% in the 1958–78 period. The Liberals still retained their status as majority party. Examining only the seven competitive elections of 1974–86, the Liberal and Conservative shares both increased slightly to 54.6% and 38.0%, respectively, because of the decline of votes for opposition movements. After 1970, the electoral arena failed to translate regime opposition into votes for opposition movements. Overall, these percentages indicate that average party shares for the two traditional parties changed little over nearly five decades.

But, the bulwark of continuity in electoral patterns was in rural areas. With parity requiring bipartisan staffing of municipal posts and alternation leading voters to twice elect presidents from the opposing party, one might logically expect both polarization of the vote and the stability of its pattern to decline considerably by the end of the National Front years. The evidence suggests this did in fact occur in urban areas. But electoral statistics at the municipal level in rural areas support the argument that they did not in the countryside. A random sample of 219 rural municipalities was drawn and results for the presidential elections of 1946 and 1978 were compared (see Tables 6.3 and 6.4). Examining polarization first, we see that in 1946, 16.9% of the municipalities in the sample gave the Conservative Party 80% or more of their total vote; in 1978 that figure actually increased to 23.7% (Table 6.3). In contrast, the percentage of municipalities giving the Liberal Party 80% or more of the vote declined slightly from 21.0% in 1946 to 16.0% in 1978 (Table 6.4). Continuity was also very high and appears to be highest in the most polarized municipalities (the top left and bottom right cells). As Table 6.3 shows, 89% of the municipalities that voted 80% or more Conservative in 1946, did so as well in 1978. The equivalent figure for the Liberal Party in Table 6.4 is 63%. In the case of the Conservative Party, 62% of the municipalities remained in the same category in the two elections (the diagonal running from top left to bottom right); the equivalent figure for the Liberals is 61%.[9]

The changing electorate and campaign strategies

These continuities in participation rates and party shares, however, are a less important part of the electoral picture compared to the changes that occurred during this period. In that sense, the emphasis on electoral continuity by scholars such as Losada (1976; 1979) seems misplaced. The National Front structure itself, the country's significant urbanization and other demographic, social and economic changes, as well as the nature of the elections and specific circumstances surrounding them led to significant vote fluctuations from one election to another as in the pre-National Front period. These were partially a result of the nature and particular circumstances of each election and of party campaign strategies, the focus of the next few paragraphs. But, these factors also led to two new realities in Colombia. One was the emergence of a new segment of the electorate, a mostly urban group, often abstentionist but potentially mobilizable by either traditional political party and even by movements with no links to the traditional parties. The other was the growth of opposition that expressed itself outside of electoral channels.

First let us examine the vote fluctuations during these years. The National Front structure and the centralizing economic processes encouraged by the regime led to a decline in the administrative and financial importance of municipalities and departments. And since 1972, with the extension of the term of members of the House to 4 years, mid-term (*mitaca*) elections have been held only for posts in the increasingly less significant departmental assemblies and municipal councils. Thus, as shown in Figure 6.1, it is not surprising that national-level elections have had much higher turnouts than mid-term and local level ones. Indeed, turnout for mid-term elections has varied within a fairly narrow band from 1958 to 1984, from a high of only 39.6% in 1960 to an astonishing low of 31.2% in 1976 climbing to 39.8% in 1984.

Elections held during presidential election years had much greater fluctuations in participation rates. During the National Front period congressional elections preceded the presidential

Table 6.3 *Rural vote continuity: Conservative Party*

% Conservative vote in 1946 presidential election by % Conservative vote in 1978 presidential election for a sample of rural municipalities

% Conservative vote 1978	% Conservative vote 1946					Row %
	0–20%	20–40%	40–60%	60–80%	80–100%	
0–20%	67.4	14.3	0.0	0.0	0.0	18.3
20–40%	19.6	50.8	17.4	0.0	0.0	22.4
40–60%	6.5	25.4	54.3	14.8	0.0	21.9
60–80%	2.2	4.8	15.2	55.6	10.8	13.7
80–100%	4.3	4.8	13.0	29.6	89.2	23.7
Total%	100.0%	100.0%	100.0%	100.0%	100.0%	100.0%
Column%	21.0	28.8	21.0	12.3	16.9	
(N)	(46)	(63)	(46)	(27)	(37)	(219)

Chi square = 284.4 p<.001
Tau B = 0.73 p<.001

Table 6.4 *Rural vote continuity: Liberal Party*

% Liberal vote in 1946 presidential election by % Liberal vote in 1978 election for a sample of rural municipalities

	% Liberal vote 1946					
% Liberal vote 1978	0–20%	20–40%	40–60%	60–80%	80–100%	Row %
0–20%	89.2	29.6	13.0	4.8	4.3	23.7
20–40%	10.8	59.3	15.2	7.9	2.2	15.1
40–60%	0.0	11.1	60.9	33.3	10.9	26.0
60–80%	0.0	0.0	10.9	44.4	19.6	19.2
80–100%	0.0	0.0	0.0	9.5	63.0	16.0
Total%	100.0%	100.0%	100.0%	100.0%	100.0%	100.0%
Column%	16.9%	12.3%	21.0%	28.8%	21.0%	100.0%
(N)	(37)	(27)	(46)	(63)	(46)	(219)

Chi square = 285.5   p<.001
Tau B = 0.72   p<.001

ones by a few weeks in 1958, 1962 and 1966. In these years, the congressional elections generated a slightly higher voter turnout, probably reflecting the de-mobilizing impact of single-party presidential races and the lack of incentive for regional leaders to get out the vote once they had achieved their own election. Elections were held on the same day in 1970 and 1974, but when they were separated again for the 1978, 1982 and 1986 elections, the opposite phenomenon occurred (see Figure 6.1). This reflected the importance of competitive presidential races, the perception of the increased importance of the post and changes in the electorate that facilitated their mobilization to vote in non-clientelist fashion using media image and programmatic appeals, particularly in urban areas that contributed proportionally more of the vote increase.[10] Higher turnout presidential elections occurred in 1958, 1970, 1974 and 1982. Each can be explained partially by particular issues and circumstances. In 1958, legal restrictions on voting were eased and public interest was high since these were the first elections for public office since Rojas was overthrown. The 1970 elections reflected the mobilization of voters who perceived an alternative in the populist candidacy of Rojas and the fact that the Conservatives presented three additional candidates (electoral fraud may also have contributed some to the total vote count). The first inter-party competitive presidential elections since 1946 were held in 1974 and the Liberal candidate, López, was particularly attractive due to the reformist image of his father and his own leadership of the MRL in the 1960s. The 1982 elections reflected a Liberal Party that was divided and an attractive and well-organized campaign by the Conservative candidate spearheading a "National Movement" (see Hoskin, 1985). The 1962 and 1978 elections, in turn, had extremely low participation rates. From 1958 to 1962, participation in presidential elections declined 12%, and from 1974 to 1978, a dramatic 15%!

The vote fluctuations reflected changes in party campaign strategies and in the electorate as well as circumstances peculiar to each election. As the nature of the division between the two traditional parties was not ethnic, linguistic, religious or class-based, the National Front agreement gradually fostered a decline in party identification. The curbs on inter-party competition and the limits of sectarian party appeals led to important modifications in party identification and in the country's voting patterns, especially in the major cities. In addition to these factors,

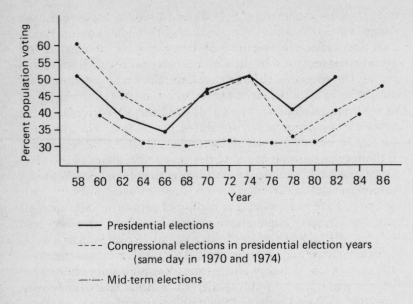

Figure 6.1 Electoral participation rates (1958–86).
Source: Tables 6.1 and 6.2

the emergence of a younger, better educated electorate raised in a period of presidential alternation and coalition governments was also very important.

Party leaders sought a large turnout in support of the National Front agreement in the 1957 plebiscite and the 1958 elections. However, one of the intentions of the National Front system was to demobilize the mass following of the traditional parties, defusing the conflict between them. Many party leaders that previously generated enthusiasm (*mistica*) for their party by virulently attacking the other party extolled the virtues of alternation and parity, and of peace and co-existence (*paz y concordia*). A decrease in party polarization and violence was one of the desired aims of the National Front. A natural result, not fully expected at the time, was a decline in voter turnout from the initial enthusiastic response to the National Front agreement, a decline further accelerated by the reimposition of legal requirements for voting and a predictable deflation of expectations following the euphoria of regime change.

Sectarian appeals were common by dissident party factions, particularly in the early years of the National Front. This permitted the more aggressive party faithful to express their views at the ballot box. Conservative stalwart Jorge Leyva received nearly 20% of the vote in 1958 and 11.7% in 1962, much of it regionally concentrated. Campaigns during this period by the Alza–Ospinistas (in 1960) and by the MRL were also sectarian in nature. López' candidacy in 1962 against Valencia and Leyva was especially successful in Liberal rural areas affected by *la violencia* as well as in some urban areas.[11]

As the National Front continued, non-sectarianism in government made attempts to revive party *mística* at election time increasingly untenable. The initial historically high participation rates were unsustainable. At the same time, in a context of declining legislative power, brokerage politics and high abstention elections, there was a proliferation of party lists at election time, of factional and sub-factional dissidences for electoral purposes (see Table 6.5).[12] The proliferation of lists during the years of presidential alternation and legislative parity reflected in part the existence of opposition factions such as the MRL and ANAPO. Yet, they also reflected the inability of national party or even party-faction leaders to impose discipline.

The role of national party leaders in list preparation varied by faction and election. Politicians unhappy with the placement of their name on a list sometimes prepared a new list even within the same faction or negotiated with other factions. Sometimes a faction would purposely present two lists in order to try to gain an extra seat by means of a higher "remainder" vote. More commonly, however, the dissident sub-factions allowed opposing factions to win (see Latorre Rueda, 1974: 137–70; Payne, 1968: 185–237; Kline, 1980: 74–9; and especially Losada, 1982). The persistence of two major factions in the Conservative Party throughout the National Front period, around Laureano and then Alvaro Gómez and around Mariano Ospina, appears to have inhibited factionalism in that party somewhat more than in the Liberal Party (see Table 6.5). With a return to competitive politics in 1974, there was a slight decline in factionalism, though the parties were still far from united (which would have meant only one list per department). In fact, after the 1974 elections, the number of lists again increased. This process led to an increase in the number of departments in which "uninominal" lists, often with strengths in particular regions or municipalities, have been victorious (see Table 6.5).[13] This phenomenon has reflected an individualistic political strategy of developing a dependable captive electorate and illustrates the strengthening of electoral power by regional party leaders and their increased autonomy from national leaders.[14] It has been a logical response by individual politicians to high abstention elections. Candidates have carefully nurtured and employed personal and public resources to muster the small number of votes necessary to get elected. They have not actively sought to incorporate broad sectors of the population into the political process. This phenomenon in some ways has been a consequence of high abstention. However, it also has been partially, though only partially, a cause of high abstention because as it developed its momentum it helped prevent the development of more broadly based and institutionally established parties. These dissidences did little to increase voter turnout, whereas factional and opposition movement candidacies (such as the MRL or ANAPO) probably did.[15]

Differentiation of the electorate and opposition movements

The most significant political phenomenon that emerged during the National Front years has been the decline in party segmentation. All survey evidence points to a population-wide decline in identification and attachment with either of the two traditional parties though these have continued to dominate the party landscape. Within urban areas, surveys have demonstrated that the younger and the poorer groups vote much less, and that their identification with traditional parties has been declining, without being replaced by identification with other parties or movements. As Table 6.6 indicates, the proportion of respondents identifying with either of the two traditional parties in electoral surveys in Bogotá has declined from 87% in 1970 to 67% in 1978. In one study carried out in 1976–7, only 59% of those surveyed in urban areas claimed a party affiliation while 74% in rural areas did (Losada, 1977: 32).

Voting behavior in urban areas experienced more dramatic changes than in rural areas during this period. During mid-term

Table 6.5 *Party lists and elections for the House 1949–82*

Year	Liberals		Conservatives	
	No. of lists/ department	Only uninominal lists victorious department	No. of lists/ department	Only uninominal lists victorious department
1949	2.2		1.1	
1958	1.6		3.1	
1960	3.8		2.9	
1962	5.0		2.7	
1964	6.3		3.5	
1966	5.5	32%	5.0	37%
1968	4.9	18%	4.8	18%
1970	7.1	50%	5.8	54%
1974	4.6	59%[1]	3.1	50%[2]
1978	5.6	73%[1]	3.8	76%[3]
1982	6.6	74%[1]	4.6	86%[3]

[1]In one department, only one Liberal elected.
[2]In six departments, only one Conservative elected.
[3]One department excluded as no Conservatives elected; in three, only one elected.
Sources: For 1949 through 1964, Payne (1968: 202), based on the fifteen departments in existence in 1949; for 1962 and 1964 ANAPO lists are excluded. For subsequent years, compiled from information provided by the Registraduría Nacional del Estado Civil. For the 1966 election, calculated on nineteen departments, for the 1968, 1970, 1974 and 1978 elections, calculated on twenty-two departments, and for 1982, on twenty-three departments.

elections, urban areas have had significantly higher rates of decline in participation than rural areas. This has been especially true of Bogotá (Losada, 1976: 13). In presidential election years, though, urban turnout has occasionally reached levels higher than in rural areas. It is in the country's urban areas that the emergence of a new floating electorate has been felt most sharply.

During the National Front the country's electorate could be viewed as consisting of three broad groups. First, a "captive electorate" that consistently voted in all elections for traditional party candidates, though not necessarily in support of National Front candidates. This group, as suggested by the tremendous con-

Table 6.6 *Party affiliation in Bogotá: 1970–82*

Party	Year					
	1970		1972	1974	1978	1982
	A	B				
Liberal	61.6	50.1	54.4	59.9	40.8	36.3
Conservative	25.3	21.1	16.6	13.8	16.6	18.9
Other	11.2	14.7	8.3	8.0	9.5	3.2
No party	0.0	5.3	16.3	15.9	30.6	38.2
Refused	2.0	8.7	4.4	3.0	2.5	3.3
Total	100%	100%	100%	100%	100%	100%
N	(700)	(700)	(699)	(1463)	(601)	(2035)

Sources: Williams & Losada, 1972: 12, 33 (the two listings for 1970 reflect different question wording); Murillo & Williams, 1975: 25; Hoskin, 1979b: 29; and Gómez Gómez, 1982: 43.

tinuities in rural voting patterns, was stronger in the countryside. It probably has represented around 25% of the electorate.[16] Second, a group of "hard-core abstentionists," who have never voted in elections for a variety of different reasons. Some abstention can be viewed as "structural," reflecting rural isolation or an inability to vote for related reasons. More relevant in urban areas as primary causes for abstention have been apathy, disinterest and alienation.[17] This group probably represented around 20% to 30% of the electorate at the beginning of the National Front.[18] A decade later, due to the effects of the National Front limitations on voting and the country's demographic changes (a younger, more urban electorate de-linked from the traditional parties), it probably increased to between 30% and 40% of the electorate. This estimate is based on the fact that in the high turnout elections of 1970 and 1974, some 45–55% of the electorate did not vote.

The third category in the electorate, proportionally larger in urban than in rural areas, is of "potentially mobilizable voters," of those who voted in some elections but not in others. Their decision has depended upon factors such as their perception of the importance of the election, the appeals of specific candidates or whether a Liberal or Conservative was to be elected president. Many Liberals probably abstained from voting in 1962 and 1970, as did Conservatives in 1966. Within this third category, in a process facilitated by the National Front electoral requirements of parity and alternation, a new group emerged, a *floating electorate* potentially mobilizable by groups or parties other than the one single traditional party to which they had previously been wedded. The presence of this group was first acutely felt when Rojas and his ANAPO movement nearly scored an upset victory in 1970. Its turn toward López in 1974 and toward abstention in 1978 belied many of the simplistic analyses of "realignment" along class lines that appeared after the 1970 elections (see, for example, Talbot Campos & McCamant, 1972). At the same time, as we shall see in chapter 7, fear of electoral advances within this group by parties associated with guerrilla movements spawned opposition to democratic reforms among traditional politicians in the 1980s.

The nature of ANAPO, the most serious opposition movement to the National Front, was shaped by the form of the National Front pact itself as well as by the characteristics of its founder. In 1970, the last year in which the National Front requirement of alternation for presidential elections was in effect, Rojas could maintain the ambiguous stature of populist opposition figure and of candidate within the Conservative Party. Voters in urban areas, predominantly Liberal, had no Liberal presidential candidate for whom to vote; if there had been one or more Liberal presidential candidates, it is difficult to imagine Rojas' urban vote would have been nearly as large. Regional politicians were displeased with Lleras' attempts to curb their influence. ANAPO lists for Congress and for local assemblies and councils were listed under either party rubric, and dissident traditional figures could run under the ANAPO banner, yet remain within their party.

Rojas' ANAPO was a heterogeneous collection of populists, socialists and traditional party figures. Bearing the stamp of its leader, it was more Conservative than Liberal. Its ideology was vaguely "Christian," "national" and "socialist." It promised concrete material benefits and immediate relief from economic hardship, not class struggle. By the 1970 elections, ANAPO had a considerable organizational network in urban areas, dispensing social services and basic necessities at low cost, even while being focused around a *caudillo* figure (see Premo, 1972). The movement effectively capitalized upon growing discontent, especially in urban areas affected by increasing unemployment. Survey studies all confirm that ANAPO was overwhelmingly a lower class phenomenon concentrated in urban areas.[19]

After the narrow and questionable defeat of 1970, the movement quickly faded.[20] The *caudillo*'s health deteriorated and he passed away in 1975. His daughter, María Eugenia, assumed the leadership post, but could not prevent the fragmentation of ANAPO. The paucity of resources at the departmental and municipal level, obstructionism from other parts of government and internal divisions within ANAPO all prevented ANAPO from being able to capitalize more fully on the local electoral representation it won in 1970. At the same time, the Pastrana government developed short-term programs targeted at poor urban neighborhoods[21] and then implanted its urban construction program.

After the 1970 elections, a share of Anapista voters probably joined the permanent abstentionists, especially in Bogotá. Others may have followed regional figures as they moved back to the traditional parties.[22] A survey study of the 1974 elections in Bogotá suggests that the majority of those who voted for Rojas in 1970 either abstained or voted for the Liberal López in 1974. The study found that 36.3% of its respondents who said they voted for Rojas in 1970 abstained in 1974. Another 30.4% said they voted for López. Of the remaining Rojas voters in 1970, only 18.7% voted for María Eugenia Rojas, 10.5% for the Conservative candidate, Alvaro Gómez, and 4.1% for the leftist candidate.[23]

In Colombia, the consociational agreement appears to have aided the decline in partisanship and of segmentation in the country because of its electoral requirement of parity and especially alternation. At the same time, the regime stability provided by the consociational agreement also permitted other social processes – urbanization and population growth – to affect partisanship. In many consociational regimes in which the segmental division is of a different nature, such as ethnicity, or in which segmental conflicts develop international linkages, this type of decline appears much less likely to occur. In others, where the divisive issues revolve more around questions of religion or religiosity as in the Netherlands, the salience of the segments is more likely to decline through time. Certainly, declines in partisanship are neither unique to Colombia nor particular to consociational regimes. In other less developed countries, urbanization has had effects similar to those in Colombia, concentrating electoral opposition movements in urban areas even as urban residents tend to be difficult to organize and mobilize to vote (cf. Nelson, 1979: especially 318–80). Yet, in Colombia it was because the consociational agreement provided a framework for a return to civilian rule that these other processes could operate. In addition, the inability of either party to claim credit for city projects (or to blame poor performance on the other) due to the strictures of parity partially inhibited the ability of Colombian party leaders to organize in urban areas. In practice, though, party leaders committed to brokerage politics expressed little interest in developing strong party organizations or expanding internal party democratization.

Regime-sponsored organizations and "state pluralism"

Although the factionalized traditional political parties did little to link themselves organizationally with broader groups in the population, there were two major regime-initiated organizational efforts in this direction during the National Front period. These were the Communal Action Boards (Juntas de Acción Comunal) and the peasant association ANUC. The evolution of the two demonstrated the ambivalence of the regime, the weakness of state corporatist efforts, and ultimately a pattern more akin through time to a "divide and conquer" strategy of state pluralism (see Schmitter, 1979).

The Communal Action program emerged from efforts to defuse conflict in the country's rural areas most deeply affected by *la violencia*. A National Commission to study the violence was appointed by the military junta that deposed Rojas. In addition, a French priest, Louis Lebret, headed a mission to Colombia which made numerous suggestions regarding pacification. Under President Alberto Lleras, a Rehabilitation Committee was formed to coordinate government attention to the most affected areas. In areas of violence, special public works programs, and housing and credit programs were established. In addition, community action programs assisted by special teams of experts were also created.[24]

These experiences ultimately led to legislation establishing the national program of Communal Action Boards. These Juntas were intended to encourage community participation and to foster self-help projects ranging from construction of educational and health facilities to agricultural improvement programs. In fact, many Juntas were not established as the result of community effort, but were created under the stimulus of state "promoters", priests, or even US Peace Corps volunteers (Henderson, 1985b: 232). Ostensibly non-political entities, politicians increasingly played a prominent role in their funding and running, employing the Juntas as bases for electoral support. In some cases, though, due to state neglect, inefficiency or corruption, Junta members became vocal anti-regime proponents.

President Carlos Lleras partially de-emphasized the Juntas, increasingly dominated by the brokerage politics of traditional politicians, during his government. Lleras attempted to impose greater control over the Juntas' funding, even as he sought unsuccessfully to eliminate congressional patronage funds. At the same time, Lleras created ANUC, a new peasant organization, separate from local power structures, which he hoped would mobilize peasant opinion in favor of land reform. This bold move reflected Lleras' conviction that it was necessary to stem rural to urban migration as industrial growth slowed and unemployment grew in the cities and to create a larger internal market for industrial goods. It was supplemented by new legislation intended to accelerate agrarian reform which granted tenants and sharecroppers increased rights. At the same time, Lleras probably hoped that ANUC could provide an important base of support for a re-election bid four years later (Zamosc, 1986; Bagley & Botero, 1978).

Under Lleras, ANUC expanded quickly. According to the ministry of agriculture, its membership grew from 600,000 members in March, 1968 to 989,000 in October, 1971. One month before stepping down from office, in July, 1970, Lleras personally inaugurated the first National Congress of the new semi-official organization (Zamosc, 1986: 60–1). ANUC's membership expanded with the help of state "promoters" who created local associations, encouraging members to seek independence from local political leaders and instructing them regarding their rights to state services and to land (Zamosc, 1986). In some regions, to the disapproval of local politicians, bureaucrats themselves effectively became "brokers" of state services (see Schmidt, 1974a).

However, ANUC rapidly became radicalized. Those elected to leadership posts in the first National Congress called for a dramatic acceleration of the agrarian reform. At the same time, the peasantry and many ANUC associations had supported

Pastrana's election in April 1970. With the transition to the Conservative Pastrana presidency (in August 1970), bureaucratic control over the organization was also loosened even as the new Conservative administration distrusted the organization created by Lleras as a mechanism of Liberal clientelism. Pastrana also began slowing down implementation of agrarian reform. The regime requirement of presidential alternation and counter-pressure by landowners worked against continuity essential for corporatist control. And ANUC responded in late 1970 with a coordinated series of demonstrations, rallies and land seizures. Finally, with a more radical faction in control, ANUC opted for direct confrontation with the state and organized numerous land occupations. In February 1971, peasant groups linked to ANUC mobilized more than 15,000 families occupying 350 landed estates, particularly on the Atlantic Coast and in Huila and Tolima. A second wave of invasions took place later in the year.[25]

Corporatism was replaced by "state pluralism" and hard-line policies. As ANUC became radicalized, its government financing, staff and office support were eventually stopped. INCORA, the land reform agency, stopped playing a mediating role in the land occupations. And, at the same time, the government helped promote a split in the movement in 1972, supporting to a lesser extent the less militant "ANUC – Linea Armenia," which gradually became a weak and ineffectual organization. Legal recognition was withdrawn from the more radical "ANUC – Linea Sincelejo," which also declined organizationally, as some of its members were thrown off the land, harassed, sometimes co-opted and occasionally murdered. Ignored by the mass media, as most opposition movements and parties, financially impoverished as it lost state support and wracked by internal ideological conflicts and divisions, the organization was increasingly dismissed by the regime as it became apparent that it no longer represented a threat.[26]

As ANUC declined, and as the technocratic vision of Lleras receded, the Communal Action Boards (Juntas) regained attention as entities to be employed by local politicians. The Juntas and brokerage politics by the traditional parties played a major role in weakening ANUC. The number of new Juntas continued to grow in the 1970s. Of the 21,752 Juntas registered in a national census in 1978, 48% were created after 1970, 31% of them during the Pastrana administration.[27] Their most rapid expansion took place in the regions where ANUC had been strongest and most radical (Zamosc, 1986: 195). The census reported 1.3 million affiliates and 2.2 million participants (Ungar, 1981a: 17–18), with the overwhelming majority of the Juntas in rural areas (80%). In over half of the cases (54.1%), the Juntas reported being the only form of organization serving the community, concentrating on the provision of basic services such as schools, electrification, water and sewage, roads and housing.

The regime structure encouraged Juntas, especially in rural areas, to develop political ties to seek resources from the regime, sometimes with figures of both parties. Approximately half of their resources came from the state, often from congressional pork-barrel funds.[28] In the larger cities, Junta leaders often petitioned directly for services from the appropriate government bureaucracies. In both cases, the linkages established were usually at a personal "patron–client" level. The effect has been to fragment demands across neighborhoods or communities seeking to prevent the emergence of broader movements with demands beyond the immediate ones of basic services. Indeed, in many communities, once the basic services have been provided, the Junta organizations have lapsed (Ungar, 1981b).

Brokerage and clientelist politics

Colombia has been a centralized polity since the 1886 Constitution. The president through the minister of government has appointed all departmental governors who in turn have named all municipal mayors (as discussed in chapter 7, the popular election of mayors is due to begin in 1988). In addition to this political centralization, in the post-World War II era and especially during the National Front years there was a dramatic administrative and financial centralization, as municipalities and especially departments lost their economic role to national agencies (discussed in chapter 5). At the same time, municipal councils, departmental assemblies and the Congress increasingly lost functions to executive branch agencies. Congress lost its initiative in public expenditures as a result of the 1968 Constitutional Reform. At the same time, for political reasons related to brokerage it was unable to form the special commission legislated by that Reform intended to oversee the country's development plan. Immobilism fueled by parity and the two-thirds majority vote requirement also fed these processes. Congressmen increasingly devoted their attention to electoral, patronage and brokerage matters, particularly pork-barrel funds and the placement of job holders. Given the near total absence of influence on policy matters at the departmental level, assemblymen also have devoted almost all of their attention to these kinds of issues, seeking "quotas" for their party faction in departmental ministries (*secretarías*) or decentralized agencies. Access to the executive branch at the congressional and local level – participation in government – has been necessary in order to be able to put key electoral workers and other followers into government posts. These selective placements became more important by the mid-1970s as the growth of public sector employment declined considerably. Access to the executive branch also increased the possibilities of serving as a broker for government revenues. A more select group of politicians has been able to employ positions as ministers or heads of agencies to channel major state investments into their region, subsequently gaining election to Congress.[29] Due to these factors and other advantages of having access to executive power, politicians of both parties have been reluctant to move away from coalition rule.

Politicians have sought to gain electoral advantage from the channelling of state investments into their regions. From their perspective, the smaller and more dispersed the amounts, the wider the impact and the more the personal role they could claim for its distribution. This particularistic, decentralized vision clashed with a more centralized, rationalized, planning-oriented vision propounded by international agencies and supported by several major National Front politicians, particularly Carlos Lleras. In chapter 4 we saw how the 1968 Constitutional Reform almost failed to pass in part because of congressional demands that Congress continue to control its own budget and because of resistance to executive attempts to eliminate pork-barrel funds (*auxilios*). Lleras had multiple objections to these funds, including the lack of rational expenditure and the fact that due to the absence of effective oversight they were prone to misuse and corruption.[30] In the end, though he capitulated to their continued existence, Lleras sought unsuccessfully to insure greater control over their expenditure. Efforts to assure greater oversight and control over their use have continued into the present.[31]

Congressmen fought hard to retain their right to these pork-barrel funds. Prior to the 1968 Reform, congressional *auxilios* formed a direct part of the central budget and an examination of the budget itself is insufficient to distinguish *auxilios* from other expenditures. In part, this reflected the lesser importance of planning and the larger role of congressmen in determining allocations.[32] Trends in the amount and distribution of the *auxilios* are given in Table 6.7. They show that the funds available for this purpose have been relatively small, fluctuating around 1% and 2% of the initial central budget. They appear to have been high under Valencia, decreased slightly under Lleras, grew slightly under Pastrana and López, under whom they again declined to remain around 1% under Turbay and for the first years of Betancur.[33]

The *auxilios* have been negotiated year by year between Congress and the president, usually represented by the minister of finance and the director of the National Planning Department (DNP). In addition to the *auxilios*, in recent years congressmen have also negotiated certain larger amounts with DNP, planned in a more careful and rational fashion (buried in the central budget, they do not approximate the total figure for *auxilios*). The budgetary law normally begins in Commission IV of the House, goes to the full House, then passes to Commission IV of the Senate and then to the full Senate, before going to the president for his signature. Once the global figure for *auxilios* is agreed upon, it is divided by the number of departments, and then within each department by the number of congressmen. Each congressman types up a list of his *auxilios* by ministry and sends it to the respective Commission IV. The officers (*mesas directivas*) of each chamber, the officers and to a lesser extent the members of each chamber's Commission IV (fifty in the House and twenty-five in the Senate), and the presenter (*ponente*) of the budget law in each chamber all also have received additional *auxilios*. Some of them may have promised part of their additional funds to other congressmen in exchange for their support or in support of specific projects. The amount they have received, thus, is not easily estimated, and like the global figure is open to negotiation year by year.[34] Minority parties or movements may also gain access to these posts, as ANAPO did in negotiations prior to the vote on the 1968 Constitutional Reform.

The *auxilios* have been especially concentrated in the ministry of government (through which funds to Juntas are provided), with an average of 45.3% from 1975 to 1983, and the ministry of education, with an average of 37.5% during that period (see Table

6.7). Funds have been allocated to Juntas for purposes such as: the provision of water supply for schools or other community buildings; marketplaces; construction and provision of health clinics; sewage; electrification; roads; construction or provision of classrooms; bridges; parks; paving; building of water tanks; construction of sports facilities; and even uniforms and musical instruments for neighborhood or school bands. Congressmen have rarely given seed money to begin a project; they have preferred to provide funds that will complete a project thus receiving more visibility from their aid. Funds channelled through the ministry of education were for specific schools, for scholarships, administration and supplies. As publicity over abuses regarding the actual allocation of these funds multiplied, changes have slowly been enacted. In 1977, it was specified that at least 60% of the money given to a school must be employed for scholarships (Law 25). The year before a special program was started through the Colombian Institute for Educational Credit and Technical Studies Abroad (ICETEX – Instituto Colombiano de Crédito Educativo y Estudios Técnicos en el Exterior) by means of which congressmen could provide scholarships for specific students. In this way, schools were not forced to accept certain students because they were receiving congressional scholarship support, as had been true in the past. The program grew rapidly from 686 scholarships in 1977 to 85,205 in 1983.[35] Congressional funds allocated through the ministry of health were usually assigned to hospitals, clinics, old people's homes, and first aid stations, whereas those channelled through the ministry of public works were typically employed to build roads, provide for street repairs, fire stations and fire fighting equipment, or conserve churches and support parish work.[36]

Many politicians have viewed the *auxilios* and scholarships as crucial to their electoral survival. They have also argued (with some degree of truth), that these funds, a very small part of total public expenditures, are often the only major state effort that reaches many isolated communities. In reality, the number of people affected by the *auxilios* and scholarships has been far from representing a majority of voters.[37] And, without follow-up organizational efforts to try to get people to vote on election day, there has been little guarantee that this aid would translate into actual ballots. A number of Juntas have received money from both Liberals and Conservatives and especially in urban areas,

Table 6.7 Congressional *"auxilios regionales"* by administrative unit (%)

Ministry or administrative department	1970	1975	1976	1977	1978	1979	1980	1981	1982	1983
Government	48.2	42.6	42.4	51.8	43.5	44.7	42.7	44.2	40.5	39.1
Health	2.4	3.1	4.8	4.7	4.1	6.0	5.0	5.3	5.6	5.4
Economic development	0.2	1.8	3.0	2.6	1.4	1.9	2.1	0.8	1.2	5.8
Education	43.6	35.3	29.2	29.3	38.2	35.1	39.6	45.1	45.3	42.6
Public works	5.4	9.5	13.5	6.8	6.4	8.1	6.9	3.0	4.7	4.7
Others[1]	0.2	7.7	7.1	4.8	6.4	4.2	3.7	1.6	2.7	2.4
Total	100.0	100.0	100.0	100.0	100.0	100.0	100.0	100.0	100.0	100.0
Total (thousands of current Col $)	297,078	490,644	986,302	1,000,000	900,000	1,100,000	1,389,274	1,798,115	2,349,700	3,000,000
Total *auxilios* as % of initial central sector budget	1.98	1.26	1.85	1.59	1.04	1.02	0.94	0.91	0.90	0.98

[1]Others include Aeronautics, Security and Police, Justice, Defense, Agriculture, Labor, Mines and Communications.
Source: Calculated by author from budget documents.

several Juntas have had leadership posts claimed by followers of radical movements.[38]

Thus, politicians have also relied on other patronage resources. A critical factor has been the ability to provide jobs in state agencies for key followers who could employ these positions to promote electoral activities (more extensively discussed in the next section). These have included congressional offices, the regional offices of some national level decentralized agencies (especially subsequent to the Carlos Lleras administration when patronage possibilities partially reasserted themselves) as well as departmental agencies and offices. This, too, has been a powerful incentive for the retention of coalition rule given the fact that departmental governors are all appointed in Bogotá. Deputies in departmental assemblies also have budgeted small amounts for scholarships and *auxilios* and have sought "quotas" from departmental governors. In addition, congressmen have used their skills – as lawyers or doctors – to provide services to their constituents.[39]

Traditional party leaders have had relatively greater success in rural areas where traditional ties of party identification and dependency based upon poverty and relative isolation have been strongest, as the electoral statistics presented earlier indicate. In urban centers, politicians have been increasingly relegated to the role of brokers competing with alternative politician-brokers or with government bureaucracies themselves, which could be approached directly. Individual politicians could serve as intermediaries, helping with land title legalization, provision of utilities or public transportation. But, neighborhood groups could also transact these with the appropriate bureaucracy without party mediation (see Losada, 1984; Ungar, 1981a). Because of coalition governments and the fact that all mayors have been appointed from the center, neither party could use government resources to develop single-party machines in any of the cities.

In the 1970s and 1980s, a smaller group of politicians was also able to employ their appointments to upper-level executive branch positions for electoral purposes. As ministers or as managers of certain decentralized institutes they have completed public works in their region and then reaped the political benefits in a subsequent election. There are two examples from the period of the López administration. One is a minister of mines who completed certain electrification projects in his department and then successfully ran for senator and another is a manager of the municipal public works agency (INSFOPAL) who completed numerous projects in his Atlantic Coast department and then was successfully elected senator from his department.[40]

Overall, though, this activity generated by the *auxilios*, the scholarships and even larger projects, suggests a relatively low penetration of the country as a whole. The funds have not reached many areas of the country at all and even if they were spent well they have been woefully inadequate for the basic needs of the population. Politically, though, they have been so critical that few politicians could conceive of living without them. In a context of high abstention and an increasing turn to the election of uninominal lists, the mobilization of a few thousand votes one way or another has sometimes spelled the difference between victory and defeat.

The parties and the state bureaucracy

The historic importance placed on control of the state and state jobs by the two political parties was discussed in chapters 2 and 3. The staffing of government positions was such a sensitive issue between the two parties that three of the fourteen articles of the 1957 plebiscite dealt with government employees and civil service (*carrera administrativa*). These stated that political affiliation was not to be considered in naming a person to a civil service post (article 7), that such appointments had to be made within the framework of laws enacted by Congress (article 5) and that all civil service employees were prohibited from taking part in partisan political activities, although they were guaranteed the right to vote (article 6). In addition, three of the four subsequent presidents decreed administrative reforms, those of the two Liberals being more sweeping in nature. Yet, by the end of the National Front period it was clear that civil service reform existed largely on paper, lacked support among any of the major affected groups and was unlikely to be widely implemented in the near future. At the same time, the ability of regional politicians to employ the bureaucracy for employment increasingly came under challenge by restrictions on the growth of public sector employment, by technocrats and by unionization.

The "patronage mentality" of the past was replaced during the National Front period by an analogous "parity mentality"

(Groves, 1974). In the early years of the National Front, parity between the parties was established not by wholesale dismissals, which would primarily have involved Conservatives, but by a rapid expansion of government employment (Dix, 1967: 197). Throughout the National Front period public employment grew faster than the economically active population (see Table 6.8). From 4.9% of the economically active population in 1966, by 1976 the public sector had expanded to employ around 10% of that population. Reflecting the country's growing centralization, the greatest growth was at the national level and the lowest at the municipal level, though the phenomenon was exaggerated by the transfer of teacher payrolls to the central state. As in other consociational cases, careful use of proportional representation defused a major source of conflict between the original segments in conflict with each other (cf. Lijphart, 1977). However, conflicts arose between politicians and professionalized state agents objecting to chaotic, unplanned growth of the state encouraged by patronage. And, disaffected state workers increasingly unionized to protest low pay and poor working conditions. Beginning in the mid-1970s, the rate of growth of public sector employment slowed considerably (see Table 6.8). This reflected a bipartisan consensus at top party leadership levels about political and labor problems in the state sector and pressure from producer associations. As a consequence, the country's public employment levels have been somewhat lower than those of other countries at equivalent levels of development.[41]

Some observers have argued that those appointed to positions in state institutions have continued to be politically liable for their job (see the discussion in ANIF, 1980: 30). In support of this argument is the fact that there has been very little progress on civil service reform in spite of considerable legislation and administrative effort. Under President Alberto Lleras legislation (drafted by the indomitable rationalizer Carlos Lleras) was approved creating an Administrative Department for Civil Service (DASC – Departamento Administrativo del Servicio Civil) and establishing a framework to place most public employees in an administrative career structure beyond the reach of partisan patronage. Implementing regulations were finally approved by the Valencia government. Then President Carlos Lleras developed sweeping new legislation which facilitated entry of eligible government employees into what was termed career service

Table 6.8 *Estimates of public employment in Colombia*

Year	Total government	National central and decentralized	Departmental	Territorial	Municipal	% Economically active population
1966	262,420					4.9
1970	339,837	178,339	106,891	1,500	53,110	5.9
1971	378,591					6.5
1976	696,543	566,624	47,815	3,787	78,317	9.5
1976	725,233	620,253	78,692	n.a.	26,288	10.0
1981	891,337	756,760	107,229	n.a.	27,348	n.a.
1985	913,359	780,905	105,068	n.a.	27,386	9.5

Note: The sharp increase at the national level and the decline at the departmental level in 1976 are due in part to the "nationalization" of public education, which transferred approximately 160,000 educators from the departmental level to the national one.

Sources: For 1966, Payne (1968: 52); for 1970 and 1971, DANE, Boletin Mensual de Estadistica, No. 299, June, 1976; for 1976, from DASC, mimeo provided me by the manager, 1978; for the second set of figures for 1976, and those for 1981 and 1985, Chenery, Ocampo & Ramirez, 1986: 56.

(positions protected by civil service) by seniority rather than by competitive examinations. Implementing regulations, though, were not completed until 1973. By 1976, only 13,000 people had joined career service, and of those who had done so, almost all were already job holders in the public sector guaranteeing their tenure, rather than new appointees.[42] Politicians resisted civil service legislation because they feared it would limit their patronage possibilities. Gradually, however, opposition also spread to high government officials who logically should have been among its strongest supporters. Their opposition stemmed from the fact that the wording of civil service legislation was such that it became almost legally impossible to fire a person who entered career service.[43] And, the group that should have been the most concerned, government employees, increasingly focused their attention on alternatives to civil service, though they continued to pressure for expanded civil service coverage.[44] Contrary to the view that the vast majority of state employees were still in a precarious clientelist relationship, their concerns went beyond job stability to include poor working conditions and low pay. They preferred unionization, with the right to collective bargaining, to civil service measures that prohibited such actions.

The National Front agreement made partisan based large-scale dismissals more difficult.[45] These still occurred, though infrequently and concentrated in municipal and departmental agencies. In the 1960s and early 1970s, patronage relied more on the creation of new jobs than on forcible large-scale replacement of current job-holders. Initially, it was primarily the bad publicity and the risk to the consociational agreement that could result from such dismissals that prevented such action. In addition the ability of politicians to name job holders to certain state agencies declined through the National Front period, as state technocratization increased and as public employment levelled off. Politicians held greater influence in certain areas of the bureaucracy at the national level: in some of the line ministries, decentralized agencies involved in public works and social services, parts of the judiciary and especially posts in Congress and its dependencies. At the departmental and municipal levels, with regional variations, nearly all agencies were open to patronage possibilities, particularly the departmental liquor companies and lotteries. As one Liberal politician noted in expressing his disapproval of civil service:

I'll support civil service only if employees' duties and responsibilities are clearly spelled out. . . The truth is that the ability of congressmen to use the government for clientelist purposes is becoming more and more limited. An increasing number of managers of decentralized agencies simply ignore their letters of recommendation. . . That's why congressmen defend so fiercely their right to patronage in the *contraloria* and to a lesser extent in the *procuraduria*. (Interview, May 17, 1978)

The extent to which ministers, managers and directors changed personnel and brought in friends, relatives and associates from their own party and region reflected both the tone of the particular presidential administration as well as the personality of the new head. Several of the fourteen managers of decentralized agencies interviewed in 1977 and 1978 went out of their way to assert that changes in top leadership no longer meant widespread changes in middle-level, much less lower-level personnel. Five of these managers had only held posts in the public sector, indicating that a professional state bureaucratic class was beginning to emerge for the first time in Colombia by the end of the National Front. Only three had held extensive political posts prior to their appointment; not surprisingly, they headed executive agencies in public works and social security.

Yet if professionalization and depoliticization encouraged by the National Front structure limited large-scale replacements for partisan purposes, unionization and other activity by state employees also played an increasingly more important role. At the national level, there have been two main categories of workers, "official workers" (*trabajadores oficiales*) and "public employees" (*empleados públicos*). Official workers, employed for the most part in the decentralized sector, have been free to form unions and seek labor contracts (though because they work in a "public service" most technically do not have the right to strike). Public employees, on the other hand, work primarily in the central sector of the government and in one kind of organization in the decentralized sector (*establecimientos públicos*). Public employees are eligible for career service; however, for that reason, they are not eligible to unionize and to seek collective bargaining pacts.

In an ultimately counterproductive attempt to curb unionization and strike activity in the public sector, President Carlos Lleras expanded the groups of workers defined as public employees. In subsequent years, many of the struggles of state workers revolved around seeking a redefinition of their status so they would be eligible for collective bargaining. Special career tracks gradually appeared in the judiciary, in education, in the foreign service, in health and elsewhere (see Moncayo & Rojas, 1978: 222; and Perry, Gómez & Londoño, 1982: 181–3, 189–91). Unions mushroomed throughout all of the public sector as workers sought improvement in their dismal working conditions and improved salaries.[46] By the mid 1970s, about one third of all union members in Colombia worked for the state and slightly over half of the bureaucracy was unionized.[47]

Naturally, if these union organizations were controlled by the parties or by the state, they would represent a powerful source of regime support. The opposite, however, was true, as most state labor unions formed part of independent labor federations with radical leadership. From 1974 to 1980, there were 258 strikes in the public sector, all technically illegal.[48] The strongest unions were often found, as in other Latin American countries, in areas of economic activity central to the running of the state and among workers who were geographically isolated and where the overlap of workplace and community ties was especially strong. This was particularly true of the workers of the state petroleum company, ECOPETROL, in the refinery town of Barrancabermeja. Their Workers Syndical Union (USO – Unión Sindical Obrera) had carried out major strikes in 1963 and 1977 (Caicedo, 1971: 123–5; Urrutia, 1984). Important unions are also found in the ports, the national railroads and among medical workers of the social security system.[49] Yet, unions flourished throughout the state– in central ministries and decentralized agencies at the national, departmental and municipal levels.

In sum, the state became the site of three contradictory processes during the National Front: increased state capacity as technocrats sought to set goals, specify investments and direct the economy in a comprehensive, planned fashion; a source for jobs, resources and particularistic benefits employed by politicians; and aggressive organizing and protest by state workers. This three-way clash among efforts at rational planning, patronage and public employees seeking protection by union activity is well illustrated in the situation of the public teachers. Public education teachers have gradually become organized by labor federations associated with the umbrella organization FECODE (Federación Colombiana de Educadores). Initially dominated by leaders with ties to the two traditional parties, by the 1970s FECODE was controlled by various leftist groups often bitterly divided among themselves. FECODE gradually gained organizational strength through experience and by reducing the number of negotiating sites. This process was facilitated when labor federations of secondary school teachers joined FECODE in massive numbers during the López administration years as the central government completed its takeover of the financing of education with the "nationalization" of secondary school education.[50] Throughout the National Front, FECODE and its associated federations organized numerous and occasionally large protests, all technically illegal: strikes of national proportions were carried out in every year from 1970 to 1978 except for 1974 and 44% of the 258 strikes in the public sector in the 1974–80 period were carried out by teachers. (Gómez Buendía & Losada Lora, 1984: 226; Fonseca, 1982: 97).

Even as the national government increasingly paid the educational bills, departments continued to insist upon their hiring prerogatives. Teachers would be hired by the dozens, sometimes around election time and usually with little regard to whether funds were available for their salaries (Blutstein et al., 1977: 181; for a cautionary note regarding the scope of clientelism, see Gómez Buendía & Losada Lora, 1984: 71–7). President Carlos Lleras attempted to institute greater national control to insure adequate and prompt salary payments, thus reducing a central cause for labor strife. He imposed contracts between the central and departmental levels through newly created Regional Educational Funds (Fondos Educacionales Regionales), with restrictive provisions concerning teacher appointments. As already noted, efforts such as this one to limit clientelist practices gained him the enmity of regional party figures. In fact, in many cases departments continued, on their own account, to hire teachers whose salaries they could not pay, forcing the national government opposed to their initial hiring to take on the financial burden to mitigate labor protests (speech by President López in 1977 in Colombia, Presidente, 1978: 82–5). The threat of punishing recalcitrant departments by withholding national funds could not realistically be applied. Thus, delays in the payment of the abysmally low and declining salaries was the major cause of teacher strikes in the 1974–80 period (92% according to Fonseca, 1982: 97). The radical national leadership of FECODE led technically illegal national work stoppages based on these economic issues as well as against government attempts to rationalize the teacher career ladder. However, they also challenged the regime linking their work stoppages to broader national issues, for which they were condemned by successive administrations as "subversives" (Gómez Buendía & Losada Lora, 1984: 221–91).

The National Front system of coalition rule prevented massive dismissals similar to those of the 1930s and 1940s. At the same time, the strength of clientelist ties between politicians and the vast majority of state employees appeared quite weak; initially, politicians relied on the creation of additional jobs to satisfy their desires to employ the government for clientelist purposes. By the end of the National Front, politicians were employing the public sector less to provide massive numbers of jobs to party faithful who could be counted on to support them at election time, than to give selected posts to party loyalists and campaign assistants. And the difficulties the state had with labor organizations of state employees reflected the growth of anti-regime labor unions in other areas of the economy.

Organized labor and civic movements

The National Front regime initially reinforced the existing pattern of a weak, divided, dispersed labor movement. The structure of the economy, including the importance of the agricultural sector, high levels of unemployment and subemployment and the importance of the informal sector in urban areas, worked against high levels of unionization, though these did increase during the first years of the National Front. In addition to its small size organized labor in 1958 belonged overwhelmingly to the two traditional labor confederations, the UTC and the CTC. All this was combined with a regime strategy of demobilizing labor through legal restrictions to limit labor militancy during the National Front years. However, coalition rule also weakened the ties between labor and the traditional parties, even as it contributed to the tensions between labor and the regime discussed above. As unionized labor expanded in the early 1960s, the ties between the traditional labor confederations and the political parties weakened. The labor challenge in the 1965 crisis was resolved not by the parties but through the intervention of ANDI and other producer associations, as discussed in chapter 5. With the sharpening conflicts within the state sector resulting from tensions across rationalizers, machine politicians and workers, and the higher inflation and decline in real wages of the 1970s, labor organization and militancy passed increasingly to the more radical union confederations.

The UTC, founded as an "apolitical" labor federation by Jesuits in 1946, first took a "political" stance in its cautious support for the overthrow of Rojas in 1957. During the National Front, it was to continue to take more open political positions and even tried briefly and unsuccessfully to form a labor party. It maintained itself as the single most important labor confederation in the country. Its leadership circles contained both Liberals and Conservatives, although for most of the period its head was linked to the Ospinista Conservatives. The CTC, which had begun by organizing primarily among transport workers, construction workers and public service workers, had once maintained extensive links with the Liberal Party. These were strained during Alberto Lleras' brief presidency in 1945, when he repelled a call for a general strike by the CTC and then repressed its most powerful union. The CTC suffered further repression under Ospina and Gómez. In the early 1960s, the CTC ejected many unions from its organization, and these along with other Communist-oriented unions formed a new confederation, the Syndical Confederation of Colombian Workers (CSTC– Confederación Sindical de Trabajadores de Colombia), in 1964. A fourth socialist labor confederation, the CGT (Confederación General de Trabajo), was formed in 1971. Other unions, especially in the public sector, remained firmly anti-regime, but unaffiliated with any of the confederations (González, 1975b: 78–122). Yet the UTC and the CTC together contained between 70% and 75% of all union affiliates in 1967. The CSTC and CGT were finally granted legal recognition by President Alfonso López.

Organized labor also was weak because in addition to being divided it represented a relatively small proportion of the total work force. The percentage of the labor force which was unionized expanded slowly from 4.7% in 1947 to 5.5% in 1959 and then more quickly to between 12% and 13% in 1964 (Urrutia, 1969: 184). Ten years later, though, this figure remained unchanged.[51] Furthermore, in nearly all sectors with a high percentage of organized workers, the right to strike was sharply curbed. Colombian labor legislation promoted the development of enterprise unions and weakened the possibilities for industry-wide unions. This "state pluralist" pattern, distinct from the more centralized corporatist pattern of other Latin American countries such as Brazil or Mexico (cf. Mericle, 1977 and Stepan, 1978: 61–9), also sought to demobilize workers and channel labor conflict within the existing political regime. It reflected the other demobilizing elements of the National Front agreement. Unlike the labor movements in Argentina, Brazil or Chile prior to the imposition of bureaucratic–authoritarian rule, organized labor had very little influence on economic policy in Colombia during the National Front period (Perry, Gómez & Londoño, 1982).

Most of the changes in labor legislation during the National Front period served to strengthen the role of enterprise unions and to decrease the likelihood of strikes, while expanding certain guarantees for unions and their workers. As such, these changes were facilitated by and consonant with the demobilizing and depoliticizing intent of the National Front, though eventually with somewhat counter-productive results for the regime itself. Some of the most important changes in labor legislation resulted from work carried out by the 1965 Gran Comisión (see chapter 5). President Valencia eliminated the "reserve clause" which made it easier to fire a worker and the "test period" in work contracts, two factors which had been central to many worker protests in the early 1960s (Gómez & Losada, 1977: 132). The legislation he decreed employing state of siege powers (Decree-Law 2352 of 1965) also protected union leaders in the process of bargaining from being summarily fired and provided sanctions for employers that excessively delayed the process of collective bargaining. It also prohibited non-union or minority groups of workers from continuing to work while a strike was in progress.

The legislation also increased the likelihood that binding arbitration rather than strikes would occur. If the first stages of conciliation failed then workers could vote either to go on strike or call for binding arbitration. Both the UTC and the CTC enthusiastically supported this measure, for many of their firm level unions were weak, lacking organization or funds for a sustained strike. Industrialists initially opposed the measure (Moncayo & Rojas, 1978: 207–11). A subsequent government decree (Decree-Law 939 of 1966) established binding arbitration (in which managers, the workers and the ministry of labor each appointed one arbitrator) and a return to work by strikers forty-three days after the official declaration of a strike. These changes in legislation appear to have been a major factor in the reduced strike levels under President Carlos Lleras (see Table 6.9). Under President Carlos Lleras the use of tribunals of binding arbitration increased dramatically; in 1966, forty-five were convened, jumping in 1967 to ninety-five.[52]

There have been other important legal restrictions on labor activity. Strikes have been prohibited within any activity considered a "public service," such as public utilities, transportation, communications, or since 1959, the financial sector. The president has been empowered to suspend a strike and impose binding arbitration anytime in which "the interests of the national economy considered as a whole" have been considered vitally affected. Even those few unions sufficiently well-organized to attempt to bargain at an industry-wide level have been hampered by the lack of legislation.[53] As we saw in the discussion of workers in the state sector, legal prohibitions have not prevented workers from striking. In the manufacturing sector, even though binding arbitration has been legally required forty-three days after a strike is officially declared, 50% of the 219 strikes between 1974 and 1980 lasted over forty-three days. The government decided for political reasons not to impose arbitration, in some cases without management objection (due to excess inventory, for example). However, legal restrictions have often been employed to restrict the activities of organized labor. Different administrations have employed labor legislation or more specific measures passed using state of siege powers to remove or suspend a confederation's legal recognition (*personería jurídica*), freeze its bank accounts, refuse to allow unions to employ advisers from non-recognized federations or confederations and permit the dismissal of union leaders (Tenjo, 1975b: 141–4; Caicedo, 1971: 178–9; Lara, 1976: 35–46; Gallón Giraldo, 1979: 96–100, 172, 181–3, 186; Urrutia, 1984; also interviews with a former high official of the ministry of labor, other officials of the ministry of labor and a Communist Party leader, Summer 1982). All these various factors have meant that Colombia has had a comparatively low level of strikes. Strike levels in Colombia have been considerably lower than those of other Latin American countries prior to the imposition of corporatist controls or bureaucratic–authoritarian coups. Thus, as Table 6.10 shows, strike activity in Colombia during the National Front was much lower than for Peru or Chile (prior to 1973).

Nevertheless, by the mid-1970s several important changes in the Colombian labor movement were apparent. Labor organization shifted toward the independent labor federations – especially in the public sector – and the CSTC. By 1974, union affiliates of the UTC and CTC had declined to 65% of all organized workers and these continued to fall through the following years (Tenjo, 1975: 22–3; interview with a high official of the ministry of labor, Summer 1982). Similarly, a disproportionate percentage of strikes were carried out by unions of the non-traditional labor confederations.[54] As we saw in the previous section, regime efforts to prevent unionization in the public sector were counterproductive and may have accelerated radicalization and labor organization as workers mobilized for the right to collective bargaining. With the de-linking between the traditional parties and the UTC and CTC, the increase in inflation and declines in real wages in urban areas in the early and mid-1970s also augmented labor militancy and the strength of the more radical confederations.[55] Faced with a continued loss of membership and an economic situation markedly unfavorable for most of its membership, the UTC and CTC took the unprecedented step in 1977 of joining the CSTC and CGT in carrying out a joint National Civic Strike in September. Defined by the government as a "subversive act" rather than a protest action, the strike succeeded in paralyzing economic activities in many cities but resulted in dozens of casualties as security forces clashed with strikers (Delgado, 1978).[56]

Thus, by the end of the National Front period, organized labor was gradually becoming a somewhat more autonomous force, in spite of its limited size. The links between the traditional parties and the UTC and CTC had weakened, although along with the CGT they remained pro-regime. Yet, the growing strength of the CSTC and of independent labor federations marked the emergence of a more important non-electoral opposition to the regime.

Another indicator of urban discontent and party decline was the growth of civic strikes (*paros cívicos*) in the 1970s. From 1958 to 1973, thirty-nine such strikes had taken place; in the period from 1974 to 1978 these jumped to eighty-four, exploding to even higher numbers in subsequent years (Fonseca, 1982: 140; see Medina, 1977; and Cartier, 1986). These strikes occurred most commonly in the country's smaller cities and towns. Demands usually revolved around basic services, such as improved water and sewage facilities, electrical energy, communications and

Table 6.9 *Colombia: strike data 1962–80*

Year	Total no. of strikes	% Strikes manufacturing	% Strikes[1] services	No. of workers in strikes	% Workers in services in strikes
1962	36	36.1	52.8	48,000	65.5
1963[2]	59	32.2	30.5	110,000	32.2
1964	75	25.3	62.7	118,000	46.6
1965	84	51.2	40.5	172,000	85.6
1966	111	18.0	60.4	n.a.	n.a.
1967	66	25.7	50.0	n.a.	n.a.
1968	44	50.0	45.4	41,500	86.4
1969[3]	59	40.7	44.1	58,000	23.2
1970	64	21.9	70.3	143,000	91.4
1971[4]	51	33.3	45.1	152,000	85.9
1972	67	31.3	52.2	162,000	85.3
1973	54	37.0	51.8	105,000	87.6
1974	75	37.3	46.7	82,800	63.7
1975	111	29.7	54.9	197,500	75.2
1976	58	53.4	34.5	117,100	84.6
1977[5]	93	47.3	39.8	210,200	84.2
1978	68	36.8	51.5	366,000	91.1
1979	60	41.7	45.0	90,200	64.3
1980	49	42.9	46.9	303,380	90.3

Notes:

[1] Services includes government, education, ports, hospitals, financial institutions and commerce. For 1971–80, includes education and "other services."

[2] Three partially effective general strikes were called, estimated to have involved 27,300 workers.

[3] One partially effective general strike with 15,000 workers is included.

[4] One partially effective general strike with 10,000 workers is included.

[5] The National Civic Strike is not included in these figures.

Sources: Gómez and Losada, 1977: 124 (first 3 columns, 1962–76); Delgado, 1974: 60–71 (last 2 columns, 1962–70); Delgado, 1982: 14–16 (first 2 columns, 1977–80; last 3 columns, 1971–80). The total number of strikes for 1962–76 reported by Delgado, 1982 differs only slightly from figures above except for 1971 when he lists 37 strikes.

Table 6.10 *Cross-national comparisons of strike activity*

	Colombia	Chile	Peru
Average no. strikes per year[1]	68	478	331
Average no. strikers per strike[2]	116	141	n.a.
Strikes as % non-agricultural work-force[3]	3.6	9.3	n.a.
Strikes as % economically active population[4]	2.02	n.a.	3.07

Notes:
[1]For Colombia, 1962–76; Chile, 9 selected years between 1952 and 1969; Peru, 1957–67.
[2]For Colombia, 1962–5, 1968–76; for Chile 9 selected years between 1952 and 1969.
[3]For Colombia, 1964 and 1973; for Chile, 1952, 1960 and 1964.
[4]For Colombia, 1962–5, 1968–76; for Peru, 1957–67.
Sources: Previous table; Stepan (1978: 310); Valenzuela (1978: 31).

education or in protest over increases in tariff or transportation rates. These strikes reflected the frustration of entire communities over state inefficiency and illustrated the decreasing ability of politicians and the traditional parties to serve as effective intermediaries and of local municipal authorities to satisfy demands. Rapid upward mobility for flashy drug traffickers, increases in real terms for public utility tariffs since around 1976, numerous newspaper accounts of alleged corruption by high government officials and declining real incomes for many urban groups fueled the protests.

These civic protests represented a new form of non-electoral opposition not channelled through the traditional political parties. They also called into question the country's growing fiscal centralization and lack of responsiveness to regional and local demands. At the same time, they were largely multi-class phenomena, focused on particular demands and lacking national coordination. The government usually negotiated with the movements and reached a compromise, though at times protests were met with repression (Ungar, 1981a). A significant form of political mobilization challenging the regime and another indicator of the growing inability of the regime to channel demands through established electoral, party or bureaucratic channels, these civic strikes were less threatening than the emergence of new guerrilla movements and the strengthening of older ones.

Guerrilla opposition

Underlying the formation of guerrilla movements in Colombia in each decade was a sense of social injustice and political blockage as a consequence of the National Front regime. At the same time, the role and importance of precipitating factors, linkages to earlier guerrilla experiences and social conflicts, international orientation and general ideology of each movement varied considerably. Some of the guerrillas that fought in the 1950s were never completely disbanded nor totally defeated. From these were formed the oldest operating guerrilla movement in the country, and the most significant, the Revolutionary Armed Forces of Colombia (FARC – Fuerzas Armadas Revolucionarias de Colombia). Two other guerrilla movements emerged in the 1960s. The National Liberation Army (ELN – Ejército de Liberación Nacional) emanated from the student movement influenced by the Cuban Revolution, and the Popular Liberation Army (EPL – Ejército Popular de Liberación) was created by Maoist-oriented dissidents from the Communist Party. Other guerrilla movements emerged in the 1970s. The group that gained the most visibility during this decade was the Movement of April 19 [1970] (M-19 – Movimiento del 19 de abril (de 1970)), which took its name from the date of the elections it felt fraudulently prevented an ANAPO victory in 1970. The much smaller Workers' Self-Defense (ADO – Auto Defensa Obrera) emerged from student and working-class circles in 1974.

The FARC was formally established in 1966 by Communist guerrilla groups and peasants that survived the military attacks on the so-called "independent republics," particularly the attacks on Marquetalia (Tolima) in May and June, 1964. In 1961, then Senator Alvaro Gómez, as a means of disparaging the Lleras administration, asserted there were "independent republics" in the country where the Colombian state and its armed forces could not operate. These areas included Sumapaz, Planadas, Riochiquito, Guayabero, El Pato and Vichada. In these or surrounding regions, relatively autonomous peasant communities had organized around struggles for control of agricultural land in the 1930s under the influence of members of Gaitán's short-lived UNIR and of the Communist Party (Alape, 1985: 171–4). They were consolidated during the period of *la violencia* in struggles for self-defense against large landowners. The FARC was a relatively small, cautious, rural-based and oriented movement in the late 1960s. Its major leaders, who had all been active during the years of *la violencia*, gradually established small "fronts" in isolated rural areas throughout the country, including southern Tolima and northern Cauca, Huila, Caquetá, Meta and the middle Magdalena valley.[57] By the mid-1970s, it had gradually developed new fronts facilitated by the end of the Lleras reform effort in agrarian reform. It increasingly financed its activities by kidnappings and extortion in rural areas, activities facilitated in the late 1970s and early 1980s by the decline in state capacity resulting from the rapid growth of drug trafficking and coca cultivation in areas of FARC influence. The FARC has always maintained an ambiguous linkage with the Soviet-oriented Colombian Communist Party, and followed its political line, though both groups have claimed autonomy from each other (valuable testimonies by FARC leaders are in Arango, 1984 and Arenas, 1985).

The ELN and the EPL both emerged from disaffected student and university groups in the 1960s. The leadership of the ELN was influenced by the example of the Cuban Revolution and emerged from the youth movement of the MRL as well as from the short-lived Workers Student Movement of Colombia (MOEC – Movimiento Obrero Estudiantil de Colombia). The ELN decided to establish operations initially in Santander, in a region of extensive guerrilla activity in the 1950s. It made its first public appearance in January, 1965. Probably its most well-known adherent was Camilo Torres, who was killed in an army ambush in February, 1966 shortly after he joined the movement. The ELN continued to draw its followers principally from the student movement in the late 1960s, even though it suffered serious internal divisions and then a substantial military setback in 1973 (in Anorí).[58]

The EPL emerged as the military arm of a Maoist splinter group from the Communist Party which established itself in 1965 as the Colombian Communist Party – Marxist Leninist (PCC-ML – Partido Comunista de Colombia – Marxista Leninista). As such the EPL was more heavily influenced by Maoist notions of prolonged people's war than the *foquista* theories of the Cuban Revolution propagated by Che Guevara and Regis Debray which influenced the ELN. Peasant-based units of the EPL first emerged in December 1967 in areas of Sinú and San Jorge (Cauca) where Liberal guerrillas had been active in the 1950s. However, the movement suffered military defeats and factionalism as it gradually attempted to establish an urban guerrilla force though still subjugated to a rural-based strategy. In 1980, the PCC-ML and the EPL carried out a "self-criticism" regarding their earlier Maoist positions and refocused their attention away from the peasantry toward the urban and rural working class (see the interviews in Alape, 1985: 296–314; and Behar, 1985: 43–51).

The M-19 emerged as an effort to create an urban-based, unified "anti-oligarchical and anti-imperialist" movement that would be both mass-based and committed to armed struggle. The M-19 was formed in 1973 by radicalized Anapistas joined by elements from the FARC, the ELN, revolutionary Christians and other popular organizations. In part, they were frustrated by the divisions, sectarianism, international alliances and caution among other leftist movements combating the political regime. At the same time, the experience of Rojas in the 1970 elections and then the overthrow of Allende in Chile in 1973 convinced them that "the only possibility of breaking the oligarchy's monopoly of power is by means of revolutionary violence" (Alvaro Fayad, an M-19 leader, in Alape, 1985: 321). Their attempt to become the military arm of ANAPO (which they viewed as the largest anti-oligarchical mass based movement in the country at the time) without clear knowledge of the party's directorate eventually led to the expulsion of the Anapistas associated with the M-19 from the party.

The M-19's ideology thus was a radical and nationalist hybrid. This was reflected in the movement's first action, the theft of Simón Bolívar's sword, a national treasure, from its museum display case on April 19, 1974. Their next actions were more violent. In 1976, they kidnapped, "sentenced" and then killed the corrupt head of the pro-regime CTC labor confederation. A few months later they kidnapped the head of a firm whose workers were on strike, releasing him after the firm acceded to the workers' demands to the satisfaction of the M-19.

The ADO, an urban terrorist group, was born from a similar sense of political frustration. As one of its founders noted:

We see armed struggle as a necessity because it is the result... of having uselessly travelled the path of legal struggle; that has been our experience in the unions, the popular neighborhoods and student circles (in Alape, 1985: 333).

Their most dramatic action was the assassination of the man who had been the minister of government during the 1977 national civic strike on the first anniversary of the date of its occurrence.

The apparent exclusionary form and exhaustion of the political model underscored the regime's apparent lack of popular responsiveness. The popularity of the López government and the legitimacy of the political regime were both eroded as the state confronted the growing guerrilla activity of the 1970s and challenges to its authority by drug trafficking and other emboldened criminal enterprises. The different responses of the next two administrations to the growing regime crisis are analyzed in the next chapter.

Concluding reflections

This chapter has explored the principal means by which the political regime sought to maintain continued legitimacy and popular support. It has also analyzed the increasing challenges confronted by the regime as the political realities that led to the establishment of consociationalism were superseded due to the regime structure itself, and to massive social and economic changes in the country over the twenty-year period. These changes, combined with short-term economic pressures, increasingly impaired the ability of the regime and the parties to maintain a perception of popular responsiveness.

From the beginning, the National Front agreement was viewed as a means of mass demobilization, even as the parties sought partial mobilization of their electorate at election time. To preclude the possibility of a struggle over state resources reviving inter-party conflict, parity was employed in the distribution of government jobs. This, in turn, encouraged party factionalism as the arena of partisan conflict shifted from inter-party relations to intra-party negotiations. Brokerage ties increasingly served as the major linkage between party leaders and followers as traditional patron–client ties broke down in rural areas due to migration, the commercialization of agriculture and a greater institutional presence of the state. In Colombia, as in other countries, "machine-style politics . . . represents a conservative response to its dynamic environment" (Scott, 1972: 145). By focusing on short-term and particularistic goals, these practices linked individuals and groups in the electorate to individual politicians, sometimes reinforcing traditional party identification, while working against the creation of class solidarities at the mass level. Yet in this way vast sectors of the population remained untouched by the political parties. The parties became dominated by regional politicians in control of small captive electorates and thus lacked substantial links to mass organizations.

Congress and local-level political arenas lost importance as sites for discussion and decisions on policy issues. Their attention focused especially on narrow issues of direct interest to them: *auxilios*, "quotas" in government agencies, scholarships, factional politics and placement on electoral lists. Yet, political leaders at local levels and congressmen at the national level found themselves constrained. A "technocratic" state sector, encouraged by certain political leaders, international agencies and structural pressures, expanded. This sector opposed and sought to restrict the particularistic and patronage aims of politicians, even as it occasionally provided an alternative channel to state resources. At the same time, autonomous radical unionization sharply increased in the public sector, serving as another constraint on the usage of the state for patronage. Politicians retained a critical brokerage function especially in rural areas where the role of other state institutions was less prominent. However, their penetration even in these areas was fairly limited. And the parties largely failed to develop new organizations or methods to appeal to the country's growing urban population.

There were ambivalent and only partially successful efforts at state-sponsored organization of the lower classes. Attempts at autonomy and greater coordination by popular sector organizations were met with "divide and conquer" strategies, a kind of state corporatism shifting to state pluralism. This was particularly evident in the case of the peasant association ANUC. The presumably apolitical Juntas de Acción Comunal instead became the preferred channels for the disbursement of political patronage. The traditional parties did not develop stronger party institutions or mass organizations. In part this reflected the difficulty of generating party organizations employing state resources in a consociational system. But primarily, this fact appeared to reflect concern about the potential autonomous capabilities of mass organizations, as the examination of Communal Action and ANUC suggest.

Most significantly, there was a decline in party segmentation, a result of the regime structure, which twice required voters to elect a presidential candidate from the opposing party due to the requirement of alternation, and of socio-economic changes. And, in spite of continuities in party electoral shares, a new urban electorate, largely abstentionist but potentially mobilizable by any party or movement, emerged for the first time in the country's modern history.

The political regime of shared rule with its access to resources and the electoral system of high abstention made politicians reluctant to change the model of coalition rule. Ironically, with a return to competitive elections, this made it more difficult for opposition movements to gain electoral representation even as the traditional parties were increasingly incapable of channelling dissent. In the more difficult economic context of the 1970s, in which higher inflation and economic policy affected middle and popular sector urban groups most seriously and with a certain deflation of state authority due to the drug trafficking, increased corruption and criminal violence, non-electoral opposition groups emerged or were strengthened. Perhaps modest by continental standards, they appeared significant in the Colombian context. Labor organizations in and out of the public sector independent from the traditional parties and the regime gained in strength at the expense of the traditional labor confederations which also distanced themselves from the regime. The result was the historic 1977 civic strike. Further reflecting the economic frustration of urban groups, particularly in smaller cities, and the declining role of the traditional parties as intermediaries in the political process was the sharp rise in civic movements and protests in the 1970s. And finally, and most threatening, was the growing strength of guerrilla groups, particularly of the emerging M-19. By the late 1970s, the political realities that led to the establishment of consociationalism had changed and regime arrangements required transformation.

7

Toward the dismantling of coalition rule: exclusion or reform?

We have been living, without realizing it, by relying upon old solidarities, which the parties managed to establish, not without great difficulty, in order to return to institutional order. But these solidarities have not been renewed nor much less revitalized. (Alvaro Gómez Hurtado, 1972: 21–2)

Today we have class struggle more than party struggle. The division is between those who wish to end the system and those who wish to preserve it. Thus, the theme of how to make peace between Liberals and Conservatives is no longer topical; rather the debate is between friends of the "status quo" and those who aspire to a different order. (President Alfonso López Michelsen in an interview in *Revista Causa Común*, No. 1 (April–May, 1977), p. 19)

The issue of consociational transformation has not been adequately addressed by the consociational literature. The initial literature on consociational democracy, because it addressed Western European cases, tacitly assumed these regimes would indefinitely remain consociational or would evolve into stable, consolidated majoritarian democratic regimes. When the analysis was extended to Third World countries, the cases examined were primarily ones in which the segments in conflict were ethnic or religious. Here, the assumption was that if these countries were to retain open political regimes they would have to remain consociational almost indefinitely (Lijphart, 1977). The alternatives were violence or authoritarian domination by one group over another. The range of possibilities of consociational transformation, however, is more extensive.

Consociational regimes may revert to open conflict between the same segments either because of a breakdown of consociationalism at the elite level, because of mass pressure or due to a combination of both of these. Consociational rule may also break down if one or more segments break the consociational agreement in order to try to impose hegemonic rule over the other segment(s). Violent conflict may result from the interjection of new segments and issues. It may also be a consequence of the inability to move beyond an initial consociational agreement in spite of the necessity to do so due to significant societal transformation. Whether consociational rule strengthens the particular segmental divisions upon which it is built in a particular country depends upon the nature of the segmental cleavage, the specific political arrangement and the impact of economic and societal change on these two factors. In Colombia, all of these have operated to weaken the traditional party segments.

In chapter 3 it was argued that consociational mechanisms were necessary in order to establish the civilian regime in Colombia in 1958. Yet, the saliency of the original segments in conflict – the political parties – has declined considerably over a twenty-year period as new conflicts have emerged. This change is clearly observed in the quotations by two leading politicians at the beginning of this chapter. Was continued shared rule in these circumstances a benign result of party elites overestimating the danger of inter-party violence if there was a shift to competitive rule, perhaps combined with institutional inertia? Or was it more a result of the fact that the arrangement benefited the immediate interests of entrenched party leaders and major producer groups, while serving to control in increasingly authoritarian and counterproductive fashion other potentially more explosive kinds of conflicts? The electoral advantages of continued coalition rule for party leaders, the very modest social reforms during this period and the increase in repression during the presidency of Julio César Turbay (1978–2) suggest that "control" rather than "benign" inertia was more significant. Yet, the emergence of electoral counter-reactions to traditional machine politics within both parties, the victory of Belisario Betancur in 1982 and the steps taken during his administration toward opening the political model, however hesitant and uneven, suggest some regime leaders sought a regime transformation that recognized the country's new political realities. And coalition rule finally came to an end in 1986. Virgilio Barco, the Liberal presidential candidate for the 1986 elections, campaigned on the theme of a "program" or "party" government. When Barco formed a single party Cabinet shortly after his inauguration, the country finally returned to a "government–opposition" form of government.

The regime confronted a growing legitimacy crisis as political actors sought to justify and retain a political model– coalition rule – that no longer responded to the country's social structure, in important respects because of changes induced by the regime structure itself. The crisis was accentuated because urban middle-sector groups most alienated by the sectarian appeals and brokerage practices of regional politicians and the corruption associated with new drug wealth suffered a relative economic decline in the mid-1970s in a period of presumed national economic bonanza (for income distribution data, see Urrutia, 1985). Underlying this regime crisis was a partial deflation of state capacity brought about by drug trafficking, growing criminal violence and guerrilla activity. A more fundamental challenge to the state and economically dominant groups, built upon the country's glaring social and economic inequalities, though, was still distant. The growing problems of the 1970s responded to the predicaments of an unchanged regime in a changed society. The state was not in danger of collapse, though the regime was in danger.

Contradictions sharpened as the country's economy went through a painful period of adjustment in the late 1970s and early 1980s. As discussed in the next section that examines economic policy during the Turbay and Betancur administrations, Colombia postponed and mitigated, but could not fully avoid, the financial crisis that affected its continental neighbors. As in the past, the regime generated within its political leadership not only the forces seeking re-accommodation but also those of blockage. This is analyzed in the two sections that follow the review of economic policy. One analyzes the different electoral experiences of 1978 and 1982 and the other the "strategies" of exclusion and inclusion practiced toward the guerrillas and attitudes toward the issue of political reform by Turbay and Betancur. In the case of both administrations there are important elements of continuity that help explain, in addition to the growing economic problems, the sharp constraints that operated particularly on Betancur. A final section considers the country's possible future evolution in the context of alternative transformations of the consociational regime discussed in chapter 1 and summarized in this chapter's opening paragraphs.

Economic policy-making: recession and austerity "moderately"

Colombia's economic growth record suffered and economic policy-making was strained in the late 1970s and early 1980s, as public deficits grew, balance of payments problems increased and unemployment inched upward. The country slipped into its worst recession since the 1930s, in large part due to external conditions. Betancur was finally forced to impose an austerity program, cutting back public expenditures and social programs. By Colombian standards and for the segments of the population that suffered most directly the effects of the country's economic decline, the downturn was serious; in comparison to the crushing debt burdens, public sector deficits, inflation and jarring adjustment programs of many other Latin American countries, however, the country's economic problems were less severe (for comparative data on growth and inflation, see Table 7.1 and for public sector deficits, see Table 7.2). An upturn in world coffee prices in late 1985 also helped pull the country out of balance of payments difficulties. And, in the medium term, coal exports from the massive Cerrejón project and important oil discoveries suggested that the country's future foreign exchange situation could improve further, though uncertainty about world prices for these commodities as well as for coffee meant the country could not bank on a full-scale "bonanza."

Economic policy-making during the Turbay period reflected a tilt toward greater public investment in response to the growing effects of the international recession. The country's coffee bonanza that had begun in 1975 and peaked in 1977 ended in mid-1980, and the Turbay administration based its "National Integration Plan" (PIN – Plan de Integración Nacional) on an expansion of government spending for basic infrastructure projects, particularly in transportation, communications, mining and energy. During the Turbay years, though, the decline in industrial expansion that had begun in the López government turned into an outright industrial recession. Several factors appear to have played a role: reduced world demand for industrial goods; continued reliance on tight monetary policy to control inflation, reducing credit and driving up interest rates (exacerbated by increased domestic government borrowing); reductions in some levels of industrial protection and the granting of import licenses for a

Table 7.1 *Selected Latin American countries: economic growth rates and inflation 1981–4*

Table 7.1.A Economic growth (% change in GDP)

Year	Argentina	Chile	Peru	Brazil	Colombia	Mexico	Venezuela
1981	-6.2	5.5	3.0	-1.6	2.3	8.0	-0.3
1982	-5.1	-14.1	0.9	0.9	1.0	-0.5	0.7
1983	2.9	-0.7	-11.8	-3.2	1.0	-5.3	-4.8
1984	2.0	6.0	3.5	4.1	3.0	3.5	-1.7
1984/80	-6.4	-3.3	-4.4	0.3	7.2	5.6	-6.1

Table 7.1.B Change in consumer price index (%)

Year	Argentina	Chile	Peru	Brazil	Colombia	Mexico	Venezuela
1981	104.5	19.7	75.4	105.6	26.7	27.9	16.0
1982	164.8	9.9	64.4	97.9	23.9	58.9	9.7
1983	343.8	27.2	111.1	142.0	16.7	101.9	6.3
1984	625.6	19.9	110.2	196.6	– 18.3	65.6	12.2

Source: IDB, 1985: 71, 86

Table 7.2 *Selected Latin American countries: public sector deficits (% of GDP) 1980–4*

	Argentina	Chile	Peru	Brazil	Colombia	Mexico	Venezuela
1980	−7.6	5.5	−5.3	−9.1	−2.4	−7.0	−13.5
1981	−15.9	0.8	−8.4	−7.2	−5.9	−13.5	1.3
1982	−16.7	−3.4	−9.1	−6.2	−6.8	−17.6	−3.9
1983	−15.7	−2.5	−11.6	−2.7	−6.8	−8.9	3.0
1984	−12.4	−4.1	−8.1	0.2	−7.5	−6.9	3.6

Source: IDB, 1985: 66, based on non-financial public sector revenues and expenditures excluding capital revenue for all countries except Mexico.

number of industrial goods; contraband, sometimes facilitated by the abuse of import licenses; and a continued sluggishness of the exchange rate in relation to major world currencies. As government revenues flattened, a result of the changes in tax legislation discussed in chapter 5 and of continued evasion, the government financed part of its growing budget deficit by means of the country's "special exchange account," which included principally revenue generated by the buying and selling of foreign exchange and interest on international reserves (see Mercedes de Martínez, 1981). The Turbay administration increased government borrowing, both internally and abroad. The public sector deficit climbed steadily under Turbay, jumping from 2.4% of GDP in 1980, to 5.9% in 1981 and 6.8% in 1982 (see Table 7.2).

Reactions to the deteriorating economic situation and government policies by producer groups were sharp. Dissatisfied particularly by policies of trade liberalization, tight credit and heavy government borrowing, the major producer associations joined in a common *ad hoc* front in February 1981 (known as the Frente Gremial). Formation of the front illustrated the associations' frustration not only with government but also with the parties as policy intermediaries.

The administration's relations with the Frente Gremial pointed to the state's apparent strength but continuing limited autonomy. For several months Turbay refused to meet formally with the Frente Gremial to discuss their demands. He even sought to have the heads of several of the producer associations removed, though their boards of directors refused to comply (Urrutia,

1981: 211–18). Furthermore, while the Frente could not meet with the president, the textile and cotton sectors, important regional economic interests in crisis due in part to international economic conditions, conferred with the administration. Turbay met personally with the heads of the major textile firms (who were important figures in ANDI, a major Frente association) in July 1981, in the midst of his conflict with the associations (interviews with the heads of two major textile firms in the Summer 1982). Subsequently, in conversations with appropriate state officials, measures of support and relief were negotiated for these firms, as also occurred slightly later for the cotton sector (already discussed in chapter 5).

The government–business deadlock was broken by a call for a new general strike by the CSTC and CTC for October 1981. The outcome showed once again the divided political allegiances and relative weakness of organized labor. The government and the private sector perceived a mutual interest in preventing such a strike. The president and the heads of the producer associations met both separately and jointly with labor leaders to seek to prevent the strike. As in 1965, an agreement was reached to create a tripartite forum with several study subcommissions and the CTC opted not to participate in the general strike. Although the CSTC and several independent federations proceeded with the strike, it was not nearly as successful as the joint action four years earlier.[1]

Complaints by industrialists also focused on the massive underground economy fueled primarily by drug trafficking.[2] Around US$1.1 billion in foreign exchange resulted from drug trafficking between 1975 and 1982, a figure that is not higher because a large proportion of drug profits were not repatriated (Gómez, 1986). When this foreign exchange was combined with the coffee bonanza the consequence was that the black market dollar exchange fell below the official rate, which served as a powerful incentive for the smuggling of textiles and other consumer goods into the country and for speculative investments, especially in real estate. The peso became increasingly overvalued relative to the dollar. The resulting industrial recession combined with government deregulation of the burgeoning financial sector led to a crisis in that sector in the final weeks of Turbay's administration sparked by the questionable loans of a number of banks to associated conglomerate firms. The crisis dragged into Betancur's first year in office threatening confidence in the financial system. The Betancur administration declared a state of national economic emergency and used its powers to liquidate one financial group, intervene in another and shore up several banks.[3]

Betancur's economic team was more involved in crisis management than in strategic planning for almost its whole first year in office. In part due to growing trade deficits, economic policy tilted back toward protectionism. Import restrictions were imposed and new export subsidies provided. The swing in this direction, like the earlier shift toward more monetarist and less protectionist policies under López and Turbay, was "moderate" by continental standards. The country's trade deficits, however, continued to deteriorate. One reason was the narrowing of important markets in Ecuador and Venezuela as these countries imposed their own import restrictions. The Venezuelan market virtually closed following a massive devaluation of the bolívar in February 1983. This also led to a massive decline in Colombian migrants to Venezuela in search for better employment opportunities.

Government efforts to re-establish public finances on a sound footing met unexpected difficulty. The administration declared a second state of national economic emergency at the end of 1982 in order to enact a broad tax reform, imitating the example of López in 1974. By declaring a tax amnesty, lowering personal income tax rates, improving procedures and introducing several new taxes, the government hoped to reduce evasion and augment state revenues. It also reformed the way the government could employ the special exchange account (for a detailed analysis of the tax measures, see Ocampo & Perry, 1983). To the government's shock and dismay, the Supreme Court unexpectedly declared the government's tax measures unconstitutional in February 1983.[4] The country was in fiscal chaos and capital flight accelerated as rumors of a maxi-devaluation increased.

Betancur was forced to shift his political strategy as a result of the Supreme Court action. He had formed his first cabinet by incorporating mainstream and dissident Liberals directly, some of whom were more technocrats than politicians, rather than in negotiations with the leadership of the Liberal party. Now, in order to insure passage of the necessary tax measures in the Liberal dominated Congress, Betancur was forced to negotiate with the Liberal leadership directly.[5] His hopes of consolidating the "National Movement" into a more permanent political organization gradually declined. Although Congress eventually approved the tax reform virtually intact, government finances remained in serious disarray because of the fiscal confusion even as the country's balance of payments continued to deteriorate.[6]

The Betancur government's ambitious development plan, "Change With Equity" (*Cambio con equidad*), presented nearly a year after the government came to power, never became more than a "wish list" of good intentions. Over 1983 and 1984, almost all economic indices deteriorated as the country's long promised economic reactivation never appeared. Most disturbing were the continued loss of foreign exchange reserves (net reserves fell steadily from US$5.6 billion in 1981 to US$1.8 billion in 1984), fiscal problems and increased unemployment. Colombia was particularly affected by the reluctance of foreign commercial banks to extend loans in support of the administration's development plans. This was due to these banks' general policy of withdrawal from Latin America, a process accelerated by the Mexican crisis of late 1982. In more normal times, Colombia would have been perceived as creditworthy.

By mid-1984, it was becoming evident that Colombia would be joining its Latin American neighbors in the implementation of an austerity program to try to correct its balance of payments and fiscal deficit problems. Colombia's total foreign debt at the time was relatively more manageable than that of other Latin American countries (around US$12.5 billion) and was heavily weighted toward long-term fixed interest loans from international agencies. Yet, its under-reported private debt contracted with foreign commercial banks was problematic. The country was rapidly losing reserves and the government was printing money in order to cover its deficit (equivalent to 6.8% of GDP in 1983 and 7.5% in 1984). But the situation never degenerated to the extent it had in many of the other major Latin American countries (see Table 7.2). In a dramatic turnaround, the president admitted the country's serious economic problems. His new minister of finance, a respected economist who had been the head of SAC, began serious discussions with the IMF and the World Bank. Producer groups, hoping to tie the president's hands, strongly urged an agreement with the IMF.

The president refused a formal accord with the IMF on nationalist grounds, but pragmatically acceded to austerity measures including cutbacks in public expenditures and a sharp increase in the rate of devaluation. Although these adjustment measures initially were timid and for many observers came a year too late, the government acted sooner than governments in other Latin American countries in similar circumstances had been known to act. And as if to prove his non-populist credentials, government funds committed to the bailout of certain private banks continued to flow. New fiscal measures were pushed through Congress at the end of 1984. And in the Spring 1985, the government agreed to "enhanced surveillance" by the IMF on a quarterly basis while the World Bank accelerated its disbursements of funds to the country. Private commercial banks reopened lines of credit to the country. The government reduced its deficit to below 4% of GDP by cutting expenditures, increasing tariffs on public utilities and increasing taxes. It also eased restrictions on foreign investment, dismounted trade restrictions and accelerated the rate of devaluation of the peso (see Schloss & Thomas, 1986: 15–20).

The government's austerity measures accelerated discontent in urban areas and made it impossible to implement promised social and economic reforms in rural areas of guerrilla activity. Unemployment reached new highs for Colombia (around 15% for the four major cities). The labor movement, spearheaded by the CSTC, planned a national strike for June 20, 1985. The proposed action was condemned by the Church, the traditional parties and producer groups. As in 1981, the government again succeeded in preventing several of the labor confederations from joining the strike action: the UTC, CTC and CGT, organized in a Democratic Syndical Front (FSD – Frente Sindical Democrático), withheld their participation. In turn, the government promised these confederations it would make additional expenditures in health, channel more credit to small farmers, freeze prices of some basic food items and invite a special foreign mission to make recommendations on reducing unemployment. The civic strike failed, as it had in 1981, in its objective of shutting down the major urban centers.

However, the impact of the recession on labor led to further steps toward unity which had begun with the 1977 civic strike. These were spearheaded by Jorge Carrillo who had been one of the principal leaders of the Democratic Syndical Front and minister of labor under Betancur in 1985-6. Upon leaving office, he joined

with leaders of FECODE, CSTC, other independent labor federations and a few UTC unions to create a new umbrella labor
organization, the Unified Workers Central (CUT – Central
Unitaria de Trabajadores). At least initially, the CUT reflected a
tenuous coalition rather than effective unity within organized
labor. However, it provided further evidence of the declining role
of the political parties as effective interlocutors between the state
and society.

Betancur's actions in the economic field as well as those of Turbay
before him continued to reflect the moderating influence of the
political regime. Administration policy responses stayed within a
fairly narrow band. Differences in government policy between
the two administrations represented in part differences in
economic conditions – less protectionist in times of foreign
exchange abundance and more so in times of relative scarcity.
They also represented regional and ideological predilections, as
Betancur was committed to resurrecting traditional industry,
especially affected in his own region of Antioquia.[7] In neither case
was the policy swing – toward liberal economic orthodoxy or
toward protectionism – especially sharp. And in Betancur's case,
even with his popularity sharply eroded, the country initiated a
stabilization process in late 1984.[8] The Liberals sought to capitalize
politically from the crisis, but in the end gave the administration
much of what it sought from Congress in terms of additional
revenues. Although it was little solace to the country's population, Colombia joined its continental neighbors in financial and
economic crisis relatively late and its economic indicators were
only "moderately" bad in comparison to many of these countries
at the height of their respective crises. Similarly, Colombia's painful
adjustment process, although postponed somewhat by Betancur,
was initiated comparatively earlier in the country's crisis and
could be implemented less brusquely because key factors – the fiscal
deficit, exchange rate, existing debt, inflation – were lower or less
out of control.

The country's medium-term prospects appeared more hopeful.
In Betancur's final months in office there was a brief explosion of
public spending – in preparation for a possible political comeback
– facilitated by a sharp upturn in coffee prices. In spite of difficulties in acquiring outside funding and lower world coal prices
than originally projected, plans appeared on schedule for the
development of the massive US$3.2 billion Cerrejón coal project

on the Atlantic Coast, a joint venture of Exxon and the Colombian government.[9] Similarly, important oil discoveries were found in the early 1980s in the Eastern Plains, unfortunately as world oil prices declined. These were to be exploited jointly by ECOPETROL, the Colombian state oil company, Occidental Petroleum and Shell Oil. Depending on world prices, significant growth in these two export products and continued expansion in other non-traditional exports could lead total Colombian exports nearly to double between 1985 and 1990.

This possible bonanza would differ from the bonanza of coffee and illegal drugs of the 1970s in at least two significant ways. First, it would have been forecast for several years, rather than resulting suddenly and unexpectedly. Second, it is to be channelled directly through the state, rather than largely through private hands as occurred with the earlier boom. Yet, given the vagaries of the world market, the "bonanza" could be more disappointing than initially expected, and original expectations have already been trimmed back. The historically cautious Colombian attitude has also been affected by the negative experiences of previously "moderate" oil-exporting countries such as Mexico and Venezuela. In spite of these more hopeful medium-term economic prospects, though, the crucial issue of political re-accommodation was demanding immediate attention.

The 1978 and 1982 elections: the limits of machine politics

The 1978 elections heralded the regime's growing legitimacy crisis. Marred by accusations of fraud and of legislative races funded by drug money, they had an extremely low turnout and the victory by Liberal Julio César Turbay Ayala appeared to confirm that clientelist and machine politics effectively dominated the electoral landscape.

In turn, the victory of Conservative Belisario Betancur at the head of a "National Movement" in the 1982 presidential elections came like a breath of fresh air. The 1982 elections may have been a watershed in Colombian politics, for they represented the victory of a clever blending of modern campaign techniques with traditional politics over dependence on informal campaign planning and reliance on traditional party machinery. An effective if only partial mobilization of the urban electorate not open to sectarian appeals provided the necessary edge for Betancur's victory.

Though significant, the result represented a "deviating" rather than a "realigning" election and was helped by the disrepute of the previous López and Turbay governments and the division within the Liberal Party.

The Liberal Party division reflected the diverging views of reformist versus machine politicians. Carlos Lleras represented the sector of the party most opposed to machine politics and Turbay the regional politicians most identified with it. López, who ably bridged the two, had gained the party's nomination for the 1974 campaign by pledging to run a "Liberal campaign" rather than a bipartisan "National Unity" campaign as suggested by Lleras in his own bid for re-election. López' nomination in the 1973 Liberal convention was due to the support of Turbay, even though in the 1972 mid-term elections Turbayista lists had been opposed by joint Llero-Lopista lists.[10] During López' presidency, Lleristas joined Conservative Ospino-Pastranistas in opposition.

The 1978 elections intensified the party division and became embroiled in an effort by López to carry out extensive institutional reforms to facilitate the regime's political re-accommodation. López sought to establish a Constitutional Assembly that would carry out far-reaching changes in two areas. It was intended to revamp the administrative structure of the country, financially strengthening the departments and municipalities. This reform could encourage a more normal political process of government–opposition by reducing the country's suffocating centralization that led most politicians to want to form part of the government. It could also reduce political irresponsibility at the local level as the central government would no longer be financially liable for local programs. The Assembly was also intended to reform the country's archaic and increasingly inoperative civilian judicial system that had not expanded sufficiently with respect to the country's increased population and had not modernized its facilities, equipment or procedures. The judicial system was easily subverted by captured drug traffickers and guerrillas. Its problems were a major reason for the pressure to expand the scope of crimes to be tried under military justice.

López proposed that the presidential and congressional elections in 1978 be separated. Delegates to the Assembly, who could not also be congressmen, would be elected along with the president, employing a formula that practically guaranteed parity between the two traditional parties as well as exclusion of opposition groups. López chose this mechanism of an Assembly in part to try to avoid a repeat of the political crises that had punctuated passage of the 1968 Constitutional Reform (Cepeda, 1977: 10). Liberal Lleristas and Conservative Ospino-Pastranistas accused López of fueling a further decline of the Congress without specifying clearly the functions of the Assembly. Leftist opposition groups criticized it as a means of continuing the exclusionary National Front since opposition parties would be absent from an important policy decision arena. Debate revolved almost exclusively around the mechanism rather than any proposed reforms.

At the same time, the two major Liberal presidential aspirants, Lleras and Turbay, could not agree on the means by which the party would choose its presidential candidate. Turbay favored a party convention, which would largely comprise congressmen and departmental and municipal delegations under their influence. By July, 1977, about 75% of all Liberal congressmen supported him. For that reason and adducing arguments of greater party democracy, Lleras favored a party primary. He felt he could win the nomination if he appealed directly to Liberal voters over the heads of the regional politicians. In a typical summit negotiation, a compromise was worked out with the assistance of the editor of the Liberal daily *El Tiempo* in the Presidential Palace. The Consenso de San Carlos, as the agreement was named, called for the separation of congressional and presidential elections (opening the way for an election of delegates to the Constitutional Assembly, initially opposed by Lleristas) and for the congressional elections to serve as a primary for the Liberals to determine their presidential candidate (initially opposed by the Turbayistas).[11] After tortuous maneuvering, congressional approval for the Constitutional Assembly and the separation of elections was achieved. Then, just weeks before the presidential elections, the proposal for the Assembly was declared unconstitutional by the Supreme Court. An important opportunity for political reform was lost.[12]

As the Liberals achieved agreement on candidate selection, the Conservatives coalesced around Belisario Betancur as their presidential candidate. With the party still divided, each Conservative faction held its own convention. Each convention agreed that Betancur would be free to organize his campaign as the "National Candidate" and not only as the Conservative candidate.[13]

The congressional elections demonstrated again the strength of machine-style politics in high abstention elections. In the weeks prior to the elections, Turbay campaigned with vague populist rhetoric while regional and local Liberal leaders supporting him used government resources to mobilize votes. Lleras, in turn, focused on his proven ability for leadership and administration and attacked the "progressive deterioration of political customs" in the country, including clientelism, vote buying and corruption.[14]

Turbayista lists received twice as many votes as those of Lleras nationwide, though the opposite phenomenon occurred in Bogotá. Conservative Alvaristas, who were governing in coalition with López, edged out Ospino-Pastranista lists for the first time since the 1958 elections (*El Tiempo*, April 3, 1978, and June 29, 1978). The Liberals again showed that they were the majority party with 55.1% of the total vote to the Conservatives' 39.4%. The abstention rate of 66.8% was the highest ever for a congressional election held the same year as a presidential election. It was especially high in urban areas. In terms of actual votes cast, the national Liberal vote declined by 19% from the 1974 elections; in Bogotá, it declined by a whopping 37%! Leftist parties were only able to win one senate seat and five house seats.

The presidential elections represented another victory for traditional politics, though a narrow one. Turbay eked out a narrow victory over Betancur in elections in which only 41.2% of the electorate participated (for the results, see Table 6.2). And for the first time, the Liberals actually lost the popular vote in Bogotá.[15] Because of the larger percentage of the electorate identified with the Liberal party, the focus of Turbay's campaign was in preventing high levels of Liberal abstention. Turbay's campaign sought ineffectually to mobilize Liberals to vote by reviving fears of renewed violence and instability with a Conservative victory. His campaign's major slogan was "Liberal Vote Liberal; Liberal Vote Turbay." However, Turbay was closely identified with the unpopular López government, and though Lleras withdrew from the race after the February elections, he refused to endorse Turbay.[16]

"Belisario" in turn, responding to the new realities in the electorate brought about by the National Front and to the fact that a smaller percentage of the electorate identified with the Conservative Party, sought to appeal to a wider set of voters as a "multiparty" candidate. Thus, he campaigned not only for the traditional and potentially mobilizable Conservative vote, but also for part of the growing urban independent electorate as well as disgruntled Liberals who could not accept Turbay. Betancur also raised the spectre of violence – with a Liberal victory leading to a possible sectarian hegemonic "Liberal Republic" – and promised peace with his more open multi-party candidacy.

The 1978 elections showed the declining centrality of the two political parties in the name of which thousands had been killed just a few decades earlier. The National Front and the country's significant social changes had accomplished a remarkable de-segmentation, and the high rates of abstention in these elections and the emergence of significant non-electoral opposition during this period in the face of continued coalition rule showed the regime's need for transformation. Yet, the victory of Turbayistas and Alvaristas in the congressional elections and of Turbay over Betancur a few months later strengthened the perception particularly among regional party figures that it was difficult for parties or factions to survive as a "loyal opposition" (cf. Linz, 1978: 36–7). This increased opposition to long-overdue regime modification.

This perception was widely held among businessmen and high government officials as well as politicians. Almost two thirds of a sample of private sector, government and party leaders taken in 1977 and 1978 stated unequivocally that in their view a political party needed to participate in government in order to maintain itself or strengthen itself; representation in Congress was deemed insufficient.[17] A prominent Liberal politician who had been active in the MRL argued that opposition movements or party factions could survive only four to five years without access to state resources and bureaucratic posts (interview, April 1978). Conservatives, who had struggled to guarantee a continued share of government in the 1968 Constitutional Reform (see chapter 4), were among the most ardent believers of this need:

Here it is important to participate in government. Look at the last elections. The government is of fundamental importance for it controls the budget, it has the capacity to give out jobs, to control the popular will... The parties in Colombia are really sums of factions at the departmental level. (Interview with a Conservative Alvarista politician, recently re-elected Senator, April 5, 1978)

Congress has little power ... The competition for votes is at an economic level. There is a lack of resources at all levels and the government can buy consciences. The opposition can only penetrate in urban areas, for rural areas are managed by government authority. ANAPO collapsed in the opposition. People got bored and the discontented didn't vote. (Interview with an Ospinista congressman, July 29, 1978)

The 1978 elections, however, had shown that the "National Movement" strategy was viable. Thus, Betancur remained outside of government free to criticize it during the Turbay years. At the same time, both major factions of the Conservative party entered government. Betancur successfully overcame an attempt by Alvaro Gómez to capture the nomination at the Conservative convention (the factions were able to agree to hold only one), and by late 1981 was once again running for the presidency as the head of a "National Movement."

Within the Liberal Party, there was no clear presidential candidate for 1982. The principal aspirant, Virgilio Barco, appeared to be more of a technocrat than a politician and to lack the stamina for the drawn-out campaign. He was distrusted by most regional party figures. The other major aspirant, however, Alberto Santofimio, was a traditional regional politician from Tolima with almost no national presence. He was also trying to gain popularity by seeking the candidacy outside of the party rules, established by a party directorate formed by three ex-Presidents, Alfonso López, Alberto Lleras and Carlos Lleras, and the Cauca Senator, Victor Mosquera Chaux.

López' name began to emerge as a likely candidate. The two Lleras sought assurances that López would help them oversee the party nomination and not participate in it. After complex maneuvering, however, López emerged as the candidate with Santofimio as one of his campaign managers. This split the Liberal party (for López' explanation of the selection process, see *El Tiempo*, November 15, 1981). Barco, who had received support from many former Lleristas, refused to run as an anti-Lopista candidate, but a young collaborator of Carlos Lleras, Luis Carlos Galán Sarmiento, eagerly jumped in.

Galán's movement of New Liberalism (Nuevo Liberalismo), formed in 1979, attacked the Turbay government and forces behind the López candidacy as reflecting an opportunistic, clientelist, corrupt and calculating political caste: his was the voice of urban middle and upper sector groups that rejected the traditional political mores and also were upset by the drug trafficking and associated corruption. Lopistas countered that Galán represented an urban elitist rejection of emerging social groups in society, wrapped in a moralistic package with potentially fascist overtones.

At the same time Belisario's campaign possessed advantages it had lacked four years earlier. Because of growing dissatisfaction with the eight years of Liberal rule and the intense antagonism many felt toward López, Betancur's campaign enjoyed a significant increase in financial resources. Furthermore, the Conservative party was more united behind his candidacy whereas the split in the Liberal ranks was now openly represented by a candidate.

Given the extensive violence in the country – guerrillas, drug trafficking, kidnappings, and other organized and street crime– it was not surprising both candidates emphasized "peace" in their campaigns. As in 1978, Betancur emphasized that his multi-party "National Movement" was the best guarantee of continued peace in the country. Given the constitutional requirements, the appeals for continued coalition rule were somewhat artificial, though extremely well-managed. As in 1978, in addition to dissident Liberal groups, he also brought in Anapistas and the minute Christian Democratic Party. In his upbeat, optimistic campaign, Betancur also attacked clientelism and corruption and focused on selected popular issues such as housing with no down payments and more accessible university education. His populist credentials were strengthened by repeat endorsements from Gloria Gaitán, daughter of Jorge Eliécer Gaitán, and from María Eugenia Rojas.

The Lopista campaign was predicated on attempts to mobilize Liberal sympathizers more effectively than Turbay had four years earlier. The campaign sought to polarize the electorate, both to prevent votes for Galán and to convince Liberal Party identifiers to go to the polls. López' major slogan was that "Peace is Liberal," an ambiguous attempt both to revive sectarian fears of a Conservative victory and to benefit from concerns about guerrilla and criminal violence. He called for the incorporation of former guerrilla groups into the political process. López also argued that the country needed to rescind the constitutional clause on coalition governments and move to a clearer pattern of government and opposition between the two traditional parties. In addition, López called for the Liberal Party to enter the Socialist International, a way of indicating a desire to move away from the extremely pro-US foreign policy of the Turbay government, evident in Central American issues and elsewhere.

The congressional elections in March appeared to confirm that machine politics and the country's normal voting patterns continued to hold. Liberals maintained a comfortable majority over the Conservatives, and Lopistas handily defeated Galanistas throughout the country. After these results, López was confident of victory. However, in the months between these elections and the presidential ones, Betancur carried out a methodically planned campaign, strategically criss-crossing the country, employing a targeted media campaign and being careful not to over-identify with the Conservative Party. For example, during this period, he made no campaign appearances with Misael Pastrana or Alvaro Gómez, the leaders of the two major Conservative factions. And fearing that Turbay might not permit a Liberal defeat, his campaign also mounted an elaborate machinery to guarantee that fraud would not rob them of their expected victory (interviews with two figures prominent in Betancur's campaign, Summer 1982).

As the results came in, it was clear that Betancur had won a convincing victory, receiving 46.8% of the vote to López' 41.0% (Galán received 10.9%). Abstention declined by 9% compared with the 1978 elections. Major electoral shifts in three areas of the country between March and May were especially significant in explaining Belisario's victory: on the Atlantic Coast, in Bogotá and in Antioquia. López' vote on the Atlantic Coast – the region where vote-buying and machine favors are most deeply entrenched – fell by 230,000 votes compared to the March elections. This was probably due to a combination of a lack of funds and a lack of effort by the traditional regional politicians who had already been elected themselves in March. In contrast, Betancur's vote increased over 200,000 with major concentrations in the leading urban centers where image and programmatic appeals were as significant as machine favors. In Bogotá, López' vote rose over 100,000 votes, but Belisario's increased over 200,000. And in Antioquia, Betancur's birthplace, his candidacy received some 170,000 more votes than the Conservatives had won in March. Betancur's strategy of seeking to mobilize a high percentage of Conservative votes while convincing some Liberals and segments of those without party affiliation to vote for him succeeded.[18]

As in earlier elections, the left was unable to make significant electoral inroads. In March, leftist parties won only one senate seat and two seats in the chamber of representatives. In seeking a joint presidential candidate, many leftist groups agreed to support Gerardo Molina, a widely regarded scholar and social democratic critic of the Liberal Party. However, ideological divisions and personality conflicts basically reduced Molina's support to the Communist Party, and he was only able to garner 1.2% of the vote. [19]

For Colombia, the 1982 elections reflected "an unsuspected institutional maturity" (Enrique Santos Calderón in *El Tiempo*, June 2, 1982). They also reflected the varying legacies of the National Front and the ambiguities of the regime. Sectarianism was largely relegated to older generations who still remembered *la violencia* and to rural communities which had been affected by it. More significant was the mix of machine-style electoral mobilization combined with appeals based on mass media image and programmatic appeals.

At the presidential level, the results indicated that the candidate most likely to win was the one that could retain the support of regional political figures so they would "deliver" their electorates yet maintain sufficient national prominence and an image of independence in order to mobilize the increasingly more important loosely affiliated or unaffiliated electorate in urban areas. The elections also reflected the continuing inability of leftist parties to channel the country's growing social unrest to their electoral advantage.

Behind the campaign's major theme of "peace" lay the issue of regime transformation. Political blockage, immobilism and lack of popular responsiveness had combined with economic decline and a rise in violence due to the drug trafficking to generate a serious guerrilla challenge during Turbay's administration.

Guerrillas and political reform: the politics of exclusion and inclusion

During Turbay's period in office, the role of the military expanded considerably as the country faced its most serious guerrilla threat since the 1950s. As we saw above this occurred in the midst of a serious industrial recession wedded to financial speculation fueled by drug money. The scope and extent of repression in the country during Turbay's period in office was probably intensified because of the unfortunate coincidence of the particular presidential and military leadership, but at some level it may have been inevitable. Most of those who benefited from the political regime's specific arrangement – regional political leaders, economic actors, judges – responded narrowly to preserve their privileges. And Turbay was greeted by the M-19 shortly after his inauguration with an attempt on his life. Belisario's efforts to open up the regime, consonant with those preached by López in his campaign, demonstrated that elements of the national political leadership recognized the need for regime transformation. As with previous efforts toward more than gradual change in Colombia, this was to be far less successful than intended. Its unintended consequences included a strengthening of the guerrilla opposition and a hardening of attitudes by fearful elements on the right, even as state coherence suffered as well as a consequence of the vast sums of money manipulated by a small number of drug barons.

Military power increased shortly after Turbay came to office when his administration enacted a tough "statute on security" by presidential fiat using state of siege powers. The Colombian armed forces, especially the aggressive new minister of defense, General Luis Carlos Camacho Leyva, played a major role in the statute's enactment. The statute increased the kinds of crimes to be tried in military courts-martial, substantially augmented the powers of arrest of the armed forces, lengthened sentences for crimes like kidnappings and extortion, and prohibited news reports on public disturbances while they were occurring. The initial justification for the statute was that it was a tool to combat the drug traffic; in fact, it was invoked primarily in the struggle against the guerrillas.

Over the National Front years, the institutional identity and coherence of the armed forces and their growing autonomy from the two traditional parties increased. At the same time, the National Security Doctrine which flourished particularly in Brazil and the Southern Cone countries was never fully adopted in Colombia. Due to the extensive links that exist among the Latin American military, it is difficult to assert this was due to their lack of knowledge of the doctrine. Rather, consonant with the focus here on the impact of the country's political regime, Leal (1984: 263) has argued "[t]he difference of political regime and the ideological effect over the military that this has are more important than international military identity. The Colombian military themselves recognize they belong to another school."[20]

The first dramatic sign of a shift in the Colombian military occurred in December 1977. Thirty-three generals and admirals headed by General Camacho Leyva took the unprecedented step of demanding from President López emergency measures to improve the country's internal security, granting the armed forces greater powers. The civilian judicial system was harshly rebuked and the mass media criticized for their attacks on the military. López side-stepped their demands, claiming that the recently approved Constitutional Assembly would deal with the issues that concerned them. The Assembly, however, was declared unconstitutional. And Turbay had maintained close ties with the military since the 1950s. As a cabinet minister of the military junta he had been a key intermediary between the armed forces and the political parties (interviews with two retired generals who occupied important posts during the period of the military junta, Summer 1984). During the National Front he often headed congressional efforts to increase military salaries (Leal, 1984: 265).

The statute on security was used extensively during the Turbay government. Soon after its enactment, several dozen students were arrested by the military and allegedly tortured during interrogation. Then, in January 1979, the M-19 removed 4,000 arms from an army arsenal in Bogotá. Employing powers granted them by the statute, the military seized thousands of people with leftist sympathies for questioning. Torture became more prevalent; it may well have become a part of the military's institutional process as at the same time mysterious deaths and disappearances increased (see Amnistía Internacional, 1980; Leal, 1984: 266–7). The military did recover the stolen arms and broke up a large number of urban guerrilla cells. Rural violence also accelerated, especially in the Magdalena Medio, in areas of Indian lands and subsequently in Caquetá and the Putumayo. Rural assassinations and violent struggle over land increased dramatically. In some cases, taking advantage of the security statute, landowners were throwing peasants off land or seeking to consolidate their hold where tenants, squatters and Indian groups were challenging their title.

Some feared the country was beginning a process of "Uruguayization," similar to the slide toward complete military domination initiated in that country by Bordaberry. In an attempt to gain world attention and the release of many of their imprisoned leaders, the M-19 took fourteen ambassadors hostage in the Dominican Embassy in February 1980. However, the peaceful resolution of that crisis – the release of the hostages in return for safe conduct out of the country for the guerrillas, an undisclosed sum of money ostensibly raised through private channels and the promise to permit human rights groups greater access to military trials – revealed a certain weakness in the guerrillas and the continued ability of Colombian leaders to muddle through difficult situations.[21]

The guerrillas gained some public sympathy, a situation that was to increase over 1981 and 1982. At the same time, the deteriorating human rights situation was condemned by prominent members of both traditional parties in association with members of other parties and movements. The distinguished Conservative political leader, Alfredo Vázquez Carrizosa, became a key voice of protest and condemnation. The government responded to political pressure by enacting a very limited amnesty in March 1981. Rejection of the amnesty by the M-19 came only weeks later. In a shift in strategy from urban to rural guerrilla warfare, 100 guerrillas landed on the country's Pacific coast. However, most of the group was quickly killed or captured; the remnants ended up in isolated areas of the Chocó, Putumayo and Caquetá. The Caquetá became a virtual war zone, as military operations against remaining M-19 guerrillas and FARC groups in the area intensified. Equally disturbing was the appearance at the end of 1981 of the paramilitary death squad Death to Kidnappers (MAS – Muerte a Secuestradores) in Cali and Medellín.

In late 1981, though, Turbay pragmatically became more conciliatory. He appointed an *ad hoc* "peace commission" with Carlos Lleras as its head to negotiate a new amnesty with the guerrillas. Most of the M-19 leadership was dead or in jail and most military trials against the guerrillas were completed or in process. Yet the work of the peace commission met opposition from the military and from Conservatives and became embroiled in electoral politics. Some observers felt Turbay was worried that the commission's success could hurt López' ongoing campaign as the candidate was arguing that with a firm mandate he would bring "peace" to the country. Frustrated, the commission members resigned two weeks before the presidential elections. A week after Betancur's victory, Turbay announced the lifting of the state of siege, thus automatically repealing the statute on security. By that move, Turbay preempted the new president; at the time, critics also believed the move would complicate the process of negotiating a new amnesty, which would now have to be approved by Congress instead of being enacted by executive decree.

Much of the national political leadership, though, had decided that a serious effort at amnesty and political incorporation was now necessary. Carlos Lleras had acceded to head a peace commission under Turbay, and López had campaigned on the issue.[22] Official government statistics showed that the total number of armed guerrillas increased from 1,495 in 1976 to 1,895 in 1980 (Colombia, Ministerio de Gobierno, 1985: 12; other sources point to a more realistic range of between 10,000 to 15,000 during this time period). Political violence increased dramatically in 1981 and 1982 relative to Turbay's first two years. And reflecting the realities of polarization, unrealized expectations and declining state capacity, the "peace process" was to provoke even greater numbers of guerrillas (3,682 in 1984 according to the ministry of government; from 15,000 to 20,000 according to other sources) and even higher levels of violence (Table 7.3).

Betancur seized the "peace" issue and doggedly remained with it with an intensity that surprised everyone. In some respects, the period was propitious. In addition to a degree of consensus at the level of national political leadership, the M-19 was militarily decimated and the FARC had let it be known that after decades of rural struggle it was ready to talk. However, there were many obstacles. As became evident, Betancur lacked a clear strategy, and relations between him and the Liberal-dominated Congress were often tense. There were also numerous divisions within each of the guerrilla groups, exacerbated by the M-19's politically inept leadership. Links between guerrilla groups and drug traffickers and the relationship between the internal peace process and Belisario's prominent role in the Contadora Group seeking a negotiated peace to the conflicts in Central America further complicated the effort. Growing economic constraints were to prevent the implementation of promised programs in areas of guerrilla activity. And from the beginning the military had indicated their skepticism which often led to obstructionism. That skepticism was shared by some political leaders and businessmen, particularly in regions hard hit by violence and guerrilla threats, a group that grew larger as Betancur's administration progressed but the peace process dragged.

The peace process began auspiciously. In November 1982, Congress approved and the president sanctioned the broadest amnesty law ever passed in the country's history. Although prominent Liberal congressional representatives presented an

Table 7.3 *Political violence in Colombia 1975–85*

			López 1975–8				Turbay 1979–82					Betancur 1983–5		
	1975	1976	1977	1978	Total	1979	1980	1981	1982	Total	1983	1984	1985[1]	Total
Assaults	21	13	7	10	51	22	62	167	198	449	180	153	88	421
Kidnappings	7	5	9	7	28	5	11	62	93	171	113	299	177	589
Ambushes	5	2	7	3	17	8	10	13	12	43	15	13	50	78
Terrorist acts	n.a.	n.a.	2	8	10	15	31	53	126	225	115	52	390	557
Military and police casualties (dead and wounded)	39	38	62	36	175	81	46	155	123	405	164	260	462	886
Civilian casualties (dead and wounded)	44	60	47	76	227	121	79	339	396	935	412	409	554	1,375

[1]Figures only until September, 1985.
Source: Colombia, Ministerio de Gobierno, 1985.

amnesty bill, the president successfully urged passage of the bill presented by Gerardo Molina, the 1982 left opposition presidential candidate (elected to Congress). The amnesty law passed prior to any serious conversations with the guerrillas and with no promises from them regarding the handing over of arms (see Vázquez Carrizosa, 1985). And there were no legal provisions for registering or determining how many people had accepted the government's amnesty offer and no clear plans regarding what the next step should be. Some 900 jailed rebels, including top leaders of the M-19, were freed and an estimated additional 1,100 guerrillas accepted the amnesty (*New York Times*, May 22, 1984). Earlier, Betancur had named a new peace commission headed first by Carlos Lleras and then by Otto Morales Benítez, who had been active in peace efforts and Alberto Lleras' amnesty offer at the beginning of the National Front, and his attorney general had initiated an investigation of the right-wing death squad MAS (Leal, 1984: 278). The military grudgingly accepted the amnesty, but responded furiously several months later to the attorney-general's report implicating dozens of military with the MAS. The military received endorsements of support from different private sector groups, especially from cattlemen. In a compromise, it was agreed that cases involving the military and the MAS would be tried by military justice (none were).

The peace process soon seemed stalemated. The M-19 found itself politically "disarmed" by the amnesty and the president's more independent and nationalist foreign policy. The government, in turn, did not fully follow through on promises of social and political reform and, as occurred in the late 1950s and early 1960s, several amnestied leaders were assassinated. Then, in April 1983, the M-19's charismatic leader Jaime Bateman died in a plane accident. Apparently, no figure was able to emerge as a clear successor and the M-19 suffered from the lack of a unified leadership structure and a coherent strategy. It announced it was breaking the truce it had initiated several months earlier, strengthening the hand of hard-liners within the regime. In May, the head of the peace commission resigned in frustration, indirectly accusing the military of obstructionism. Bloody conflicts intensified in the Magdalena Medio, as the army remained in place in Tolima, Caquetá and elsewhere.

But Betancur did not relent. At the same time, he devoted increased energies to the Central American conflict and the

Contadora group which Colombia helped form in January 1983 (along with Mexico, Venezuela and Panama). For Betancur, the two efforts reflected a symmetry of belief: that the guerrilla struggles responded to internal social and political problems and were best resolved by negotiation. At the same time, his more independent foreign policy was intended to provide support for his domestic policy and to distance himself from a US policy which focused on military solutions to guerrilla problems. His policy was also expected to reduce the country's diplomatic isolation on the continent, a consequence of Turbay's pro-US foreign policy, and to gain Cuba's acceptance for Colombia's own peace process. Cuba had earlier provided a safe haven for the M-19 which had led Turbay to break relations with the island republic following the 1981 M-19 invasion. As part of his Central American peace effort, Betancur met with representatives of Salvadoran guerrilla groups in Bogotá. In October, he met secretly with leaders of the M-19 in Spain. He pushed the peace commission, now headed by John Agudelo Ríos, to continue negotiations toward a truce with the guerrillas. The commission focused its attention on the larger and more "professional" FARC (interview with a member of the peace commission, Bogotá, Summer 1986).

At the same time, the military became bolder in their pronouncements against the peace process. The minister of defense, General Fernando Landazábal, openly criticized the Communist Party for its presumed links to the FARC and in November 1983 claimed the amnesty granted the previous November had expired. Tensions built into a major confrontation between Landazábal and Betancur in January 1984, which led to the resignation of Landazábal and four other generals. However, in respecting military hierarchy and promoting General Gustavo Matamoros to the cabinet, Betancur replaced one hard-liner by another. A seeming final blow to the process came in March 1984 when a splinter group of the M-19 brazenly attacked Florencia, the capital of Caquetá, forcing Betancur to impose a partial state of siege.

However, shortly after that attack, on March 28, 1984, the government's peace commission signed a truce with the FARC, which was to begin two months later. The document expressed the peace commission's belief that the government was willing to seek political and socio-economic reforms and to guarantee appropriate conditions for the FARC to devote itself to political and electoral activities. Violence from a different direction then threatened the peace process. The state of siege was extended to the whole country in April when the minister of justice, Rodrigo Lara Bonilla, was killed. Lara had been carrying out an increasingly more effective campaign against drug-traffickers, who it was presumed had him killed.[23]

In August, the peace commission signed a truce with the M-19, the EPL and the ADO. This occurred in spite of fears about the reimplantation of the state of siege, the assassination of Carlos Toledo Plata, a prominent amnestied M-19 leader, and an audacious attack by the M-19 on a Cali suburb. This agreement differed from the one with the FARC in March in that it called for a "great national dialogue" to discuss and propose political, social and economic reforms. Yet, as with the truce signed in March, this one also fell considerably short of being a peace treaty. Considerable ambiguity remained regarding weapons in possession of guerrillas and how subsequent steps would be taken. However, only a few minor guerrilla groups now remained outside of the peace process.

By the Fall 1984, though, it had become clear that the government would have to take drastic action to reduce its growing deficit, and to address the country's precarious balance of payments. There would be no money for social reforms or for public works in areas of guerrilla activity. Attention focused increasingly on political reforms, the "democratic opening" (*apertura democrática*) that political leaders had been discussing for several years. With the signing of the agreements with the guerrillas and the call for a "national dialogue," the two processes – of peace and political reform – became linked more directly (Santamaría & Silva, 1984: 68).

Betancur and political reform

During the López and Turbay periods various suggestions for political reform were presented, though none prospered. The most significant was López' Constitutional Assembly, discussed above. Subsequently, bills seeking to institutionalize the parties, to provide guarantees so political parties would be more willing to serve as opposition and to improve the electoral system were presented in Congress without gaining approval (Santamaría &

Silva, 1984: 51). Discussions during the López and Turbay administrations to remove the constitutional requirement that participation in government be offered to the party receiving the second highest number of votes (article 120) did not prosper. Mutual distrust (and differences between national and regional leaders) marked these conversations between Liberals and Conservatives over civil service reforms, guaranteed media access and suggestions that the minority party be guaranteed control of the Contraloría and the Procuraduría, oversight agencies that could paralyze the state and were also rich sources of patronage.

Early in Turbay's administration there was an effort to correct some of the more glaring congressional and judicial institutional flaws, though without breaking out of the constraining mold of coalition rule. The 1979 Constitutional Reform sought to improve the agility of Congress and permit it to regain some of the power it had lost as a consequence of the 1968 Constitutional Reform.[24] The reform also sought to reduce the power of judges to select themselves and removed the requirement for political parity from all but the top judicial levels.

Two years after its enactment the Supreme Court declared the Reform unconstitutional, provoking a major crisis. The primary reason alleged by the Court were procedural flaws in the Reform's passage by Congress. As with López' Constitutional Assembly, however, many observers felt that the Reform's curtailment of judicial power may well have played a role in the court's decision. When news leaked out several days prior to the formal announcement that by a bare majority of fifteen votes (of twenty-eight) the Reform had been found unconstitutional, Turbay sought to save the Reform by decreeing that a three-fourths majority was necessary to declare constitutional reforms unconstitutional. The Supreme Court and leading political figures firmly rejected Turbay's effort to block the decision (*El Tiempo*, November 3 and 4, 1981; Arboleda, 1981: 79–81).

There was a growing realization among the national political leadership of both parties that political reforms were necessary. In addition to the frustrated efforts discussed above, in the final months of Turbay's government, the minister of government and prominent Liberal leader, Jorge Mario Eastman, published extensive studies regarding various reforms to open up the political process to other parties and movements, increase participation and modernize the country's political and electoral structures

(Santamaría & Silva, 1984: 57). The government had also sponsored another foreign tax mission, headed by Richard Bird and
the minister of finance Eduardo Wiesner Durán, to study issues of
public finance, particularly relating to financial and administrative decentralization. More effective popular participation, including the direct election of mayors, would only be meaningful if
combined with administrative decentralization and the financial
strengthening of the country's departments and municipalities
(see Bird et al., 1981; Botero, 1980; and Santamaría & Silva, 1984:
129–36).

From the beginning of his administration Betancur also insisted
on the need for reform to open up the political process, though he
devoted less attention to this topic than to the amnesty or foreign
policy. The political reforms did not have even the early successes
that the amnesty and the shifts in foreign policy had. Through the
ministry of government, the administration promoted meetings–
an *ad hoc* forum – of the traditional parties and other political
movements to discuss transforming a broad set of reform proposals into new legislation. These included measures such as the
institutionalization of political parties, guarantees to opposition
movements, partial state financing of campaigns, improvements
in the electoral process to minimize fraud, civil service reform,
improved access of political movements to the mass media,
administrative decentralization and the popular election of
mayors. In the end, the government only presented a few
measures to the 1983 session and none achieved passage. The
administration did not put its full weight behind the measures and
congressmen did not perceive changes in the political rules of the
game to be to their advantage (Santamaría & Silva, 1984; interviews with two leading congressmen, Summer 1984).

In 1984, consideration of the political reforms and the peace
process were more directly joined following the signing of the
agreements with the major guerrilla groups. Yet, Betancur was
now in a far weaker position than when he was inaugurated.
Opposition to the peace process was expanding far beyond the
military and initially skeptical political and economic groups
while the president's popularity had plummeted from its initial
highs. With the signing of the truce, guerrilla groups, particularly
the M-19, organized demonstrations in the country's major cities.
At the same time, the "national dialogue" with a large number of
participants (forty) and sub-commissions (ten, each with thirty

members) soon became bogged down due to resistance from government and political circles (see Colombia, Ministerio de Gobierno, 1986; and Restrepo, 1986: 128–39). The armed forces and many producer groups and political leaders feared that guerrilla groups were gaining inordinate strength. In their view the president's capacity to negotiate was weak, the process too drawn out and the economic situation unpromising. A president spearheading an effort at a negotiated settlement in Central America could not effectively negotiate – using sticks as well as carrots – with guerrilla groups in his own country. The drawn-out negotiating process had permitted guerrilla groups that had been decimated or isolated in outlying rural areas to re-group, and, especially after the truce agreements, to expand in size and develop more coherent urban networks. Businessmen complained of being threatened if they did not provide "campaign contributions"; cattlemen and ranchers asserted that "voluntary quotas" were still being required of them; and traditional politicians claimed that peasants were being warned not to attend their campaign functions.[25] Tensions were exacerbated as the government began imposing an austerity program in late 1984 and had to go to Congress to request additional tax revenues. Betancur's influence over Congress was waning and Liberals, though divided, were positioning themselves for the 1986 elections (see Deas, 1986).

By the end of 1984, the peace process was languishing. In typically dramatic last-minute maneuverings, though, the administration was able to push the popular election of mayors through the first of two necessary congressional approvals (because it was a constitutional reform) as well as gain passage for several other minor political reforms. In extra sessions called by the president in early 1985, a bill calling for a pardon for past political crimes was approved only due to firm government determination, even though ostensibly it was supported by the national directorates of both traditional parties, by the Galanistas and the Communists. The government was less successful regarding the political reforms, most of which were postponed for consideration in the subsequent session of Congress.

The M-19 continued to confront government, especially military, hostility as it retained its status as a guerrilla movement but increasingly operated as a political organization. From its perspective, the minister of government was attempting to

replace the agreement of a national dialogue leading to a democratic opening and then to legalization of the guerrilla forces by
an exclusionary process that would lead to a timetable for
legalization, handing over of weapons by the guerrillas and only
then political reform (Restrepo, 1986: 219; subsequently, the
M-19 nearly succeeded in an assassination attempt on the minister).
The military encircled a major M-19 base and in February 1985,
the government prohibited and the military sought to restrict
access to an M-19 "congress" in rural Valle. Similarly, a growing
network of M-19 "peace bases" (*campamentos de paz*) in poor urban
neighborhoods in Cali and other cities became a focus of growing
regime concern. Fearing they were guerrilla recruitment centers,
for which no evidence was presented, many were invaded and
closed down by the military. In May 1985, less than a year after
the assassination of Carlos Toleda Plata, the M-19 top leadership
in Cali narrowly missed being killed in a grenade attack.

One day before a national strike called by the CSTC in June, the
M-19 declared it was breaking the truce as its "legal" representatives went underground (*El Tiempo*, June 23, 1985). Although the
day of the strike evolved relatively peacefully, in the subsequent
weeks clashes between the army and the M-19 intensified. The M-
19 sought to unify all guerrilla movements in an umbrella
guerrilla organization, the National Guerrilla Coordinator (CNG
– Coordinadora Nacional Guerrillera). It was joined by the ELN,
the "Ricardo Franco" splinter group from the FARC, the new
indigenously based "Quintín Lame", and by the EPL after one of
its major leaders was assassinated following his emergence from
clandestinity.[26] The M-19's return to a military strategy combined
with an apparent effort to regain the political offensive set the
scene for its dramatic takeover in November of the country's
Palace of Justice which faced Congress on the main plaza in
downtown Bogotá. The ensuing military assault resulted in the
death of half the country's Supreme Court judges, all of the M-19
participants and scores of others. President Betancur was left
assuming responsibility for a military action many asserted he did
not fully control.

The tenuous truce with the largest guerrilla group, the FARC,
continued to hold. In March, 1985, the FARC established a political
party, Patriotic Unity (UP – Unión Patriótica). Yet business,
military and church opposition to FARC-UP participation in elections without handing over its weapons intensified. Ultimately,

though, the ambiguity of FARC's status was allowed to stand as the government desired the truce to continue and could not force the FARC to hand over its arms. Instead, a new agreement was signed simply extending the earlier truce agreement. As the UP prepared for elections, the Communist Party served as a crucial logistical support. The UP also arranged for a number of coalition lists with factions of the Liberal Party. In the 1986 congressional elections, the total vote of single and coalition UP lists approached 300,000. In absolute numbers this was around twice as many votes as the left had received in preceding elections, though in percentage terms (4.4%) it was similar to results in 1976, 1978 and 1980 (see Table 6.1). As a consequence of these elections, the UP was able to gain eight congressional seats (and the possibility of six others as substitutes), 22 deputies in departmental assemblies and representation in 150 municipal councils (*El Tiempo*, March 16, 1986). The UP gained a plurality or a majority in over a dozen municipalities.

The FARC's principal leaders did not participate actively in the elections. Due to the activities of right-wing death squads and the lack of guarantees, Jacobo Arenas and Manuel Marulanda, the legendary FARC leaders, opted to remain in their jungle hideout. Their concern was not misplaced as a number of elected UP legislators were assassinated in the months following the elections. After Arenas rejected a presidential bid, the UP chose Jaime Pardo Leal, an independent left-wing labor activist, as their presidential candidate. His vote of 4.5% reflected considerable growth over that of previous leftist presidential candidates (see Table 6.2).

As the election campaign proceeded, modest progress was being achieved in advancing political reforms that reduced centralization and exclusionary bipartisanship. The most significant step was the successful passage (for the critical second time) in December 1985 of the constitutional amendment calling for the popular election of mayors. Political resistance was eased by delaying implementation of the measure until 1988. The reform was given added meaning by various fiscal measures that were intended to increase the flow of resources to the departmental and municipal levels, although these will probably affect primarily the larger cities and municipalities that can charge special natural resource taxes. Other laws, some considerably weakened in congressional debate and others passed with little attention to detail, touched on electoral reform, civil service, party structure, campaign financing, regionalization and access to television and to public information (see Colombia, Ministerio de Gobierno, 1986; interviews with political figures, Bogotá, Summer 1986). Some of the more dramatic features of bipartisan rule were removed. For example, a more powerful National Electoral Council (Consejo Nacional Electoral) that replaced the Electoral Court (Corte Electoral) was to be formed not only by three members of the two major parties but also by one member from a third party (Law 96 of 1985).

Yet, more far-reaching political reforms, such as large-scale, multi-level implementation of civil service, or openness, accountability and limits to campaign financing or electoral reforms to provide minority parties more access to legislative posts, did not pass. And, the two traditional parties could still not agree on a formula to dismantle the constitutional formula requiring the winning party to offer the party coming in second participation in government. Furthermore, none of the socio-economic reforms presented in Congress were approved.

In this tumultuous context, preparations for the 1986 elections within the traditional parties continued. Virgilio Barco quickly emerged as the Liberal candidate for the presidency, this time with the endorsement of all the Liberal ex-presidents including López. Galán opted to continue as the head of his separate Nuevo Liberalismo movements. And in the Conservative Party, Alvaro Gómez again gained the nomination to seek the presidency. The relatively high participation rate in congressional elections reflected somewhat easier registration procedures in urban areas and growing politicization in the country. Results showed the continuing traditional Liberal dominance (see Table 6.1), though the extremely poor showing of Nuevo Liberalismo lists (6.6% of the vote) convinced Galán to withdraw from the presidential race. With an increasingly discredited Betancur administration, the peace process in shambles, violence of all kinds in ascendance, and with Gómez unable to shake his sectarian Conservative image, the stage was set for an overwhelming victory by Barco (see Table 6.2). The Liberal candidate successfully mobilized large elements of the potentially mobilizable Liberal and independent urban vote while maintaining a high provincial and rural vote through the support of regional leaders.

Barco's overwhelming victory led to another significant political event: formation of a single party government and return to a "government–opposition" form of government. Barco campaigned on the pledge to pursue a Liberal "government-program" which potential Conservative Party collaborators would have to accept if they were to participate in his government. Following the Conservative defeat, Pastrana called for Conservative refusal to participate at top levels of government, though he insisted that oversight agencies should remain in Conservative hands (*El Tiempo*, May 2, 1986). Technically following the requirements of article 120, Barco named three Conservatives to Cabinet positions upon his inauguration, though (as Betancur before him) he did not consult with the opposing party's directorate regarding the appointments. The Conservatives rejected the positions, criticized the government for its refusal to dialogue and entered into "reflexive opposition." To attempt to manage the transition to a "government–opposition" form of government, Barco appointed Fernando Cepeda as his minister of government. Cepeda was a legal scholar and political scientist who had been advocating the need for this change (see Lewin, 1986).

Barco's government confronted three major challenges. First, it was attempting to reaffirm more democratic "rules of the game," reclaiming a legitimate role for opposition, opening up the political process to minority groups and trying to restore the importance of the national Congress as a center of national debate. The risk was that the "government–opposition" formula could be perceived as an attempt merely to reinvigorate and refurbish an exclusionary bipartisanship. Second, it was seeking to regain state coherence and strengthen vital state institutions, such as the judiciary, under challenge from guerrillas, drug lords and criminal violence. And finally, it was seeking to make some progress on the socio-economic front, particularly by developing rehabilitation programs for areas of guerrilla activity. The administration was also seeking agrarian and urban reforms, though these were not likely to progress in Congress. Conservatives were maintaining a polemical political opposition while preparing for the 1988 mayoral elections and the FARC remained in an armed truce, retaining its guerrilla status as it began to separate organizationally from the UP. The Colombian state was under challenge and the country's limited democratic consociational regime, its legitimacy eroded but its capacity for change not yet exhausted, was in the midst of a process of redefinition and re-accommodation.

Possible regime directions

The direction the transformation of the Colombian consociational political regime will take is still in flux. Certain of the alternatives discussed in chapter 1 and presented at the beginning of this chapter can be largely discarded. A reversion to conflict between the segments that formed the consociational agreement in Colombia, between the two traditional parties, is not conceivable. Although the Conservatives are still the minority party in Colombia, the issue that precipitated the breakdown in 1949 – fear of permanent exclusion from power – is no longer salient. The rhetorical excesses of the contemporary period between the two parties will not help spawn consequences similar to those of the 1940s. No major issues separate the two parties at the elite level. The centrality of the parties to elite–mass relations has also declined, particularly in urban areas where an increasing share of the population now resides. Sectarianism, patron–client and brokerage ties mobilize an important but declining percentage of the population, and the parties have made little progress toward establishing themselves on a more institutional and participatory basis.

Another scenario that can be discarded is that one party will unilaterally seek to impose its rule in some hegemonic, dictatorial fashion over the other party and over the country as a whole. Producer associations have links with both parties and both parties receive support from all social groups in society. Factions across parties often have had more in common than factions within the same party on social and economic issues and bipartisan coalitions on regional issues have been common. At the same time, over the period of the National Front, national political leaders have lost influence within their parties relative to regional leaders. These regional politicians have delayed and resisted the dismantling of coalition rule and other political reforms because of the overwhelming importance of participation in government for their brokerage function and possibilities of re-election, even as national leaders have recognized the growth of non-electoral opposition as a symptom of the need to transform the regime. As discussed in this chapter, a possible transformation of the regime could result from the emergence of violent conflict by the interjection of new segments and other issues. From its inception, National Front leaders had as one concern the potential of class-oriented or revolutionary struggle. In 1957–8, consociationalism was a response to crisis, permitting the establishment of a limited democratic regime. The nature of that regime's political process has permitted substantial economic progress, though with little redistributive impact. That regime is now in crisis as the social and political bases for its existence have been sharply eroded, in important respects because of the agreement itself. During its almost thirty-year existence the regime has appeared more contingent than consolidated because of the nature of the bipartisan agreement which encouraged crisis decision-making, because of the social tensions associated with the country's uneven process of development and because of the increasing perception of its politically exclusionary nature.

With a decline in party segmentation, the country initiated a process of polarization in the late 1970s as different forms of non-electoral opposition de-linked from the traditional parties gained in importance. At the same time, drug trafficking, the growing ineffectiveness of the judicial system as well as increased criminal violence facilitated by these factors and the declining economic situation have led to a decline in state coherence.

The Turbay and Betancur administrations responded to the situation with a mix of exclusionary and inclusionary policies. Turbay's period in office was marked by a sharp increase in exclusionary, repressive policies and the clearer emergence of a more institutionally coherent armed forces differentiated from both of the traditional parties. Yet, during Turbay's period in office there was some resistance to his policies from within both traditional parties. By the end of his term, with part of the guerrilla forces militarily weakened, Turbay was striving toward a more conciliatory pose. Betancur unambiguously sought a negotiated peace with the guerrilla forces and an opening up of the political process, though he never chose a strategy of mobilizing sectors of the population in support of his policies. Paradoxically, his term in office witnessed increased violence and a stronger guerrilla movement. The reasons his efforts largely failed are complex. One problem was an evident lack of clarity regarding his administration's strategy and goals. This intensified existing resistance from the military, as well as from within the traditional parties and from producer groups as the peace process dragged on and the guerrilla groups appeared to be regaining strength. The difficulty of seeking an end to guerrilla violence was compounded by the challenges to the viability of the state represented by the presence of high levels of criminal and drug-related violence from which guerrilla activity was not always easily differentiated and by the intense economic problems that affected his administration.

What is the regime's most likely transformation? In late 1986, Colombians feared the degeneration of the current state of violence into civil war ("Salvadorization") or reactive repression and military terror ("Argentinization"). The activities of urban and rural guerrilla and terrorist groups could augment the fears of business groups regarding their safety, generate continued official repression and strengthen rightist paramilitary groups, leading to an increasing spiral of reaction and counter-reaction that in a context of declining state coherence could conceivably lead to military domination. During the Turbay period, some observers feared what they then termed the "Uruguayization" of Colombia, a gradual military takeover of government. Then came the surprising shift under Betancur supported by elements of both traditional parties. Although constraints on Betancur showed that the military have gained a certain autonomy in the regime, civilians still appear to have maintained an important degree of control. A military intervention could not be entirely ruled out, though it appears especially unlikely in the current period of democratization throughout Latin America.

Could Colombia move in the direction of consolidating a more competitive democratic political regime? As occurred with Austria and the Netherlands in the 1960s, in Colombia in the 1980s consociational mechanisms were still in place long after any clear need for them. Unlike the Austrian and Dutch cases, however, Colombia is a less-developed country with substantial social and economic inequalities, a high degree of violence, and a weak state under challenge. The resistance to Betancur's efforts to promote amnesty and political reform, the continuing wave of guerrilla violence, the challenge to state authority represented by drug trafficking and the country's short-term economic problems indicate the regime is still far from state coherence and democratic consolidation. At the same time, the efforts by Presidents Betancur and Barco to seek a political opening, though only partially successful, and the existence of bipartisan support for these reforms, though far from unanimous, are significant. They indicate there is a growing consciousness that if the route of reform and incorporation is not at least partially taken the alternative is a continuing spiral of polarization and violence.

Democratic consolidation would almost certainly be centered on the country's two traditional parties, though not in their current form. It would require broader political participation both by other political movements and within the two parties and greater access to the economic benefits of the regime for wider sectors of the population. The struggle for an alternative political basis for the regime is still in process. It involves a means of moving away from the remaining strictures of coalition rule while striking a balance between traditional brokerage politics and a politics that effectively reaches out to new groups and movements. The campaigns of Betancur in 1982 and of Barco in 1986, the electoral results for the UP in 1986 and the emergence of Galán as Carlos Lleras' generational successor in the Liberal Party are indications of such an effort, though still with a limited base. The popular election of mayors combined with guarantees for the physical safety of all parties to campaign and with financial and administrative decentralization could reduce the advantages of traditional coalition brokerage politics, at least in the larger population centers. This could help loosen the stranglehold of the two traditional parties on the country's electoral and political process. Confronted with more vigorous electoral opposition, the two parties might seek to rebuild themselves organizationally and more effectively reach out to the urban electorate. However, many elements cloud the picture. The state faces severe challenges, regional economic and political interests feel insecure, the military resists conciliation and the short-term economic situation is uncertain.

The Colombian political process has confounded pessimists and disappointed optimists. If the recent past is the best indicator of the immediate future, then the process of consociational transformation, of political re-accommodation, will be drawn-out, resisted and uneven.

8

Consociationalism and political conflict in comparative perspective

Consociationalism is a model for democratic politics in countries wracked by violence or threatened by it. Conceptually distinct from democracy, its practices partially circumscribe a regime's democratic nature, even as they often facilitate the practice of at least a qualified kind of democratic politics in certain countries. In this book, I have employed a regime-centered analysis to examine consociationalism in Colombia in an integrated fashion, analyzing the importance of consociational practices for the establishment of limited democratic rule in the country, the management of its tensions and predicaments and the prospects of alternative kinds of transformation.

In the next section, this chapter analyzes comparatively some of the central issues raised by the Colombian case regarding consociationalism and the establishment of open civilian regimes. Colombia is a clear and intriguing case of consociationalism with several distinctive features. Consociational practices appeared necessary rather than simply helpful for a successful transition to civilian rule in 1958. At the same time, the conflict was centered around two political parties with a long history of violent inter-action and accommodation, rather than being based upon religious, ethnic, linguistic, regional or ideological issues traditionally considered in the literature. And unlike the European cases of consociationalism, the regime was based upon a rigid, constitutionally-mandated agreement.

At the most basic level, the regime has been successful: it has survived, inter-party violence has receded and the country as a whole has prospered, if unevenly. Yet, as we have argued, after more than twenty-five years the regime remains some distance from being a consolidated democracy. In that respect, unfortunately, Colombia has considerable company among less-developed countries. In the chapters above, the Colombian regime's response to its consociational predicaments in a changing society has been emphasized in explaining the difficulties in moving toward broader and more consolidated democratic rule. In sections below, this chapter considers issues of consociationalism and democratic consolidation in a comparative setting. First it explores the relationship between consociationalism and corporatism in different consociational cases. Then, it turns to an examination of issues in consociational transformation and democracy.

Consociationalism and the transition to democracy

The need for and the usefulness of consociational mechanisms for democratic rule, as distinct from simply a general atmosphere of commitment to democratic principles and to accommodation, depends upon the nature and intensity of prior or potential conflict between identifiable groups in society and upon whether these mechanisms are to be applied in the context of an ongoing political regime or in a transition from military rule, colonial rule, foreign occupation or some other context. In Colombia, and commonly in other Latin American cases, the consociational literature is applied in the context of transition from military rule. In contrast, the European cases have involved ongoing regimes (such as the Netherlands) or new regimes following foreign occupation (such as Austria). The Third World cases of Cyprus, Lebanon and Malaysia have all consisted of regimes formed immediately following independence from colonial rule. In countries where regime breakdown occurred because of violent conflict between readily identifiable groups a strong argument can be made that consociational mechanisms may be necessary, rather than simply helpful, for a democratic transition: this we have argued is the case for Colombia, and a strong argument can also be made for the Austrian case. Few would disagree that if Cyprus or Lebanon today are to be reconstituted as single states, much less as democratic polities, consociational mechanisms will almost certainly be necessary. These are cases in which the likelihood of democratic politics is small but much more favorable with consociational mechanisms.

In the Latin American context, where societal conflict has largely not fallen along the ethnic or religious lines analyzed by the consociational literature, the relevant question is more whether in some cases consociational mechanisms may be helpful, even if not strictly necessary, in a transition from military to civilian rule. The Colombian case is somewhat anomalous in Latin America in that no other country on the continent has had a similar patterning of structured identification around two political parties with deep historical roots combined with such intensive civil strife. Thus, *consociational regimes* are much less likely to emerge or necessarily to be desirable (more on that later) in other Latin American countries. However, where conflict channelled by political parties played a central role in regime breakdown as in Chile, Venezuela and to a lesser extent Uruguay, it would appear that consociational mechanisms could play a useful role in a democratic transition.

Venezuela underwent a successful transition to democracy around the same time as Colombia with a number of striking similarities. Bitter conflict sparked by the reformist efforts of the governing Acción Democrática (AD) party and the fears of other parties that they could never electorally defeat the AD during the brief democratic interlude of the *trienio* (1945–8) paved the way for military rule. However, in Venezuela all the major parties were new organizations and there had been nothing comparable to the Colombian *violencia*. Furthermore, party figures from all the major parties had suffered exile or imprisonment under what was the longer, more brutal and repressive government of Pérez Jiménez in contrast to the more benign rule of Rojas in Colombia. A less rigid and more limited agreement to respect the elections, support a common minimum program and agree to form part of a coalition government was also expressed in a formal pact (the Pact of Punto Fijo) signed by the three major parties. As in Colombia, though an over-arching coalition was formed, parties on the left (namely, the Communist Party) were excluded. The military were provided with guarantees that examination of corruption would focus on the deposed military leader and not the military institution. And the more secular AD party provided specific guarantees to the Church. In both Colombia and Venezuela the electorally stronger party had lost power in the 1940s, in one case fueled by internal divisions and in another by excessive zeal, and subsequently accepted a reduced role in a coalition to assure broad civilian support for the overthrow of the military and the establishment of a civilian regime, though AD did not tie its hands the way the Liberal Party felt forced to in Colombia. A significant difference was that mass mobilization played a limited but significant role in the overthrow of Pérez Jiménez in contrast to the totally marginal role it played in the overthrow of Rojas.

The rituals of pact-making certainly provided crucial assurances in Venezuela. Ultimately, though, the willingness to compromise and conciliate expressed in the ways in which opposition politics was carried out and in specific policy arenas such as educational reform may have been more important than formal pacts. By the next presidential election in 1963, the Christian Democratic party (COPEI), which received the second highest number of votes, refused to form part of a coalition government. At the same time, it continued to have access to some patronage and faithfully played the role of a "loyal opposition" (on the Venezuelan transition, see Levine, 1978; Karl, 1981; and Kelley, 1977).

A transition process with a more limited role for formal interparty pacts occurred in Uruguay over the 1980–5 period. As in Colombia, in Uruguay two parties formed in the nineteenth century have dominated the political landscape. Similarly, the Uruguayan Blanco and Colorado parties were both factionalized and dependent upon patronage and machine politics for electoral mobilization. Also, consociational practices, such as the granting of regional autonomy to the Blanco party by the governing Colorado party or a bipartisan plural executive, have also been present in different periods of Uruguayan history. Economic decline, the emergence of the urban terrorist Tupamaros, military "new professionalism" oriented toward internal security and a more powerful, independent and radical organized labor movement all played a role in the deterioration and ultimate breakdown in 1973 of what had been Latin America's most democratic polity (see Gillespie, 1984 and Gillespie & González, 1985). Yet, a central factor was the declining linkages of the two political parties with Uruguayan society. The parties were factionalized, poorly organized and entrenched in an increasingly bankrupt large state apparatus which constrained their access to patronage. And Uruguay's unusual electoral system apparently did not help. This system has permitted different factions within each party to present presidential candidates and to have all votes cast for a party to go to the candidate within that party with the most votes. In 1971, that meant that the conservative Colorado

Bordaberry won the election with the help of votes cast for a moderate Colorado in spite of the fact that the reformist Blanco candidate Ferreira had received a plurality of the votes cast. Bordaberry formed a coalition government with conservative Blancos and governed in increasingly anti-democratic fashion, brutally confronting guerrilla activity and labor strife.

Breakdown in Uruguay, unlike the situation in Colombia and Venezuela, had less to do with the confrontational interaction between leaders or members of the two major parties *per se* than it did with other factors. It had not been open conflict between adherents of the two parties fueled by a breakdown of party elite negotiations (as in Colombia) or bitter policy, ideological and electoral debates between the two parties threatening key constituencies (as in Venezuela) that had precipitated regime breakdown. For that reason, the transition from military to civilian rule which culminated with the inauguration in 1985 of a Colorado President, though it involved extensive negotiation and compromise, could succeed while possessing fewer consociational elements. Although disorganized at the time due to military repression, the two parties in Uruguay did cooperate in an unparalleled defeat of a regime plebiscite in 1980 to ratify a Constitution that would have entrenched military control, and they held joint rallies such as one that drew over a quarter of a million people in Montevideo in November, 1983. Yet, given the different nature and continued coherence of this bureaucratic–authoritarian regime compared to the military regimes of the 1950s, pact-making occurred primarily *between the parties and the military*, who were negotiating their exit from power. Unlike the personalistic governments of Pérez Jiménez and Rojas, in Uruguay the military as an institution were in control of the state apparatus in a far more complex society.[1]

As the process unfolded, the unusual circumstance of the Blanco party refusing to join other parties in negotiating with the military ostensibly because of a more extreme democratic position (reflecting their insistence that the political rights of their leader Ferreira be fully restored) permitted the other parties, including those on the left, to appear more moderate and reasonable (see Gillespie, 1985: 1–15). Blanco intransigence was fueled in part by the desire for electoral advantage. Although disturbing to the military, the Blanco posture was less threatening to economically dominant groups because it did not revolve primarily around socio-economic issues. Furthermore, the potential for terrorist violence was low and the left opposition groups sought to provide assurances of their commitment to democratic practices. As in Colombia, the political–electoral dominance of these two heterogeneous parties increased the confidence of economically dominant classes that they would not be at risk in a democratic transition; on the contrary, in Uruguay the fear was that continued military rule could affect the viability of this relatively "safe" system with two dominant parties (see Stepan, 1985: 325–9).

Consociationalism is of potentially greater relevance in contemporary Chile than in Uruguay, though of much more difficult application than it was in Venezuela. To a much greater extent than in the Uruguayan case in Chile regime breakdown in 1973 was fueled by escalating conflict between readily identifiable groups – social classes – channelled through political parties (though all major political parties were to some extent multi-class parties, their political, ideological and class perspectives were quite clearly differentiated). Because the extent of polarization prior to the coup that ushered the bureaucratic–authoritarian regime into power in Chile was considerably higher than in Uruguay, support among upper and middle classes for the Pinochet regime and fear of the possible consequences of a democratic transition (with its polarized party system) have been far higher than was true in Uruguay (not to mention the earlier cases of Colombia and Venezuela) (see O'Donnell, 1978). The Chilean military have remained institutionally coherent though dominated largely by the figure of Pinochet. As in Uruguay and distinct from the focus of the consociational model, any successful, real democratic transition would almost certainly have to result from an extended period of negotiation with the armed forces, facilitated perhaps by divisions within them (such as over leadership succession). The likelihood of a military collapse such as in the Argentine case appears remote. Yet, in either case, in spite of the Chilean military's efforts to reshape Chilean society and thus the country's party system, the dangers of renewed polarization remain high.

The nature and intensity of the prior conflict between the parties currently militates against a consociational pact encompassing all the major political parties active in the Allende period. Ideological differences among the main opposition groups have been heightened by the absence of elections and uncertainty about the timing of a political opening (cf. Valenzuela & Valenzuela, 1983: 35; see also Fleet, 1985: 194–210). The pursuit of "maximalist" socio-economic goals by insurrectional means by some leftist groups (in contrast to events in Uruguay) has strengthened the resolve of the military who have a "constitutional" transition in place as a result of a 1980 plebiscite.[2] Consociational pacts may be easier when the conflict is over how to agree to "live and let live" (group autonomy) or over how to share divisible goods (patronage); in the Chilean case, the experience of polarization and repression has not induced all groups to agree to recommit to a democratic process in part due to fears of some parties that their participation could be effectively constrained by the military. Unlike the Colombian and Venezuelan cases, there is not a sufficiently dominant "moderate" over-sized party willing to underplay its potential power to help facilitate an agreement and there is a far more organized and class-oriented left.

The differences between the transition to civilian rule in Colombia in 1958 and current transitions in Latin American countries reflects the nature of the country's social structure with its two hierarchical, multi-class, deeply entrenched and historically antagonistic political parties, the ferocity and degeneration of violence in the 1950s as well as the nature of the military regime that was replaced. In other Latin American countries, consociational practices may provide important assurances and guarantees that strengthen the hand of opposition forces joined together to oppose both continued military rule as well as other potential opponents to the democratic transition (whether from the right or the left) – at the moment of transition and shortly afterwards – without being absolutely necessary. Thus, democratic transitions employing consociational pacts are, strictly speaking, probably necessary in only a few country cases; and that very fact often means that any kind of democratic transition in these cases is improbable. However, forces opposed to military rule and in favor of a democratic transition may find consociational pacts to be helpful in two kinds of situations. To the extent political parties are an important part of a country's social structure and regime breakdown was associated (in the not too distant past) with their past interaction, the extension of mutual guarantees via consociational mechanisms could be of crucial importance in a transition effort. And to the extent military withdrawal is occurring by means of gradual steps or by uncertain negotiations with a relatively coherent military institution, opposition unity and thus consociational guarantees may also prove helpful.

Consociationalism and corporatism

Consociational mechanisms provide political guarantees and assurances across groups in conflict or potential conflict. Consociationalism entails the granting of considerable autonomy to leaders to negotiate with each other. Particularly in Latin American cases, it has entailed assurances (whether implicitly or explicitly) to economically dominant groups and the military that the socio-economic order would not be radically threatened, a threat that played a role – with considerable variation and filtered through other political processes – in initial regime breakdown in many cases. In Colombia, the support of industrial, commercial and financial elites was crucial for the overthrow of Rojas and successful establishment of the National Front. And in Venezuela, the political parties' common minimum program provided assurances to economic elites that had felt threatened by the policies of Acción Democrática in the *trienio* period. The center and right coalition in Venezuela in the early 1960s was strengthened by fear of a left committed to a strategy of insurrection.

Indeed, one characteristic of consociational arrangements in most countries is that even at a formal political level they are not completely inclusionary. In Colombia, the parity requirement effectively excluded leftist forces, that were, in any event, electorally insignificant. In Venezuela, the older party leadership in exile, over the wishes of younger party activists collaborating with leftist groups in the overthrow of Pérez Jiménez, excluded the Communists from the coalition. In Austria, the Communists were a minor partner of the consociational coalition between the conservative and socialist "camps" only for a two-year period until they left the government following disappointing electoral results. And, in spite of socialist participation in coalition governments from 1945 to 1966 and several subsequent socialist governments, issues of social redistribution have been "dormant" (Katzenstein, 1985: 247). Similarly, in the Netherlands, the socialists, the second largest party, were excluded from forming part of the government until just before World War II. In

Lebanon, the economically dominant Christian (Maronite) groups were given substantial guarantees and a prominent role in government by means of a "National Pact" understanding in 1943, which also strengthened the political role of traditional leaders. Given the nature of the consociational agreement and the predicaments inherent to it, this conservative bias is not unexpected. Nevertheless, the extent to which and the way in which popular sector groups participate in political and economic decisions have varied considerably across these countries, for numerous historical and structural reasons. One hypothesis that emerges from contrasting the Western European cases of corporatism with the Colombian case is that in the more industrialized countries consociationalism has helped foster corporatism and policy concertation with an active role for organized labor, whereas in less developed countries it is more likely to promote a pattern more akin to state pluralism.

What is the relationship between consociational processes and corporatist ones? Consociational pacts almost always comprise agreements between or among political parties and their top leadership; corporatist accords are struck between heads of specialized interest groups, often with influential participation by high government officals.[3] Thus, of the two, consociationalism is a broader, more inclusive process, not as issue-specific as corporatism. Both consociationalism and corporatism rely on interelite accommodation between or among leaders of large groups of people with a strong potential for conflict. Both rely on decision-making processes that contrast sharply with competitive decision rules with an emphasis on majority control: rather, they stress negotiation, cooperation and consensus. In both there is a tension between elite accords and the ability of these elites to carry along their mass following (for example, splinter parties or wildcat strikes). The overlap between the two is such that in some consociational cases, major state institutions have been claimed by theorists of both camps as examples of their conceptual mechanism at work.[4]

Such characteristics of consociationalism as grand coalitions, mutual vetoes and a high degree of autonomy for each segment to run its own affairs, are not only compatible with corporatism, but could help foster conditions for its success. The fact that in consociationalism important policy-making decisions are often made in other forums and then brought to parliament for ratification, could facilitate corporatist agreements following the same procedure. Corporatism implies extensive societal organization, widespread patterns of accommodation at leadership levels to prevent potential conflict from escalating, and the need for leaders to have stable support from their followers in order to make commitments and agreements. In all these ways it shares important characteristics with consociational agreements. Yet, unlike consociationalism in some cases, corporatism addresses what are essentially ongoing tensions and potential conflicts between employers and workers in capitalist societies.

What then can we state about the relationship between consociational political pacts and corporatist socio-economic pacts? There have been a number of Western European countries with significant corporatist structures and processes, yet with no consociational arrangements, such as many of the Scandinavian countries. Thus, there is no *necessary* relationship from one to the other. Yet, consociationalism may have fostered the development of corporatist patterns of policy-making in European countries in which it was present (see also Lehmbruch, 1979). Thus, though consociational predicaments have been present in these regimes as well,[5] some of the tensions have been more successfully managed by the employment of corporatist techniques. In the Dutch case, consociationalism gradually became transformed into a more competitive model, a shift that had its counterpart in the industrial relations system, which moved from one of peaceful cooperation to more conflictual negotiation (Akkermans & Grootings, 1978). In Austria, the corporatist arrangements had never been as extensive as in the Netherlands and the end of coalition governments in 1966 did not spell the end of collaboration between industrialists and labor leaders on the Joint Commission for Prices and Wages (Steiner, 1972: 306–17).

In less-developed countries, corporatism has been seen as involving much more unilateral, deliberate state-initiated measures upon a variety of interest associations, particularly labor. Schmitter has termed this "state corporatism" and he views it as a response to the problems of delayed, dependent capitalist development as well as non-hegemonic class relations. Stepan (1978) has viewed it more generally as an elite response to crisis which can take two forms, an inclusionary one, incorporating and co-opting major working-class groups into a new political mode, and an exclusionary one, relying primarily on coercive policies to deactivate and then reorganize major working-class groups. In these cases, corporatism is viewed essentially as a major mechanism employed by the state to co-opt an incipient organized labor force, or to repress and control one that is already politically active. There is less likelihood for socio-economic agreements akin to those of the European cases in nascent Latin American democratic regimes. And consociational cases in less-developed countries rather than confronting potential problems of class polarization by means of state corporatism, may have a more logical response in what Schmitter has termed "state pluralism," in which "multiple, overlapping and competing associations" are promoted by government in a "classic *divide et impera* strategy" (Schmitter, 1979: 68). As we saw in chapter 6, the regime's ability to control state-created labor or peasant organizations could weaken due to differences across the major segments or parties, in which case state pluralism would be a logical response. And since control of the state apparatus is usually one of the most sensitive issues dividing segments in conflict, they may well decide not to move toward state-created labor organizations. Furthermore, state corporatist patterns are often, though not inevitably, associated with strongly anti-liberal and undemocratic political regimes. Consociationalism, on the other hand, is usually associated with some form of democratic politics.

Consociational transformation

Questions can be raised regarding the extent to which consociational arrangements can provide stable, long-term political arrangements. This is true both because of the predicaments entailed by the consociational model as well as by the problems generated by societal transformations often encouraged by the very agreement. In analyzing the breakdown of consociationalism in the Netherlands, Lijphart noted that "not the least of the virtues of the politics of accommodation [consociationalism] is that it provides the means for its own abolition" (Lijphart, 1977: 219). Unfortunately, this does not always lead in a more democratic direction.

A critical issue is whether the regime structure and societal transformation in consociational regimes blur old segmental divisions and conflicts – as occurred in Austria, the Netherlands and increasingly in Colombia – or if these divisions are reinforced

– as occurred in Cyprus or Lebanon, partially as a result of international factors. In both Austria and the Netherlands there was eventual desegmentation, although the pattern was smoother in Austria. In the 1960s, the independent electorate or "floating vote" (Pappalardo, 1981: 371) increased in both countries, though far more in the Netherlands. Partially in an effort to appeal to this new electorate and partially because as a result of the concomitant desegmentation new issues and conflicts emerged, party competition became more lively and governments more unstable (Pappalardo, 1981: 372–4; cf. Lijphart, 1975: 196–219). In Austria, in part due to the continuities provided by the corporatist arrangements between the same two groups that were a part of the consociational agreement, the transition to single-party governments was relatively smooth. Thus, even in industrially developed countries, the impact of societal change on the political regime can generate institutional re-accommodation that is relatively conflictual.

In contrast, in Cyprus and Lebanon, in part due to the role of foreign intervention, the tensions between the segments were heightened. The Lebanese case, as it was longer lasting, may be of greater interest. The informal "National Pact" divided government among the major social groups, though with predominant Maronite Christian representation in government though they comprised no more than about 30% of the population (a Maronite was to be elected president and representatives to parliament were to be majority Christian in a 6:5 proportion). The Maronite appeal for special status built not only upon their greater economic dominance but also on the argument that Middle East Christians had a claim to a special status and role in Lebanon. The initial agreement was then held onto by an intransigent, fearful and powerful minority that through time found itself confronting unfavorable demographic, ideological and international circumstances: an increasingly larger and more vocal, organized and ideologized poor Moslem majority as well as a more radicalized Arab world, including a significant Palestinian presence within Lebanon (see Khalidi, 1979).

The prospects for democratic consolidation in Colombia are more promising than they were for Cyprus or Lebanon. There are no external powers with major influence over specific communities within the country and geopolitical objectives tied to them. At a more general level, the ideological legitimacy of

democracy is high on the Latin American continent, whereas
military regimes have found no world models (such as fascism in
an earlier era) to emulate. Similarly, insurrectional strategies and
revolutionary struggles have lost some– though by no means all–
of the appeal they had in earlier decades. Closer to Colombia
geographically and in other respects, Venezuela did successfully
make a transition from a pact-oriented form of political interaction toward one of more inter-party competition. In Venezuela
the major political parties were able to shift to a pattern of
government–opposition through the 1960s, while Colombia
remained within its National Front strictures. In part because the
role of mass mobilization in the overthrow of Pérez Jiménez was
more important and in part because "fear" of the masses was not
as apparent as in Colombia reeling from *la violencia*, the parties in
Venezuela retained more effective links to various mass groups
(labor unions, peasant associations, etc.). Both these factors also
facilitated the efforts of the country's two major parties to reach
out more effectively to the country's growing urban electorate,
primarily by media and image campaigning. In Colombia, the two
parties are only now beginning to devise a way to break out of the
coalition mold and form a government and opposition. And they
have yet to develop vigorous auxiliary organizations or to incorporate successfully the increasingly larger and more independent urban electorate. As significantly, the guerrilla struggle
of the 1960s in Venezuela was brief and occurred at a time when
state capacity and regime legitimacy were in ascendance and
when economic resources were bountiful. In all these ways, the
Colombian experience of the 1980s offers a stark contrast. Thus,
in Colombia intolerance and resistance to the incorporation of
former guerrillas into the political process from the armed forces,
producer groups and regional party leaders has been substantially
higher than it was in Venezuela, even as the political aspirations
and tactics of various Colombian guerrilla groups have also
been different.

The built-in biases of consociationalism toward conservative
rather than innovative or redistributive policies, combined with
its strong possibilities for immobilism and policy incoherence,
all point to the difficulty of consolidating democratic politics in
less developed countries from a consociational beginning. In
countries where vast sectors of the population still have basic
unmet material needs, effective democratic consolidation would

appear to require not only a strengthening of democratic institutions so that social groups do not perceive going outside of the democratic process as an appropriate response in a crisis situation, but also progress and perception of that progress toward meeting socio-economic needs. Consociational practices in certain developing countries often provide a more humane politics than likely alternatives. Yet, their inevitable requirement of considerable elite autonomy and their fear of mass mobilization may inhibit development of broader democratic practices. Regime elites and their allies may seek to use consociationalism not as a democratic solution but as a means of halting significant democratization by defending privilege. Understanding a painful reality, though, does not always point to a better alternative.

Some time ago, in a critique of another book on Colombia (Payne, 1968), Albert O. Hirschman warned against *la rage de vouloir conclure* (1971: 349). His warning had two facets. One was that there are limits to what our theories can explain about social reality. In the pages above we have not set out to create a new "model" to explain all of Latin American or even Colombian political and economic behavior. Rather, our more modest goal has been to seek to show the value of a regime-centered analysis by exploring the ways in which the predicaments of consociationalism and the response to them by the regime – shaped by historical, structural and international factors particular to the country – contribute to an explanation of central economic and political phenomena in the country. The other warning was more normative than methodological. It was an appeal for consideration of "reform-mongering" over the call for revolutionary upheaval and total solutions. Although this book has shown the difficulties of reform in Colombia, it has not shown reform-mongering to be doomed inevitably to failure due to structural factors. The possibilities for reform of conservative regimes – inevitably gradual and uneven – may provide better hope than an uncertain revolutionary cataclysm. Especially given the country's history of violence without social change, it is not at all evident that promotion of violent revolutionary change is a preferred option in Colombia to pressuring for continued change within an open, though resistant, regime.

Appendix A
Elite sample: aggregated responses

Table A.1 *Views on power capabilities of major groups and organizations: "Please indicate for each group if in your judgement its power to act or to negotiate increased or decreased during the National Front."*

Group or organization	(1) Increased %	(2) No change %	(3) Decreased %	(1–3) %	(N)
The Church	2	2	89	−87	64
Armed forces	38	32	30	8	60
International agencies	42	14	44	−2	59
FEDERACAFE (coffee)	36	45	19	17	58
SAC (agriculture)	33	29	38	−5	61
FENALCO (commerce)	30	33	37	−7	60
ANDI (industry & others)	31	23	45	−14	64
UTC-CTC (traditional labor)	57	15	28	29	60
Left opposition	41	31	28	13	61
Traditional parties	29	32	40	−11	63
Congress	10	16	74	−64	62

Others not on card cited as having increased:
Government/Executive Branch/Technocracy, 9 respondents
ANIF/Financial sector, 4 respondents
ACOPI (small industrialists), mafias, the press, politicians and
abstention, 1 respondent each

Table A.2 *Elite opinion: party participation in government. Views on parties' abilities to maintain themselves without participating in government, by sector*

Respondents	Participation in government is necessary	Representation in Congress is sufficient	Depends on whether or not it is a good government	Not really necessary but some feel it is
Government leaders	13	2	1	2
Party leaders	7	2	1	4
Private sector:				
Agriculture–Coffee	8	3	0	0
Industry–Finance–Commerce	11	7	2	0
Total (N)	39	14	4	6 (63)
Total (%)	62%	22%	6%	10% (100%)

Table A.3 *Do you believe that the range of activities of the public sector have extended themselves excessively over the private sector?*

Respondents	Yes	No, but the public sector is inefficient	No	Total	N
Government officials	16%	32%	53%	100%	19
Party leaders	46%	8%	46%	100%	13
Private sector	74%	19%	6%	100%	31
N	32	13	18		63

chi^2 = 20.73   p < 0.001 (3 cells have N < 5)

Appendix B
Interviewees

This book is based in part on interviews conducted during a twenty month stay in Colombia in 1977 and 1978 and during additional trips in the summers of 1982, 1984 and 1986. Interviews and in some cases re-interviews with over one hundred and sixty people and informal conversations with dozens more were carried out during these periods. The interviews in 1977 and 1978 were conducted while I was affiliated as a Visiting Professor at the Universidad de los Andes and with the understanding that the identity of the respondents would not be divulged. Similarly, interviews with politicians, businessmen and others in the summers of 1982, 1984 and 1986 regarding campaign strategies, and contemporary political and policy issues were also carried out with the understanding that their names would remain confidential. In contrast, only a few of the retired military officers, businessmen and politicians interviewed in the Summer 1982 with regard to the transition from military to civilian rule and the establishment of the National Front requested confidentiality and in those cases their wishes have been respected.

Interviews were employed to acquire information regarding the establishment of the National Front, to supplement other sources regarding the selected policy case studies, for issues of brokerage and unionization and on the electoral campaigns of 1978 and 1982. Standard positional and decisional methodologies were employed. In addition, a selected sample of 64 (of an intended sample of 86) high government officials, leading businessmen with ties to the major producer associations and political party leaders was interviewed in 1977 and 1978. Respondents' views were elicited on processes of political and policy-level inter-elite accommodation as well as opinions on substantive issues. Many of their views are cited throughout the text and several of the aggregated responses are included in Appendix A. For that reason, a few words on how the sample was selected are in order.

The sub-sample of high government officials was chosen from agencies ranked as the most influential policy-making institutions by a panel of 31 academic experts (collected by Bruce Bagley and reported in Bagley & Laun, 1977) and from the largest decentralized institutes in the country (based upon their 1976 budgets). The ministries and agencies are listed below. In all cases, I attempted to interview the chief executive officer:

255

minister, general manager, director general or president. From the list of twenty-six institutions, nineteen interviews were successfully completed:

Major state institutions in Colombia

1. Ministry of Finance
2. Ministry of Economic Development
3. Ministry of Agriculture
4. National Planning Department
5. Bank of the Republic
6. Colombian Petroleum Enterprise (ECOPETROL)
7. Institute for Industrial Promotion (IFI)
8. Colombian Institute for Electrical Energy (ICEL)
9. Colombian Company of Alcalis (ALCO)
10. National Institute for Municipal Promotion (INSFOPAL)
11. Electrical Corporation of the Atlantic Coast (CORELCA)
12. National Telecommunications Enterprise (TELECOM)
13. National Railroad of Colombia (FNC)
14. National Highway Fund (FVN)
15. Enterprise of the Ports of Colombia (COLPUERTOS)
16. Financial Transportation Corporation (CFT)
17. Institute for Agricultural Marketing (IDEMA)
18. Regional Autonomous Corporation of Cauca (CVC)
19. Colombian Institute for Agrarian Reform (INCORA)
20. Colombian Institute for Social Security (ICSS)
21. National Public Social Security Agency (CAJANAL)
22. Institute for Territorial Credit (ICT)
23. National Savings Fund (FNA)
24. National Apprenticeship Service (SENA)
25. Colombian Institute for School Construction (ICCE)
26. Export Promotion Fund (PROEXPO)

The sub-sample of businessmen was determined in a two-step process. First, eight of the country's major producer associations (ranked by the same panel study reported in Bagley & Laun, 1977 and considered in light of data regarding the contribution of the particular sector to the country's GDP) were visited to collect lists of the boards of directors for the past 10 years.[1] This also permitted me to ask the officials of these associations how their organizations were structured and operated. Then I sought to interview those who had served the longest on the boards of the different associations.[2] Of the 40 projected interviews, 31 were carried out.

The most challenging sub-sample to define and interview was that of political party leaders. Two methods that did not work were to sample from National Party Directorates or to sample from Committee Chairmen in Congress. There were no central party headquarters where information on party directorates was maintained, itself an indicator of the low organizational level of the parties. In addition, factional politics sometimes led to the creation of dual directorates (the Conservative

Party in 1977) or to an agreement not to have one (the Liberals in 1977). Committee Chairmen in Congress are not selected by seniority for the post is generally considered as an undesirable administrative burden, except for Commission IV (Budget) as discussed in chapter 6. Instead, interviews were sought with the major factional leaders (in early 1978) and the heads of their congressional party lists in the departments with the country's four largest urban centers (Cundinamarca, Antioquia, Valle and Atlántico). Fourteen of the projected twenty interviews were completed.[3]

Because I personally conducted all the interviews (accompanied in some cases by a research assistant), I was able to pursue interesting themes, elicit specific examples and then follow up in interviews with actors outside the formal sample and through published and unpublished material. Since what I garnered were views at one point in time from a sample of limited size, the focus of the book has been on historical and policy case studies. The sample has been used as corroborative evidence, though the interviews provided tremendous exposure to the views, hopes and frustrations of respondents central to many economic and political processes in the country.

Notes

1 Introduction

1 Colombian social scientists are also perplexed. As Mario Arrubla noted, "La democracia politica colombiana, con todo y sus recortes, tiene que ser vista ... come un hecho sorprendente" (1978: 218). Leal (1984) refers to it as a *democracia restringida*, a restricted or limited democracy.

2 As we shall see in subsequent chapters, the Colombian state has had an extensive and generally supportive relationship with these social groups, as is true in most other capitalist countries. However, it is quite possible for the state to pursue policies which damage the long-run interests of all or nearly all capitalists. Gillespie (1984: 23) notes this for the case of Uruguay, especially in the period from the mid-1950s to the mid-1960s, as does Stepan (1985: 330) for the Argentine case in the period from 1976 to 1981.

3 *State autonomy* refers to the ability of the state to formulate and pursue objectives independent of societal demands or interests; *state capacity* refers to the ability of the state to implement its goals or objectives and depends upon such essential factors as the integrity of its sovereignty and military control of its territory, as well as its internal coherence and administrative and financial capabilities (Skocpol, 1985). Naturally, both autonomy and capacity can vary considerably dependent upon the strength and intensity of support and opposition by other actors or social groups on particular issues. Thus, it is often useful to determine the extent to which autonomy or capacity is present in particular contexts. At the same time, it makes sense – especially in comparative contexts – to talk in a more aggregated fashion of "weak" or "strong" states recognizing that state power is likely to be uneven across policy areas. Furthermore, "state autonomy" can come and go; it is not a fixed structural feature of any governmental system but one dependent upon "structural potentials" for state actions that change over time (Skocpol, 1985: 14).

4 For example in what has been justifiably recognized as an outstanding work of political economy, Evans (1979) notes: "Repression is especially necessary in those countries which have passed through the

258

phase of 'easy import substitution' and are trying to push the process of dependent industrialization further." And in the following paragraph: "In the context of dependent development, the need for repression is great while the need for democracy is small" (49).

5 Examples include scholars such as Guillermo O'Donnell who previously wrote from substantially different analytical viewpoints (see O'Donnell, 1982, 1986 and other articles in O'Donnell, Schmitter & Whitehead, 1986).

6 See Dix 1980a; Wilde, 1978; Berry & Solaún, 1980; Peeler, 1985. Some Latin American scholars, particularly in the Southern Cone, have begun to discuss the consociational literature (e.g. Van Klaveren, 1983).

7 In defining a plural society, Lijphart chooses to employ only the first half of Harry Eckstein's definition of "segmental cleavages", which notes these exist "where political divisions follow very closely, and especially concern lines of objective social differentiation, especially those particularly salient in a society" (cited in Lijphart, 1977: 3). Yet, Eckstein expands this definition by noting "[o]ther sorts of segmental cleavages might be based on rural–urban conflicts, on sex, generation, religion, language or occupation" (in Eckstein, 1966: 34). Thus, even employing Eckstein's concept of segmental cleavages Lijphart's rejection of Colombia as a plural society may be unwarranted (in Lijphart, 1977: 33).

8 In this sense, I am sympathetic to part of Lijphart's response to Steiner's critique from which the quotation is taken (Lijphart, 1981: 357). The analytical process entailed in making the distinction is analogous to that required in characterizing a state as "strong" or "weak." Yet, in his reply Lijphart *is* ambiguous about his earlier insistence that consociationalism is applicable only to plural societies.

9 Democracy is defined in this book along procedural lines, as discussed in Dahl (1971) or Linz (1978: especially 5).

10 A similar point is made in Bridge (1977: 343n) in an analysis of political change in Yugoslavia from the point of view of consociationalism. Lijphart also implicitly recognizes this point when he argues for example that "it is doubtful that Malaysia after 1971 can be regarded as either fully democratic or fully consociational . . ." (Lijphart, 1977: 153).

11 Nordlinger (1972) discusses "open" regimes as a category encompassing both limited democratic and fully democratic regimes.

12 In a brilliant analysis, Nordlinger (1972) does point to *necessary* factors, emphasizing the critical role of segmental leaders, the need for conciliatory attitudes and practices among them and their ability to bring along their mass following.

13 These are discussed in the concluding section of chapter 3.

14 For example, only some forty pages after arguing that consociational democracy is a form of stable democracy (Lijphart, 1977: 104–9), Lijphart describes "three clear examples . . . where consociational democracy was initiated in the Third World," in two of which

"consociationalism was reasonably successful for an extended period of time (that is, at least ten years)" (1977: 147)!

15 See Lustick, 1979. He has argued that in some cases attempts to implement consociationalism may be counterproductive and more costly to a society than "control" by one segment.

16 In the Western European cases, an analogous argument is sometimes made. Lijphart's analysis of Dutch politics has been criticized for ignoring the extent to which the societal "pillars" have served as a means of political control (Bakvis, 1984; see also Obler, Steiner & Dierickx, 1977: especially 41).

17 See Lijphart, 1975: 196–219; and Stiefbold, 1974. In both these cases, the rise of corporatist mechanisms during their consociational period meant that the demise of consociationalism did not lead to a return to strict majoritarian practices with a central role for the legislature (see also Lehmbruch, 1977). The relationship between consociationalism and corporatism is considered in the concluding chapter.

2 Political parties and consociational practices in Colombia: a selective history

1 As suggested by Tirado Mejia in the preface to Santamaría and Silva (1984) and below in chapters 3 and 7, these quarter-century cycles of institutional readjustments have continued, with the establishment of the National Front in the 1950s and with the effort to open up the political regime in the 1980s.

2 The western half of Colombia is traversed by three Andean mountain ranges and the country's highest peaks are located off the Caribbean coast in the Sierra Nevada. South and east from the Eastern Plains (*llanos orientales*) are the mostly depopulated Amazon territories. The country's capital and department, Bogotá, Cundinamarca, have never overshadowed other major urban centers – Medellín, Antoquia; Cali, Valle; and Barranquilla, Atlántico – to the extent found in other Latin American countries.

3 The artisans supported the brief dictatorship of General Melo for they were seeing their livelihood threatened by the free trade policies of previous governments. Melo's overthrow was also their defeat.

4 Oquist, 1980: 21–88. I have modified certain of his dates in accordance with more customary Colombia historiography, discussed in Delpar, 1981. Payne does not include the conflicts of 1885 and 1895 in his list of national-scale conflicts (1967: 4).

5 The meager fiscal resources of the nineteenth-century Colombian state are discussed in Deas, 1982; on Colombia's limited external trade and its boom-and-bust cycles, see McGreevey, 1971: 99.

6 A comprehensive compilation and analysis of Colombian constitutions is Uribe, 1977. English translations may be found in Gibson, 1948.

7 A recent analysis has underscored that the issue of free trade did not

divide Liberals and Conservatives as clearly as previously argued (Palacios, 1983: 30).

8 With adoption of the more centralized new Constitution, the previously more autonomous "states" became "departments." The country also adopted the name of Republic of Colombia. From 1819 to 1830, it was called New Granada, forming Gran Colombia with Venezuela and Ecuador. With the disintegration of the larger unit, it became the independent nation of New Granada. Reflecting federalist principles, it was called the Granadine Confederation from 1858 to 1861 and the United States of Colombia from 1861 to 1886 (Delpar, 1981: 193n).

9 Fals, 1955: 210–11. The powerful role of violent conflict in marking political patterns is apparent in the experience of the South of the United States, in which a *single* Civil War "produced a regional cohesion with impressive qualities of persistence" (Key, 1964: 239; cf. 228–53).

10 Palacios, 1983: 457, on the basis of 1932 coffee census data, estimates that 98% of all coffee *fincas* at that time could be considered in this category (*campesinas*), and they produced between 70%–78% of the country's total coffee production. See also Parsons, 1968; McGreevey, 1971: 196; and Machado, 1977: 108–9.

11 Rojas, 1970: 109. For a more sustained examination of this point, in the context of a general argument about the importance of the labor force in a peripheral economy's export sector in determining a country's trajectory, see Bergquist, 1986. Certainly there is something to his argument regarding the importance of coffee workers and small producers in determining the nature of the country's labor movement as they sought to acquire or expand their control over land, though I would choose to emphasize that political factors such as less-entrenched partisan identification and a less co-optative strategy from government in the 1930s – as well as different structural factors – could also have led to a different kind of labor movement. The clientelist links forged by party leaders were retained in regions where small growers of a cash crop predominated, as these often developed ties of dependency to local merchants and hoped that party links could help them in conflicts over land, credit and other issues. Yet, this *reinforced* strong party identification and its clientelist basis (which also remained strong in latifundista regions of the country), it did not create it.

12 Commercialization initially was largely in foreign hands. Palacios (1979: 404) estimated that in 1933 approximately 47% of Colombian coffee exports were conducted by foreign firms. Thereafter, there was a relatively steady decline: 35% in 1940–1, 28% in 1944, 18% in 1954, 15% in 1961, 18% in 1966, and 12% in 1970.

13 Bergquist, 1986: 253–7; Melo, 1978: 95–9. For a detailed study of Olaya's presidency, see Horgan, 1983.

14 During the years of the Liberal Republic, Conservatives practiced opposition as the Liberals had in earlier years. Electorally, this

included a refusal to participate in elections (*retraimiento*) (1934, 1938), support for a dissident figure from the other party (1942) and, ultimately and successfully, presentation of their own candidate (1946).

15 See Comité Central del Partido Comunista de Colombia, 1960; Montaña, 1977; and, on UNIR, Sharpless, 1978: 71–84; and Robinson, 1976: 67–81.

16 Many have seen López' presidency as a period in which new industrialists and organized labor confronted traditional landowners and the Church. Although possessing an element of truth, this view tends to exaggerate López' support from industrialists and to a lesser extent the opposition from landowners (see Palacios, 1983: 401–11, 505–9; contrast to interpretations by Bagley, 1979; Gilhodès, 1970; or Walton, 1984).

17 Attempts to limit the Church's influence on education were largely unsuccessful and though civil marriage and divorce were contemplated, they were never legislated. The Liberal-dominated Congress voted them down in an attempt to reduce conflict on religious issues (Tirado, 1978: 149). They were legislated only forty years later, when López' son held the presidency!

18 Palacios, 1983: 401. See also Bergquist, 1986: 340–2; LeGrand, 1984: 43–6; Urrutia, 1969: 129–33. The radical tradition of peasant self-defense communities in regions of Cundinamarca such as Viotá dates from this period.

19 See UN/ECLA, 1957: 262. Increased tariffs probably played a less significant role than the devaluations during these years which substantially aided industries with installed machinery (Palacios, 1983: 507).

20 For an overview of the early history of Colombian labor, see Urrutia, 1969: 55–109. In the 1920s, there was increased labor activity primarily in public services and major strikes against US companies such as Tropical Oil and United Fruit.

21 On the coup attempt, see Leal, 1970: 174–6; following the coup attempt, López enacted broad-ranging labor legislation using state of siege powers (see Moncayo & Rojas: 1978, 63–77).

22 See Table 6.2 on pp. 152–3 for the electoral results.

23 Wilde, 1978: 46–7. This article, which also borrows from the consociational literature, contains much valuable material on this period of regime breakdown.

24 The directorates of the two parties issued a joint manifesto in October 1951 condemning the violence and Liberal leaders even visited Liberal guerrilla areas to seek negotiated settlements. By 1952, relations between the directorates of the two parties were completely broken (Oquist, 1980: 176).

25 Quote from Bishop Miguel Angel Builes of Santa Rosa de Osos in his Lenten message of 1949, cited in Wilde, 1978: 49; see also Ortiz, 1985: 196–207.

26 Other analysts that share this emphasis on the central role of party leadership include Wilde, 1978; Molina, 1977: see especially 251–3;

Pollock, 1975; and Christie, 1986: 229–34; see also Ortiz, 1985. In my view, Payne (1968: 159–82) overestimates the desires of all major elements of top party leadership to seek peaceful solutions and thus appears to underestimate the extent to which different factional leaders mobilized followers to violence, rather than being dragged behind them.

27 There were police under the administrative control of the national ministry of government, of the departments and of municipalities. Conservatives had been horrified to discover that some Liberal policemen had joined the rioters during the *bogotazo*. Increasingly, Liberal policemen were purged as police recruits were sought from strongly Conservative minifundio areas of Santander and of Boyacá such as the municipalities of La Uvita and Boavita (particularly the regions of Chulavo and Chulavita). The brutal, intensely anti-Liberal police thus came to be known generically as *chulavitas*. General Rojas Pinilla "nationalized" nearly all of the country's various police forces with administrative control passing to the ministry of war (subsequently defense). This process was consolidated in the early years of the National Front (Ortiz, 1985: 142–62).

28 Oquist (1980: 273–317) notes the "collective amnesia" he encountered regarding this period in major coffee cities such as Pereira, Armenia, Caicedonia and Sevilla; see also Ortiz, 1985: 309–21.

29 Oquist, 1980: 235. Oquist also cites the remarkable case of a peaceful municipality in Caldas surrounded by intense violence whose "majority Conservatives and minority Liberals periodically renewed their mutual allegiance in ceremonious meetings conducted in the public square with massive attendance."

30 There does not appear to be a simple causal relationship between violence, land concentration and the expansion of agrarian capitalism. Depressed world coffee prices apparently had as much or more impact than *la violencia* on land concentration; the violence, rather than always favoring landowners occasionally allowed peasants to gain at the expense of landowners or other peasants; and, commercial agriculture expanded most in areas largely unaffected by *la violencia* (see Zamosc, 1986: 17–18; contrast to Kalmanovitz, 1978: 31–4).

31 SENDAS, run by Rojas' daughter María Eugenia Rojas de Moreno Díaz, was an attempt to emulate the Fundación Evita Perón in Argentina (Martz, 1962: 194).

32 In October, 1956, the World Bank suspended all further loans to the country because of its dissatisfaction with government policies (Cepeda & Mitchell, 1980; their source is David Lilienthal's diary). Rojas steadfastly refused to devalue (interview with Antonio Alvarez, president of one of the public banks created by Rojas and the subsequent junta's minister of finance, Summer, 1982).

33 Perón's relationship with the Church had begun to deteriorate since 1951, and in November 1954, he had launched an open attack on it. Perón was excommunicated by the Church in June 1955 (see Bailey, 1967: 145).

34 On Brazil, see Erickson (1977: 49–93) who traces how Vargas' more

controlled "paternalistic–administrative" populism led to a more "radical populist" politics. For the Argentine case, see O'Donnell, 1973: 115–99. For a systematic analysis of how the Colombian development path contrasts to the pattern for Argentina and Brazil drawn in the bureaucratic–authoritarian model, see Hartlyn, 1984b.

3 The establishment of the National Front

1 See the discussion in chapter 8.
2 The additional structural variables I emphasize that facilitated the establishment of the National Front in 1958 when political compromise had failed years earlier overlap to some extent the set of explanatory factors Dix (1980a) employs (as an alternative to those presented by Lijphart) to explain consociational democracy in Colombia. Dix's excellent article appropriately emphasizes socio-economic elite coalescence and the specifically partisan advantages resulting from political compromise for all actors. In my view developed below, though, he overemphasizes the importance of a third factor, "subcultural elite cohesion" (leadership unity within the parties), for Conservative divisions nearly destroyed the agreement at several points and the party entered the National Front period bitterly divided. Furthermore, the Liberal division at the top had begun to mend following Gaitán's assassination in 1948 and thus was present for much of the period of *la violencia*. Similarly, in my view, he underplays the extent to which the rigid institutionalization of the agreement resulted from fear of mass mobilization and does not consider adequately the fact that two processes were at work: removal of a military regime and establishment of a new civilian regime. Most crucially, as is true of other authors who have examined Colombia in the context of the consociational literature, Dix does not consider the implications of the nature of the regime for its subsequent transformation (in part, admittedly, because it was not his goal to do so in one short article). Yet, his suggestion that the most critical problem in the post-National Front era would be the maintenance of a "spirit of inter-party collaboration" (cf. Dix, 1980a: 310) is not borne out, as is evident from the discussion in chapters 6 and 7.
3 This was not relevant in the four Western European cases considered in the literature – Belgium, Switzerland, the Netherlands or Austria – though the Austrian case is the most analogous as a new regime was established in the aftermath of World War II. In the Third World cases of Cyprus, Lebanon and Malaysia, consociational regimes emerged directly from the colonial period.
4 Lleras had played no direct role in the failed negotiations from 1948 on and probably was capable of easier personal access to Conservative leaders for that reason. This information comes from a taped interview of Carlos Lleras Restrepo with Luis Pinilla, 1979, to which I was graciously provided access; see also Pinilla, 1980.
5 Interview with a leading military officer from the period, Summer 1982; see also *El Tiempo*, November 13, 1957. The Liberal willingness

to seek an agreement under these conditions is consistent with the public goods literature that indicates that the actor who most stands to gain from an accord is usually willing to and thus generally "pays" a greater share of the cost for doing so (cf. Olson, 1971).

6 This was an important symbolic gesture. The Liberal Party agreed to reinsert language it had removed in the Constitutional Reform of the 1930s. At the same time, the Church, reacting to the bitter denunciations from Gómez and to *la violencia* shifted from partisan support of the Conservative Party to support of the National Front idea (cf. Levine & Wilde, 1977).

7 Interviews with José Gutiérrez Gómez, president of ANDI at the time, Jaime Tobón Villegas, president of FENALCO (the merchants association) at the time, and Jaime Posada Angel, a Medellin industrialist who played a major role in organizing the strike, Summer 1982. Many Antioquian businessmen had endorsed the parties' Pact of March on April 8, 1957 (Ediciones Documentos Colombianos, 1957: 161–7).

8 Interviews with high military officers from that period, Summer 1982. Some suggested that a talk with Monsignor Builes was significant in convincing an ambivalent Rojas to step down (interview with a close civilian adviser to Rojas, Summer 1982). Also important was the fact that senior military officers informed Rojas they would not instruct their troops to fire upon the civilian demonstrators (interview with a leading general during the period, Summer 1982). See also the letter to the armed forces by three former civilian ministers of war, dated May 7, 1957, and the statement by Alberto Lleras and Guillermo León Valencia promising guarantees and asking the military's help in finding a solution to the country's crisis without bloodshed in Ediciones Documentos Colombianos (1957: 161–7).

9 The concerns of the military were noted by Rafael Navas and Hernán Jaramillo in interviews with the author 1982. Navas stressed he thought it would have been difficult for the junta to have turned over power to Valencia. See also Vázquez (n.d.: 265–6) and Pinilla (1980: 47–50).

10 This Commission was established by the junta to determine the fate of legislation passed during the Rojas years by the Constituent Assembly. Gómez told his followers not to participate in it with fellow Conservatives who once cooperated with Rojas (see *El Tiempo*, June 12, 1957).

11 Alfonso López Pumarejo was fearful of a Conservative ploy to keep Liberals out of local office by keeping parity only in the cabinet. He was also insistent that no time limit be placed on this aspect of the National Front agreement (see *El Tiempo*, September 11 and 12, 1957). López' fears were not unfounded. Complaints were expressed that Liberal ministers could not hire Liberals or fire Conservatives (in Alberto Galindo's column, *El Tiempo*, August 28 and September 9, 1957). Ricardo Uribe Escobar, a Liberal lawyer on the Commission, suggested a Swiss-style plural executive, but found little support (*Semana*, August 23–30, 1957).

12 Dix, 1967: 133. Approximately 70% of the country's population over 21 cast a vote. Women voted for the first time.

13 The Communist Party was in a quandary. The plebiscite, by nullifying certain of Rojas' decrees, would return legal status to the party; at the same time, the measures on parity would reduce the party's future role in politics. In the end the party called for its adherents to cast blank ballots (Comité Central del Partido Comunista de Colombia, 1960: 138–9).

14 Belisario Betancur, a prominent Laureanista politician at the time, noted there had been "general panic" among Conservative congressmen as a result of Gómez' invitation to Lleras (interview with Pinilla, 1979). Many politicians argue that as a result of this maneuver Gómez lost his standing within the Conservative Party, permitting the Ospinistas to regain majority status in the next elections (interviews with Raimundo Emiliani [prominent Laureanista politician], Jaramillo and another Conservative politician, Summer 1982). Gómez' byzantine political (mis)calculation appears to have been that the Conservative Party could strengthen itself better *under his direction* with a Liberal President and only Laureanistas in executive positions. Conservatives would be forced to unite around him in search of patronage.

15 See in particular the editorial by an "anonymous military officer" in *El Tiempo*, June 29, 1957, and the speech by Alberto Lleras to military officers in February 1958 reprinted in Junta Militar de Gobierno, 1958. Upon the request of the junta, the transition coalition changed its name from "Civic Front" to "National Front" (interview with Navas, 1982).

16 Regarding complaints of obstructionism, see *El Tiempo*, May 22, June 29, July 2, September 3, and November 13, 16 and 17, 1957. Yet, the junta's first minister of justice, a pro-Rojas officer, apparently resigned because of the anti-Rojista tone of the investigations (interview with a high military officer from that period, Summer 1982).

17 Forero noted in an interview (1982) that he was told Rojas did not follow through for astrological reasons. On Rojas and astrology, see also Premo, 1972: 71n.

18 Interviews with Antonio Alvarez and Hernán Jaramillo, Summer 1982; *Semana*, April 19–25, 1958. Soon after assuming the ministry of finance, Alvarez noted there were no significant differences in economic policy between the two parties (*Semana*, May 24–31, 1957). As a result of IMF drawings, World Bank loans and US assistance, foreign aid to Colombia in 1958 jumped to $108.2 m, considerably more than previous years: 1953, $24.1 m; 1954, $42.7 m; 1955, $18.2 m; 1956, $30.7 m; 1957, $39.0 m (Wilkie & Haber, 1981: 518 ["all drawings"], 514 ["actual loans"], 371 ["gross actual assistance"]). Simultaneously, Colombia followed Brazil's lead in seeking cooperation from the US for a coffee producers association that would prevent prices from falling even more sharply by voluntarily keeping stocks off the world market (see Zuleta, 1975; Delfim Netto & Andrade Pinto, 1973).

4 The National Front political regime: an introduction

1 The political regime's essential continuity and the only partial dismantling of the National Front requirements makes it difficult to
specify when the National Front "ended" and the post-National
Front period "began." National level competitive elections were first
held in 1974, but parity in the executive branch was mandated until
1978. Even after 1978, coalition governments were retained, in part
due to constitutional requirements, until 1986. At that time, the
newly inaugurated administration of Liberal Virgilio Barco and the
defeated Conservatives agreed to a "government–opposition" form
of government (see Chapter 7). In this chapter and in chapters 5 and
6, analysis will concentrate on the 1958–78 "National Front" period,
though occasionally material from later periods will be incorporated.

2 Of course, the possibility of a deadlock in executive–legislative relations is a dilemma of presidential systems like Colombia's; in
parliamentary systems, common to most other consociational
regimes, the risk is of executive instability (cf. Lijphart, 1984: 74–85).

3 Business associations or organizations are referred to in Colombia as
gremios de producción, a term I will usually translate as producer associations. In referring to activities of firms or businessmen, either alone
or in conjunction with the associations, I employ the term producer
groups.

4 An obvious contrast is the case of Fedecámaras in Venezuela.

5 Other examples can be cited: numerous middle-sized and small commercial firms are not members of FENALCO; FEDEGAN has lived in
penury as its regional federations have fallen months behind in paying their quotas; SAC for many years was almost entirely a regional
association (interviews with high officers in these associations, 1977).
Furthermore, many groups have been further weakened by organizational splits. For example, dissatisfied with ANDI's lukewarm
endorsement of land reform, the sugar producers left that organization for many years, and the cotton sector has been wracked by
organizational splits.

6 See Gilhodès, 1979: 114, 120; and Bejarano, 1985: 227, 276. Bejarano
noted that the SAC purposely chose to shy away from partisan
controversies. In the 1950s it already alternated its board among
members of both parties, though unofficially; in 1960, it established
partisan alternation of the presidency and vice-presidency of the
board and parity of board membership as official policy.

7 Interview with one of the founding managers of ANDI, July, 1977.
ANDI was formed with the encouragement of then President López,
who sought a means to interact more effectively with the industrialists. Another basic principle was that the organization would not
intervene in labor matters at the firm level. Earlier attempts to
establish industrial associations failed and an effort by President Santos
and his minister of finance Carlos Lleras Restrepo to require firms to
join a National Association of Manufacturers created by law was
declared unconstitutional by the Supreme Court (Poveda, 1984:
1–16).

8 In fact, regional disputes have almost always been more acrimonious than partisan ones, often reflecting diverging economic interests. In the case of ANDI, these disputes have represented a conflict between primarily national industrialists in Medellín versus emerging industrial firms with more foreign investment in Bogotá and Cali. These disputes led to several changes in the way that membership to the association's board was to be determined as well as crises in the presidency of the association (interviews with members of ANDI's board, 1977; Poveda, 1984: 84–5; 252–5). In the cotton sector, organizational splits reflected the diverging interests of the more export-oriented cotton growers on the Atlantic Coast as opposed to cotton growers in the interior more oriented toward the domestic market (Hartlyn, 1978).

9 Early examples of producer associations relying on political figures include FENALCO's appointment of Hernando Agudelo Villa as its president during the period of the military junta, as FEDEMETAL had Carlos Lleras as its president. Alfonso López Michelsen has served on the board of FEDEARROZ. From the other side, López brought the managers of different cotton federations to serve as his successive ministers of agriculture, one of whom subsequently became his minister of government. A manager of ASOCAÑA became mayor of Cali and subsequently minister of government under Betancur, who also took the manager of SAC as his first minister of agriculture.

10 It was very fortuitous that the politically moderate Luis Concha Córdoba became Archbishop of Bogotá in 1958 (Wilde, 1980: 211).

11 Camilo Torres gradually shifted from an activist stance within the system, principally as chaplain at the National University and Church representative on the board of the agrarian reform institute, to open though still legal opposition. In 1965 he helped form a United Front which sought to mobilize alienated abstentionists into a coherent political force. Torres' growing conviction that the political regime would not respond to peaceful efforts to change it led him to join a guerrilla movement, the Ejercito de Liberación Nacional (ELN), in October 1965 after having given up the priesthood in June. He was killed in an army ambush in February 1966 (see Broderick, 1975; Guzmán, 1969; and for events surrounding his death by the army officer responsible for the battalion that killed him, Valencia, 1976).

12 The cautious views of the Colombian bishops regarding the role of the Church in political and social action are discussed in Levine, 1981: especially 82–95; 171–210.

13 In the sample of businessmen linked to major producer associations, high government officials and political party leaders I interviewed in 1977 and 1978, 89% (of 64) felt the Church had declined in influence during the National Front years. It was followed by Congress, which 74% (of 62) felt had lost influence during those years. Table A.1 in Appendix A provides the full results. Appendix B explains how the sample was chosen.

14 Colombia has consistently ranked below the Latin American average

on comparative measures such as military expenditure as a percentage of GNP or soldiers per thousand population; see US/ACDA, 1985.

15 Laureano Gómez died in 1965, and his son Alvaro inherited his leadership. Followers of Gómez were known as Laureanistas, Doctrinarios, Lauro-Alvaristas, Independientes, and increasingly after Laureano's death, simply as Alvaristas. Followers of Ospina were known variously as Ospinistas or Unionistas. Later, during López' term of office, they allied themselves with followers of former President Pastrana, an Ospina protégé, and the group was known as Ospino-Pastranistas. With the death of Mariano Ospina in 1980, the core of the group remained Pastranista.

16 See Dix, 1967: 257–69; Sánchez & Meertens, 1983: 49–52. Parity required that all candidates register as Liberals or Conservatives. However, since the parties were not even legal entities and had no formal registries, legal challenges against candidates such as Juan de la Cruz Varela could not prosper.

17 López' basic commitment to the regime was made clear by various speeches in 1962. For example at one point he noted: "we will not permit the unhappiness and frustration being incubated by the National Front to find refuge under the sign of the hammer and sickle" (cited in Sánchez & Meertens, 1983: 214).

18 The ways in which the regime facilitated ANAPO's successes and worked for its decline are discussed in chapter 6.

19 It is also significant that during the Gómez presidency (1950–3) economic policies were non-ideological, supportive of industry and of foreign investment. A caustic commentary on Gómez' decision to pull out of the National Front coalition in 1960 is Lleras Restrepo, 1963b: 529–35.

20 López also pursued a variety of social reforms, yet one participant in cabinet meetings during his presidency noted programmatic differences aired on these occasions had never fallen along party or party-faction lines (interview, July 1978).

21 Congressmen surveyed in 1968–9 perceived both intra-factional and inter-factional partisan conflict as more important sources of conflict than inter-party conflict (Hoskin, 1976: 6). As discussed in chapter 2, Colombian history provides several examples of inter-party factional alliances stronger than intra-party unity.

22 An exception occurred in 1975 when the first non-parity Congress with an ample Liberal majority imposed a Liberal *contralor* against the wishes of President López and the Conservatives.

23 Through time, ex-presidents were sometimes called upon in periods of crisis to play a mediating or supportive role, as they ambiguously symbolized "national" figures; ambiguously, for some were still leaders of major party factions and occasionally themselves presidential aspirants.

24 For only a little over five years spread over the period from 1958 to 1978 has the country not technically been under a partial or total state of siege (Gallón Giraldó, 1979: 27–8).

25 Augusto Espinosa Valderrama, at a Liberal Convention 8 years later,

asserted "Carlos Lleras Restrepo negotiated [*pactó*] with Mariano Ospina Pérez the election of Guillermo León Valencia" (in *Criterio político*, Jan. 1970, 18). See also Lleras Restrepo, 1963b: 587–699 and Dix, 1967: 139–43. Carlos Lleras and Mariano Ospina also put the finishing touches on a programmatic bipartisan platform, which, however, was neither ratified by the Conservatives nor accepted by Valencia (Ramírez Aljure, 1986: 19–34).

26 Liberal politicians talked of an *escalafón liberal*, a hierarchy of leadership within the party which could be identified by examining the placement of names on Senate and House electoral lists and the order of speech-giving in conventions among other means. Interview with a leading Liberal politician, March, 1978.

27 Sourdís had served as Ospina's minister of foreign relations and had sided openly with him in his struggle against Gómez in the 1950s. Pastrana had been Ospina's personal secretary.

28 Systematic review of *El Espectador*, November 1969; a bitter retelling of the Conservative Convention is in García, 1977: 89–97; see also Ramírez Aljure, 1986: 56–7.

29 A politician present at Sourdís' house the evening of the 1970 election returns informed me Sourdís was convinced his candidacy had played that role. Confidential interview with a Conservative politician, Summer 1984.

30 Determination of which chamber to present a bill in first was usually based on political, tactical or administrative criteria. In this case, the most controversial packages were first presented where less political opposition was expected.

31 Two matters that the review committee could not reach agreement on – one ethereal and the other practical – were what the constitutional wording should be regarding the role of the state in the economy and the manner of determining the future size of the Congress (Vidal, 1970: 39).

32 This congressional power dates back at least to the 1886 Constitution (article 76 paragraph 18). The 1968 Reform in its final form explicitly specified that Congressmen could initiate legislation regarding matters specified by the mandate "[t]o encourage useful and beneficial work deemed worthy of support and stimulation, with strict adherence however to the proper plans and programs" (article 76, paragraph 20), since they had lost all other initiative regarding budgetary matters as well as in matters regarding personal exemptions from taxes (for Constitutional texts, see Gibson, 1948 and Colombia, 1972; see also Vidal, 1970: 222–6). For a discussion of the importance of these *auxilios* to the functioning of the political process, see chapter 6.

33 The original proposal was that the Senate be formed by 2 members from each department plus an additional member for each 500,000 inhabitants or fraction greater than 250,000 and the House, by 2 members from each department plus an additional member for each 300,000 inhabitants or fraction greater than 150,000, with a 20% adjustment in these figures each time a new census was approved. The

compromise reduced the population figures for the Senate to 200,000, and those of the House to 100,000, and determined that the adjustment in size would be proportional to the increase determined by each census. See articles 93 and 99 of the Constitution and Vidal, 1970: 14–15.

34 A state of siege can only be declared "in cases of foreign war or domestic disturbance" (article 121), yet in 1956 the Supreme Court asserted that decisions to declare or end a state of siege were purely a matter of executive discretion not subject to judicial review (Findley, 1973: 426). Under article 76 (12), Congress could delegate extraordinary powers to the President to issue legislation in specific areas. However, until the 1968 Reform, article 32 precluded such delegation of legislative authority to intervene in the economy. Because Valencia and Lleras had enacted considerable legislation employing state of siege powers, Lleras had to wait until Congress had approved a series of measures to replace these decrees before lifting in December, 1968 the state of siege implanted due to student riots back in 1965.

5 Economic policy-making: thwarted reformism and moderation

1 See Hartlyn & Morley, 1986a, especially Hartlyn & Morley, 1986b; Revéiz, 1986; Schydlowsky, 1986; and Diamand, 1986. Fernando Cepeda emphasized Colombia's "moderate" nature in oral comments at an International Conference on Models of Political and Economic Change in Latin America held on the Vanderbilt campus in November 1983. The pendular sequence in Argentina, Chile and Peru is apparent in an analysis of redistributive efforts in Latin America by Ascher (1984) which focuses on regime shifts from "authoritarian populists" (Perón, Ibáñez and Odría, respectively), to "centrist reformers" (Frondizi, Frei and Belaúnde), to " 'radicals' " (Perón, Allende and Velasco). These three countries, it should be added, swung sharply to economic orthodoxy following their "radical" experience. An argument might be made that Brazil followed this pattern to some extent, though earlier and in more compressed fashion (Vargas, Kubitschek, Goulart). Other major Latin American countries have not followed this pattern, particularly the "moderate" cases of Colombia, Mexico and Venezuela.

2 The statistics that might be most questioned are those for public sector deficits. In a subsequent publication, the estimates of the Inter-American Development Bank for the public sector for these countries over the 1980–4 period are somewhat higher for various countries, including Colombia (see Table 7.1). Even if all Colombian budget deficits were underestimated by 1% of GDP or so and *none* of those of its continental neighbors were (an unlikely occurrence), the central points regarding the relative size *and fluctuation* of these deficits in comparative perspective would not be affected (see IDB, 1985: 66–9).

3 As we saw, this played a role in the downfall of Rojas in 1957. For a

number of careful studies of *democratic* regime breakdown, with varying degrees of economic determinism, see Linz and Stepan (1978). Economic problems may be necessary in some cases for regime crisis, but it is political factors – the failure of regime structures, statecraft and leadership – that almost always provide the sufficient conditions for regime breakdown or overthrow.

4 A strong case that the National Front regime structure played a central role in this remarkable phenomenon in what is a very traditional and Catholic country is made in McGreevey (1980).

5 As elsewhere in Latin America, this protection also helped generate direct foreign investment which eventually dominated a number of the most dynamic and fastest growing branches of industry (Arango, 1978; Matter, 1977; and Misas, 1975). The new tariffs had both protectionist intentions (Díaz-Alejandro, 1976) and served to increase public revenues (for some analysts such as Fuentes & Villaveces (1976), their principal goal). At the same time, Colombia's average tariff rates and real interest rates in the late 1950s were "moderate," as they were substantially lower than those of Argentina, Brazil and Chile, though higher than those of Mexico and Peru (personal communication, John Sheahan).

6 Berry, 1983a: 91n, in referring particularly to the 1957–68 period argues "[t]he stop-go nature of growth in manufacturing was reminiscent of the Argentine pattern . . ."

7 Among the reasons for the latter move, the two most important appear to have been a desire to diversify the country's commercial relations and an expectation that normal relations with the Soviets could facilitate agreement with the FARC guerrilla group associated with the country's Moscow-line Communist Party. This latter logic with regard to Cuba and in the context of a much higher profile foreign policy was pursued in the 1980s by president Belisario Betancur (see chapter 7).

8 The growing economic difficulties of the Turbay and Betancur years in the context of the continent's external debt crisis are analyzed in chapter 7.

9 These "rules of the game" for inter-elite accommodation and to seek broader political support and legitimacy are discussed in chapter 4. They consist of mechanisms employed to circumvent the predicaments generated by the consociational regime and include increased presidential authority, secrecy, *ad hoc* policy-making forums and summit negotiations.

10 For a detailed description of passage of the agrarian reform law, see Bagley, 1979; also Hirschman, 1973b. On Ospina's summit meeting with Lleras, reported publicly only ten years later, see Bagley, 1979: 169–70. Ultimate passage of the reform was only made possible by the fact that abiding by the National Front plebiscite Congress had agreed in September, 1959 to permit social reform legislation to pass with a majority vote rather than a two-thirds vote for a two-year period.

11 This was particularly clear on the Atlantic Coast where extensive

livestock latifundia were turned over to cotton cultivation (interview with a prominent cotton grower from the Coast, May 1978).

12 In signing the bill, Lleras attacked the landowners and "old-style political bosses" from both parties and especially from the Atlantic Coast that had held up passage of the bill (see Bagley, 1979: 199–226, especially 216–17; see also Findley, 1973). Most of the land acquired by INCORA for redistribution occurred under the Lleras presidency. Yet, after 16 years of agrarian reform, only 2.7% of potentially cultivable land had been acquired by the agency for redistribution and much of that land was actually unfit for cultivation (see Colombia, INCORA, 1978).

13 The legal justification for declaring the emergency is in Colombia Presidente (1974–8), 1974; see also Findley, 1980: especially 451–64. López had set up an economic team to begin work on these measures, building upon ideas presented by the Musgrave Commission report and elsewhere, some 3 months prior to his inauguration (interviews with several of these economic policy-makers, 1977 and 1978).

14 Agricultural groups had finally acquiesced to a modest presumptive income tax in the 1973 agrarian legislation, but it was based on such low tax rates and assessed land values that its potential for augmenting state revenues or encouraging inefficient producers to sell or rent their land was largely lost. In addition, even after it was decreed, its application was suspended by the minister of agriculture (see Berry & Urrutia, 1976: 239–40; for an explanation of the tax, see Berry, 1972; see also Bird, 1974).

15 Interviews with two businessmen on ANDI's board and one on SAC's board and interviews with two high government officials, 1977 and 1978. Among those favored by concessions at this time were the coffee growers (see Perry, 1977: 128–9, which is an excellent analysis of the reform by one of its technical authors).

16 For a critique of the tax reform and its stimulus of evasion from ANDI, see Munera, 1977; SAC's argument that the measures exceeded the country's "level of fiscal tolerance" are in *Revista Nacional de Agricultura*, November–December, 1977: 18.

17 See Urrutia, 1981: 196–8; he argues the tax reform survived, "although somewhat weakened." More negative assessments are based upon interviews in July, 1982 with other economists who were also high government officials during the López government. See also the interview of Guillermo Perry in *Estrategia* 7 (December 1977–January 1978): 23–5.

Probably the most lasting measure of those decreed in 1974 had little to do with tax reform; taking advantage of the "state of national emergency" powers, a new more liberal regime of oil and gas exploration was enacted. This led to a sharp increase in exploration by foreign oil companies and to several major new discoveries.

18 Growth was facilitated and foreign exchange constraints eased by foreign funds. The US provided an Export-Import Bank loan of $45.4 million in May 1961 and an AID program loan of $35.0 million in April 1962. Lleras also signed IMF standby agreements in December

1960 ($65 million were disbursed in 1961) and in January 1962 ($7.5 million were disbursed that year) (see Wilkie, 1974).

19 The devaluation involved different adjustments to each of the country's exchange rates, which are not discussed here. For more details, see Diaz-Alejandro, 1976 and Dunkerley, 1968.

20 See Dunkerley, 1968: 128. Reflecting the state's low autonomy, the board of directors of the country's central bank was dominated by private sector interests. Dissatisfaction with their management of the money supply during this period, though, led to the creation of a Monetary Board (Junta Monetaria) in 1963 to insure greater state control over monetary policy. This new organism was comprised entirely of government officials (the ministers of finance, economic development and agriculture, the manager of the National Planning Department and the Bank of the Republic, and since 1968 the director of the Colombian Foreign Trade Institute). Establishment of the Monetary Board was an important step in increasing state capacity, although it effectively handed power over monetary policy to the administration in power as the leading figure on the Board has been the minister of finance appointed by the president.

21 In spite of low coffee prices, the coffee sector was able to maintain its real income levels during this period (chiefly by increasing domestic support prices) at the expense of other sectors and at an inflationary cost. In 1964, export prices were actually below internal support prices (Bird, 1968: 80). The large growers and major merchants who reaped much of the benefit were aided by the fact that economic protection of the coffee sector could be justified by the existence of so many small and medium-sized coffee growers.

22 One prominent industrialist told me during a July 1982 interview that he had been offered a cabinet post in a potential new government.

23 Interviews with a number of the major actors, including the Conservative president of ANDI at the time and the Liberal president of ANDI's board of directors (in July 1977, February 1978, and July 1982). According to two Medellín industrialists, the situation in January 1965 was deemed so serious that Bogotá industrialists had accepted the inevitability of a coup prior to the arrival of ANDI officials from Medellín. It is also likely that Alvaristas, bitterly opposed to Valencia's government, may have welcomed a military coup. See also *El Tiempo*, January 16, 19 and 20, 1965.

24 Ostensibly, Ruiz Novoa resigned because other high army officers felt he was threatening "the unity of the Armed Forces" (*El Tiempo*, January 29, 1965). See also Dix, 1967: 160; Ruhl, 1980: 192–3; and Maullin, 1973.

25 For a review of the contents of Decree-Law 2351 of 1965 see chapter 6. The state of siege had been re-imposed in the country in May 1965, in response to student demonstrations in Medellín against the US invasion of the Dominican Republic.

26 See Cepeda, 1977: 94–5; confirmed by an unpublished 1972 World Bank document evaluating bank operations in Colombia to which I was provided access (further citations will be to IBRD, 1972).

27 Interviews with several members of the Commission. Other suggestions included increased efforts at national planning. One of the key
authors of these reports went on to become President Carlos Lleras'
first director of the National Planning Department. Cepeda (1977:
142n) notes the gasoline tax was imposed by the Lleras government
upon the suggestion of the international agencies. The reports can be
found in Colombia, Comisión Especial de Estudios Económicos y
Sociales, 1965a and 1965b.

28 In late 1964 because of the country's tight foreign exchange position,
the Bank of the Republic (central bank) announced that it would no
longer sell any foreign exchange; would-be importers were told to
buy what they needed from exporters, thus briefly creating a free
market. The price of a dollar shot up from the official rate of Col\$9 to
around Col\$18, with no announced devaluation. The IMF was dis-
pleased with the duality and sought that the official rate be made an
actual rate again (details from John Sheahan [an adviser to the
National Planning Department in the 1960s], personal communication, 1985). See also Dunkerley, 1968: 138–9; Díaz-Alejandro,
1976: 195–205; and Wiesner, 1978: 80–4; also interview with the
minister in question, 1978.

29 This episode is still fraught with controversy. The president and high
government officials continue to insist they acted autonomously; yet
confidential interviews carried out in July 1982 confirm the views
expressed in Currie (1981) and Díaz-Alejandro (1976). Currie (1981:
99) notes that in 1965 the IMF was urging devaluation in terms of a
flexible exchange rate, not a fixed unalterable rate. Indeed, even as
Lleras augmented state capacity, in part with the encouragement of
international agencies, these agencies continued to play an essential
role in Colombia. Standby agreements with the IMF were signed in
April 1968, May 1969 and April 1970, and in related actions,
memoranda of understanding were signed with the World Bank each
year specifying targets for quarterly performance reviews (IBRD,
1972).

30 As Díaz-Alejandro notes: "It seems difficult to argue that without the
1966–68 pressure of foreign creditors Colombian exchange-rate
policy, particularly the pace of devaluation, would have been the
same as that actually observed" (1976: 208).

31 Growth or decline in public expenditures must be viewed in context
to determine their impact on state capacity. The conscious reduction
in the size of the state sector in Chile under Pinochet did not mean a
decline in state capacity (see Stepan, 1985), and the massive increase
in the size of the state sector in Nicaragua with the expropriation of
Somoza's holdings did not lead to as much control over the economy
as the figures would lead one to expect due to the state's uneven holdings in different sectors (see Dore, 1986).

32 Among the new agencies created during the Lleras presidency were:
in 1967, the CFT (Financial Transportation Corporation); in 1968,
the National Transportation Institute (INTRA) and the Institute for
the Defense of Non-renewable Resources (INDERENA); in 1969, the

Electrical Corporation of the Atlantic Coast (CORELCA), the National Savings Fund (FNA), the Colombian Institute for Family Welfare (ICBF), the Colombian Institute for School Construction (ICCE), the Colombian Institute of Culture (COLCULTURA), the Colombian Institute of Youth and Sports (COLDEPORTES), the Export Promotion Fund (PROEXPO), the Colombian Foreign Trade Institute (INCOMEX), the Colombian Mining Company (ECOMINAS) and others of lesser importance.

Lleras' belief in an active state role and his penchant for the creation of agencies of this nature was evident during his term as minister of finance for president Santos in 1938–42. In those years, he was instrumental in creating the Institute for Industrial Promotion (IFI), the National Institute for Municipal Development (INSFOPAL), the Institute for Territorial Credit (housing agency, ICT), and a geographical institute (Instituto Geográfico "Agustín Codazzi").

33 See Losada, 1973. Lleras' felt need to "protect" the agencies by providing them with earmarked funds reflects "low stateness" and the fear of what future incumbents of the presidency might do to dismantle or politicize them.

34 Based upon a review in 1977 of World Bank loan documents in the uncatalogued AID archives at the Universidad de los Andes library and others to which I was provided access; see also Cepeda & Mitchell, 1980.

35 CONPES is comprised of the president and the ministers of development, finance, agriculture, public works, foreign relations and labor, the director of the DNP, the manager of the Bank of the Republic, the manager of the Coffee Federation and the director of the Foreign Trade Institute.

36 Perry, 1974 identified nine major document-studies intended as economic models for Colombia of which three were completed by international consultants, one was a further analysis of a study prepared by international consultants, three were elaborated with international technical assistance, one was written by a former international consultant on his own initiative, and essential elements of this last plan were later adopted and written into a new plan. None was fully implemented.

37 Based on my interviews with a sample of members of ANDI's board of directors as well as additional interviews with members of ANDI's administrative staff, in 1977 and 1978.

38 See Findley, 1980: 432–3; also interviews with two leading ANDI officials in July 1977 and with an official of the Fondo in December 1977, and a review of stories in *El Espectador*.

39 For a complete listing, see Revéiz, 1981: 53–60; see also Revéiz & Pérez, 1986. Public sector representatives have comprised between two thirds and three fourths of the membership of these various boards, private sector representatives between one fifth and one third and workers, consumers and congressional representatives have had only marginal representation.

40 Interviews with members of ANDI's administrative staff, 1978. An effort at planning in the cement sector failed, for example, when industry backed out of a commitment to an expansion plan when the government re-imposed price controls (interview with businessman, July 1978). Cases where the government was less likely to feel the need to impose price controls, or in which negotiations were among limited numbers of parties because the sectors were heavily oligopolized, met with somewhat greater success. Such appears to have been the case with the paper sector during the subsequent López government (interview with industrialist, July 1977).

41 Currie had directed the first World Bank Mission to Colombia in 1949 and had stayed in the country, becoming a Colombian citizen. Under his impetus, key aspects of the Mission study, particularly investments in transportation and power, were carried out in the 1950s.

42 Rivera Ortiz, 1975: 81–105. As a means of presenting an overall critique to the plan, a conference of noted economists was organized in which many of these points were presented (see CORP, 1972). A number of the economists presenting critiques went on to serve in high positions in the subsequent López government.

43 The clause was article 120 (14) of the Constitution. See Findley et al., 1983: 72–83 for a description of the legislation decreed by the president and of the constitutional issues involved.

44 See Currie, 1981: 50. The other members of the Junta, ex officio, were the ministers of finance and development, the manager of the central bank and the director of the National Planning Department (all members of the Monetary Board).

45 This discussion on the Coffee Federation is based in part on interviews with three members of the board and two staff members in 1977 and 1978. Between 1964 and 1978, of the six private representatives, four served the entire period, though one served the first two years as a *suplente*.

46 In the elite sample interviewed in 1977 and 1978, 74% of the businessmen felt the public sector was too large; in contrast, 85% of the government officials did not, though 32% of them did feel it was inefficient. Party leaders were split, though not along party lines (see Table A.3 in Appendix A).

47 This explanation was given me by the manager of an unprofitable state enterprise owned by IFI (interview, November 8, 1977).

48 For a detailed study of the Federation of Cotton Growers, based on a review of Federation documents and interviews with leading members of the Federation and appropriate government officials, see Hartlyn, 1978. In 1982, additional interviews were carried out with managers of various cotton federations and government officials and access to government documents and correspondence between the cotton-growers and the state was provided me. In addition, interviews with the heads of the country's leading textile firms were carried out.

49 Hectares of cultivated cotton expanded from 281,000 in 1975 to

377,000 in 1977, to fall (with a slight rebound in 1980 and 1981) to only 80,000 hectares in 1983 (see Federación Nacional de Algodoneros, 1984: 26).

50 Colombia was due to "graduate" from such aid as its GNP/per capita had increased, and AID officials had thought the announcement would be made jointly (interviews, 1978).

51 State capacity to control economic transactions had always been limited on the Atlantic Coast and some other regions of the country where smuggling and contraband were a way of life. In addition to drug trafficking, major forms of contraband have revolved around coffee, cattle, emeralds, gold, platinum and other frontier trade (see Junguito & Caballero, 1978).

52 The *cafeteros* consist of four major groups: exporters, commercial growers, rural wage-earners and peasants. Of these, the small group of private exporters appears to have garnered around half of all additional income earned and commercial farmers also appear to have done extremely well. Rural wage-earners did see their real wages increase whereas peasants do not appear to have increased their standard of living (see Ocampo & Revéiz, 1979: 244–5).

6 Political support: elections, brokerage and popular sector organizations

1 This is not to imply that social reforms always lead to greater regime support by their beneficiaries, though they often do. In Latin America, one of the more prominent cases of a regime that failed to generate support among groups favored by its reforms is that of the Peruvian military in their reformist 1968–75 phase (see McClintock & Lowenthal, 1983). For discussions on the political impact of reform, see Hirschman, 1973a, Huntington, 1968 and Ascher, 1984.

2 Clientelism can be viewed as an asymmetric dependency relationship between a patron and a client, in which the material benefits the patron gives the client in exchange for certain services and his/her vote can be of two different types: traditionally, they belong to the patron himself (such as land); or, as a broker, the patron may serve as a mediator for outside, usually state, resources, which the patron-broker then controls and dispenses. Brokerage is a hierarchical relationship which does not possess the affective quality of patron-client relationships, and in which concrete benefits not personally owned by the broker, whether of an individual nature (such as a job or a scholarship) or of a collective nature (such as a school or a health clinic) are promised in return for votes (see Schmidt et al., 1977 and Scott, 1972). Brokerage is an important political function even in political regimes with more polarized and ideological parties as studies on Chile (Valenzuela, 1977; and Valenzuela & Wilde, 1979) and Italy (Di Palma, 1977; Zuckerman, 1979) have indicated.

3 For a discussion of "state" versus "societal" pluralism, see Schmitter, 1979: 67–8.

4 Although the emphasis in this chapter is on regime policies and the

impact of the regime structure on patterns of legitimacy and support during the National Front period (1958–78), data from the 1978–85 period is included in appropriate sections where available to provide a more comprehensive picture. The 1978–86 period is analyzed extensively in chapter 7.

5 Both estimates of participation rates provided in the tables are fraught with inaccuracies. However, those of the Registraduría are known to be based on highly incomplete and not fully updated records of citizen national identification cards (*cédulas de ciudadanía*). For that reason, whenever possible, participation rates based upon population figures will be employed in the text. The system of national identification cards began under President Olaya Herrera and was first used in the 1933 congressional elections (Lleras Restrepo, 1975: 207). Conservatives opposed the *cédulas* because they felt Liberal government officials would refuse them to Conservative party faithful. In fact, many sectors of the population never took out a card, thus becoming excluded automatically from the possibility of voting. This naturally tended to exaggerate the true extent of electoral participation. In the 1940s, this overestimation was probably overcompensated for by the fact that many women who were not given the right to vote until 1953 were receiving the *cédulas* and thus being counted as part of the eligible voting population and by the fact that files were not updated as people died, moved or changed their civil status. In the National Front period, the earlier problem of many eligible voters lacking a *cédula* probably became accentuated, especially following the 1976 law that gave 18–21 year olds the vote, since large percentages of these young people did not possess *cédulas*.

6 The system appeared to be designed almost as if low participation rates were desired, as congressional, departmental and municipal elections were held on different days in the same year. Some 28 elections or an average of 1.47 per year, were held between June, 1930 and June, 1949 (Henderson, 1985: 253).

7 A survey study of the 1978 elections in Bogotá found that 84% of the 18–21 year old group abstained; the average of all other age groups was 58% (based upon computer printouts of survey results); see Sánchez et al., 1981; and Losada, 1980.

8 Once the MRL divided into a *linea dura* and a *linea blanda*, the latter was essentially a Liberal faction, which is why the vote of the *linea blanda* was included in the Liberal tally in Table 6.1.

9 The continuities found in this Table are similar to those found between the 1930 and 1946 elections reported in Table 2.2.

10 For example, in 1978 the country's three major cities of Bogotá, Medellín and Cali contributed 15.1% of the total vote in the legislative elections and 17.4% in the presidential elections; in 1982, they contributed 16.7% of the total vote in the legislative elections and 21.9% for the presidential elections. Reflecting the general importance of vote-buying and other questionable electoral practices on the Atlantic Coast, and in contrast to the national trend, the vote in the country's other major city located on the coast, Barranquilla (as in the

seven departments of the Coast as a whole), declined somewhat from the legislative to the presidential elections in both 1978 and 1982.

11 See chapter 4. MRL leaders were surprised by their rural successes and had run more of an urban-centered campaign. Mainstream Liberals concerned with the López candidacy in 1962 had the Supreme Court declare that all votes cast for López were "void." During the campaign they sought to combat the MRL by suggesting that "void" votes for López favored the sectarian Leyva candidacy whose victory would be a "true crime against Liberalism and against its people" (see Johnson, 1965: 19–22 [quote on 22]).

12 The Colombian electoral system is based on proportional representation with candidates winning elections based on their rank order on their respective list. During elections in which parity was in effect, the total vote received by each party was divided by the number of seats allotted to the party in order to determine the electoral quotient. If a list did not receive at least one half of the quotient, then the votes of that list went to the list with the same label that received the most votes within the same party. Each faction's vote was then divided by the electoral quotient. The last seat was assigned to the faction that had the largest "remainder" after dividing by the electoral quotient.

13 "Uninominal lists" are those in which the only candidate elected is the one who appears as the first name on the list. Party lists contain the names of both *principales* and *suplentes*. The latter replace the *principales* according to their rank order on the list when called upon to do so. Sometimes prior arrangements have been reached to share a post if elected; other times, prominent names are placed at the head of a list with the understanding that the *suplente* will serve the term if elected (based upon interviews with politicians in the 1978 and 1982 campaigns). Candidates need not live in the department in which they seek election, and one tactic factions have followed is to place prominent names at the head of lists throughout the country.

14 Because the phenomenon has been most prevalent on the Atlantic Coast, where machine-style politics and vote-buying practices are most common, one politician termed the process the *costeñización* of the parties (interview in Medellín, July 6, 1978).

15 In my view, these incentives provided by the regime structure are far more important sources of explanation for the political behavior of politicians than a personal incentive for "status" rather than "program" presented in Payne's culturalist argument (1968).

16 In the absence of national-level survey data through time, these figures and those that follow are rough approximations. The pitfalls in imputing individual behavior from aggregate data preclude making more detailed estimates. The 25% figure is based on the fact that participation rates in mid-term elections have been around 30%.

17 See the results of the survey studies of elections in Bogotá: Williams & Losada, 1972; Losada & Murillo, 1973; Murillo & Williams, 1975; Sánchez et al., 1981; Gómez Gómez, 1982.

18 Based upon the fact that even in the heavily polarized 1949 election, some 25% of the electorate did not vote and that in the 1957 plebiscite some 30% abstained.

19 A survey study taken after the 1970 elections in Bogotá showed that 24% of the respondents that identified themselves as Liberal and voted cast their ballots for Rojas (Williams & Losada, 1972). The survey had substantial under-representation of the Rojas vote, probably because in the tense weeks following the elections many who had voted for Rojas denied it in the survey. In the Bogotá survey study, Rojas voters overwhelmingly evaluated the National Front negatively and claimed their support for Rojas was based on his promise of economic help for poor people (Williams & Losada, 1972: 23, 28). Rojas received 64.5% of the vote in polls located in low stratum neighborhoods in Medellín and 63.9% of the vote in polls located in the two lowest stratum neighborhoods in Bogotá (see Colombia, DANE, 1972: 298, 396; see also Talbot Campos and McCamant, 1972:60).

20 Confronted with a firm attitude on the part of President Lleras, who immediately declared a state of siege, Rojas did not call upon his supporters to protest the decision. In that sense, he repeated the pattern of behavior of May, 1957, when, confronted with the fact that bloodshed would be the likely result of seeking to manage the existing demonstrations and an ultimatum from his high command, he opted to leave. The ambivalence of populist figures in critical moments such as these has been noted in other cases, such as that of Goulart in Brazil in 1964 (cf. Stepan, 1978).

21 See Trapido (1979) for a description of a program created at this time aimed at providing food in urban areas at reduced prices with clear political aims.

22 See Dix, 1980: 162–3. Of the 488 candidates elected to legislative, departmental or municipal posts as Anapistas in 1970, only fifty-one were re-elected to some post in 1974: thirty-six as Anapistas, four as Conservatives, eight as Liberals and three as members of the left opposition coalition (UNO). (Data compiled from information provided by the Registraduría Nacional del Estado Civil).

23 Murillo & Williams, 1975: 37. Although in broad outline these results appear valid, they must be accepted cautiously both because they refer only to Bogotá and because respondents' recall of how they voted in past elections has been shown to be imperfect.

24 Some of the first agrarian reform programs were in areas most affected by violence, and links between these programs and the other pacification efforts were developed (Duff, 1968: 182–7).

25 For a detailed analysis of ANUC and of the invasions, see Zamosc, 1986: especially 68–96. Land invasions jumped from forty-seven in 1970 to 645 in 1971, declining to fifty-four in 1972. The invasions took place primarily as a result of conflicts between tenants or sharecroppers and large landowners or between colonists and landowners over unused and public lands. Significantly, there was little overlap between areas of *la violencia* and areas of land struggles in the 1970s.

26 Bagley & Botero, 1978: 74–5. The more radical ANUC was stronger in areas of latifundia and new colonization zones in which struggles were principally over land rather than services, as was true of minifundia

or older colonization areas. Its decline was caused not only by the switch from government support to repression but by political factionalism and by the fact that the most active groups within it had succeeded in gaining land in earlier invasions. President López gradually revived ANUC-Armenia beginning in 1976. The effort by ANUC-Sincelejo to compete in the 1978 elections with its own political party met with dismal failure, as it mobilized only an estimated 15,000 votes. Brokerage politics by the traditional parties and repression of several activists were critical factors. Finally, in 1981, a weakened ANUC-Sincelejo was reincorporated into the semi-official ANUC (Zamosc, 1986: 100–4; 179–201).

27 The census recovered information from an estimated 24,803 Juntas in the country; of the Juntas covered in the census, 10% gave no information on date of establishment (see Ungar, 1981a: 10; also Ungar, 1981b). Some of these new Juntas may have represented the reorganization or the re-creation of older Juntas. Henderson (1985b: 232) estimates there were 15,000 Juntas in 1970.

28 Even during the Lleras administration the relationship between politicians and the Juntas was very strong. In the 1968 congressional session, the group that visited the highest percentage of congressmen (72%) were Acción Comunal representatives. Indicating the brokerage role of these legislators, Junta leaders were followed by representatives of municipal governments (62%) and peasants (59%). Reflecting the declining importance of Congress in economic policy-making, producer associations ranked last (Kline, 1974).

29 Most Congressmen have been "local notables" overwhelmingly recruited from lower level political posts such as municipal councils, departmental assemblies and local-level party directorates. Few have previously held any administrative post in the public sector and turnover – due to fierce competition and the multitude of lists – has been high. See Hoskin & Swanson, 1974. The most extensive study of Colombian congressional behavior is Hoskin, Leal & Kline, 1976.

30 Congressmen occasionally found means to pocket the money, augmenting their salaries or employing them to fund "Foundations" whose basic goal was to support their re-election efforts. They sometimes created fictitious Juntas or schools, or made agreements with existing ones that a certain amount would be returned to the congressmen (interviews with a former budget director (Director de la Dirección General del Presupuesto, Ministerio de Hacienda), and interviews and conversations with politicians during my observation of the 1978 electoral campaign and in the Summer 1984). One Congressman was reviewing a list of names of a party census of a "foundation" just before his interview with me (interview, April 6, 1978). Protest over the abuse of *auxilios* have continued. López' minister of finance (who had also served Lleras in that capacity) unsuccessfully sought to exclude any funds for *auxilios* in the 1978 budget, asserting that he did not "share the theory regarding the convenience of atomizing the budgets of the nation, the departments or the municipalities" (*El Tiempo*, September 2, 1977).

31 In the first years of the National Front, controls of any kind were essentially non-existent. For example, Law 93 of 1965, establishing the 1966 Budget simply noted that: "the regional *auxilios* . . . will be guided to their beneficiaries through legally constituted organisms . . ." (article 24) without providing for any oversight by any agency whatsoever. A subsequent article (51) noted that *auxilios* channelled through the housing agency (ICT), the municipal public works agency (Instituto de Fomento Municipal) and the electrification agency (Instituto de Fomento Eléctrico) must be invested as indicated in the budget; if the funds were not spent after one year, then they should be sent to the appropriate municipal treasurer. By 1970, the budget laws specified that the Congressional Contraloría General de la República was responsible for oversight and control. Although this probably added considerably to the paperwork, it is likely that it added inefficiency rather than assured appropriate expenditure; as a dependency of the Congress, the Contraloría was itself a major source of patronage for congressmen. During the López administration, for example, congressmen were guaranteed a certain number of jobs in the agency if they voted to support a particular candidate for the position of *Contralor*.

32 In examining the initial budgets for the central sector of 1964 and 1966 (both prepared under President Valencia), it was not possible to separate out *auxilios* from other expenditures in any of the ministries except education (or for 1966, government and justice as well as education). Nevertheless, I sought to identify bare minimum and medium estimates of what budgeted *auxilios* may have been: the minimum estimates for 1964 and 1966 were $86,430,000 pesos (2.2% of initial central budget) and $126,514,000 pesos (2.3% of initial central budget), respectively. The expenditures for *auxilios* were not placed separately in the budget law until 1975, and beginning in 1978 they were published as a separate volume of the central budget: "Aportes para el plan de programas de fomento a empresas útiles y benéficos de desarrollo regional."

33 The budgetary process in Colombia has been extremely complex. This initial central budget is usually added to during the fiscal year (same as calendar year); between 1965 and 1980, the final budget for the central sector of government was as much as 144.4% of the initial budget (1979), and as little as 106.8% of it (1976). Actual expenditures, on the other hand, were usually far less that the final budget, fluctuating from a low of 68.7% in 1975 to a high of 84.7% in 1980 (Bird et al., 1981: 74). I could not ascertain definitively the extent to which *auxilios* that are budgeted are actually spent, though a Conservative senator asserted that nearly all were spent, for other congressmen would employ the funds if the politician to whom they were initially provided did not, a view confirmed by a leading Liberal politician (interviews, Summer 1984).

34 In 1983, approximately 15% of the *auxilios*, or $458.5 million pesos, was to be distributed as additional funds for the 83 congressmen entitled to them. (Details based upon extensive conversations and

examination of letters from Juntas, requests for scholarships and the lists of requested *auxilios* of a Conservative Senator for 1983 and 1984, Summer 1984; essential points confirmed in an interview with a former Liberal president of the House of Representatives, Summer 1984).

35 ICETEX, 1984: 52–3. A typical scholarship in 1984 at the primary or secondary level was for a mere $5,000 pesos; for university students they were often in the $10,000 to $20,000 range, though they could go as high as $100,000 (based upon an examination of lists of students receiving scholarships of a senator, August 1984).

36 Congressional *auxilios* have also been employed for such purposes as supporting union conventions, peasant organizations such as FANAL, and landowner and livestock associations (review of the central budget law for 1964, 1966, 1970 and each year from 1975 to 1984).

37 A rough estimate for 1983 would be that 985,000 voters were reached in this way, a figure equivalent to 17% of the total vote in the 1984 mid-term election. The calculation was made by assuming that only the minimum permitted of $100,000 was given to each Junta and thus that through the ministries of government, health and development, funds were distributed to 15,078 Juntas. Although not completely true, it was also assumed that no single Junta received more than one congressional *auxilio*. Based upon the fact that the average number of affiliates of Juntas in the 1978 census was sixty-one, then approximately 900,000 voters were reached by these funds (rounding numbers to 15,000 x 60). Then, making the further heroic assumption that none of the scholarships went to beneficiaries of *auxilios* to Juntas, but the minimalist assumption that each scholarship only translated into one vote, adding the 85,000 scholarships to the earlier figure totals 985,000.

38 One politician told me he organized a get out the vote campaign to insure that leadership posts in numerous urban Juntas in his department capital city would be taken away from the MOIR (a Maoist movement) (interview, Summer 1984). In contrast, a political activist seeking to help radical Juntas link up and coordinate their activities in the capital city reported government hostility (interview, Summer 1982).

39 See Reyes, 1978: 128–37.

40 Interviews with both individuals (in 1984 and 1977, respectively) and with a former president of the House of Representatives (1984). When I interviewed the manager of INSFOPAL in his office, I was struck by a large map of the country on the wall with pins for each project his agency was involved in; the pins were densely packed in his department and the Atlantic Coast region as a whole and disbursed more widely elsewhere in the country.

41 Chenery, Ocampo & Ramirez, 1986: 54–8. In spite of improvement in the informational capacities of the Colombian state, figures on total state employment have all been estimates. This has been due to the lack of an effective central reporting agency, to the number of levels and the growing number of legal structures under which employees

have operated and desires by various agencies to circumvent regulations. In the period from 1964 to 1982, contract personnel (*super-
numerarios*) grew from 2.4% of the public sector to 22.4% (González,
1986: 33).

42 Interviews with two former managers of DASC (in November, 1977
and March, 1978) and extended conversations with a number of
DASC employees. In his annual report to Congress in 1977, the then
manager of DASC reported 15,136 government employees in career
service (Colombia, DASC, 1977: 26); in a document he prepared
around the same time for the Turbay campaign (to which I was provided access), though, the same author used the figure of 13,000, also
cited in an interview with another DASC official. Thus, of 200,000
national level employees who could potentially join the civil service
at that time only 6.5% chose to do so.

43 A cabinet minister during the López government, reflecting on his
experience within his own ministry, noted that if in earlier years in
Colombia the bureaucracy was a source of spoils and posts for the
parties, that by the mid-1970s the situation was the opposite, one of
total immobilism and inertia in public administration caused by existing civil service laws (interview, October 10, 1977). In 1976 the López
government used state of siege powers to suspend all civil service
measures primarily so it could deal with work stoppages and radical
union activity in tax collection and other key areas of the public sector (interview with a leading Liberal politician, November 1, 1978,
and with a DASC official, November 29, 1977). These suspensions
were declared illegal by the Council of State in 1978.

44 The easing of legal requirements under President Betancur finally
facilitated the entry of an additional 52,000 employees into civil service between 1984 and 1986, though no progress was made at the
municipal or departmental level (Chenery, Ocampo & Ramírez,
1986: 106).

45 This point was confirmed in numerous interviews with politicians and
government officials. Hartwig (1985) notes there were no party-line
purges and little turnover in the ministry of public works below top
policy-making levels.

46 State salaries were extremely low: in 1964 the average income per
employed person for the urban employed labor force for the lowest
decile was Col$1,140 (for the second decile it jumped to $4,200), and
in 1966, 63% of all employees at the national level earned less than
$1,000 a month (Berry & Urrutia, 1976: 34 and DANE, *Boletín Mensual
de Estadística*, no. 227). As Urrutia notes, "labor leaders and officials of
the Labor Ministry, including the Labor Minister himself agreed that
the state was the worst employer in Colombia" (1969: 48–9). The
situation did not improve in the next decade. In fact, real average
public sector wages fell precipitously from 1971 to 1977, and by the
mid-1980s were only at levels equivalent to those at the beginning of
National Front in 1958. At the same time, the public sector employed
proportionally greater percentages of the working force with higher
levels of education, including 12.4% of all those with some high

school education and 29.6% of all those with some university education (Chenery, Ocampo & Ramirez, 1986: 30, 58).

47 As with other statistics involving the public sector, the extent of unionization is known only approximately. A 1976 census by DASC of union membership at the national level in the executive branch, excluding teachers, found seventy-two unions with a membership of 135,013 (Colombia, DASC, 1976: 53–4). The various unions that comprise the umbrella teachers' union had a membership of around 150,000 in 1976. As there were also important unions at the departmental and municipal level, particularly in public utilities, conservatively around 15,000 workers at this level can be considered unionized. Dividing this figure (300,000) by the total number of union members given in Chenery, Ramírez & Ocampo (1986: 118) of 835,000 in 1974 generates the figure of roughly one third.

48 During this same period, there were only 219 strikes in all of the manufacturing sector (Fonseca, 1982: 79).

49 In the 1970s, the state social security system employed around one fourth of all medical personnel in the country; 26% of all strikes in the public sector in the 1974–80 period were called by this group (Perry, Gómez & Londoño, 1982: 182, 187–92; Fonseca, 1982: 97).

50 For a thorough analysis of the political and administrative issues surrounding public education, see Gómez Buendía & Losada Lora, 1984: especially 203–20 for a brief history of FECODE. For a different perspective, see Coral Quintero, 1980.

51 Chenery, Ocampo & Ramírez, 1986: 107–10. And according to this same study, by 1984 this figure had actually fallen to 9.3% as a consequence of the economic recession, especially in the manufacturing sector. This analysis corrects earlier overestimates (such as Tenjo, 1975a) which had union members comprising around 17% of the Colombian labor force in 1974.

52 The Lleras Restrepo administration convened about 36% of all such tribunals for the 1960–82 period. Under the impact of higher inflation in the 1970s and a probably accurate perception of a pro-management bias on the part of the tribunals, workers increasingly resisted their invocation (see Epstein, 1982).

53 It was not until 1966 that the *first* multi-firm agreement was signed, in the cement industry (Caicedo, 1971: 148). Of the 219 strikes in the manufacturing sector from 1974 to 1980, only 19 affected more than 1 plant (Fonseca, 1982: 61).

54 Between 1969 and 1976, UTC and CTC affiliated unions only carried out 22.1% of the strikes in the country (Gómez & Losada, 1977: 129).

55 Although real average urban wages experienced an average rate of growth of 2% from 1958 to the mid-1980s, they fell steadily from 1972 to 1977 (see Chenery, Ocampo & Ramírez, 1986: 30–3; Urrutia, 1985: 9–54).

56 Top CTC and UTC leaders proceeded with the strike in spite of their active involvement in support of different traditional party presidential contenders in the ongoing campaign – all of whom con-

demned the planned strike. Subsequently, in 1981 and in 1985, the "democratic" UTC, CTC and CGT refused to join the CSTC in carrying out announced national strikes in part due to government promises of labor and social reform (see Hartlyn, 1985; and the columns by Enrique Santos Calderón, *El Tiempo*, June 23, 1985, and Alfredo Vázquez Carrizosa, *El Espectador*, June 25, 1985).

57 The Magdalena river is one of the most important in Colombia. It runs between the eastern and central Andean mountain ranges and flows into the Caribbean at Barranquilla. The middle Magdalena valley comprises western parts of the departments of Caldas and Antioquia, eastern parts of Boyacá and Santander and southern parts of Cesar and Magdalena (see Acosta & López, 1984: 153–4). For a discussion of the early struggles of Communist guerrilla groups, see Montaña Cuéllar, 1977: 171–82, 272–8; and Alape, 1985: 170–278.

58 Many of the captured guerrillas were eventually released as they passed from mistreatment and procedural irregularities at the hands of military justice to civilian courts. Other key leaders were captured or killed in the mid-1970s but an effort to negotiate a settlement with remaining elements was frustrated during the López administration partially due to military obstructionism (see the interview with López' intermediary with the ELN, Alvaro Escallón Villa, in Behar, 1985: 287–90). The ELN began to re-emerge in the late 1970s (see Behar, 1985: 51–67; Alape, 1985: 279–96).

7 Toward the dismantling of coalition rule: exclusion or reform?

1 The UTC and the CGT did not consider joining a possible strike for they feared a possible military coup if they went ahead with the strike. The security forces were also far more extensively deployed in 1981 than they had been in 1977, minimizing the effects – as well as the casualties – of the strike. Eventually an agreement was reached to increase the minimum wage at a level somewhat higher in relation to inflation than in previous years (Urrutia, 1981: 219–25).

2 Estimates of the value of drug trafficking are obviously fraught with difficulty. Gómez (1986), based on US government estimates, asserts that by 1977 Colombia supplied over half of the marihuana consumed in the US. Marihuana cultivation in Colombia was concentrated on the Atlantic Coast and probably covered a maximum of 10,000 hectares when it peaked in 1981. It declined sharply thereafter as a consequence of drought, increased production in the US and elsewhere and the decision by the Betancur administration to spray crops with the pesticide glyphosate. The maximum annual income to traffickers was around US$250 million. Cocaine exports to the US from Colombia apparently began to expand dramatically in 1980 to a high point in 1982, when total revenues from cocaine may have been US$1.1 billion. The cocaine traffic has been centered in Medellín. Initially consisting primarily of the processing and trans-shipment of coca paste from Peru and Ecuador, it expanded into coca cultivation in Caquetá, Vichada and other regions of Colombia (to around 15,000

hectares), though the crops were of a lower quality. According to these figures, total drug traffic as a percentage of GDP climbed from 4.1% in 1981 to a high of 6.4% in 1982, declining to 2.6% in 1985. These are conservative estimates.

3 Political favoritism appeared to have played a role in determining how different banks were treated. The absence of a strong state ideology is apparent in the contrast between the measured steps taken by the Colombian authorities versus the state takeover of financial institutions in Mexico in that same year.

4 Changes in Supreme Court judges, not well analyzed by Betancur's legal advisers, led to a change in jurisprudence from 1974 when the Court ruled that the executive could enact a tax reform by decree using its powers to declare a state of national economic emergency (see Latorre, 1983).

5 Upset by the way Betancur had brought Liberals into his government but unwilling to forego the posts, the Liberal party directorate at the time explained that Liberal participation in government was "personal and technical." As a result of the new accommodation with Betancur, it was termed "cooperation with oversight (*fiscalización*)." After the 1984 mid-term elections, seeking both continued participation in government and freedom to criticize with an eye toward the 1986 elections, the directorate explained that Liberal participation was "constitutional collaboration with critical independence" (see *El Mundo*, April 27, 1984).

6 Congress was especially interested in approving the tax reform because the Supreme Court had declared unconstitutional decrees that gave additional resources to the departments, while leaving intact those that took resources away. As a leading Liberal congressman told me, the departments were being left without resources and individuals were not paying taxes (interview, Summer 1984). Reflecting the continued strength of agrarian interests in Congress, the final law was more beneficial to landowners than the measures decreed using emergency powers.

7 A partial indicator of administration similarities and differences is the fact that Turbay's last finance minister went from government to a post in the IMF, whereas Betancur's first finance minister left government for a position with the World Bank. Both were technocrats with international ties, but one was more economically orthodox than the other.

8 Betancur's positive ratings fell from 71.1% in January, 1983 to 34.8% in September, 1984, while his negative ratings grew from 3.4% to 22.3% in that same time period (survey data by Centro Nacional de Consultoría, mimeo, October, 1984).

9 For details of the Cerrejón project (including the smaller central Cerrejón project) and of the contract between the state and Exxon, see Kline, 1982.

10 For a history of the 1974 campaign, see Ungar & Gómez de Martínez, 1977 and Cepeda, 1976; useful insights on the Liberal nomination process are in Lara, 1983: 145–7.

11 No party was organizationally capable of actually running a separate party primary. The use of congressional elections as surrogate "primaries" was well entrenched in the parties' history. A prominent example noted in chapter 3 occurred in 1958, when the victory of Laureanista congressional lists doomed Valencia's 1958 candidacy.

12 The Court based its judgement in part on the failure of Congress to follow rigorously requirements for congressional quorum and voting majorities (*El Tiempo,* May 26, 1978). However, many political observers felt it may also have stemmed from fear of the potential changes that would be made to the judicial system. Under the existing system, judges of the Supreme Court replaced themselves (known as *cooptación*) and elected judges of the lower court, who in turn elected the judges of the lowest courts.

13 General Alvaro Valencia Tovar, forced into early retirement by López, organized a Movement for National Restoration and campaigned on themes of moralization and the need for congressional reform. The left was sharply divided and both the Communist Party and the Maoist MOIR formed separate electoral coalitions with smaller groups, promoting Anapistas as their respective presidential candidates. Eventually, a coalition of mostly Trotskyite groups also presented a presidential candidate. Out of frustration with these divisions, a political movement seeking "a single candidate against the system" known as Firmes! emerged, but postponed its organizational activities until after the presidential elections.

14 Delgado, 1978: 248; this book is a useful compilation of major speeches and interviews with the principal 1978 presidential candidates. The two major Liberal dailies of the capital endorsed Lleras, a fact Turbay used to buttress his argument that he was the people's candidate against the oligarchy. In fact, most regional newspapers, radio stations and television news shows (the latter leased from the state) endorsed Turbay.

15 An indicator of Turbay's weakness is the fact that 57% of the respondents to an electoral survey study of Bogotá who identified themselves as Liberals opted not to vote in the presidential elections and another 7% voted for other candidates. The data is taken from computer printouts; see also Sánchez et al., 1981.

16 Lleras bitterly denounced the government partiality toward Turbay; one week after the elections he wrote: "I considered the past 'mitaca' [1976] elections to be dirty, but what happened then was child's play compared to what happened this time . . . The government machine exerted pressure in every imaginable way" (*Nueva Frontera,* March 18–24, 1978, p. 171).

17 For a more complete breakdown, see Table A.2 in Appendix A.

18 A panel study of the elections in Bogotá indicated that Liberal efforts to "polarize" the vote between Betancur and López did not cause many who intended to vote for Galán to switch (only 2.9% of those who were Galán sympathizers a few weeks before the election voted for López). However, the López strategy may have convinced some abstainers to vote for López, as 21% of his vote was comprised of

voters who made their decision to vote in the week before the election (the respective figures for Betancur and Galán were 12.4% and 11.6%) (Gómez Gómez, 1982: 171). According to this study, Belisario convinced 8.3% of those who identified as Liberals to vote for him, providing him with 18.6% of his total vote in the city; similarly, 14.1% of those with no party affiliation voted for him, which represented 21.9% of his total Bogotá vote. These figures dramatically illustrate the importance of the floating electorate that emerged during the National Front and the success of Betancur's strategy. Among Conservatives, Betancur mobilized 53.7% of all party identifiers who gave him 54.5% of his total Bogotá vote. In sharp contrast, López received votes only from Liberals. In addition to Liberals and a negligible percentage of Conservatives, Galán was able to motivate 8.3% [sic] of those without party affiliation to vote for him, which represented 16.1% of his total Bogotá vote (Gómez Gómez, 1982: 151, 160).

19 In the 1982 Bogotá panel study, only 2.9% of the sample identified with leftist parties. When asked to place themselves on an ideological side, only 9.4% of the sample asserted they were "leftists," while 28.7% placed themselves on the right, 20.9% in the center and 41.0% said they had no position. Most remarkably, of the large group (39.5%) that expressed no party affiliation, none considered themselves "leftists."

This group tended to be younger and from lower socio-economic strata; it was less politically informed and less willing to express opinions on political issues. Abstentionism was largely not the reflection of a coherent ideological position of rejection of the regime (see Gómez Gómez, 1982: 48, 61–5).

20 Yet, as Linz has noted, because "[a] primary requirement of a stable democratic regime is retention of its legitimacy among those in direct control of the instruments of coercion ... [i]n certain respects the armed forces in a modern society are a concurrent minority, in the sense that Calhoun uses the term" (Linz, 1978: 85). In Colombia by the late 1970s, the military were institutionally more prepared to demand that role.

21 Eyewitness accounts have been written by the US Ambassador held hostage (Asencio, 1982) and by the leader of the M-19 operation (Pabón Pabón, 1984). Reflecting the extent of risk the political regime was under, Asencio notes candidly that Turbay faced a "complicated and sophisticated problem" including "the nagging threat of the possibility of a military coup" (: 58).

22 Thinking that López was the most likely candidate to revamp the political regime and incorporate the guerrillas and other social forces into the political process, the noted leftist Colombian writer Gabriel García Márquez shocked many opposition groups by endorsing the establishment figure of López in the 1982 presidential race. García Márquez had fled Colombia in March, 1981 fearing that his connections with Cuba could lead to his arrest. Betancur, however, cultivated him assiduously and his receipt of the 1982 Nobel Prize in

Literature was officially celebrated in the country. In fact, García Márquez became a major intermediary in Colombia's foreign policy and internal peace process, in part because of his close friendship with Fidel Castro (see Cepeda, 1985).

23 In mid-March, the government had apparently carried out one of the largest drug raids in the world, shutting down a jungle cocaine processing plant and seizing 13.8 tons of cocaine (*New York Times*, March 21, 1984). This was the first successful assassination of a cabinet minister while in office. As a consequence of the assassination, Betancur decided to follow through on the terms of an extradition treaty signed under Turbay which permitted Colombian nationals to be sent to the US to face drug charges there. Convinced they could evade justice in Colombia, the extradition treaty was the only legal tool the major drug traffickers feared.

24 The Reform facilitated the formation of the congressional commissions responsible for reviewing the executive's development plans that had been created by the 1968 Reform yet had never been able to convene. The 1979 Reform also enshrined congressional control over funds for *auxilios*, but prohibited the re-election of key patronage and oversight posts such as congressional officers, the *Procurador, Contralor* and newly-created *Fiscal*. It resolved the problem of immobilism due to congressional absenteeism by eliminating the need for a quorum to meet and reducing the quorum needed to take a vote from one half plus one to one third of a chamber's members. The text of the Reform is in Arboleda, 1981: 86–100; see also Botero, 1980.

25 With a strong endorsement from the Reagan administration, the Colombian military insisted on the existence of a connection between guerrillas and drug traffickers, a "narco-guerrilla." Evidence suggests not extensive unity but occasional points of collaboration between the M-19 and some drug traffickers and that jungle coca plantations and cocaine laboratories may have paid "protection money" to FARC guerrillas active in the same area.

26 The descent into violence became macabre. The CNG ousted the "Ricardo Franco" following confirmation that the organization had massacred over 100 peasants and followers claiming they were infiltrators. This internecine violence on the left was occurring as the country continued to debate the report by the attorney general regarding the participation of members of the police and of the army in some of the several hundred cases of "disappearances."

8 Consociationalism and political conflict in comparative perspective

1 Of course, not all transitions from bureaucratic–authoritarian rule have necessitated extensive negotiation with the military institution. The complete collapse of the Argentine military following the Falklands/Malvinas débâcle on the heels of economic crisis obviated any need for a negotiated process with them. At the same time, the

sobering experience of military rule and the lack of any revolutionary threat produced a shift toward moderation and tolerance among most parties and interest groups (see Waisman, 1985: 89–101).

2 As a result of that plebiscite, which approved a new constitution, Pinochet is to remain in office until 1989 and could serve until 1997.

3 Schmitter's often cited conceptualization of corporatism refers to it as a form of interest intermediation that is "singular, concentrated, functionally differentiated, hierarchical and compulsory." In the Western European context, it is often employed to describe the "concertation" of public policy among major functional interests (cf. Schmitter, 1982: 263–4). I am emphasizing the phenomenon where both are present.

4 For example, the Social and Economic Council in the Netherlands and the Joint Commission for Prices and Wages in Austria.

5 For example, in Austria "*immobilisme* in the policy area delayed legislation and reforms for years" (Dreijmanis, 1982: 258) as the coalition system of government earned a reputation for "stalemate, inefficiency and corruption" (Obler, Steiner & Dierickx, 1977: 26).

Appendix B

1 All the associations listed in Table 4.1 with the exception of CAMACOL and FASECOLDA were visited. In two cases, I was unable to get complete lists for the full ten years.

2 Of the over 400 names collected, only eighteen had served on more than one board during the ten-year period. Of these eighteen, nine had served on boards of different interest groups within the same sector, either in agriculture or commerce and another three had moved from ASOBANCARIA to ANIF when the organizational rift occurred. Of the remaining six, two served only briefly as *suplentes*; three of the other four as well as several other relevant members of this small group were interviewed. The flow of information and interaction across sectors did not operate by means of interlocking directorates at the level of producer associations.

3 Given my analytical focus on consociationalism, opposition leaders were interviewed on an informal basis rather than as part of this sample.

Bibliography

Abel, Christopher. 1974. "Conservative party in Colombia, 1930–1953." PhD dissertation. University of Oxford.

Acosta, Daniel & López, Gilma. 1984. "Violencia capitalista en el Magdalena Medio." In *La realidad del "sí se puede": Demagogia y violencia.* Bogotá: Comité de Solidaridad con los Presos Políticos.

Agudelo Ramírez, Luis E., ed. 1958. *El Frente Nacional: síntesis doctrinal e histórica.* Bogotá: Ediciones Lasguram.

Akkermans, Tinie & Grootings, Peter. 1978. "From corporatism to polarization: elements of the development of Dutch industrial relations." In Colin Crouch and Alessandro Pizzorno, eds., *The Resurgence of Class Conflict in Western Europe Since 1968: vol. 1 National Studies.* New York: Holmes and Meier.

Alape, Arturo, ed. 1985. *La paz, la violencia: testigos de excepción.* Bogotá: Planeta Colombiana Editorial, S.A.

Amézquita, Saul & Fernández, Javier. 1977. "La economía colombiana, 1950–1975." *Revista de Planeación y Desarrollo* 9 (October–December), pp. 1–278.

Amnistía Internacional, 1980. "Recomendaciones al Gobierno Colombiano de una Misión de Amnistía Internacional a la República de Colombia (15 de enero–31 de enero de 1980)." London (April).

Anderson, Charles. 1979. "Political design and the representation of interests." In Philippe C. Schmitter and Gerhard Lehmbruch, eds., *Trends Toward Corporatist Intermediation.* Beverly Hills: Sage Publications.

ANIF. 1980. *La abstención.* Bogotá: Fondo Editorial ANIF.

Arango, Juan Ignacio. 1978. *Inversión extranjera en la industria manufacturera nacional.* Bogotá: Departamento Administrativo Nacional de Estadísticas.

Arango F., Sebastián. Bueno M., Jaime & Gómez de Arango, Florangela, eds. 1979. *La estructura fiscal colombiana: los impuestos y el gasto público.* Bogotá: Universidad Javeriana.

Araya A., Juan Enrique, et al. 1975. *La política agraria en Colombia.* Bogotá: FEDESARROLLO.

Arboleda Perdomo, Enrique. 1981. *La reforma constitucional de 1979: su inexequibilidad.* Bogotá: Editorial Dintel.

Arenas, Jacobo. 1985. *Cese el fuego: una historia politica de las FARC.* Bogotá: Editorial Oveja Negra.

Arocha, Jaime. 1979. *La violencia en el Quindío*. Bogotá: Ediciones Tercer Mundo.

Arriaga Andrade, Adán. 1946. "La obra social del Partido Liberal." In Plinio Mendoza Niera and Alberto Camacho Angarita, eds., *El liberalismo en el gobierno, tomo II: sus realizaciones, 1930–1946*. Bogotá: Editorial Minerva.

Arrubla, Mario, ed. 1976. *La agricultura en Colombia, Siglo XX*. Bogotá: Ediciones Colcultura.

Arrubla, Mario, et al. 1978. *Colombia hoy*. Bogotá: Siglo XXI.

Ascher, William. 1984. *Scheming for the Poor: The Politics of Redistribution in Latin America*. Cambridge, Mass.: Harvard University Press.

Asencio, Diego & Nancy. 1982. *Our Man is Inside*. Boston: Atlantic Monthly Press.

Avramovic, D. 1972. *Economic Growth of Colombia*. Baltimore: The Johns Hopkins University Press.

Bagley, Bruce M. 1979. "Political power, public policy and the state in Colombia: case studies of the urban and agrarian reforms during the National Front, 1958–1974." PhD dissertation, University of California–Los Angeles.

 1984. "Colombia: National Front and economic development." In Robert Wesson, ed., *Politics, Policies and Economic Development in Latin America*. Stanford: The Hoover Institution.

Bagley, Bruce M. & Botero, Fernando. 1978. "Organizaciones campesinas contemporáneas en Colombia: un estudio de la Asociación Nacional de Usuarios Campesinos (ANUC)." *Estudios rurales latinoamericanos* 1 (January–April), pp. 59–96.

Bagley, Bruce M. & Edel, Matthew. 1980. "Popular mobilization programs of the National Front: co-optation and radicalization." In Albert Berry, Ronald Hellman and Mauricio Solaún, eds., *Politics of Compromise: Coalition Government in Colombia*. New Brunswick: Transaction Books.

Bagley, Bruce M. & Laun, John I. 1977. "Political power and agricultural policy in Colombia: a case study of Laws 4 and 5 of 1973." Bogotá: Department of Political Science, Universidad de los Andes, mimeo.

Bailey, John J. 1976. "Bureaucratic politics and social security policy in Colombia." *Inter-American Economic Affairs*, 29 (Spring), pp. 3–20.

 1977. "Pluralist and corporatist dimensions of interest representation in Colombia." In James M. Malloy, ed., *Authoritarianism and Corporatism in Latin America*. University of Pittsburgh Press.

Bailey, Norman. 1965. "The Colombian 'Black Hand': a case study of neo-liberalism in Latin America." *Review of Politics* 27 (October), pp. 445–64.

Bailey, Samuel J. 1967. *Labor, Nationalism and Politics in Argentina*. New Brunswick: Rutgers University Press.

Baklanoff, Eric N. 1969. "External factors in the economic development of Brazil's heartland." In Eric N. Baklanoff, ed., *The Shaping of Modern Brazil*. Baton Rouge: Louisiana State University Press.

Bakvis, Herman. 1984. "Toward a political economy of

consociationalism: a commentary on Marxist views of pillarization in the Netherlands." *Comparative Politics* 16 (April), pp. 315–34.

Balassa, Bela & Associates. (n.d.). *The Structure of Protection in Developing Countries*. Baltimore: The Johns Hopkins University Press.

Baloyra, Enrique. 1983. "Reactionary despotism in Central America." *Journal of Latin American Studies* 15 (November), pp. 295–319.

Barry, Brian. 1975a. "The consociational model and its dangers." *European Journal of Political Research* 3 (December), pp. 393–412.

1975b. "Review article: political accommodation and consociational democracy." *British Journal of Political Science* 5 (October), pp. 477–505.

Behar, Olga, ed. 1985. *Las guerras de la paz*. Bogotá: Planeta Colombiana Editorial, SA.

Bejarano, Jesús A., ed. 1982. *Deficit fiscal*. Bogotá: Talleres Gráficos de la Contraloría General de la República.

1985. *Economía y Poder: La SAC y el desarrollo agropecuario colombiano 1871–1984*. Bogotá: Fondo Editorial CEREC and SAC.

Bergquist, Charles W. 1978. *Coffee and Conflict in Colombia, 1886–1910*. Durham, NC: Duke University Press.

1986. *Labor in Latin America: Comparative Essays on Chile, Argentina, Venezuela, and Colombia*. Stanford University Press.

Bergsman, Joel. 1970. *Brazil: Industrialization and Trade Policies*. London: Oxford University Press.

Berry, Albert. 1971. "Some implications of elitist rule for development in Colombia." In Gustav Ranis, ed., *Government and Economic Development*. New Haven: Yale University Press.

1972. "A presumptive income tax on agricultural land: Colombia." *National Tax Journal* 25 (June), pp. 169–81.

1983a. "A brief summary of twentieth-century industrial policy." In *Essays on Industrialization in Colombia*. Tempe: Center for Latin American Studies, Arizona State University.

ed. 1983b. *Essays on Industrialization in Colombia*. Tempe: Center for Latin American Studies, Arizona State University.

Berry, Albert, Hellman, Ronald G. & Solaún, Mauricio, eds. 1980. *Politics of Compromise: Coalition Government in Colombia*. New Brunswick: Transaction Books.

Berry, Albert & Solaún, Mauricio. 1980. "Notes toward an interpretation of the National Front." In Albert Berry, Ronald Hellman and Mauricio Solaún, eds., *Politics of Compromise: Coalition Government in Colombia*. New Brunswick: Transaction Books.

Berry, Albert & Soligo, Ronald, eds. 1980. *Economic Policy and Income Distribution in Colombia*. Boulder: Westview Press.

Berry, Albert & Thoumi, Francisco. 1977. "Import substitution and beyond: Colombia." *World Development* 5 (January–February), pp. 89–109.

Berry, Albert & Urrutia Montoya, Miguel. 1976. *Income Distribution in Colombia*. New Haven: Yale University Press.

Bird, Richard M. 1968a. "Coffee tax policy in Colombia." *Inter-American Economic Affairs* 22 (Summer), pp. 75–86.

1968b. "Sales tax and development planning – Colombia." In Gustav F. Papanek, ed., *Development Policy – Theory and Practice*. Cambridge, Mass.: Harvard University Press.

1974. *Taxing Agricultural Lands in Developing Countries*. Cambridge, Mass.: Harvard University Press.

Bird, Richard M., et al. 1981. *Finanzas intergubernamentales en Colombia*. Bogotá: Departamento Nacional de Planeación.

Bluhm, William T. 1973. *Building an Austrian Nation: The Political Integration of a Western State*. New Haven: Yale University Press.

Blutstein, Howard I., et al. 1977. *Area Handbook for Colombia, 3rd Edition*. Washington, DC: United States Government Printing Office.

Botero, Camila. 1980. "La Reforma Constitucional de 1979." *Coyuntura Económica* 10 (April), pp. 83–103.

ed. 1983. *Propuestas sobre descentralización*. Bogotá: Universidad de los Andes, CIDER.

Bridge, Susan. 1977. "Some causes of political change in modern Yugoslavia." In Milton J. Esman, ed., *Ethnic Conflict in the Western World*. Ithaca: Cornell University Press.

Broderick, Walter J. 1975. *Camilo Torres: A Biography of the Priest-Guerrilla*. New York: Doubleday.

Bushnell, David. 1967. *Eduardo Santos and the Good Neighbor, 1938–1942*. Gainesville: University of Florida Press.

1970. "Elecciones presidenciales colombianas 1825–1856." In Miguel Urrutia M. and Mario Arrubla, eds., *Compendio de Estadísticas Históricas de Colombia*. Bogotá: Universidad Nacional de Colombia, Dirección de Divulgación Cultural.

1975. "Bolivarismo y Santanderismo." In David Bushnell, *Política y sociedad en el siglo XIX, Lecturas de historia No. 3*. Tunja: Ediciones Pato Marino.

Caicedo, Edgar. 1971. *Historia de las luchas sindicales en Colombia*. Bogotá: Ediciones CEIS.

Camacho Guizado, Alvaro. 1977. *La organización social de la centralización del capital en Colombia*. Cali: Universidad del Valle.

Cano, Augusto. 1974. "Antecedentes constitucionales y legales de la planeación en Colombia." In Hernando Gómez and Eduardo Wiesner, eds., *Lecturas sobre el desarrollo económico colombiano*. Bogotá: FEDESAROLLO.

Cardoso, Fernando Henrique. 1979. "On the characterization of authoritarian regimes in Latin America." In David Collier, ed., *The New Authoritarianism in Latin America*. Princeton University Press.

Cardoso, Fernando Henrique & Faletto, Enzo. 1979. *Dependency and Development in Latin America*. Berkeley: University of California Press.

Carnoy, Martin. 1984. *The State and Political Theory*. Princeton University Press.

Cartier, William. 1986. "Civic movements and *paros cívicos* in Colombia, 1958–1986." University of Toronto, Department of Political Science, ms.

Cepeda Ulloa, Fernando. 1976. *Ensayos políticos*. Bogotá: Universidad de los Andes, Programa de Alta Gerencia, September.

1977a. "Colombia and the World Bank." In *The Impact of International Organizations on Legal and Institutional Change in the Developing Countries*. New York: International Legal Center.

1977b. "Liberales y conservadores contra los trabajadores?" *Estrategia* No. 5 (October), pp. 41–3.

1985. "Contadora, Colombia y Centroamérica." Presented to a Conference on Regional Approaches to the Central American Crisis, Tolima, Mexico.

Cepeda Ulloa, Fernando & González de Lecaros, Claudia. 1976. *Comportamiento del voto urbano en Colombia: una approximación*. Bogotá: Universidad de los Andes.

Cepeda Ulloa, Fernando & Mitchell, Christopher. 1980. "The trend toward technocracy." In Albert Berry, Ronald Hellman and Mauricio Solaún, eds., *Politics of Compromise: Coalition Government in Colombia*. New Brunswick: Transaction Books.

Chalmers, Douglas A. 1977. "The politicized state in Latin America." In James M. Malloy, ed., *Authoritarianism and Corporatism in Latin America*. University of Pittsburgh Press.

Chenery, Hollis B., Ocampo, José Antonio & Ramírez, Manuel. 1986. "El problema laboral colombiano: diagnóstica, perspectivas y políticas. Informe Final de la Misión de Empleo." *Economía Colombiana*, Serie Documento No. 10 (August–September), pp. 1–156.

Christie, Keith. 1986. *Oligarcas, campesinos y política de la frontera antioqueña*. Bogotá: Universidad Nacional de Colombia.

Coleman, James S. 1960. "Conclusion: the political systems of the developing areas." In Gabriel A. Almond and James S. Coleman, eds., *The Politics of the Developing Areas*. Princeton University Press.

Collier, David. 1979a. "Overview of the bureaucratic–authoritarian model." In David Collier, ed., *The New Authoriarianism in Latin America*. Princeton University Press.

1979b. "The bureaucratic–authoritarian model: synthesis and priorities for future research." In David Collier, ed., *The New Authoritarianism in Latin America*. Princeton University Press.

ed. 1979c. *The New Authoritarianism in Latin America*. Princeton University Press.

Collier, Ruth. 1982. *Regimes in Tropical Africa*. Berkeley: University of California Press.

Colmenares, Germán. 1968. *Partidos políticos y clases sociales*. Bogotá: Ediciones Universidad de los Andes.

Colombia. Cámara de Representantes, Secretaría. 1959. *Por qué y cómo se forjó el Frente Nacional*. Bogotá: Imprenta Nacional.

Colombia. Comisión de Estudios Económicos y Sociales. 1965a. *Aspectos Económicos y Sociales*. Bogotá: Talleres Gráficos del Banco de la República.

Colombia. Comisión de Estudios Económicos y Sociales. 1965b. *Conclusiones*. Bogotá: Talleres Gráficos del Banco de la República.

Colombia. 1972. *Constitución política de la República de Colombia*. Eduardo López Villa, ed. Bogotá: Imprenta Nacional.

Colombia. Departamento Administrativo del Servicio Civil. [Carlos Ramírez Cardona]. 1976a. "La administración pública como instrumento del desarrollo: medidas adoptadas en Colombia para mejorar los niveles de eficiencia y acelerar el progreso nacional." Bogotá: Departamento Administrativo del Servicio Civil.

Colombia. Departamento Administrativo del Servicio Civil. [Jaime Lopera Gutiérrez]. 1976b. "Informe del Jefe del Departamento Administrativo del Servicio Civil al Congreso Nacional: Agosto 1974–Julio 1976." Bogotá.

Colombia. Departamento Administrativo del Servicio Civil. [Jaime Lopera Gutiérrez]. 1977. "Informe del Jefe del Departamento Administrativo del Servicio Civil al Congreso Nacional." Bogotá.

Colombia. Departamento Administrativo Nacional de Estadísticas (DANE). 1971. *Estadísticas 1935–1970*. Bogotá.

Colombia. Departamento Administrativo Nacional de Estadísticas (DANE). 1978. *Indice de precios al consumidor, 1954–Junio, 1977*. Bogotá.

Colombia. Fondo de Promoción de Exportaciones (PROEXPO). 1977. "1967–1977: Informe presentado por la Dirección." Bogotá.

Colombia. Ministerio de Agricultura. INCORA. 1977. "Informe de actividades – 1976." Bogotá.

Colombia. Ministerio de Agricultura. INCORA. 1978. "Informe de actividades – 1977." Bogotá.

Colombia. Ministerio de Gobierno. Dirección General de Integración y Desarrollo de la Comunidad. 1970. "La acción comunal en Colombia." Bogotá: Imprenta Nacional.

Colombia. Ministerio de Gobierno. 1985. *Paz: Política de paz del Presidente Betancur*. Bogotá.

Colombia. Ministerio de Gobierno (Jaime Castro). 1986. *Proceso a la violencia y proceso de paz: memoria ministerial*. Bogotá.

Colombia. Ministerio de Educación Nacional. ICETEX. 1984. "Informe de Labores, 1983–1984."

Colombia. Presidencia (Alfonso López Michelsen). 1974. "Informe presidencial sobre el estado de emergencia económica." Bogotá: Banco de la República.

Colombia. Presidencia (Alfonso López Michelson). 1978. *Testimonio Final: Mensaje al Congreso Nacional, 1978, vol. I*. Bogotá: Talleres Gráficos del Banco de la República.

Colombia. Presidencia de la República (Virgilio Barco). 1987a. *Así estamos cumpliendo: cuatro meses de gobierno–programa agosto a diciembre 1986, tomo I*. Bogotá: Imprenta Nacional.

Colombia. Presidencia de la República (Virgilio Barco). 1987b. *Así estamos cumpliendo: cuatro meses de gobierno–programa agosto a diciembre 1986, tomo II*. Bogotá: Imprenta Nacional.

Colombia. Presidencia (Secretaría Jurídica). 1969. *Historia de la Reforma Constitucional de 1968*. Bogotá: Imprenta Nacional.

Colombia. Registraduría Nacional del Estado Civil. 1964. *Organización y estadísticas electorales: 15 de marzo de 1964*. Bogotá.

Colombia. Registraduría Nacional del Estado Civil. 1966. *Organización y estadísticas electorales: marzo 17 de 1966*. Bogotá.

Colombia. Registraduría Nacional del Estado Civil. 1968. *Organización y estadísticas electorales: marzo 17 de 1968*. Bogotá.

Colombia. Registraduría Nacional del Estado Civil. 1970. *Estadísticas electorales: 19 de abril de 1970*. Bogotá.

Colombia. Registraduría Nacional del Estado Civil. 1974. *Estadísticas electorales: abril 12, 1974*. Bogotá.

Colombia. Registraduría Nacional del Estado Civil. 1976. *Estadísticas electorales: abril 18, 1976*. Bogotá.

Colombia. Registraduría Nacional del Estado Civil. 1978. *Estadísticas electorales: corporaciones públicas, 26 de febrero de 1978*. Bogotá.

Colombia. Registraduría Nacional del Estado Civil. 1978. *Estadísticas electorales: junio 4, 1978*. Bogotá.

Colombia. Senado de la República. Comisión Instructora. 1960. *El proceso contra Gustavo Rojas Pinilla ante el Congreso de Colombia*. Bogotá: Imprenta Nacional.

Colombia. Superintendencia de Sociedades. 1978. *Conglomerados de sociedades en Colombia*. Bogotá.

Comité Central del Partido Comunista de Colombia. 1960. *Treinta años de lucha del Partido Comunista de Colombia*. Bogotá: Ediciones Paz y Socialismo.

Coral Quintero, Laureano. 1980. *Historia del Movimiento Sindical del Magisterio*. Bogotá: Fondo Editorial Suramérica.

Corporación para el Fomento de Investigaciones Económicos (CORP). 1972. *Controversia sobre el plan de desarrollo*. Bogotá: Editorial La Oveja Negra.

Craig, Richard B. 1983. "Domestic implications of illicit Colombian drug production and trafficking." *Journal of Inter-American Studies and World Affairs* 25 (August) pp. 325–50.

Currie, Lauchlin. 1981. *The Role of Economic Advisers in Developing Countries*. Westport, Ct: Greenwood Press.

    1983. "La unidad de poder adquisitivo constante: una breve historia acerca de su nacimiento." *Desarrollo y Sociedad* Cuaderno 6 (August), pp. 5–12.

Daalder, Hans. 1973. "Building consociational nations." In S. N. Eisenstadt and Stein Rokkan, eds., *Building States and Nations, Vol. II*. Beverly Hills: Sage Publications.

    1974. "The consociational democracy theme." *World Politics* 26 (July), pp. 604–21.

Dahl, Robert A. 1971. *Polyarchy: Participation and Opposition*. New Haven: Yale University Press.

    1978. "Pluralism revisited." *Comparative Politics* 10 (January), pp. 191–203.

Deas, Malcolm. 1982. "The fiscal problems of nineteenth-century Colombia." *Journal of Latin American Studies* 14 (May), pp. 287–328.

    1986. "The troubled course of Colombian peacemaking." *Third World Quarterly* 8 (April), pp. 639–57.

Dekmejian, R. 1978. "Consociational democracy in crisis: the case of Lebanon." *Comparative Politics* 10 (January), pp. 251–65.

Delfim Netto, Antônio & Andrade Pinto, Carlos Alberto de. 1973. "The Brazilian coffee: twenty years of set-backs in the competition on the world market, 1945/65." In C. M. Peláez, ed., *Essays on Coffee and Development*. Rio de Janeiro: Instituto Brasileiro de Café.

Delgado, Alvaro. 1974. "Doce años de luchas obreras." *Estudios Marxistas* (Separata). Bogotá: Editorial Nueva Colombia.
    1978. "El paro cívico nacional." *Estudios Marxistas* No. 15, pp. 58–115.
    1982. "El decenio huelguístico 1971–80." *Estudios Marxistas* No. 23, pp. 3–82.
Delgado, Oscar, ed. 1973. *Ideologías políticas y agrarias en Colombia, Tomo I. La burguesía conservadora: burguesía dependiente, patriciado político, tecnoburocracia desarrollista.* Bogotá: Ediciones Tercer Mundo.
    1978. *La campaña por la presidencia, 1978–1982: los temas en controversia.* Bogotá: Ediciones Tercer Mundo.
Delpar, Helen. 1981. *Red Against Blue: The Liberal Party in Colombian Politics 1863–1899.* The University of Alabama Press.
Diamand, Marcelo. 1986. "Overcoming Argentina's stop and go economic cycles." In Jonathan Hartlyn and Samuel A. Morley, eds., *Latin American Political Economy.* Boulder: Westview Press.
Díaz-Alejandro, Carlos F. 1976. *Foreign Trade Regimes and Economic Development: Colombia.* New York: Columbia University Press.
Di Palma, Guiseppe. 1977. *Surviving Without Governing: The Italian Parties in Parliament.* Berkeley: University of California Press.
Di Tella, Torcuato. 1969. "Populism and reform in Latin America." In Claudio Veliz, ed. *Obstacles to Change in Latin America.* Oxford University Press.
Dix, Robert H. 1967. *Colombia: The Political Dimensions of Change.* New Haven: Yale University Press.
    1980a. "Consociational democracy: the case of Colombia." *Comparative Politics* 12 (April), pp. 303–21.
    1980b. "Political oppositions under the National Front." In Albert Berry, Ronald Hellman and Mauricio Solaún, eds., *Politics of Compromise: Coalition Government in Colombia.* New Brunswick: Transaction Books.
Dore, Elizabeth. 1986. "Nicaragua: the experience of the mixed economy." In Jonathan Hartlyn and Samuel A. Morley, eds., *Latin American Political Economy.* Boulder: Westview Press.
Drake, Paul. 1979. "The origins of United States economic supremacy in South America: Colombia's Dance of the Millions, 1923–33." Washington, DC: Wilson Center, Latin American Program, Working Papers No. 40.
Dreijmanis, John. 1982. "Austria: the 'Black'–'Red' Coalitions." In Eric C. Browne and John Dreijmanis, eds. *Government Coalitions in Western Democracies.* New York: Longman Inc.
Drekonja, Gerhard & Cepeda, Fernando. 1982. "Colombia." In Gerhard Drekonja and Juan G. Tokatlian, eds., *Teoría y práctica de la política exterior latinoamericana.* Bogotá: Fondo Editorial CEREC.
Duff, Ernest A. 1968. *Agrarian Reform in Colombia.* New York: Praeger.
    1971. "The role of Congress in the Colombian political system." In Weston H. Agor, ed., *Latin American Legislatures: Their Role and Influence.* New York: Praeger Publishers.
Dunkerley, Harold B. 1968. "Exchange-rate systems in conditions of

continuing inflation – Lessons from Colombian experience." In Gustav F. Papanek, ed., *Development Policy – Theory and Practice*, Cambridge, Mass.: Harvard University Press.

Eckstein, Harry. 1966. *Divisions and Cohesion in Democracy: A Study of Norway*. Princeton University Press.

Edel, Matthew. 1968. "Mobilizing human resources: the Colombian Community Development Program." In Frank T. Bachmura, ed., *Human Resources in Latin America*. Bloomington: Bureau of Business Research, Indiana University.

Edelman, Alexander T. 1969. "The rise and demise of Uruguay's second Plural Executive." *The Journal of Politics* 31 (February), pp. 119–39.

Ediciones Documentos Colombianos. 1957. *Las Jornadas de Mayo*. Bogotá: Antares.

Engelmann, Frederick C. 1966. "Austria: the pooling of opposition." In Robert A. Dahl, ed., *Political Oppositions in Western Democracies*. New Haven: Yale University Press.

Epstein, Edward. 1982. "Compulsory labor arbitration and wage policy in Colombia: 1960–1982," ms.

Erickson, Kenneth Paul. 1977. *The Brazilian Corporative State and Working-Class Politics*. Berkeley: University of California Press.

Evans, Peter. 1979. *Dependent Development: The Alliance of Multinational, State and Local Capital in Brazil*. Princeton University Press.

Evans, Peter B., Rueschemeyer, Dietrich & Skocpol, Theda. 1985. "On the road toward a more adequate understanding of the state." In Peter B. Evans, Dietrich Rueschemeyer and Theda Skocpol, eds., *Bringing the State Back In*. Cambridge University Press.

Fals Borda, Orlando. 1955. *Peasant Society in the Colombian Andes: A Sociological Study of Saucío*. Gainesville: University of Florida Press.

1969a. *Subversion and Social Change in Colombia*. Translated by Jacqueline D. Skiles. New York: Columbia University Press.

1969b. "Violence and the break-up of tradition in Colombia." In Claudio Veliz, ed., *Obstacles to Change in Latin America*. Oxford University Press.

Federación Nacional de Algodoneros. 1984. "Informe del Gerente al XXIII Congreso Nacional de Algodoneros, 1983–84." Valledupar.

FEDESARROLLO. 1975. "La política agraria en Colombia, 1950–1975." In Banco de Bogotá, *Informe Segundo Semestre de 1974*. Bogotá.

Figueroa J., Alejandro. 1977. "El sector financiero y el desarrollo industrial." *Revista Bimestral ANDI* No. 36 (November), pp. 28–42.

Finch, Henry J. 1977. "Three perspectives on the crisis in Uruguay." *Journal of Latin American Studies* 3, Part 2 (November), pp. 173–90.

Findley, Roger W. 1973. "Problems faced by Colombia's Agrarian Reform Institute in acquiring and distributing land." In Robert E. Scott, ed., *Latin American Modernization Problems*. Urbana, Illinois: University of Illinois Press.

1980. "Presidential intervention in the economy and the rule of law in Colombia." *The American Journal of Comparative Law* 28 (Summer), pp. 423–73.

Findley, Roger W., Cepeda Ulloa, Fernando & Gamboa Morales,

Nicolás. 1983. *Intervención presidencial en la Economía y el Estado de Derecho en Colombia*. Bogotá: Universidad de los Andes, CIDER.

Finegold, Kenneth & Skocpol, Theda. 1982. "State capacity and economic intervention in the early New Deal." *Political Science Quarterly* 97 (Summer), pp. 255–78.

Fleet, Michael. 1985. *The Rise and Fall of Chilean Christian Democracy*. Princeton University Press.

Fluharty, Vernon Lee. 1957. *Dance of the Millions: Military Rule and the Social Revolution in Colombia, 1930–1956*. University of Pittsburgh Press.

Fonseca, Luz Amparo. 1982. "Huelgas y paros cívicos en Colombia." Postgraduate thesis, Universidad de los Andes, Facultad de Economía.

Fuentes Hernández, Alfredo & Villaveces Pardo, Ricardo. 1976. "La liberación actual de importaciones y su perspectiva histórica." *Coyuntura Económica* 6 (July), pp. 87–98.

Furtado, Celso. 1963. *The Economic Growth of Brazil*. Berkeley: University of California Press.

1970. *Economic Development of Latin America*. Cambridge University Press.

Gallón Giraldo, Gustavo. 1979. *Quince años de estado de sitio en Colombia: 1958–1978*. Bogotá: Editorial América Latina.

Gallón Restrepo, Octavio. 1978. *Ruptura histórica*. Bogotá: Ediciones Tercer Mundo.

Garcia, J. J. 1977. *Epocas y gentes*. Bogotá: Ediciones Tercer Mundo.

Gerschenkron, Alexander. 1962. *Economic Backwardness in Historical Perspective* Cambridge, Mass.: Harvard University Press.

Gibson, William Marion. 1948. *The Constitutions of Colombia*. Durham, NC: Duke University Press.

Gilhodès, Pierre. 1970. "Agrarian struggles in Colombia." In Rodolfo Stavenhagen, ed. *Agrarian Problems and Peasant Movements in Latin America*. Garden City, NY: Doubleday and Co., Anchor Books.

1979. *Fuerzas e instituciones políticas en América Latina*. Bogotá: Editorial Colombia Nueva, 1979.

Gillespie, Charles G. 1984. "The breakdown of democracy in Uruguay: alternative political models." Washington, DC: The Wilson Center, Latin American Program.

1985. " 'Democradura' or 'reforma pactada'? comparative perspectives on democratic restoration in Uruguay." Presented to the International Political Science Association, July.

Gillespie, Charles & González, Luis. 1985. "Democracy in Uruguay." Presented to a Conference on Democracy in Developing Countries, Stanford, California.

Gillis, Malcolm, ed., Musgrave, Richard A., President. 1971. *Fiscal Reform for Colombia: Final Report and staff papers of the Colombian Commission on Tax Reform*. Cambridge, Mass.: Law School of Harvard University.

Gómez, Hernando J. 1986. "The Colombian illegal economy: size, evolution, characteristics and economic impact," ms.

Gómez Buendía, Hernando. 1978. *Alfonso López Michelsen: un examen crítico de su pensamiento y su obra de gobierno.* Bogotá: Ediciones Tercer Mundo.

Gómez Buendía, Hernando & Losada Lora, Rodrigo. 1977. "La actividad huelguística en Colombia, 1962–1976." *Coyuntura Económica* 7 (May), pp. 120–32.

Gómez Buendía, Hernando & Losada Lora, Rodrigo. 1984. *Organización y conflicto: la educación primaria oficial en Colombia.* Ottawa: International Development Research Centre.

Gómez Gómez, Elsa. 1982. *La elección presidencial de 1982 en Bogotá. Dinámica de la opinión electoral.* Bogotá: ANIF Fondo Editorial.

Gómez Hurtado, Alvaro. 1972. "Conservatismo y populismo." In *Populismo.* Bogotá: Editorial Revista Colombiana.

Gómez Otálora, Hernando & Wiesner Durán, Eduardo, eds. 1974. *Lecturas sobre el desarrollo económico colombiano.* Bogotá: FEDESARROLLO.

González, Fernan E. 1975a. "Colombia 1974. I. La política," *Controversia.* Bogotá: CIAS, No. 33.

1975b. "Pasado y presente del sindicalismo colombiano," *Controversia.* Bogotá: CIAS, No. 35–6.

González, Jorge Iván. 1986. "Evolución del empleo público (1982–1986)." *Economia colombiana* No. 183 (July), pp. 31–5.

Groves, Roderick T. 1974. "The Colombian National Front and administrative reform." *Administration and Society* 6 (November), pp. 316–36.

Gutiérrez, Alfredo, et al. 1979. *Uruguay: Economic Memorandum.* Washington, DC: The World Bank.

Guzmán, Germán. 1969. *Camilo Torres.* Translated by John Ring. New York: Sheed & Ward, Inc.

Guzmán, Germán, Fals Borda, Orlando, & Umaña Lima, Eduardo. 1963–4. *La violencia en Colombia.* 2 vols. Bogotá: Ediciones Tercer Mundo.

Handelman, Howard. 1978. "Military authoritarianism and political change in Uruguay." *American Universities Field Staff Reports* No. 26, South America.

1980. "Labor–industrial conflict and the collapse of Uruguayan democracy." University of Wisconsin-Milwaukee, ms.

Harkess, Shirley & Lewin, Patricia Pinzón de. 1975. "Women, the vote and the party in the politics of the Colombian National Front." *Journal of Interamerican and World Affairs* 17 (November), pp. 439–64.

Hartlyn, Jonathan. 1978. "El desarrollo gremial del país: un estudio de caso." Bogotá: Department of Political Science, Universidad de los Andes, ms.

1984a. "Military governments and the transition to civilian rule: the Colombian experience of 1957–58." *Journal of Interamerican Studies and World Affairs* 26 (May), pp. 245–81.

1984b. "The impact of patterns of industrialization and of popular sector incorporation on political regime type: a case study of Colombia." *Studies in Comparative International Development* 19 (Spring), pp. 29–60.

1985. "Producer associations, the political regime and policy processes in contemporary Colombia." *Latin American Research Review* 20, No. 3, pp. 111–38.

Hartlyn, Jonathan & Morley, Samuel A., eds., 1986a. *Latin American Political Economy: Financial Crisis and Political Change.* Boulder: Westview Press.

Hartlyn, Jonathan & Morley, Samuel A. 1986b. "Political regimes and economic performance in Latin America." In Jonathan Hartlyn and Samuel A. Morley, eds., *Latin American Political Economy*, Boulder: Westview Press.

Hartwig, Richard. 1983. *Roads to Reason: Transportation, Administration and Rationality in Colombia.* University of Pittsburgh Press.

Helguera, J. León. 1961. "The changing role of the military in Colombia." *Journal of Interamerican Studies* 3 (July), pp. 351–8.

Henderson, James D. 1985a. *Las ideas de Laureano Gómez.* Bogotá: Ediciones Tercer Mundo.

1985b. *When Colombia Bled: A History of the Violencia in Tolima.* University of Alabama Press.

Hennessey, Alistair. 1969. "Latin America." In G. Ionescu and E. Gellner, eds. *Populism: Its Meanings and National Characteristics.* New York: The Macmillan Co.

Hermet, Guy. 1978. "State-controlled elections: a framework." In Guy Hermet, Richard Rose and Alain Rouquié, eds., *Elections Without Choice.* New York: John Wiley & Sons.

Hirschman, Albert O. 1971. "The search for paradigms as a hindrance to understanding." In Albert O. Hirschman, *A Bias for Hope: Essays on Development and Latin America.* New Haven: Yale University Press.

1973a. *Journeys Toward Progress: Studies of Economic Policy Making in Latin America.* New York: Twentieth Century Fund, Inc., 1963; reprint New York: W. W. Norton & Co., Inc. (page references are to reprint edition).

1973b. "Land Use and Land Reform in Colombia." In Albert O. Hirschman, *Journeys Toward Progress: Studies of Economic Policy Making in Latin America.* New York: Twentieth Century Fund, Inc., 1963; reprint New York: W. W. Norton & Co., Inc. (page references are to reprint edition).

1979. "The turn to authoritarianism in Latin America and the search for its economic determinants." In David Collier, ed., *The New Authoritarianism in Latin America.* Princeton University Press.

Hobsbawm, Eric. 1963. "The anatomy of violence," *New Society* (April 11), pp. 16–18.

Horgan, Terence. 1983. "The Liberals come to power in Colombia, *por debajo de la ruana*: a study of the Enrique Olaya Herrera administration, 1930–1934." PhD dissertation, Vanderbilt University.

Hoskin, Gary W. 1971. "Dimensions of representation in the Colombian national legislature." In Western H. Agor, ed., *Latin American Legislatures: Their Role and Influence.* New York: Praeger Publishers.

1976. "Dimensions of conflict." In Gary Hoskin, Francisco Leal and Harvey Kline, *Legislative Behavior in Colombia, Volume II.* State University of New York at Buffalo, Council on International Studies,

No. 8.

1979a. "Belief systems of Colombian party activists." *Journal of Interamerican Studies and World Affairs* 21 (November), pp. 481–504.

1979b. "Post-National Front trends in the Colombian party system: more of the same?" Presented at the Seventh National Meeting of the Latin American Studies Association, Pittsburgh, April.

1985. "Colombian political parties and electoral behavior in the post-National Front period." Presented to the XII International Congress of the Latin American Studies Association.

Hoskin, Gary W. et al. 1975. *Estudio del comportamiento legislativo en Colombia, Tomo II*. Bogotá: Departamento de Ciencia Política, Universidad de los Andes and Cámara de Comercio.

Hoskin, Gary W., Leal, Francisco & Kline, Harvey. 1979. *Legislative Behavior in Colombia, Volumes I and II*. State University of New York at Buffalo, Council on International Studies, No. 80–1.

Hoskin, Gary W. & Swanson, Gerald. 1974. "Political leadership in Colombia: a spatial analysis." *Comparative Politics* 6 (April), pp. 395–423.

Huntington, Samuel P. 1968. *Political Order in Changing Societies*. New Haven: Yale University Press.

1984. "Will more countries become democratic?" *Political Science Quarterly* 99 (Summer), pp. 193–218.

Huntington, Samuel P. & Moore, Clement H., eds. 1970. *Authoritarian Politics in Modern Society*. New York: Basic Books.

Inter-American Development Bank. 1982. *Economic and Social Progress in Latin America*. Washington, DC.

1984. *External Debt and Economic Development in Latin America*. Washington, DC.

1985. *Economic and Social Progress in Latin America*. Washington, DC.

International Bank for Reconstruction and Development (The World Bank) [IBRD]. 1972. "Bank operations in Colombia: an evaluation." Washington, DC.

1980. *World Development Report, 1980*. New York: Oxford University Press.

International Monetary Fund (IMF). 1981. *International Financial Statistics Yearbook*. Washington, DC.

Johnson, Kenneth. 1965. "Political radicalism in Colombia: electoral dynamics, 1962 and 1964." *Journal of Interamerican Studies and World Affairs* 7 (January), pp. 15–26.

Joint Tax Program of the OAS and the IDB, Fiscal Mission to Colombia. 1965. *Fiscal Survey of Colombia*. Baltimore: The Johns Hopkins University Press.

Junguito Bonnet, Roberto & Caballero Argáez, Carlos. 1978. "La otra economía." *Coyuntura Económica* 8 (December), pp. 103–39.

Junta Militar de Gobierno. 1957. *Itinerario histórico, tomo I*. Bogotá: Secretaría General de Gobierno.

1958. *Itinerario histórico, tomo II*. Bogotá: Secretaría General de Gobierno.

Kalmanovitz, Salomón. 1978. *Desarrollo de la agricultura en Colombia*.

Bogotá: Editorial La Carreta.

Karl, Terry. 1981. "Petroleum and political pacts: the transition to democracy in Venezuela." Washington, DC: Wilson Center, Latin American Program, Working Papers No. 107.

Katzenstein, Peter. 1985. "Small nations in an open international economy: the converging balance of state and society in Switzerland and Austria." In Peter B. Evans, Dietrich Rueschemeyer & Theda Skocpol, eds., *Bringing the State Back In*. Cambridge University Press.

Kaufman, Robert R. 1979. "Industrial change and authoritarian rule in Latin America: a concrete review of the bureaucratic–authoritarian model." In David Collier, ed., *The New Authoritarianism in Latin America*. Princeton University Press.

Kelley, R. Lynn. 1977. "Venezuelan constitutional forms and realities." In John Martz and David Myers, eds., *Venezuela: The Democratic Experience*. New York: Praeger.

Key, V. O. 1964. *Politics, Parties and Pressure Groups*. 5th edition. New York: Crowell.

Kieve, Ronald A. 1981. "Pillars of sand: a Marxist critique of consociational democracy in the Netherlands." *Comparative Politics* 13 (April), pp. 313–37.

Kline, Harvey F. 1974. "Interest groups in the Colombian Congress." *Journal of Interamerican Studies and World Affairs* 16 (August), pp. 274–300.

1980. "The National Front: historical perspective and overview." In Albert Berry, Ronald Hellman and Mauricio Solaún, eds., *Politics of Compromise: Coalition Government in Colombia*. New Brunswick: Transaction Books.

1982. "Energy policy and the Colombian elite: a synthesis and interpretation." Washington, DC: American Enterprise Institute for Public Policy Research, Occasional Papers Series No. 4.

1983. *Colombia: Portrait of Unity and Diversity*. Boulder: Westview Press.

Krasner, Stephen D. 1984. "Approaches to the state: alternative conceptions and historical dynamics – review article." *Comparative Politics* 16 (January), pp. 223–46.

Lara, José. 1976. "Sindicalismo de industria y conciencia de clase." *Estudios Marxistas* No. 11, pp. 35–46.

Lara Bonilla, Rodrigo. 1983. "Análisis de la organización interna de los partidos políticos colombianos." In Rodrigo Lara Bonilla, Rodrigo Losada Lora, and Humberto Uribe Toro, eds., *Los partidos políticos colombianos: presente y futuro*. Bogotá: Fundación Simón Bolívar & Pontificia Universidad Javeriana.

Lara Bonilla, Rodrigo, Losada Lora, Rodrigo, & Uribe Toro, Humberto. 1983. *Los partidos políticos colombianos: presente y futuro*. Bogotá: Fundación Simón Bolívar & Pontificia Universidad Javeriana.

Latorre Rueda, Mario. 1974. *Elecciones y partidos políticos en Colombia*. Bogotá: Universidad de los Andes.

1983. "La emergencia económica: presentación para profanos." *Estrategia* (April), pp. 19–22.

1986. *Hechos y crítica política.* Bogotá: Universidad Nacional de Colombia.

Leal Buitrago, Francisco. 1970. "Política e intervención militar en Colombia." In Rodrigo Parra Sandoval, ed., *La dependencia externa y el desarrollo político de Colombia.* Bogotá: Universidad Nacional de Colombia, Dirección de Divulgación Cultural.

1973. *Estudio del comportamiento legislativo en Colombia, Tomo I. Análisis histórico del desarrollo político nacional 1930–1970.* Bogotá: Ediciones Tercer Mundo.

1974. "Social classes, international trade and foreign capital in Colombia: an attempt at historical interpretation of the formation of the state, 1819–1935." PhD dissertation, University of Wisconsin–Madison.

1984. *Estado y política en Colombia.* Bogotá: Siglo XXI.

Leal Buitrago, Francisco, et al. 1977. *El agro en el desarrollo histórico colombiano.* Bogotá: Universidad de los Andes, Departamento de Ciencia Política.

Leff, Nathaniel H. 1968. *The Brazilian Capital Goods Industry, 1929–1964.* Cambridge, Mass.: Harvard University Press.

LeGrand, Catherine. 1984. "Labor acquisition and social conflict on the Colombian frontier, 1850–1936." *Journal of Latin American Studies* 16 (May), pp. 27–49.

Lehmbruch, Gerhard, 1975. "Consociational democracy in the international system." *European Journal of Political Research* 3 (December) pp. 377–91.

1977. "Liberal corporatism and party government." *Comparative Political Studies* 10 (April), pp. 91–126.

Lehmbruch, Gerhard & Schmitter, Philippe, eds. 1982. *Patterns of Corporatist Policy Making.* Beverly Hills: Sage Publications.

Levine, Daniel H. 1973. *Conflict and Political Change in Venezuela.* Princeton University Press.

1978. "Venezuela since 1958: the consolidation of democratic politics." In Juan Linz and Alfred Stepan, eds., *The Breakdown of Democratic Regimes: Latin America.* Baltimore: The John Hopkins University Press.

1981. *Religion and Politics in Latin America: The Catholic Church in Venezuela and Colombia.* Princeton University Press.

1985. "On the nature, sources, and future prospects of democracy in Venzuela." Presented to the Conference on Democracy in Developing Countries, Hoover Institution, Stanford University.

Levine, Daniel H. & Wilde, Alexander. 1977. "The Catholic Church, 'politics,' and violence: the Colombian case." *Review of Politics* 39 (April), pp. 220–49.

Lewin, Patricia Pinzón de, ed. 1986. *La oposición en Colombia: algunas bases para su discusión.* Bogotá: Fescol and CEI, Universidad de los Andes.

Lijphart, Arend. 1969. "Consociational democracy." *World Politics* 21 (January), pp. 207–25.

1975. *The Politics of Accommodation: Pluralism and Democracy in the Netherlands.* 2nd Edition, Revised. Berkeley: University of California Press.

1977. *Democracy in Plural Societies: A Comparative Exploration.* New Haven: Yale University Press.

1981. "Consociational theory: problems and prospects." *Comparative Politics* 13 (April), pp. 355–60.

1984. *Democracies.* New Haven: Yale University Press.

Linz, Juan J. 1978. "Crisis, breakdown and reequilibration." In Juan J. Linz and Alfred Stepan, eds., *The Breakdown of Democratic Regimes.* Baltimore: The Johns Hopkins University Press.

Linz, Juan J. & Stepan, Alfred, eds. 1978. *The Breakdown of Democratic Regimes.* Baltimore: The Johns Hopkins University Press.

Lipset, Seymour Martin. 1959. "Some social requisites of democracy: economic development and political legitimacy." *American Political Science Review* 53 (March), pp. 69–105.

Little, Ian, Scitovsky, Tibor & Scott, Maurice. 1970. *Industry and Trade in Some Developing Countries: A Comparative Study.* London: Oxford University Press.

Lleras Restrepo, Carlos. 1955. *De la República a la Dictadura.* Bogotá: Editorial Argra.

1963a. *Hacia la restauración democrática y el cambio social, vol. I, 1955–1961.* Bogotá: n.p.

1963b. *Hacia la restauración democrática y el cambio social, vol. II, 1961–1963.* Bogotá: n.p.

1964. *Hacia la restauración democrática y el cambio social.* Bogotá: Editorial Agros.

1975: *Borradores para una historia de la República Liberal, tomo I.* Bogotá: Editora Nueva Frontera.

López Michelsen, Alfonso. 1961. *M.R.L. documentos.* Bogotá: Editorial Kelly.

Losada Lora, Rodrigo. 1973. "Los institutos descentralizados de carácter financiero: aspectos políticos del caso colombiano." Bogotá: FEDESARROLLO.

1976. "Las elecciones de mitaca en 1976: participación electoral y perspectiva histórica." Bogotá: FEDESARROLLO.

1979. "El significado político de las elecciones de 1978 en Colombia." In Rodrigo Losada and Georg Leibig, ed., *Las elecciones de 1978 en Colombia.* Bogotá: Fundación Friedrich Naumann.

1982. "Evolución reciente hacia las circunscripciones uninominales en Colombia." Bogotá: Fundación Simón Bolívar.

1984. *Clientelismo y elecciones.* Bogotá: Pontificia Universidad Javeriana.

Losada, Rodrigo & Murillo, Gabriel. 1973. "Análisis de las elecciones de 1972 en Bogotá." Bogotá: Universidad de los Andes, Departamento de Ciencia Política.

Losada, Rodrigo & Vélez, Eduardo. 1982. *Identificación y participación política en Colombia.* Bogotá: FEDESARROLLO.

Lupsha, Peter A. 1981. "The political economy of drug trafficking in Colombia." Paper presented at the US State Department Conference on Colombia.

Lustick, Ian. 1979. "Stability in deeply divided societies: consociationalism versus control." *World Politics* 31, pp. 325–44.

McClintock, Cynthia & Lowenthal, Abraham, F., eds. 1983. *The Peruvian Experiment Reconsidered*. Princeton University Press.

McGreevey, William P. 1964. "Statistical series on the Colombian economy." Berkeley: University of California, Department of Geography.

1971. *An Economic History of Colombia 1845–1930*. New York: Cambridge University Press.

1980. "Population policy under the National Front." In Albert Berry, Ronald G. Hellman & Mauricio Solaún, eds., *Politics of Compromise: Coalition Government in Colombia*. New Brunswick: Transaction Books.

McRae, Kenneth, ed. 1974. *Consociational Democracy: Political Accommodation in Segmented Societies*. Toronto: The Carleton Library, McClelland and Steward Ltd.

Machado C., Absalón. 1977. *El café: de la aparcería al capitalismo*. Bogotá: Punta de Lanza.

Maingot, Anthony. 1969. "Social structure, social status and civil–military conflict in urban Colombia." In S. Thernstrom and R. Sennett, eds., *Nineteenth Century Cities*. New Haven: Yale University Press.

Martz, John D. 1962. *Colombia: A Contemporary Political Survey*. Chapel Hill: University of North Carolina Press.

Matallana, José Joaquín. 1984. *Paz o guerra: alternativas del 84*. Bogotá: Canal Ramírez-Antares.

Matter, Konrad. 1977. *Inversiones extranjeras en la economía colombiana*. Medellín: Ediciones Hombre Nuevo.

Maullin, Richard L. 1967. "The Colombia–IMF disagreement of November–December 1966: an interpretation of its place in Colombian politics." Santa Monica: The RAND Corporation, Memorandum RM–5314–RC.

1973. *Soldiers, Guerrillas and Politics in Colombia*. Lexington, Mass.: D. C. Heath & Co., Lexington Books.

Medhurst, Kenneth N. 1984. *The Church and Labour in Colombia*. Manchester University Press.

Medina, Medófilo. 1977. "Los paros cívicos en Colombia (1957–77)." *Estudios marxistas* No. 14, pp. 3–24.

Melo, Hector. 1978. "Quien controla los medios de comunicación en Colombia." *Teoría y práctica en América Latina* No. 11 (May), pp. 85–94.

Mendoza Neira, Plinio & Camacho Angarita, Alberto, eds. 1946. *El liberalismo en el gobierno, vol. I and II*. Bogotá: Editorial Minerva.

Mercedes de Martínez, Maria. 1981. "Gasto público: triste final de una historia feliz." *Estrategia* No. 51 (December), pp. 28–36.

Mericle, Kenneth S. 1977. "Corporatist control of the working class: authoritarian Brazil since 1964." In James M. Malloy, ed., *Authori-*

tarianism and Corporatism in Latin America. University of Pittsburgh Press.

Miranda Ontaneda, Néstor & González, Fernán E. 1976 "Clientelismo, 'democracia,' o poder popular." *Controversia*. Bogotá: Editorial CINEP, No. 41–2.

Misas Arango, Gabriel. 1975. *Contribución al estudio del grado de concentración en la industria colombiana*. Bogotá: Ediciones Tiempo Presente.

Molina, Gerardo. 1977. *Las ideas liberales en Colombia de 1935 a la iniciación del Frente Nacional. Tomo III*. Bogotá: Ediciones Tercer Mundo.

Moncayo, Victor Manuel. 1975. "La ley y el problema agrario en Colombia." *Ideología y Sociedad* No. 14–15 (July–December), pp. 7–46.

Moncayo, Victor Manuel & Rojas, Fernando. 1978. *Luchas obreras y política laboral en Colombia*. Bogotá: La Carreta.

Montaña Cuéllar, Diego. 1977. *Colombia: país formal y país real*. 3rd edition. Bogotá: Editorial Latina.

Morawetz, David. 1980. "Why the emperor's new clothes are not made in Colombia." Washington, DC: World Bank Staff Working Paper No. 368, January.

Munera A., Dario. 1977. "Política fiscal e inversión productiva." *Revista Bimestral ANDI* No. 36 (November), pp. 44–57.

Muri, Willy. 1975. "L'armée colombienne: étude d'une institution militaire dans ses rapports avec la societé en transition, 1930–1974." Thesis for IIIrd cycle, University of Paris, v.

Murillo, Gabriel & Williams, Miles. 1975. "Análisis de las elecciones presidenciales en 1974 en Bogotá." Bogotá: Universidad de los Andes, Departamento de Ciencia Política.

Nelson, Joan M. 1979. *Access to Power: Politics and the Urban Poor in Developing Nations*. Princeton University Press.

Nelson, Richard R., Schultz, T. Paul & Slighton, Robert L. 1971. *Structural Change in a Developing Economy: Colombia's Problems and Prospects*. Princeton University Press.

Nordlinger, Eric A. 1972. *Conflict Regulation in Divided Societies*. Cambridge: Center for International Affairs, Harvard University, Occasional Papers in International Affairs No. 29, January.

Obler, J., Steiner, J., & Dierickx, G. 1977. "Decision-making in smaller democracies: the consociational 'burden'." Beverly Hills: Sage Comparative Politics Series, vol. 6, No. 01–064.

Ocampo Zamora, Alfredo. 1978. *Hacia un nuevo compromiso del empresario en Colombia*. Bogotá: Ediciones Tercer Mundo.

Ocampo, José Antonio & Perry Rubio, Guillermo. 1983. "La reforma fiscal, 1982–1983." *Coyuntura Económica* 13 (March), pp. 215–64.

Ocampo, José Antonio & Revéiz, Edgar. 1979. "Bonanza cafetera y economia concertada." *Desarrollo y sociedad* (July), pp. 233–55.

O'Donnell, Guillermo A. 1973. *Modernization and Bureaucratic–Authoritarianism: Studies in South American Politics*. Berkeley: Institute of International Studies, University of California, Politics of Modernization Series No. 9.

1977a. "Corporatism and the question of the state." In James M.

Malloy, ed., *Authoritarianism and Corporatism in Latin America*. University of Pittsburgh Press.

1977b. "Estado y alianzas en la Argentina, 1956–1976." *Desarrollo económico* 16 (January–March), pp. 523–54.

1978. "Reflections on the patterns of change in the bureaucratic-authoritarian state." *Latin American Research Review* 13, pp. 3–38.

1979. "Tensions in the bureaucratic–authoritarian state and the question of democracy." In David Collier, ed., *The New Authoritarianism in Latin America*. Princeton University Press.

1982. "Notas para el estudio de procesos de democratización política a partir del estado burocrático–autoritario." *Desarrollo económico* 22, (July–September), pp. 231–48.

1986. "Introduction to the Latin American cases." In Guillermo A. O'Donnell, Philippe C. Schmitter and Laurence Whitehead, eds., *Transitions from Authoritarian Rule: Latin America*. Baltimore: Johns Hopkins University Press.

O'Donnell, Guillermo A., Schmitter, Philippe C., & Whitehead, Laurence, eds. 1986. *Transitions from Authoritarian Rule, vols. I–IV*. Baltimore: Johns Hopkins University Press.

Olson, Mancur. 1971. *The Logic of Collective Action*. Cambridge, Mass.: Harvard University Press.

Oquist, Paul. 1973. "Las elecciones presidenciales, 1930–1970." *Boletín Mensual de Estadística* No. 168–9 (November–December).

1980. *Violence, Conflict and Politics in Colombia*. New York: Academic Press.

Orlando Melo, Jorge. 1978. "La república conservadora." In Mario Arrubla et al., *Colombia Hoy*. Bogotá: Siglo XXI.

Ortiz Sarmiento, Carlos Miguel. 1985. *Estado y subversión en Colombia: La violencia en el Quindío años 50*. Bogotá: Fondo Editorial CEREC.

Ospina Sardi, Jorge. 1978. "Las finanzas del gobierno nacional, 1964–1976." *Coyuntura Económica* 8 (April), pp. 107–32.

Ospina Vásquez, Luis. 1955. *Industria y protección en Colombia, 1810–1930*. Medellín: Editorial Santa Fé.

Pabón Pabón, Rosemberg. 1984. *Así nos tomamos la embajada*. Bogotá: Planeta Colombiana Editorial.

Palacios, Marco. 1979. *El café en Colombia (1830–1970): una historia económica, social y política*. Bogotá: Editorial Presencia y FEDESARROLLO.

1983. *El café en Colombia, 1850–1970*. 2nd edition. Mexico & Bogotá: El Colegio de México & El Ancora Editores.

Pappalardo, Adriano. 1981. "The conditions for consociational democracy." *European Journal of Political Research* 9 (December), pp. 365–90.

Parra Sandoval, Rodrigo, ed. 1970. *La dependencia externa y el desarrollo político de Colombia*. Bogotá: Universidad Nacional de Colombia, Dirección de Divulgación Cultural.

Parsons, James J. 1968. *Antioqueño Colonization in Western Colombia*. Revised edition. Berkeley: University of California Press.

Paus, Eva. 1982. "La dinámica de la acumulación y del empleo en la industria textil colombiana durante los 70: de la promoción de exportaciones al contrabando." *Coyuntura Económica* 12 (December), pp. 129–75.

Payne, James L. 1968. *Patterns of Conflict in Colombia*. New Haven: Yale University Press.

Pecaut, Daniel. 1973. *Política y sindicalismo en Colombia*. Bogotá: Editorial la Carreta.

Peeler, John A. 1976. "Colombian parties and political development: a reassessment." *Journal of Interamerican Studies and World Affairs* 18 (May), pp. 203–24.

1985. *Latin American Democracies: Colombia, Costa Rica, Venezuela*. Chapel Hill: The University of North Carolina Press.

Perry Rubio, Guillermo. 1974. "Introducción al estudio de los planes de desarrollo en Colombia." In Hernando Gómez Otálora and Eduardo Wiesner Durán, eds., *Lecturas sobre el desarrollo económico colombiano*. Bogotá: FEDESARROLLO.

1977. "Las reformas tributarias de 1974 y 1975 en Colombia." *Coyuntura Económica* 7 (November), pp. 83–132.

Perry Rubio, Guillermo, Gómez Buendía, Hernando, and Londoño Botero, Rocío. 1982. "Sindicalismo y política económica." *Coyuntura Económica* 12 (December), pp. 176–200.

Pinilla, Luis. 1980. "Cómo se ejerce el poder en Colombia?" Master's thesis, Universidad Javeriana de Bogotá.

Pizarro, Eduardo, et al., 1981. *El patrón–estado en Colombia*. Bogotá: Editorial Colombia Nueva.

Pollock, John C. 1975. "Violence, politics and elite performance: the political sociology of *La Violencia* in Colombia." *Studies in Comparative International Development* 10 (Summer), pp. 22–50.

Poveda Ramos, Gabriel. 1967. "Antecedentes y desarrollo de la industria en Colombia." Medellín: ms.

1976. *Políticas económicas, desarrollo industrial y tecnología en Colombia 1925–1975*. Bogotá: Editora Guadalupe, Colciencias.

1984. *Andi y la industria en Colombia, 1944–1984. 40 años*. Medellín: Asociación Nacional de Industriales (ANDI).

Powell, G. Bingham, Jr. 1982. *Contemporary Democracies: Participation, Stability and Violence*. Cambridge, Mass.: Harvard University Press.

Premo, Daniel. 1972. "Alianza Nacional Popular: populism and the politics of social class in Colombia, 1961–1970." PhD dissertation, University of Texas at Austin.

Ramírez Aljure, Jorge. 1986. *Liberalismo: ideología y clientelismo, 1957–1986*. Bogotá: n.p.

Ramsey, Russell W. 1973. "Critical bibliography on *La Violencia* in Colombia." *Latin American Research Review* 8 (Spring).

Ranis, Gustav, et al. 1977. "Income distribution and growth in Colombia." Presented to the Conference on Distribution, Poverty and Development, Bogotá (June).

Restrepo, Laura. 1986. *Historia de una traición*. Bogotá: Editores Plaza & Janes.

Revéiz Roldán, Edgar. 1977. "Ensayo sobre la planeación concertada en Colombia." Bogotá: Universidad de los Andes, CEDE, No. 21.

1981. "La concertación: experiencias y posibilidades en Colombia." In

Edgar Revéiz Roldán, Fernando Cepeda Ulloa and Juan Martín Caicedo Ferré, eds., *Controversia sobre el Plan de Integración Nacional*. Bogotá: Universidad de los Andes.

Revéiz Roldán, Edgar, et al. 1977. *Poder e información*. Bogotá: Editorial Antares.

Revéiz Roldán, Edgar & Pérez, María José. 1986. "Colombia: moderate economic growth, political stability and social welfare." In Jonathan Hartlyn and Samuel A. Morley, eds., *Latin American Political Economy*. Boulder: Westview Press.

Revista de Historia, 1977. "El 2 de mayo de 1958" [interview with Hernando Forero]. 1 (August), pp. 4–11.

Reyes Posada, Alejandro. 1975. "Aparcería y capitalismo agrario." *Controversia*. Bogotá: Editorial CINEP, No. 38.

1978. *Latifundio y poder político*. Bogotá: Editorial CINEP.

Rivera Ortiz, Angel Israel. 1975. "The politics of development planning in Colombia." PhD dissertation, State University of New York, Buffalo.

Robinson, J. Cordell. 1976. *El movimiento gaitanista en Colombia, 1930–1948*. Bogotá: Editorial Tercer Mundo.

Rojas Pinilla ante el Senado. 1959. Bogotá: Editorial Excelsior.

Rojas Ruiz, Humberto. 1970. "El frente nacional: solución política a un problema de desarrollo?" In Rodrigo Parra Sandoval, ed., *La dependencia externa y el desarrollo político de Colombia*. Bogotá: Universidad Nacional de Colombia, Dirección de Divulgación Cultura.

Rothlisberger, Dora & Oquist, Paul. 1973. "Algunos aspectos de la abstención electoral." *Boletín Mensual de Estadística* No. 268–9 (November–December), pp. 80–97.

Ruhl, J. Mark. 1980. "The military." In Albert Berry, Ronald Hellman and Mauricio Solaún, eds., *Politics of Compromise: Coalition Government in Colombia*. New Brunswick: Transaction Books.

Saldarriaga V., Ana María. 1980. "Historia del desarrollo de la Federación Nacional de Comerciantes." Tésis de Grado, Facultad de Administración, Universidad de los Andes.

Sánchez, Gonzalo. 1985. "*La Violencia* in Colombia: new research, new questions." *Hispanic American Historical Review* 65 (November), pp. 789–807.

Sánchez, Gonzalo & Meertens, Danny. 1983. *Bandoleros, gamonales y campesinos: el caso de la Violencia en Colombia*. Bogotá: El Ancora Editores.

Sánchez, Ruben, with the assistance of Jonathan Hartlyn, Carlos Martínez & Gladys Delgado. 1981. "El comportamiento electoral de los bogotanos en las elecciones de 1978." Bogotá: Universidad de los Andes, Departamento de Ciencia Política.

Santamaría Salamanca, Ricardo & Silva Luján, Gabriel. 1984. *Proceso político en Colombia*. Bogotá: Fondo Editorial CEREC.

Schloss, Miguel & Thomas, Vinod. 1986. "Ajuste con crecimiento: la experiencia de Colombia." *Estrategia* No. 104 (October), pp. 15–20.

Schmidt, Steffen W. 1974a. "Bureaucrats as modernizing brokers:

clientelism in Colombia." *Comparative Politics* 6 (April), pp. 425–50.

1974b. "*La Violencia* revisited: the clientelist bases of political violence in Colombia." *Journal of Latin American Studies* 6, Part I (May), pp. 97–111.

Schmidt, Steffen W., et al. 1977. *Friends, Followers and Factions: A Reader in Political Clientelism*. Berkeley: University of California Press.

Schmitter, Philippe C. 1971. *Interest Conflict and Political Change in Brazil*. Stanford University Press.

1974. "Still the century of corporatism?" In Frederick C. Pike and Thomas Stritch, eds., *The New Corporatism*. University of Notre Dame Press.

1979. "Modes of interest intermediation and models of societal change in Western Europe." In Philippe C. Schmitter and Gerhard Lehmbruch, eds., *Trends Toward Corporatist Intermediation*. Beverly Hills: Sage Publications.

1982. "Reflections on where the theory of neo-corporatism has gone and where the praxis of neo-corporatism may be going." In Gerhard Lehmbruch and Philippe C. Schmitter, eds., *Patterns of Corporatist Policy-Making*. Beverly Hills: Sage Publications.

Schmitter, Philippe C. & Lehmbruch, Gerhard., eds. 1979. *Trends Toward Corporatist Intermediation*. Beverly Hills: Sage Publications.

Schydlowsky, Daniel M. 1986. "The tragedy of lost opportunity: Peru 1968–1983." In Jonathan Hartlyn and Samuel A. Morley, eds., *Latin American Political Economy*. Boulder: Westview Press.

Scott, James C. 1972 *Comparative Political Corruption*. Englewood Cliffs, N J: Prentice-Hall.

Selowsky, Marcelo. 1979. *Who Benefits from Government Expenditure? A Case Study of Colombia*. New York: Oxford University Press.

Serra, José. 1979. "Three mistaken theses regarding the connection between industrialization and authoritarian regimes." In David Collier, ed., *The New Authoritarianism in Latin America*. Princeton University Press.

Sharpless, Richard E. 1978. *Gaitán of Colombia: A Political Biography*. University of Pittsburgh Press.

Sheahan, John. 1968. "Imports, investment, and growth – Colombia." In Gustav F. Papanek (ed.), *Development Policy – Theory and Practice*. Cambridge, Mass.: Harvard University Press.

1980. "Market-oriented economic policies and political repression in Latin America." *Economic Development and Cultural Change* 28 (January), pp. 267–91.

Silva Colmenares, Julio. 1977. *Los verdaderos dueños del país: oligarquía y monopolios en Colombia*. Bogotá: Fondo Editorial Suramérica.

Simon. W. 1978. "Democracy in the shadow of imposed sovereignty: the first republic of Austria." In Juan Linz and Alfred Stepan, eds., *The Breakdown of Democratic Regimes: Europe*. Baltimore: The Johns Hopkins University Press.

Skidmore, Thomas E. 1973. "Politics and economic policy making in authoritarian Brazil, 1937–1971." In Alfred Stepan, ed., *Authoritarian*

Brazil. New Haven: Yale University Press.

Skidmore, Thomas E. & Smith, Peter H. 1984. *Modern Latin America*. New York and Oxford: Oxford University Press.

Skocpol, Theda. 1982. "Bringing the state back in: false leads and promising starts in current theories and research." Presented to a Conference on States and Social Structures, Mt. Kisco, New York.

1985. "Bringing the state back in: strategies of analysis in current research." In Peter B. Evans, Dietrich Rueschemeyer and Theda Skocpol, eds., *Bringing the State Back In*. Cambridge University Press.

Sojo, José Raimundo. 1970. *El comercio en la historia de Colombia*. Bogotá: Cámara de Comercio de Bogotá.

Solaún, Mauricio, Cepeda Ulloa, Fernando & Bagley, Bruce M. 1973. "Urban reform in Colombia: the impact of the 'politics of games' in public policy." In Francine R. Rabinovitz and Felicity M. Trueblood, eds., *Latin American Urban Research, Volume 3*. Beverly Hills: Sage Publications.

Stavenhagen, Rodolfo, ed. 1970. *Agrarian Problems and Peasant Movements in Latin America*. Garden City, NY: Anchor Books.

Steiner, Jurg 1974. *Amicable Agreement versus Majority Rule: Conflict Resolution in Switzerland*. Chapel Hill: University of North Carolina Press.

1981. "The consociational theory and beyond." *Comparative Politics* 13 (April), pp. 339–54.

Steiner, Jug & Obler, Jeffrey. 1977. "Does the consociational theory really hold for Switzerland?" In Milton J. Esman, ed., *Ethnic Conflict in the Western World*. Ithaca: Cornell University Press.

Steiner, Kurt. 1972. *Politics in Austria*. Boston: Little, Brown and Co.

Stepan, Alfred, 1978. "Political leadership and regime breakdown: Brazil." In Juan J. Linz and Alfred Stepan, eds., *The Breakdown of Democratic Regimes: Latin America*. Baltimore: The Johns Hopkins University Press.

1979. *The State and Society: Peru in Comparative Perspective*. Princeton University Press.

1985. "State power and the strength of civil society in the Southern Cone of Latin America." In Peter B. Evans, Dietrich Rueschemeyer and Theda Skocpol, eds., *Bringing the State Back In*. Cambridge University Press.

Stiefbold, Rodney P. 1974. "Segmented pluralism and consociational democracy in Austria: problems of political stability and change." In Martin O. Heisler, ed., *Politics in Europe*. New York: D. McKay Co.

Suleiman, Ezra N. 1974. *Politics, Power and Bureaucracy in France: The Administrative Elite*. Princeton University Press.

Szulc, Tad. 1959. *Twilight of Tyrants*. New York: Henry Holt and Co.

Talbot Campos, Judith & NcCamant, John F. 1972. "Cleavage shift in Colombia: analysis of the 1970 election." Beverly Hills: Sage Comparative Politics Series, vol. 3, No. 01–032.

Tenjo, Jaime. 1975a. "Aspectos cuantitativos del movimiento sindical colombiano." *Cuadernos Colombianos* No. 5, pp. 3–40.

1975b. "Impacto de la actividad sindical sobre los salarios: un análisis econométrico." *Revista de Planeación y Desarrollo* 7 No. 2 (July–December), pp. 129–45.

Tirado Mejía, Alvaro. 1978. "Colombia: siglo y medio de bipartidismo." In Mario Arrubla, ed., *Colombia Hoy*. Bogotá: Siglo XXI.

Torre, Cristina de la, ed. 1985. *Reformas políticas: apertura democrática*. Bogotá: Editorial Nikos and Editorial La Oveja Negra.

Torres Giraldo, Ignacio. 1974. *Los inconformes: historia de la rebelión de las masas en Colombia*. Bogotá: Editorial Margen Izquierdo.

Trapido, Paul J. 1979. "State food marketing for the urban poor in Colombia: a case study of the IDEMA's Red de Distribución Minorista." Master's Thesis, University of Texas at Austin.

Trimberger, Ellen Kay. 1978. *Revolution from Above: Military Bureaucrats and Development in Japan, Turkey, Egypt, and Peru*. New Brunswick: Transaction Books.

Ungar, Elizabeth. 1981a. "La organización popular y los servicios públicos: política de concertación o política de confrontación? (el caso de Acción Comunal)." *Carta Financiera* No. 49 (April–June), pp. 217–31.

1981b. "Las Juntas de Acción Comunal en Colombia: un diagnóstico sobre su desarrollo, actividades, logros y necesidades." Bogotá: Universidad de los Andes, Departamento de Ciencia Política, March, ms.

Ungar, Elizabeth & Gómez de Martínez, Angela. 1977. *Aspectos de la campaña presidencial de 1974: estrategias y resultados*. Bogotá: Editorial Tercer Mundo.

United Nations, Economic Commission on Latin America (UN, ECLA). 1957. *Analyses and projections of Economic Development, vol. 3. The Economic Development of Colombia*. Geneva: United Nations.

1970. *Análisis y proyección del desarrollo económico: el desarrollo económico de Colombia: anexo estadístico*. Geneva: United Nations, 1957; reprint, Bogotá: Departamento Administrativo Nacional de Estadísticas.

United States. Arms Control and Disarmament Agency (US/ACDA). 1985. *World Military Expenditures and Arms Transfer*. Washington, DC.

United States. Department of Agriculture [Horace Porter]. 1961. "The cotton industry of Colombia," Washington, DC: US Department of Agriculture.

United States. Department of State [Eileen Heaphy]. 1980. Colombia Desk Office. "US–Colombian Relations, 1980." Washington, DC, ms.

United States. US/AID-Colombia. 1975. "FY1977 Annual Budget Submission." July, ms.

United States Senate. Subcommittee on American Republic Affairs, Committee on Foreign Relations, 91st Congress, 1st Session. 1969. "Colombia – a case study of US aid." Washington, DC: US Government Printing Office.

Uribe Vargas, Diego. 1977. *Las constituciones de Colombia. tomos I y II*. Madrid: Ediciones Cultura Hispánica.

Urrutia Montoya, Miguel. 1969. *The Development of the Colombian Labor Movement*. New Haven: Yale University Press.

1977. "Políticas de distribución del ingreso en Colombia." Presented to the Conference on Distribution, Poverty and Development, Bogotá, June.

1980. "Colombia and the Andean Group: Two Essays." Washington, DC: Wilson Center, Latin American Program, Working Paper No. 65.

1981. *Gremios, política económica y democracia*. Bogotá: FEDESARROLLO.

1984. "Democracia y derecho de huelga en un servicio público esencial." *Coyuntura Económica* 14 No. 2 (June), pp. 168–83.

1985. *Winners and Losers in Colombia's Economic Growth of the 1970s*. New York and Oxford: Oxford University Press.

Urrutia M., Miguel & Arrubla, Mario, eds. 1970. *Compendio de estadísticas históricas de Colombia*. Bogotá: Universidad Nacional de Colombia, Dirección de Divulgación Cultural.

Valencia Tovar, Alvaro. 1976. *El final de Camilo*. Bogotá: Ediciones Tercer Mundo.

Valenzuela, Arturo. 1977. *Political Brokers in Chile: Local Government in a Centralized Polity*. Durham, NC: Duke University Press.

1978. *Chile*. In Juan J. Linz and Alfred Stepan, eds., *The Breakdown of Democratic Regimes*. Baltimore: The Johns Hopkins University Press.

1985. "Political science and the study of Latin America." Presented at the 12th Meeting of the Latin American Studies Association.

Valenzuela, Arturo & Valenzuela, J. Samuel. 1983. "Party oppositions under the Chilean authoritarian regime." Washington, DC: Wilson Center, Latin American Program, Working Papers No. 125.

Valenzuela, Arturo & Wilde, Alexander. 1979. "Presidential politics and the decline of the Chilean Congress." In Joel Smith and Lloyd D. Musolf, eds., *Legislatures in Development*. Durham, NC: Duke University Press.

Valenzuela Ramírez, Jaime. 1978. *Producción arrocera y clientelismo*. Bogotá: Editorial CINEP.

Van Klaveren, Alberto. 1983. "La democracia consociativa como modelo de convergencia política: la experiencia europea." *Estudios Sociales*, No. 36, 2nd Trimester, pp. 9–40.

Vasco Montoya, Eloísa. 1978. *Clientelismo y minifundio*. Bogotá: Editorial CINEP.

Vázquez Carrizosa, Alfredo. 1979. *El poder presidencial en Colombia*. Bogotá: Enrique Dobry, Editor.

1985. "Colombia entre la esperanza y la desesperación. Análisis crítico de la estrategia de la paz." In Manuel José Cepeda Espinosa, ed., *Estado de Sitio y Emergencia Económica*. Bogotá: Contraloría General de la República.

Vázquez Cobo Carrizosa, Camilo. nd. *El Frente Nacional: su origen y desarrollo*. Cali: Carvajal and Co.

Vidal Perdomo, Jaime. 1970. *La Reforma Constitucional de 1968 y sus alcances jurídicos*. Bogotá: Editorial Presencia.

Vorys, Karl von. 1975. *Democracy Without Consensus: Communalism and Political Stability in Malaysia*. Princeton University Press.

Waisman, Carlos H. 1985. "Development and democracy: the case of Argentina." Presented at a Conference on Democracy in Developing Countries, Stanford, California.

Walton, John. 1984. *Reluctant Rebels: Comparative Studies of Revolution and Underdevelopment*. New York: Columbia University Press.

Whiteford, Michael B. 1976. *The Forgotten Ones: Colombian Countrymen in an Urban Setting*. Gainesville: University Presses of Florida.

Wiarda, Howard. 1973. "Toward a framework for the study of political change in the Iberic-Latin tradition: the corporative model." *World Politics* 25 (January), pp. 206–35.

Wickizer, V. D. 1951. *Coffee, Tea and Cocoa: An Economic and Political Analysis*. Stanford University Press.

Wiesner Durán, Eduardo. 1978. "Devaluación y mecanismo de ajuste en Colombia," *Banco y Finanzas* No. 159 (March), pp. 43–123.

Wilde, Alexander W. 1978. "Conversations among gentlemen: oligarchical democracy in Colombia." In Juan Linz and Alfred Stepan, eds., *The Breakdown of Democratic Regimes: Latin America*. Baltimore: The Johns Hopkins University Press.

   1980. "The contemporary Church: the political and the pastoral." In Albert Berry, Ronald Hellman and Mauricio Solaún, eds., *Politics of Compromise: Coalition Government in Colombia*. New Brunswick: Transaction Books.

Wilkie, James W., ed. 1974. *Statistics and National Policy*. Los Angeles: University of California at Los Angeles Latin American Center.

Wilkie, James W. & Haber, Stephen, eds. 1981. *Statistical Abstract of Latin America, Vol. 21*. Los Angeles: University of California at Los Angeles Latin American Center.

Wilkie, James W. & Perkal, Adam, eds. 1984. *Statistical Abstract of Latin America, vol. 23*. Los Angeles: University of California at Los Angeles Latin American Center.

Williams, Miles. 1976. "El Frente Nacional: Colombia's experiment in controlled democracy." PhD dissertation, Vanderbilt University.

Williams, Miles & Losada Lora, Rodrigo. 1972. "Análisis de la votación presidencial: 1970." In DANE, *Colombia Política*. Bogotá.

Wogart, Jan Peter. 1978. *Industrialization in Colombia: Policies, Patterns, Perspectives*. Rubingen: Mohr, Kieler Studien No. 153.

Wynia, Gary W. 1984. *The Politics of Latin American Development*. 2nd edition. Cambridge University Press.

Zamosc, Leon. 1984. "Peasant Struggles of the 1970s in Colombia." ms.

   1986. *The Agrarian Question and the Peasant Movement in Colombia*. Cambridge University Press.

Zuckerman, Alan A. 1979. *The Politics of Faction*. New Haven: Yale University Press.

Zuleta, Luis Angel. 1975. "El sector cafetero y los fenómenos inflacionarios." *Cuadernos Colombianos* No. 7, pp. 431–519.

Index

Page numbers in *italics* refer to tables

319

CAMBRIDGE LATIN AMERICAN STUDIES